Fort Laramie and the Sioux

BOOKS BY REMI NADEAU

City-Makers

The Water Seekers

Ghost Towns and Mining Camps of California

Los Angeles

California: The New Society

Fort Laramie and the Sioux

The Real Joaquin Murieta

Stalin, Churchill and Roosevelt Divide Europe

Fort Laramie and the Sioux

ΛΛΛΛΛΛΛΛΛΛΛΛΛΛΛΛΛΛΛΛΛΛΛΛΛΛΛΛΛΛΛΛΛΛΛΛΛΛΛΛ

By Remi Nadeau

Crest Publishers
Santa Barbara, California

Originally published: Fort Laramie and the Sioux Indians. Prentice-Hall, 1967 (American Forts series). Republished as Fort Laramie and the Sioux. University of Nebraska Press, 1982 (Bison Book series).

New revised edition: Crest Publishers, Santa Barbara, California, 1997.

Library of Congress Catalog Number 97-066337

PRINTED IN THE UNITED STATES OF AMERICA

1. Fort Laramie (Wyo.). 2. Dakota Indians—Wars. 3. Indians of North America—Great Plains.

ISBN 0-9627104-6-6

Crest Publishers
P.O. Box 22614
Santa Barbara
CA 93121-2614

Front Cover: Red Cloud, fighting Oglala Sioux chief. In background is
original Fort Laramie trading post.
American Heritage Center, University of Wyoming
Cover design by Margaret Nadeau

To Bob and Jane

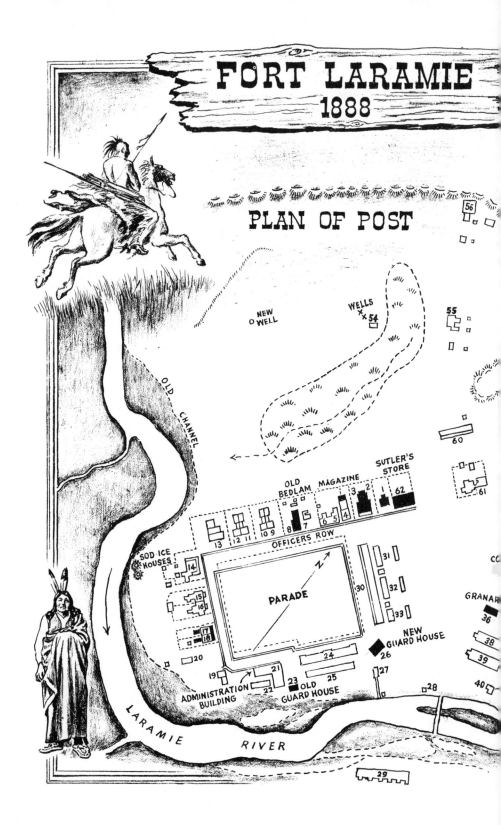

FORT LARAMIE
1888

PLAN OF POST

NEW WELL

WELLS ×× 54

OLD CHANNEL

55

56

60

61

SUTLER'S STORE

OLD BEDLAM   MAGAZINE

3 2   1 62

8 7   6 5 4

13 12 11 10 9

OFFICERS ROW

SOD ICE HOUSES

14

15

16

17 18

20

19

ADMINISTRATION BUILDING

21

22

23

OLD GUARD HOUSE

24

25

26

27

28

PARADE

N

30

31

32

33

NEW GUARD HOUSE

GRANAR

36

38

39

40

CC

29

LARAMIE   RIVER

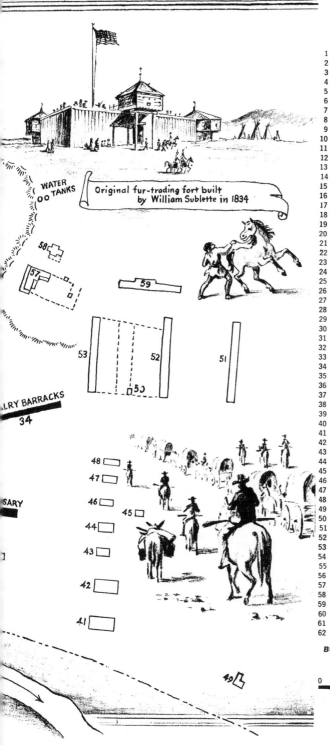

WATER ᴼᴼ TANKS

Original fur-trading fort built by William Sublette in 1834

LRY BARRACKS
34

SARY

1	OFFICERS' QUARTERS
2	" "
3	" "
4	" "
5	" "
6	" "
7	" "
8	" "
9	" "
10	" "
11	" "
12	" "
13	COMD'G OFFICER'S QUARTERS
14	OFFICERS' QUARTERS
15	" "
16	" "
17	" "
18	" "
19	" "
20	PRINTING OFFICE
21	ADMINISTRATION BUILDING
22	LIBRARY
23	MAGAZINE (OLD GUARD HOUSE)
24	BARRACKS
25	KITCHEN AND MESS HALL
26	GUARD HOUSE
27	GENERAL SINK
28	OIL HOUSE
29	MARRIED MEN'S QUARTERS
30	BARRACKS
31	KITCHEN AND MESS HALL
32	" " " "
33	" " " "
34	NEW BARRACKS
35	COMMISSARY STORE HOUSE
36	GRANARY
37	BAKERY
38	Q.M. STORE HOUSE
39	Q.M. STORE HOUSE AND OFFICE
40	TELEGRAPH OFFICE
41	Q.M. STORE HOUSE
42	" " "
43	Q.M. SHOPS
44	" "
45	Q.M. EMPLOYEES' QUARTERS
46	Q.M. SHOPS
47	" "
48	" "
49	Q.M. EMPLOYEES' QUARTERS
50	HARNESS ROOM
51	STABLES
52	"
53	"
54	SAW MILL
55	RUSTIC HOTEL
56	STAGE COACH STABLES
57	HOSPITAL
58	HOSPITAL STEWARDS' QUARTERS
59	N.C. STAFF QUARTERS
60	BATH HOUSES
61	SUTLER'S RESIDENCE
62	SUTLER'S STORE

BUILDINGS STANDING TODAY ARE SHOWN IN BLACK

0   100   300   500

SCALE IN FEET

Preface

This book is about the impact of Fort Laramie, as a spearhead of the American frontier, on the high Plains Indians. It is not a definitive history of the fort buildings as such. It has more to do with the actions of mountain men, soldiers and Indians in the surrounding country than with the daily routine inside the post.

The story told here is of the effect upon the Sioux, Cheyenne and Arapaho of the white man's westward thrust along the Overland Trail. As trading post and military fort, Laramie was the focal point of this influence, and its life from 1834 to 1890 precisely spanned the decline and fall of those Indian nations. Although the text ranges afield from the fort's vicinity, it is confined to events involving soldiers sent from Laramie or outposts commanded from the mother fort.

At the same time the book depicts the impact, not only of the traders and soldiers occupying the fort, but also the traders and Indian agents who clustered near it. For even in its military period, Laramie was to be understood as a rendezvous point and a trading center. There, or near there, the Indians brought their buffalo robes to barter with the traders, held treaty councils with the Great Father's emissaries, received provisions from the Indian Bureau, and, when the peace broke down, slew their enemies.

In covering this cavalcade of men and events, the author attempts to put the fall of the high Plains Indians in true perspective—not as a sudden military event in the 1870s but as a con-

tinuing decline beginning as far back as the 1830s. This process
was speeded not only by war but also by other factors occurring
throughout the period—the whiskey traffic, the slaughter of the
buffalo, the violation of Indian treaties, the perfidy of Indian
agents, the invasion of American settlers and, not least, the de-
moralizing influence of the soldiers sent to maintain peace. The
storm center—and one of the causes—of this epic tragedy was
old Fort Laramie.

Acknowledgments

The raw materials for this book have been the contemporary letters, diaries, reports, sworn testimony and reminiscences of those who participated in or witnessed the events described. There has been no embellishment of a story that needed none. Conversations are quoted directly from primary sources, and omissions have been indicated.

In locating these materials, I have been aided by many persons, to whom I am most grateful.

Enthusiastic assistance in providing materials and locating obscure sources was given by Dr. Gene M. Gressley, Director of the Western History Research Center at the University of Wyoming Library, Laramie.

Ready and continuing support was provided by John D. McDermott and Robert A. Murray, successive historians at Fort Laramie National Historical Site.

Efficient help in finding previously unknown materials was given by the staff of the National Archives in Washington, D.C. I am particularly indebted to Miss Jane F. Smith, Chief of the Social and Economic Branch, Office of Civil Archives, and to Elmer O. Parker, Acting Chief of the Army and Navy Branch.

Considerable research was contributed by Neal E. Miller of Rawlins, Wyoming—Past President of the Wyoming State Historical Society.

Other persons and institutions to whom I am indebted for materials, research or useful suggestions are Joseph W. Snell,

xi

Assistant State Archivist, and Miss Alberta Pantle, Librarian, of the Kansas State Historical Society, Topeka; William F. Schmidt, Archivist, Nebraska State Historical Society, Lincoln; Kenneth B. Holmes, Newspaper Librarian, State Historical Society of Missouri, Columbia; Mrs. Alys Freeze, Head of the Western History Department, Denver Public Library; J.H. Jonston III of the Leavenworth *Times;* Robert G. Athearn,University of Colorado, Boulder; J.W. Vaughn, Windsor, Colorado; Horace M. Albright, former Director of the National Park Service; Miss Nancy Carson of the Omaha Regional Office, National Park Service; Henry E. Huntington Library, San Marino, California; U.C.L.A. Library, Los Angeles; the Bancroft Library at the University of California, Berkeley; the California State Library in Sacramento; Los Angeles Public Library; Council Bluffs Free Public Library, Iowa, and the Omaha Public Library.

For assistance with photographs and historical data for the Third Edition, I wish to thank Daniel Davis, Photo Archivist, American Heritage Center, University of Wyoming; Pat Fullmer, Business Manager, Fort Laramie Historical Association; Doug McChristian, Historian, Denver Regional Office, National Park Service; and Steven Fullmer, Park Ranger, and Becky Eisenbarth, Park Ranger, Fort Laramie National Historic Site, National Park Service.

I am also obligated to the many researchers who have preceded me in these historical vineyards. Particular mention should be made of LeRoy R. Hafen—not only for his pioneer book on Fort Laramie, but more especially for his prolific spadework in compiling many volumes of first-hand documents on Rocky Mountain history. My thanks are also due to John Gudmundsen, who helped to conceive and initiate this book.

Finally, I am grateful to my wife Margaret and my daughter Christine for typing part of the manuscript and to my entire family for patience and support over a three-year period. In addition, Margaret collected new photographs, designed the cover and published this Third Edition.

                                        REMI NADEAU

Contents

ONE ♦ *There Is No Law Here*

♦ 1 ♦

In March 1834, two young tenderfeet made their way through the horses and wagons jamming the streets of waterfront St. Louis. At the outfitting headquarters of Nathaniel Wyeth, a trader preparing for the Rockies, they presented themselves as new recruits. Wyeth looked them over with a skeptical eye.

"You are both young," he answered, discouragingly. ". . . You may be devoured by grizzlies or scalped by the Indians."

If Wyeth was testing their resolve, he was not disappointed.

"We have heard all about it," one of them quickly responded. ". . . The Injun that gets our scalps will have to fight for 'em, you can bet on that!"

This scene was repeated many times in the offices of mountain traders in the St. Louis of 1834. In that spring, as in several prior seasons, the young city was bustling with the preparations of the western fur traders.

One giant among these competitors was William Sublette, descended from French Huguenots who had settled in Virginia and Kentucky and the oldest of five brothers engaged in the fur trade. At 23 he had joined Gen. William Ashley's pioneering expedition up the Missouri River to open up the fur trade and for the rest of his life was to be a tower among the mountain men. At 34 he was at the height of his physical powers. Standing six feet two, he had a long face, sandy hair, a Roman nose and a scar on the left side of his chin that earned him the Indian sobriquet "Cut Face."

A coolheaded leader who knew how to avoid trouble, Sublette was nevertheless fearless to the point of folly once the battle was joined. Two years before, when mountain men had clashed with a

1

party of Blackfeet at Pierre's Hole, Sublette had led an assault against an entrenched enemy and had drawn a shoulder wound for his trouble. Equally aggressive in business, he was alert to every opportunity for advantage over his competitors; he did not shrink from the illegal liquor traffic with the Indians, on the argument that without it he "might as well give up" the fur trade.

A year earlier Sublette and his partner Robert Campbell had dared to invade the territory of the upper Missouri River, previously monopolized by the dominant power in the western fur trade, John Jacob Astor's American Fur Company. Only a few miles from Astor's stronghold at Fort Union, near the mouth of the Yellowstone River, Sublette and Campbell had built their own trading post and had sent agents among the Indians. By early 1834 they had become such a threat that the American Fur Company had agreed to a grand division of operations: Sublette and Campbell would withdraw permanently from the upper Missouri, and the larger firm would retire from the central Rockies for one year.

With what seemed to be a clear field, Sublette was now outfitting his annual expedition to the Rockies. He would head for the summer trading fair or "rendezvous" held each year in the mountains, where he would trade goods to the Indians and trappers for their year's catch of beaver pelts. And he would build a new fort on the North Platte River, at the junction with Laramie's Fork, to consolidate his control of the central Rocky Mountain trade.

Also in St. Louis in the spring of 1834 was Nathaniel J. Wyeth, whose designs were even grander than Sublette's. Wyeth was a New Englander whose experience in the West spanned only two years. But he carried with him the Yankee's strong flare for business, his dogged enterprise, and his mastery of organizational detail. In Cambridge, Massachusetts, Wyeth had helped to pioneer the American ice industry; it was said that "there is not a single tool or machine of real value now employed in the ice harvesting, which was not invented by Mr. Wyeth." James Russell Lowell called him "a born leader of men" and "a very remarkable person whose conversation I valued highly." Washington Irving wrote, "He appears to have the mind to conceive, and the energy to execute extensive and striking plans."

Before he was thirty and never having been west in his life, Wyeth had formed a company to combine fur trading and salmon fishing in Oregon Territory. After dispatching a ship around the Horn to the mouth of the Columbia, he had personally led an expedition across the plains to meet it in 1832. But though he reached the Oregon country, his followers weakened under adversity, and his expedition failed.

On the same day that he returned to Massachusetts, Wyeth began preparing for a second expedition. In March 1834 he was back in St. Louis outfitting for the spring advance. He had already contracted to bring goods to the rendezvous in exchange for the beaver catch of Thomas Fitzpatrick, one of the chiefs among the mountain men, whose Rocky Mountain Fur Company was a leading supplier of pelts to the St. Louis traders. With the help of revenues from this transaction, Wyeth planned to press on and establish his outpost in Oregon. To his wife, who had begged him to send for her if he could, he unburdened his hopes: "I feel as much as you do the lonesomeness of my way of life but you know the success of what I have undertaken is life itself to me."

Bill Sublette knew all about Wyeth's plans and his contract with Fitzpatrick. He was aware that Fitzpatrick's Rocky Mountain Fur Company was in financial straits and was doubly aware that the company owed a large sum to the firm of Sublette & Campbell. As he wrote to his partner, Wyeth's intended transaction with Fitzpatrick would be "likely to operate against the goodness of the debt" due to them. But more than this, the success of Wyeth's mission would rob Sublette & Campbell of the sway they had won over the central Rockies fur trade through their deal with the American Fur Company.

Probably Sublette also knew that the contract allowed either party to renege on the transaction with the forfeit of a sum of money. If he were to arrive at the rendezvous before Wyeth, he would be able to bargain for Fitzpatrick's furs and deal Wyeth a reeling blow.

The New Englander himself also knew the need for haste. Being the first trader at the rendezvous gave an advantage in bargaining for pelts, and he was well aware of the loophole in the Fitzpatrick contract. As soon as he arrived in St. Louis he began hiring men and arranging for shipment of goods by steamboat up the Missouri River. His object was to leave Independence for the Indian country as soon as the prairie grass was high enough to feed the animals. He warned his eastern financial backers that

Sublette was also going to the mountains and declared his intention "to be first at the rendezvous which I consider very important."

• 2 •

In the year that Sublette and Wyeth were readying their expeditions, St. Louis was in dynamic transition from a languid French village of the eighteenth century to an American metropolis of the nineteenth century. Within a few years after the Louisiana Purchase in 1803, an American was no longer a stranger in the streets; brick buildings had joined the stone and wooden ones of the French era. By 1834 the American influx had pushed St. Louis' population from a thousand to about eight thousand; growth was headlong, and in the American section the song of hammer and saw filled the air.

Much of the change was caused by the rise of commerce in the Mississippi Valley, carried first by the keelboats and bullboats of the river men and later by that nobler and more civilized craft, the steamboat. After the arrival of the first paddle wheeler in 1817, St. Louis had become a center of steamboat traffic, second only to New Orleans. By the late 1830s as many as thirty steamboats at a time lined the levee for nearly a mile. Although most of these boats were engaged in the rising cotton trade with New Orleans, it was the western trade that made St. Louis the central Mississippi metropolis. At the turn of the nineteenth century St. Louisans were already paddling up the Missouri River to trade with the Indians for furs. After the Lewis and Clark expedition to the Pacific in 1804-1806, more traders ventured west, and, after the new Mexican republic opened entry to the central Rockies in 1822, the traffic boomed. In that year, a thousand hunters and trappers were on the tributaries of the Missouri.

Located some eighteen miles below its mouth, St. Louis was the natural entrepôt for the new West. From there French engagés boated up the Missouri to work for the American Fur Company. American mountaineers rode west to the Rockies along the Missouri, the Kansas, the Little Blue and the Platte. Both Spanish and American traders packed up for the Arkansas River and the pueblos of Taos and Santa Fe. Those returning from the Rockies brought with them Indian furs—beaver pelts for the dress hats of European dandies and buffalo robes for sleigh blankets and overcoats in the American East.

Thus in 1834 St. Louis was not only the rising emporium of the new West; it was also the point of contact between the societies of the American Indian and of the American of European descent. Already the whites were moving farther west; they had been settling along the lower Missouri since the Louisiana Purchase. St. Louis was the base, and the Missouri River settlements were the thrusting point, for the wedge of the white man's invasion beyond the Mississippi.

But in 1834 the prairies and mountains farther to the west were still recognized as one limitless hunting ground for the Indian. Any stranger entering them had to have a permit from the Superintendent of Indian Affairs in St. Louis. Since the 1820s the white man had, in fact, considered the area a vast dumping ground for Indian tribes standing in the way of settlement in the states. Already the Choctaw, Delaware, Shawnee and Kickapoo had been transferred to the Iowa country or to what would later be called "Oklahoma". The Sauk were being transferred west of the Mississippi following the Black Hawk war of 1832. Other tribes—the Creek, Chickasaw, Seminole, Miami and Potawatomi—were on the way. And beyond their adopted homes, in the plains stretching to the Rockies, were the native tribes that had seen no white men save traders and explorers—the Pawnee, Cheyenne, Arapaho, Crow and numerous bands of Sioux.

In this vast kingdom the red man ruled. The hunter or trapper who ventured from the settlements did so on the sufferance of the Indians. If he were robbed or killed, there was no law and no punishing army. For, although the Indians traded with him, they did so by their own choice, and they could as easily choose to attack him and take his goods without trading at all. That was what had happened to Fitzpatrick in 1833, when the Crow stole all his merchandise and most of his ammunition. He had kept his scalp, but his partner Jedediah Smith had already been murdered by the Comanche in 1831. According to one early estimate, of all the pioneer trappers who went into the mountains in the early 1820s, three-fifths were killed by Indians.

• 3 •

Toward this forbidding country the rival traders, Wyeth and Sublette, set out in the spring of 1834. By the end of March, Nathaniel Wyeth had signed up most of his men. Like Sublette's men, they were a hard-bitten, hard-drinking crew, but they were used to the sufferings of the trail and in a pinch could be counted on to fight. One man named Howell had been engaged to marry a St. Louis girl but at the last moment decided to sign up with Wyeth. Another named Smith was a notorious adventurer then serving time in the St. Louis jail. But Wyeth knew that he was a daring man in a crisis. On Wyeth's promise that he would take Smith where the authorities "would not hear from him again," they let him join the expedition.

On such a rough band, the New Englander staked his fortunes. To his wife he wrote a parting letter:

This is my last attempt and if I am not successfull I must come home and endeavor the best way I can to get a living and to pay my debts which will then be heavy. Still I am yet sanguine that I shall succeed. I will take good care of myself and perhaps the life which began in turmoil may yet end in quiet and peace and our sun go down from a clear sky.

On April 3 Wyeth left with his goods and some of his men on the steamer *Ioway*, a slow boat that made about thirty miles a day. Sublette did not start until April 20, seventeen days behind Wyeth. Shunning river travel, he rode west with the nucleus of his crew on horseback at the remarkable rate of sixty miles a day.

The passage from St. Louis to the "upper settlements" at the big bend of the Missouri River was an adventure in itself. As such a journey probably meant an absence of one or two years, the mountaineers customarily preceded the departure with what one chronicler called "a general debauch." While the drays rattled over the wharves, the steamers waited with engines chugging and stacks wheezing, the passengers and African boatmen adding to the pandemonium with loud chatter in several tongues. Then, as the crew members cast off, they raised the usual "river chorus". The boat, twin stacks puffing and wheels churning, parted from shore and swung into the current. At that moment the mountain men raised their rifles and filled the air with a crackling volley until the steamer was well into the mainstream beyond earshot.

In the 1830s the Missouri River steamers, then replacing the primitive keelboats, were small and hardly luxurious. Their decks were crowded with polyglot companies of mountain traders, hunters and trappers, Indians, soldiers, settlers and African slaves. Gambling, carousing and raucous singing were the standard diversions. A horrified missionary described his fellow passengers as "shockingly profane swearers and gamblers, most of whom are intemperate." Among the *engagés* bound upriver to the fur trade it was customary to pick fights with one another on deck until it had been definitely determined which man was champion.

The first stopping place up the river was St. Charles, only twenty miles from St Louis by the short-cut road. As the boat docked there, its steam engines idly panting, Wyeth's man Howell decided to return and marry his girl. Carrying his beaver traps, he stepped onto the wharf before anybody could stop him. But at that moment Smith, the rogue whom Wyeth had sprung from the St. Louis jail, stepped to the railing.

"Don't be a lovesick baby," he chided. "Act the man and stand up to your agreement."

While the two were arguing, the pilot started up the steamboat and backed it away from the wharf. Determined to have his man, Smith ordered the boat returned. The pilot refused. Smith pulled out a pistol and aimed it at the pilot's head.

"Land the boat or I will blow your brains out."

Smith's reputation was known to the pilot, who lost no time in reversing paddles and churning back to the wharf. The moment the boat touched, Smith jumped to the pier, grabbed Howell and took him back on board. On up the muddy Missouri plowed the steamboat with its cargo of mountain men.

Unlike the green and leisurely Mississippi, the Missouri swept urgently along at an average of four miles an hour and at twice that speed over sand bars. Carrying a heavy burden of silt and debris, it was scouring out fresh channels, undermining old banks, raising new islands. As artist George Catlin wrote in the 1830s, "there is a terror in its manner which is sensibly felt, the moment we enter its muddy waters from the Mississippi."

Because of the river's savage assaults on its banks, trees were continually falling into the waters, where their roots sank to the bottom and their tops floated, pointing downstream. The water was so thickly spiked with such driftwood that to the novice it appeared impossible for a steamboat to pass. As it was, paddles and paddle boxes were frequently broken by floating logs, requiring stops for repairs.

An accepted method of clearing a sand bar was to "walk" the boat across by driving down two pilings or spars at a downstream angle and raising the bow of the boat by means of a block and tackle; this procedure would reduce the boat's draft and allow it to move forward a few feet. The process was repeated until the bar was cleared, which sometimes took one or two days. Years later Mark Twain wrote in *Roughing It* about such a passage up the lower Missouri: "the boat might almost as well have gone . . . by land, for she was walking most of the time, anyhow."

So dangerous and unreliable was the river that it was usually impossible to proceed at night except in bright moonlight. With frequent accidents and groundings, most boats made only twenty to thirty miles a day and took a week or two to cross the State of Missouri.

Those who traveled the land route from St. Louis to the border took what one of them called a "horrible road" westward. Just before Sublette started, one of the regular stages was upset while fording a stream near Columbia, and as the coach floated downstream the passengers had to swim for shore. But aside from such inconveniences, the Missouri springtime was a delight to the traveler. The rolling prairie was blanketed with tall grass. In the low places and along the streams were woods of sycamore, poplar, cottonwood and pawpaw. Birds, from the wild turkey to the prairie hen, scattered at the approach of the horsemen. Parakeets, with their brilliant green and red plumage, fluttered about and screeched at the newcomers. Game was plentiful, and there was no trouble in providing the camp with fowl and venison.

The ordinary traveler, however, accepted the hospitality of the Missouri settlers, who lived in scattered log cabins on the edges of the woods. Invariably they gave the wayfarer a hearty welcome, offered him a meal and, if evening was coming on, insisted that he stay the night. The richness of the Missouri soil made every farm a cornucopia; on a half-hour's notice, the woman of the house would favor her guest with a dinner of ham, chicken, eggs, milk, honey, corn and home-made bread.

• 4 •

On April 14 Wyeth's steamboat reached the landing at Independence, the final jumping-off place for the western plains. The town itself was composed of about fifty scattered log cabins, a few clapboard stores, two taverns and several grogshops filled with a rough and raucous clientele. Immediately Wyeth fell to gathering his pack outfit for the overland trek. This included hiring more men at wages of around $300 for eighteen months, plus their board, which would consist mainly of the buffalo they could shoot along the way.

But the demand for recruits for the trading parties and government expeditions up the river was intense. Wyeth not only had to advance his men part of their wages but had to pay their debts beside; and even then they were liable to be spirited away by another party during a night's revelry in Independence. "It is like keeping a bag of fleas together," he wrote, "to keep men in this whisky country."

Yet Wyeth put together a party of seventy men; most of them were experienced mountaineers, but they included five Methodist missionaries bound for Oregon and two naturalists who had joined the trek to study the flora and fauna of the Far West. One of them was John K. Townsend, a young ornithologist from Philadelphia, who would write a most human and descriptive journal of the expedition. Also joining Wyeth's party was a small group of mountain men under Milton Sublette, one of William's younger brothers. Milton did not always work with William and in fact was one of Fitzpatrick's partners in the Rocky Mountain Fur Company. But he was suffering from an infected leg and would be able to travel with Wyeth only for a few days. Meanwhile, his experience and the strength added by his frontiersmen gave encouragement to the rest, poised on the brink of the Indian country.

By this time, William Sublette had reached the town of Lexington, an older outpost about thirty miles back of the frontier. Neither men nor animals were so scarce in Lexington, and the more experienced mountain man made it his favorite outfitting point. Within five days he had finished buying and branding his horses, had loaded his packs and had started on the road. With

him rode 37 men—most of them hard-bitten hunters and trappers.
Among them was young William Anderson, a strapping Ken-
tuckian with some education who was coming west for the first
time. He would provide the only journal of the expedition.

After two weeks in Independence, Wyeth's own men struck out
on the morning of April 28. They rode in double file, each one
leading two pack horses while the missionaries herded a band of
cattle along the flank. In the spirit of the moment, the men broke
into a tune; as if the exhilaration were contagious, the horses
pranced and pawed the ground, snorting and neighing. It was the
same as the beginnings of a hundred mountain expeditions, with
the men expressing their exuberance in whoops and songs and
startling the inhabitants of the last frontier cabins with savage
yells as they passed. The animals jumped and bucked; some of
them kicked off their packs, broke loose and had to be retrieved
with much hollering and cursing by their masters. Young Anderson, who left Independence with Sublette's party on May 5, found
time to meditate on his predicament in the unprotected wilds
beyond the frontier: "I am now out of the U.S. for the first time."

• 5 •

The route lay along the Kansas River over an undulating
prairie that was bereft of trees, except for a few cottonwoods along
the streams. This was the Indian country. Each party marched
with scouts in front and on the flanks by day; by night the men
formed their bales of goods into a square with the tents and campfires inside and the horses staked in the center.

After supper the evening's relaxation around the campfire would
be broken about eight o'clock by the sudden call, "Turn out the
first guard!" Six or eight men would then scramble into sentry
positions, each with a gun and a blanket. In some parties the
guards were ordered to stand still, as Indians were known to
sneak up and shoot anyone they saw moving. Every twenty
minutes or so the officer of the guard would cry out "All's well!"
and each guard would repeat the call in his turn. If a guard failed
to answer the officer would go and find him. If he was asleep his
gun would be taken from him, and he would have to retrieve it the
next morning from the captain of the party. Then he would gen-

erally have to pay a fine ($5 or so) and walk on foot for the next three days. One traveler reported someone footing it almost every day.

For two hours each set of guards would keep to the posts, through freezing cold or storm. At dawn the last guard would leave the encampment and ride over the surrounding hills to search for Indians. If all was still well, the animals would be turned out to graze, with hobbles on their front legs. The sleepers were roused with the order "Get up!" or, if the party was predominantly French, "Levéz! Levéz!" After breakfast the men would retrieve their animals and begin the ordeal of packing up. This scene presented the greatest confusion on the march, for the mules were determined not to be harnessed and packed. What with kicking and rearing, pulling and jerking, the camp was turned into a writhing, surging bedlam; and the silence of the prairie was broken with the most fearful chorus of braying from the mules and terrible oaths from their tormenters. At last the party would fall into line and resume its march, while the deserted campsite was invaded by waiting ravens, wolves or Indian dogs that had been skulking on the periphery.

A few days up the Kansas River Wyeth's party reached a village of the Kansas or Kaw Indians, a tribe inclined to settle in one place with more or less permanent huts made of willow branches and covered with bark and animal skins. The villagers crowded around so eagerly that progress was impeded, and, when the party had made camp, they came to trade for trinkets and tobacco, beg for food at the campfires and steal what they could from the tents. Their dogs descended upon the camps like scavengers—the first of a canine escort from successive Indian villages that would haunt the caravans the whole way to the mountains.

All the while, Sublette and his men were gaining on Wyeth. They were a week behind when they left Independence, and from the Kansas River Wyeth wrote to his backers in Boston, "I am the first as yet in the Indian country." But he tarried too long at the Kaw village. By the time Sublette reached the Kansas tribe on May 8, he was only three days behind. On the 11th Wyeth temporarily lost his way, and Sublette passed him that evening. The next day, while Wyeth and his party were resting in camp and mending equipment, his scouts came in with the news that they had discovered Sublette's trail. Packing up, Wyeth hurriedly pushed on; late in the afternoon he came across an empty camp where the Sublette party had "nooned." Thoroughly alarmed, Wyeth pressed his own party onward until darkness halted it, and sent a messenger hurrying westward with a letter addressed to Fitzpatrick "In the Rocky Mountains":

> Wm Sublette having passed me here, I am induced to write you by this opportunity and hope you will get it. You may expect me by the 1st July at the rendesvous. . . . I am not heavily loaded and shall travell as fast as possible and have a sufficient equipment of goods for you according to contract.

Because the horses had been under forced march with nothing to eat all day, Wyeth did not tether them that night but simply hobbled them within the enclosure. But other passersby were also in the vicinity. About one o'clock the animals suddenly took fright and awakened the whole camp with the most desperate whinnying and rearing. Before anyone could calm them, about a hundred horses snapped their hobbles, stampeded through camp, knocked down several tents, leaped the breastwork and galloped out into the night. Immediately the whole party turned out of bed, bridled the remaining horses and without waiting for saddles rode bareback in pursuit of the hoofbeats. It was morning before the men had rounded up the renegades—all but two.

Scarcely had the party settled down to breakfast when three Oto Indians rode into camp. Lacking an interpreter, they simply smoked the pipe with their host, who suspected strongly that they had stampeded his horses and still possessed the missing pair.

Now moving along the Little Blue River toward the Platte, Wyeth's men were a day's journey behind Sublette. Townsend wrote, "We see his deserted camps every day, and, in some cases, the fires are not yet extinguished." As they neared the Platte, they entered the country of the Pawnee, who at that time were as dreaded in the southern plains as were the Blackfeet in the northern Rockies. Though living in permanent villages and raising crops, they were expert hunters and horsemen. Tall and athletic, they combined physical strength with native cunning that made them as formidable as any cavalry on the plains.

On May 15 three Pawnee rode into Sublette's camp for a parley. Their own camp was, they said, a short way ahead on the Little

Blue. The next morning, while Sublette and his men were leaving their campsite, they saw a dust cloud descending from the distant hills to the south and heading rapidly in their direction. At first the moving forms were indistinguishable; they seemed to be either buffalo or horses and riders. Fearing the worst, Sublette hurried his cavalcade into a protective gully. Quickly the men drove down pickets for their horses, threw bales of provisions on the edge of the bank as a rude breastwork and unlimbered their rifles.

Out of the dust emerged a band of eighty to one hundred Pawnee, hurtling forward on swift ponies and wielding spears, bows and guns. In a few minutes, they arrived before Sublette's camp, their disordered array spreading almost magically into a disciplined frontal line. Young Anderson, for one, found himself shifting excitedly from one foot to another: "Twas enough to make one feel a little tremulous about the corners of the mouth—I confess that for myself."

As the invaders approached to within about 200 yards—still beyond accurate rifle range—Sublette sent out one of his scouts, who could speak the Pawnee language. At the same time the men stood up in their positions and showed their strength. The Indians halted abruptly. Sublette's interpreter asked them to send forward their chiefs. Four Indians left the others and rode out to meet Sublette.

"What do you want?" he demanded through his interpreter.

The chiefs indicated that they expected presents—apparently as a kind of toll for passing through Pawnee territory. For this very purpose Sublette had brought tobacco, powder and balls, beads and other items. When a pile of these things had been placed before the four Indians, Sublette stood quietly watching their reactions. After pondering the presents for a moment, they moved their ponies apart to form two separate pairs.

"It is very good," observed one chief, "but there is one village and there is another."

Sublette knew he was in no position to resist: "Damn the rascals!"

And he had a second pile of presents set before them. Grunts of approval indicated that the transaction was complete. First the chiefs and then some of the braves urged their ponies forward, shaking hands with Sublette and some of the other frontiersmen. One Pawnee leaned forward from his horse and hugged Anderson at the same time that he rubbed his hand over his own chest—a gesture that the tenderfoot later learned meant "My heart is made glad to see you." Then, with the permission of their hosts, Sublette and his party gathered themselves up and moved forward again.

On the 17th and 18th the two parties—still little more than a day apart—reached the Platte. Known to the Indians as the "Nebraska" or "flat" river, it was said by local plainsmen to be "a mile wide and an inch deep." When the two parties reached it in the vicinity of Grand Island it was still in low stage; ranging in width from one to three miles, it was full of sand bars and small islands. To the amazement of the tenderfeet in both parties, they could walk across it "without wetting your knees." But though the valley of the Platte was more barren of grass than was the Kansas prairie, it drew elk and antelope in large numbers. Buffalo were still three days ahead, having withdrawn westward from the lower Missouri a number of years earlier under pressure from the Indian hunters.

It was while Wyeth was pressing along the south bank of the Platte that the Pawnee turned their attention to his party. Early on the morning of May 20 two horsemen of the Grand Pawnee tribe approached to within several hundred yards of the column. Wyeth rode to meet them alone while the caravan continued to move. Their camp, they reported, was a day's march downriver and consisted of a war party about 1,500 strong. Suspecting that they had been sent out to spy on him, Wyeth became uneasy; he told them that his party would proceed only a few miles farther before stopping overnight. But, as soon as they were safely out of sight, he stirred his whole column into a fast trot. All day he kept up this strenuous pace, covering some 26 miles and stopping only at midnight. Then, after a quick supper and a three-hour sleep under doubled guard, the party pushed on steadily all next day and left the Grand Pawnee far behind.

Although Wyeth had closed some of the gap between himself and Sublette, he had still not caught him. The mountain man was half a day's march ahead when they reached the forks of the Platte on the 20th and 21st. There, suddenly, they came upon the buffalo. Anderson's first sight was of a column of animals ten to twenty wide and from ten to twelve miles long. For three days

they traveled through a veritable sea of animals. Once Wyeth's
party topped a hill and, as Townsend described the scene:

> The whole plain, as far as the eye could discern, was covered by
> one enormous mass of buffalo. . . . Our party rode up to within a
> few hundred yards of the edge of the herd, before any alarm was
> communicated; then the bulls,—which are always stationed
> around as sentinels,—began pawing the ground, and throwing
> the earth over their heads; in a few moments they started in a
> slow, clumsy canter; but as we neared them, they quickened their
> pace to an astonishingly rapid gallop, and in a few minutes were
> entirely beyond the reach of our guns. . . .

Beyond the forks of the Platte, the bill of fare for the two
parties—indeed, for all the early expeditions into the Rockies—
consisted almost entirely of buffalo meat. It was customary for the
parties to carry enough salt pork and other unperishable items to
last until they reached the buffalo country, after which they would
have more food than they could eat.

Moving first along the South Platte and then crossing to the
North Fork, the Sublette and Wyeth parties rode into higher and
rougher ground as they approached the outlying ranges of the
distant Rockies. Game in the plateau country was then rampant—
sometimes approaching in grandeur the great animal spectacles
of the African veldt. With a spyglass on a clear morning one could
see buffalo, bear, deer, elk, antelope, bighorn sheep and wolves—
all grazing or prowling about in a kind of natural pageant. One
traveler of the early 1830s wrote that the prairies were "in some
places literally covered with game. . . ."

In this plains country, other phenomena—like clouds of gnats
and merciless sandstorms—vexed the newcomers. Their animals
began to fail for lack of grass. Already such hardships had begun
to tell upon the men. From the moment they had left the settlements, there had been desertions from Wyeth's party. On the
North Platte, Anderson reported some quarreling among Sublette's
men. Partly to relieve such tensions, the captains of parties usually
held occasional "days of indulgence," in which whiskey was freely
dispensed and the cares of the trail dispatched.

But no such diversion was allowed the Sublette and Wyeth
parties on the plains; they were still plunging toward the mountains with the greatest possible speed. By May 27th Sublette had
passed Chimney Rock, and the next night he camped just below

Scotts Bluff. Wyeth nooned at the Chimney on the 29th and
passed through Scotts Bluff on the 30th—roughly a day and a
half behind Sublette.

On the same day, Sublette's party reached Laramie's Fork, a
swift and rippling stream rushing out of the Laramie Range to the
south. According to tradition, the creek was named for a French
trapper, Jacques or Joseph LaRamee, who had been killed there
by Arapaho in 1822. A mile and half upstream from its junction
with the North Platte, Sublette meant to build a fort with which
to capture the Indian trade of the central plains and the Rockies.
On the 31st, according to Anderson's journal, Sublette's party
spent the day "making arrangements for the fort builders." As the
foundation log was laid, the occasion was celebrated—in this
lonely wilderness, some 700 miles from the American frontier—
with a bottle of "good, genuine, New York imported champagne."
Anderson's journal entry for May 31 explains, "The fort on
Laramy's fork is called F. William, in honor of its founder
Mr. S."[1]

• 6 •

When Wyeth arrived on June 1, thirteen of Sublette's men
were at work on the fort, but Sublette himself had already pushed
on with his main party. Before them, gleaming on the dim horizon,
loomed the snowy crest of the Rockies—a kind of Circe to these
trail-weary adventurers. Sublette was speeded, as Wyeth observed, by leaving "one half of his goods and horses on the route,
which of course I could not do." On June 4 Sublette was only one
day ahead. By the 7th he had lengthened the gap to two days.

In that rough and sterile country, such a pace was torture.
Wyeth had already left two footworn cattle behind, and by June 8
several of his horses were ready to collapse. Next day he reached
Independence Rock, where all the travelers over the South Pass
route habitually painted their names. With alarm he discovered
Sublette's signature dated the 6th—three days earlier—and refused to believe it. Nevertheless, he dispatched a second messenger to Fitzpatrick: "I am now two days behind Wm Sublette,
who I presume is with you by this. . . . I wish that you would
defer making any contract for carrying home any surplus furs that
you have or for a further supply of goods until I come. . . ."

But on the 12th Sublette reached the rendezvous on the Green River above the mouth of the Sandy in the southwest corner of present-day Wyoming. Two days later he was shaking hands with his old friend Tom Fitzpatrick. Quickly the two mountain men concluded their transaction. Fitzpatrick also had urgent business with his own partners in the Rocky Mountain Fur Company. The beaver hunt had been disappointing, increased competition was thinning the profits of earlier years and it was already apparent that the trading firms were reaping most of the returns. All the partners but one were present at the rendezvous; they dissolved the fur company, and thus eliminated the second party to Wyeth's contract.

By that time the New Englander had left his group on the trail and had hurried ahead by himself to find Fitzpatrick. But when he arrived on the 17th Fitzpatrick refused to deal, stating that he and his company had gone out of business. He would, however, pay the forfeit.

Wyeth was outraged at Fitzpatrick and Sublette. "Gentlemen," he roared, "I will roll a stone into your garden which you will never be able to get out."

To Milton Sublette, who had accompanied him on the first part of his expedition, Wyeth wrote his suspicions: "I think he [Fitzpatrick] has been bribed to sacrifice my interests by better offers from your brother."

Sublette had won his race to the mountains and had struck down a potential rival in the central fur trade. The transaction has not added to Fitzpatrick's reputation. He had kept to the letter of the contract, but his allowing a contractor to brave the ordeal of the western passage—storms, hardships and Indians—and then refusing his goods on a technicality offers eloquent testimony to the mean and savage character to which the fur trade had sunk. As Wyeth wrote to his backers, "there is no law here."

Yet even despite the massive blow dealt him by Sublette, Wyeth could not lose heart. Leaving the rendezvous on July 2, he pressed on over the divide and established Fort Hall on the Snake River to dispose of the goods Fitzpatrick had refused. That historic trading post was his "stone" in Sublette's and Fitzpatrick's garden. Then on he pushed for the Oregon country. After founding a second fort near the mouth of the Willamette River, he strove for two years—through sickness, deprivation and Indian attack—to build a commercial empire in Oregon. But the Hudson's Bay Company —already a veteran in Oregon—was too formidable a competitor. As one observer wrote, the company "preceded him, followed him, surrounded him everywhere and cut the throat of his prosperity with . . . kindness and politeness . . ."

Beaten and broken, Wyeth abandoned his Oregon venture to his rivals and started back to Massachusetts. From the heart of the Rockies he wrote the last letter of his trip: "Keep up good spirits my dear wife for I expect when I come home to stop there and altho I shall be poor yet we can always live."

* 7 *

On July 10, 1834, Bill Sublette struck his tents at the rendezvous and started on the return trip. By the 20th his party had reached Laramie's Fork, where his men were finishing Fort William. The ramparts were of eighteen-foot-high cottonwood logs, with blockhouses at two of the corners and another over the gate. Inside were several rooms for a blacksmith's shop, a storehouse and quarters for the employees. As Anderson put it, "here she stands defying wind, rain & Indians." "She" was called "Fort William" at first but soon she would be known among the mountain men as "Fort Laramie." For two generations she would stand there, serving traders and Indians, missionaries and emigrants. She would become the principal stronghold of Uncle Sam's power in the Rockies. And if she had been able to talk she might well have said of the central West's turbulent and formative years, "All of which I saw, much of which I was."

But even at its founding in the mid-1830s, Fort Laramie had immediate influence. For, although Wyeth had failed to hurt the company's trade, the whole mountain fur traffic was faltering. The free trapper and the rendezvous were not yet dead, but their heyday had begun to pass with the disappointing meeting on the Green River and Sublette's construction of his fort on Laramie's Fork in 1834. Control of the fur trade was slipping from the hands of explorers and free spirits into those of harder businessmen located in settlements or at fixed outposts.

True, far to the north the American Fur Company had already maintained forts on the upper Missouri for several years. Southward the Bent brothers had operated a fort on the Santa Fe Trail since the late 1820s. But those routes were byways of the frontier.

The star of empire, which had moved westward across the Mississippi Valley in the infancy of the Republic, would continue to course past the bend of the Missouri to the central plains, to the central Rockies and finally to the Pacific. Of this star, Sublette's fort on the Laramie was an advance glimmer. For the first time it put a permanent society of white men in the heart of the buffalo country.

Up to 1834 the trappers in the central Rockies had lived as guests of the Indians and had embraced their ways. Like their red brothers they were nomads; they dressed as the Indians did, lived as they did and sometimes lived *with* them. But the new fort on the Laramie became a civilized enclave in the wilderness. Its palisade walls were a barrier against the red man. Its inhabitants were not guests but intruders, and its small colony of white men lived as their brothers lived in the states. There was a new finger-hold of the American-European culture within a Stone Age empire.

TWO ♦ *Bull Bear Jumps into the Fire*

A year after Fort William was founded, the American Fur Company's annual caravan from the Missouri settlements was making its way to the Rocky Mountain rendezvous. With the mountain men were Methodist missionaries bound for Oregon, making their first venture into the Indian country. On July 24, 1835, the expedition halted only a day's travel from Fort William. While dinner was being prepared, someone raised an alarm: "Secure your animals! Secure your animals!"

A mile and a half away, a mounted party of Oglala Sioux was thundering down upon the caravan. Frantically the newcomers began staking their horses and looking to their guns. But just before the Indians came within rifle shot, they abruptly fired their guns in the air. In that day of single-shot muzzle-loaders, this act was the accustomed sign of friendship on the plains—proof that the approaching party carried unloaded guns. Then the Oglala rode into camp and exchanged greetings with their trader friends.

Within a year after Fort William's beginnings the Oglala, who had previously been near-strangers on the North Platte, had become the region's overlords. The story of their migration begins with Bill Sublette's original plan to attract them south to his new trading post. He had sent two experienced traders, John Sabille and Charles E. Galpin, north to the Black Hills. At Bear Butte on the northern edge of the hills they found the encampment of the Oglala Sioux. To the chiefs the two traders described the advantages of the North Platte. There were plenty of buffalo—they were countless, like the needles of the pine. There was ample grass for Oglala horses. And at the new fort there would be trade goods

20

to take the place of those provided at Dakota outposts by the American Fur Company. Leave the Black Hills, urged Sublette's men. Move your lodges south to the North Platte and the Laramie.

To these blandishments the Oglala were vulnerable. They were traditional nomads without deep roots. They were, in fact, comparative newcomers to the plains. Together with all the Sioux tribes, they had in early times roamed the headwaters region of the Mississippi River. In that green land of lakes and woods they had hunted on foot with bows and arrows, trading at times with the English or French and battling often with the Cree. In the seventeenth century their enemies had driven them south to the Minnesota River. Exploring the vast range of the buffalo, they had drifted west, first on hunting forays and then by moving their villages. Around 1760 they had reached the Missouri River and had first come in contact with horses, which they bought or stole from the Arikara Indians. Crossing the river, they had pressed westward along the streams leading to the Black Hills. Around 1785 they had driven the Crow from the north side of the hills and had made that hunting ground, teeming with game, their home.

Capturing wild horses after the manner of the Arikara, the Sioux became a mounted nation—swift, mobile and what a later American general would call "the greatest light cavalry in the world." Buffalo had become their staple prey—useful alike for food, clothing and shelter. Horses became their mark of wealth and stealing horses from their enemies—the Crow to the west and the Pawnee to the south—their principal diversion. Although latecomers, they became in two generations the prototypes of the Plains Indians.

When Sabille and Galpin came among them in 1834, the Oglala were already familiar with the Platte Valley. For several years they had ranged southward on summer hunts as far as the domain of the Pawnee. They had refined the business of attacking the Pawnee—waiting out of sight while their enemies ran buffalo, exhausting their horses and their ammunition. Then the Oglala would swoop down upon them, massacring the braves, ransacking the villages and running off with Pawnee horses and Pawnee women.

One Oglala chief was especially charmed by the inducements of Sublette's men. He was Bull Bear, a man short and blocky in stature, swarthy in complexion, proud and willful in bearing.

Whereas other chiefs maintained their power by skillful politics, Bull Bear ignored such amenities and flaunted his strength. Whereas some warriors would steal the wives of others and then seek to placate the injured husbands by token payments, Bull Bear scorned such concessions and let his insults stand. And when a warrior objected to this or some other trespass, Bull Bear would not be content with a rebuke. He would, then and there, beat the offender or even run him through with a knife. And the act would go unchallenged; a lesser chief might have been punished with death by his tribesmen for this abuse of power. But no one dared to oppose Bull Bear.

So it was that the Oglala under Bull Bear found themselves ruled, not by tribal council, but by the overbearing and sometimes impetuous judgments of their chief. As one chronicler wrote of him, "When he had resolved on any course of conduct, he would pay to the warriors the empty compliment of calling them together to deliberate upon it, and when their debates were over, he would quietly state his own opinion, which no one disputed."

Such a chief was confident enough to be unconcerned over the selfish aims of the white traders. He looked upon contact with the whites not as a threat to Indian sovereignty but as an opportunity for Indian profit. He therefore decided to strike his lodges and follow Sublette's men south to the North Platte.

About half the Oglala—apparently those under Bull Bear's enemy Chief Smoke—at first resisted the move. They stayed behind while Bull Bear took about a hundred lodges, perhaps a thousand people, southward. After wintering at Fort William, the Bear people—as they came to be called—were probably joined by Chief Smoke and his people in the spring of 1835.

From that time on the Oglala Sioux, more than any other tribe, made the fort on the Laramie their home base. As early as 1835 they were followed by the Brulé, another Sioux tribe that had migrated westward from the Minnesota River to the Black Hills in the eighteenth century. On that move, extending over two generations, they had been caught in a prairie fire and had escaped only by jumping into a lake. Most of the tribe had suffered from burned legs—a misfortune commemorated in a new tribal name, the "Brulé" (brûlé is French for "the burned one"). Like the Oglala, they had acquired horses after reaching the Missouri and had continued their westward migration as far as the Black Hills. But by the mid-1830s the game was thinning in

their adopted domain. They joined the Oglala in veering southward to the two branches of the Platte, where the high plains
were sometimes black with buffalo and shook with the thunder
of their hooves.

For many years, in fact, the Sioux had joined other Plains
Indians in depending almost completely on the buffalo for their
way of life. The meat, preserved by drying in the sun, was their
staple food the year round. The skin was used for the coverings
of their lodges, their clothing, their beds and blankets, their saddle
leather, halters and rope. The sinews were used for the strings
of their bows and the thread with which they sewed their leather
and bound their arrowheads. The horns were turned into cups and
ladles; the bones became saddle trees, war clubs, mallets, scrapers,
chisels and needles. The hooves were boiled to obtain glue. The
long hair of the manes was braided into halters, and the tails were
converted into fly switches. The bladders were sometimes used as
water containers. Long before their use by white emigrants crossing the treeless plains, dried buffalo chips were used by the Indians
for fuel. As a German traveler wrote in the 1830s, "The Indian
and the buffalo are Siamese twins . . . both will perish together."

But, after the permanent trading posts had been established on
the upper Missouri following the War of 1812, the Sioux began
hunting buffalo for more than their own needs. A market for robes
had developed in the East, and the traders were offering every
inducement to get the Indians' business. So the Oglala and Brulé
slaughtered buffalo without end, taking the skins and perhaps the
tongues, which were also in demand as delicacies at the forts on
the Missouri River. In this way they obtained some of the white
man's possessions—guns, powder, ammunition, knives, blankets
and, the most important of all, whiskey.

Clearly, even though the Far West was still Indian country and
the farm frontier still clung to the lower Missouri River, the
Indians had already been sharply affected by their contacts with
white traders. Bartering at the annual rendezvous and at the river
forts became the goal of their year-long activities. And, as the
Sioux proved in the 1830s, whole tribes would move their villages
in order to maintain their commerce with the whites. They would
hunt out whole domains—virtually strip them of game—in order
to satisfy the white man's market. More than once the Sioux had
come near starvation in the Dakotas before moving to the Platte.

It has been commonly believed that the buffalo were plentiful until the professional white hunters began slaughtering them for the hide market in the early 1870s. But the Indians themselves, responding to demand for robes among the white men, had started the annihilation decades before. As early as the 1830s, the buffalo had retreated, under the onslaught of the Pawnee and other tribes, west of the forks of the Platte River. At the same time artist George Catlin visited the upper Missouri and warned that the Indian was slaughtering his own subsistence. On the southern plains the Catholic curate of Taos wrote to the Mexican government in 1843 that "the buffalo seems to have almost disappeared in those localities where, at first, they were thought to be inexhaustible . . ."

Through the short-term expedience of trade with the whites, the red men were committing the long-term folly of destroying their own sustenance. But for a generation it would prove possible to postpone the reckoning by moving to new hunting grounds. The Sioux hegira to the upper Platte, where the buffalo were plentiful and Bill Sublette offered a trading post, represented such a postponement. Fort William introduced to the high central plains the social pattern then shaping in the West—the diversion of the native races from their own ecology to dependence on the white man.

• 2 •

When Bull Bear and his people came to the Platte, they brought with them the techniques of buffalo hunting that they had perfected on the Dakota plains. There were two such methods —one on foot and one on horseback—and both took advantage of the peculiarities of the buffalo. Because of their relatively poor eyesight, the animals could be approached very closely but it had to be from the downwind side due to their exceptionally good sense of smell. In the older of the two methods, developed before the Indians took to horses, a hunter would cover himself with the skin of a buffalo calf, tie the front legs to his arms and approach the herd on hands and knees. As the gray wolf was familiar to the buffalo and would not attack a healthy animal while it was in the protection of the herd, the skin of a wolf could also be used.

With such a disguise the Indian might crawl as far as a mile through the grass and up to the very edge of the herd, without stirring any suspicion. Selecting a fat cow, he would position himself so close that it would be impossible to miss. Then he would take aim at a point just back of the shoulder blades and loose an arrow with such force that it was often buried up to the feathers. More than one observer in the 1830s wrote of arrows going entirely through the animals and lodging on the ground beyond or wounding other buffalo. A chronicler in Wyeth's party of 1834 reported that the arrow usually protruded on the other side, and before the wounded animal could fall the Indian would scurry around and pull the arrow through, in order to save it for his next victim. A special twist on this system was developed by the Blackfeet, who prided themselves on hunting afoot. They attacked the buffalo during the thaws of springtime, when the animals would sink deep in boggy ground and were nearly helpless before their attackers. Other tribes, including the Sioux, also stalked the buffalo on snowshoes in the winter, when the animals would sink to their bellies in the snow and the value of their robes was increased by the seasonal thickness of the hair.

With the stalking method, a few Indians working silently could bring down many buffalo before exciting alarm. But the system had disadvantages; it was dangerous, for the hunter was afoot in the midst of powerful animals that were as fleet as horses. The bulls were ill tempered and unpredictable; they might run away in the first panic, or they might turn on the hunter in defense of their cows. Furthermore, it was only a question of time before the herd would take flight; such forays had limited yields.

Although it was impossible for horsemen to approach so close to the herd without detection, the mounted hunters had one overriding advantage. With enough riders, an entire herd of several hundred buffalo could be hemmed in and methodically slaughtered.

Such a hunt was often the work of an entire village and constituted one of the best instances of community effort and group discipline among nomadic tribes. Sometimes religious ceremonies attended the chase. Along the Platte, white travelers often came across great circles of buffalo skulls with the noses turned inward —magic devices intended to lure the migrating animals back to the vicinity. On discovering a herd the Pawnee sometimes preceded their hunt with an hour or so of religious rites, including speechmaking and pipesmoking, designed to promote a successful chase.

During the ride toward the buffalo herd, the tribesmen restrained the most eager among them with stern discipline. No one was allowed to get ahead of the others and spoil the hunt by a premature attack; any impetuous youths who did get in front of the chiefs were whipped with the quirts of the older warriors. If there was a long ride before the attack the braves usually rode second horses, leading their specially trained buffalo ponies to the scene of action. According to one chronicle of a Pawnee hunt, the riders jumped off their buffalo horses from time to time and ran alongside to keep their mounts fresh for the chase. The ponies themselves, thoroughly experienced in running buffalo, pranced and snorted in their eagerness for the hunt.

After riding in as close as possible under cover of hills without disturbing their quarry, the hunters stopped to strip themselves of shields and other unnecessary encumbrances; even quivers were discarded and only a half-dozen arrows were carried loosely in the hand.

During the "stripping" process, the leaders held a council to determine their strategy. As it would have been impossible to prevent the herd from running, the objective was to start them running in the right direction, particularly away from rough ground and toward a plain less dangerous to traverse at breakneck speed. If the group was in the territory of enemy tribes, one or more young boys would be posted on nearby hills to warn of attack. Then, if the land lay favorably, parties were sent out behind hills and up dry washes to cover all sides of the herd before the attack. A successful "surround," as it was called, could yield the whole herd.

Finally the approach was made, and at a signal the charge began at a full gallop, accompanied by savage yells and much whipping of horses with the short Indian quirt. The stricken buffalo would stampede in one direction, only to be turned by a new attack. Finally, with dust filling the air, they would become a writhing mass of life surrounded and tormented by their enemy.

A good buffalo horse was so trained that, once it was clear which prey his rider had selected, he would run up on the animal's right side, the reins hanging loosely upon his own neck. The Indian would crouch forward on the left side of the horse's neck, taking aim with his bow. As they thundered over the plain, the horse would follow the quarry through every dodge and turn. When the horse was almost abreast of the buffalo, and sometimes as close as a bow's length away, the Indian would shoot his arrow into the animal's side. Then the horse would veer away to avoid further chance of collision.

Sometimes the rider would aim at the vital spot behind the shoulder blades. But, though such a shot might be fatal, it would not immediately stop the buffalo, and it was sometimes customary to deliver the first arrow in his rear quarters to cripple him, in order to return later for the kill.

The moment of shooting the buffalo was the most hazardous of all, for, beside the chance that the horse would step in a prairie-dog hole and upset his rider under the feet of the stampeding herd, there was the real danger that the buffalo would suddenly stop and, with a quick movement to the right, attempt to hook his antagonist with his horns. If he did so before the horse was fully abreast, the latter was trained to shift quickly to the left of the buffalo to avoid the horns. But sometimes it was too late to turn. Then the horse would be raised on the horns of the buffalo and would lose his entrails. The rider would be thrown to the earth, where he would scramble to his feet to avoid other trampling hooves. Generally a rope from the pony's neck was allowed to drag along the ground during the hunt, so that an unhorsed rider could grab it and retrieve his mount.

There were variations in this general mode of hunting. Sometimes spears were used, though they had nowhere near the force of the fully drawn arrow. One eyewitness told of an Indian who unexpectedly found himself next to a buffalo herd without proper weapons but, being desperate from near-starvation, rode after a fat cow, leaped on her back and killed her with his hunting knife.

The white man's gun was also used, but, though an exceptionally accurate model would later revolutionize the art of buffalo hunting, the single-shot muzzle-loader was not adaptable to the Indian's mode of attack. It was more awkward to aim at full gallop, took too long to reload and had less immediate effect on the buffalo than did the arrow. Furthermore, in the 1830s most guns sold to the Indians were long-barreled flintlocks—hardly handy weapons to wield at close quarters and at thundering speed. In the stalking method, of course, the report of the gun would ruin the Indian's whole design.

Only occasionally would the buffalo fall at the first shot. If it was a cow, it would keep running until it was weakened by its wound. If it was a bull, it would usually stand to fight, bellowing and pawing the ground with rage, eyes bloodshot and fiery, nostrils showering steam and blood.

"As I rode up within a few paces of him," wrote one white man who had been hunting Indian-style, "he would bristle up with fury enough in his *looks* alone, almost to annihilate me. . . ."

But the Indian pony would circle out of reach and allow the hunter to choose his moments to dispatch new arrows. Even after an animal was downed, he might not be counted out; on more than one instance a hunter would be bending over and cutting into the hide only to have the animal spring up ready for more battle.

At length the melee would subside; the scene would resemble a battlefield after the fight, with Indians moving among the dead and fallen, dispatching the cripples and claiming their own booty. Customarily each buffalo was claimed by the brave whose arrow had first struck it—each man's arrows were marked by special identification. Curiously, even though some buffalo could have escaped, their instincts were so gregarious that they often stood at a distance watching the scene, only to be overtaken and killed.

After the hunters had returned to the village, the squaws and children would go out to skin and butcher the game. After skinning, a robe was laid on the ground with the hair down, and upon it was piled the meat, including tongue, heart, liver, marrow and brains (the latter were obtained by cracking open the skull with a foreleg and hoof). Then the robe was tied up to serve as a bag and either slung upon a horse or carried on a squaw's back.

Butchering each animal, according to one observer, did not require fifteen minutes. What was left on the ground the hordes of Indian dogs would pounce upon and devour. And, as the squaws and canines moved through the fallen herd, there would arise arguments over particular buffalo and particular pieces of meat that virtually made up a second battle on the same field. Then, after spending the day on the ground, they would trudge their way back to their village in a long procession, like an army after the fray.

In some Indian tribes the day's work was not ended without some ceremony of thanksgiving. One resident among the Pawnee reported that the medicine men made the rounds of the village "uttering loud cries" to show appreciation to God for a successful hunt. With them they carried meat to the aged ones who had no young hunters in their lodges.

Whatever meat was not immediately cooked and eaten was preserved by drying in the sun. Cut into thin strips, it was hung on scaffolds, often with fires underneath to speed the process. As for the robes, the squaws tanned them by pegging them on the ground, removing all flesh and fat with sharp stones and thoroughly rubbing them with buffalo brains. The finished surface, smooth and pliable, was often decorated with colorful figures and designs. The robe was then ready for the Indians to trade to the white man.

• 3 •

Waiting for them at Fort William on the Laramie were some of the stalwarts of the western fur trade. In the fort's first year, from 1834 to 1835, they were mainly employees of Bill Sublette and his partner Robert Campbell. It was Campbell, in fact, who first navigated the Platte in a small boat, bringing the 1835 yield of furs from Fort William to St. Louis. But he and Sublette had no sooner put the fort on a sound footing than they sold it in the late spring of 1835 to the firm of Thomas Fitzpatrick, Jim Bridger and Milton Sublette. These worthies turned about in 1836 and sold their entire fur business, including the fort, to their arch-rival, the American Fur Company.

By that time the latter was no longer owned by John Jacob Astor. On the day after the founding of Fort William, Astor had sold the western half of his operations to the St. Louis company of Pratte, Chouteau & Co. But most of Astor's principal lieutenants in the West remained, and the operation continued to be called the American Fur Company. It was, of course, the same outfit that the Sioux had been trading with on the branches of the upper Missouri before coming down to the Platte. Before long the firm, shunning both wagon travel, and boat travel on the Platte, began delivering its furs over a new road from Fort William to its nearest post on the Missouri, Fort Pierre.

Through the late 1830s the company developed Fort William into a depot of trade with the upper Plains Indians—the Arapaho, the Cheyenne, the Crow and especially the Sioux. Within its log walls, the little city grew with its commerce. Flat-roofed houses were, in the words of a traveler of 1839, "plastered all around against the wall, like swallows' nests." Beside the trading and repair rooms, there were also dwellings "not unlike monks' cells." And in the middle of the central open area was a tall tree that served as a flagpole on special occasions.

The permanent staff of five or so men that the American Fur Company kept in charge of Fort William was hard-bitten as any pirate crew. Most of them were Frenchmen, veterans of the mountain trade. Most took Indian wives and thus gained added influence with the tribesmen. They were used to hardship and hard work, and in the rough-and-tumble competition for the Indian commerce, they lived by a code that was as far from civilization as was their fort. They had little patience, for example, with the man in distress; that was his due for not looking out for himself. But, in frontier tradition, they welcomed old friends among arriving mountain men and used the occasion for a grand debauch. Drinking, gambling, horse racing and profanity were the order of the day. One Methodist missionary bound for Oregon in 1841 tried twice to preach a sermon at the fort but admitted that he could gain little attention. "Here is plenty of talk about their damnation," he observed sadly, "but none about their salvation."

It was this same breed of men to whom Rev. Samuel Parker had preached in a Rocky Mountain camp, only to have them suddenly desert him in high excitement when someone sighted a herd of buffalo. Being Frenchmen, most of them had been raised as Catholics, but they gave little attention to the observances of their church. Their distance from civilization was, of course, the excuse. But the lack of contact apparently gave them little pain. When a priest traveled through Fort William, he confessed most of the *engagés* there. Two years later one of them commented, "I got a good clearing out myself that time, and I reckon that will do for me till I go down to the settlements again."

Usually presiding over this rough-and-ready crew was James Bordeau, a shrewd Gaul with an exceptional eye for business.[2] Born in 1812, he had spent all his adult life as a trader in the Indian country, had married a Brulé wife and was on the closest terms with the Platte River Sioux. In appearance he was short and stocky, with a round face and a dark moustache. He generally wore a regular suit and vest, rather than the leather costume of the mountain man, but as a concession to western informality the suit usually was unpressed, with noticeable bags at the knees.

Though possessed of a native Gallic civility, Bordeau had been raised in the uncultivated West. When some newcomers arrived with a letter of introduction, Bordeau simply led them to their rooms without a word. "Though not deficient in hospitable intentions," wrote one of them, "he was wholly unaccustomed to act as Master of Ceremonies."

But Bordeau could be articulate on occasion. Holding what one observer called an "inflated" sense of authority, he could bellow across the courtyard in tones that commanded obedience. Nor was he deficient in executive talents. In a country without law, he could sense danger in an instant and act as quickly. But his courage was diluted by a healthy sense of prudence. Once, in a quarrel, he and another Frenchman fell upon each other in the open yard of Fort William. Thrown down, Bordeau was saved by his brother-in-law, an old Brûlé, who pulled off his opponent. In the next instant the two combatants raced to their quarters for their rifles. Bordeau peered from his doorway while the other advanced across the court.

"Come out and fight," challenged his assailant. But Bordeau did not move.

"Go upon the prairie," called his brother-in-law, "and fight it out in the white man's manner."

Even Bordeau's wife shamed him. "You are a dog and an old woman," she cried.

His opponent stood in the middle of the yard flinging insults at him and finally left the fort in disgust.

But Bordeau was long on strategy. Once he determined to teach a lesson to an old employee named Pierre, whose duties included the selection of buffalo steaks for the meals. Bordeau considered it wasteful to lavish the best cuts on the regular *engagés*, but it was apparent that Pierre was treating himself and his messmates very favorably. Bordeau did not want to appear so miserly as to correct Pierre outright. Hiding himself behind a partition next to the store room, however, he was able to observe Pierre's movements through a hole in the wall. And, when the old man came in and held the lantern to the pile of meat, he was startled by a ghostly voice from the dark:

"Pierre! Pierre! Let that fat meat alone! Take nothing but the lean!"

Terrified, the old man dropped the lamp and burst through the door. "The devil is in the storeroom!" he shrieked.

Catching his foot on the threshold, he fell and knocked himself unconscious. Some of the others came running and were starting to enter the storeroom to confront the devil with an improvised crucifix when Bordeau sheepishly appeared in the doorway. In front of his *engagés*, he had to restore Pierre's composure by confessing the whole affair.

• 4 •

At least twice a year, Bull Bear and his Oglala brought their hairy currency to the fort on the Laramie, camping for many days at a time on the plain nearby or downstream on the North Platte. On approaching the fort to trade, they fired their guns in the customary salute of friendship, which was answered by a volley into the air from behind the log palisade. Into the fort they crowded, so numerous that had they chosen they could have captured it. But, unlike some other mountain Indians—the Crow and the Blackfeet, for example—the Sioux had accepted trading with the white man as a way of life. If they were not actually dependent on it, they had certainly shaped their culture to it. And to seize the fort would have been to cut off the very supplies to which they were accustomed.

This dependence did not prevent them from harassing the traders in other ways. As they crowded into the rooms inside the fort, their eyes and hands would be busy seeking to appropriate any loose articles. At a post later built near Fort William they jammed into one of the rooms so forcibly that there was hardly space for the traders. For relief the latter closed the doors and windows, shut the chimney damper and built a fire of half-rotted buffalo chips. In a moment the Indians, gasping and choking, made for the door. It was, they were told, the "Long Knife's medicine"—"Long Knife" being their name for a Yankee. Bellowed one, "Long Knife's medicine is strong!"

Such subtle management of the Indian did not always prevail. Against some tribes the fort was occasionally barred in defense. One party of a hundred Crow marked its arrival by invading the nearby cemetery of the Sioux, their sworn enemies, and scattering the bones. From the palisade of the fort the traders watched the orgy, and as a precaution they locked the gate. One impatient brave put a pole against a damaged section of the wall and scaled it. But James Bordeau, standing on the parapet, caught him by the neck and pushed him backward to the ground. Then the men inside opened the gate cautiously to admit only a few at a time, covering them with cocked rifles.

But with the Sioux the activity across the counters was brisk. In return for buffalo robes, the company offered a considerable variety of such necessities as blankets, calico, knives, guns, powder and balls and of such luxuries as tobacco, combs, mirrors, rings, glass beads and vermilion paints.

In the earliest years of Fort William, those items were the staples of trade. Liquor was introduced at the fort as early as 1835; when missionaries Marcus Whitman and Samuel Parker passed through late in July of that year, they found the whites dispensing alcohol to the Oglala, who proceeded to get drunk.

Whiskey had been brought to the Rockies for trade with the Indians at least as early as 1830. In that year Peter Skene Ogden of the Hudson's Bay Company had come south with a party of Rockway Indians, whom he employed as beaver trappers. Encountering the Rockways near Bear River, Thomas Fitzpatrick had tried to induce them to sell their furs to him. When all else had failed, he produced a barrel of whiskey, and, when the Rockways had tasted it, they left Ogden and sold almost their whole year's beaver catch to Fitzpatrick.

But in the early 1830s liquor was not yet the dominant item of trade in the central Rockies or even on the central plains. Southward on the Arkansas, Mexican traders had introduced brandy; northward on the upper Missouri, American whiskey competed with British rum. But most of the Fort William visitors who kept journals made no mention of the liquor trade; as late as 1839 one thorough chronicler described the fort's activities without mentioning liquor. When Col. Henry Dodge and his dragoons marched into Indian country in 1835, he told the Oto and the Pawnee that the army would "prevent the introduction of ardent spirits into your country . . ." An Englishman residing among the Pawnee in 1835 wrote that "very few Pawnees had ever tasted whisky."

Yet the tide of firewater was not far behind. Brandy had been introduced into the Great Lakes trade by the French in the middle of the seventeenth century. After the Hudson's Bay Company was founded in 1670, English rum competed with French brandy.

And, with the appearance of rival British fur companies beginning in the late eighteenth century, the flow of alcohol to the Indians of the western lakes reached near-saturation.

As early as the 1820s liquor was carried up the Missouri River by Yankee fur traders, including the American Fur Company, in competition with the Hudson's Bay Company. The United States Government banned the use of liquor in trade with the Indians but permitted the companies to carry upriver one gill per day for each employee. By this subterfuge, vast quantities were hauled into the Indian country. In 1832 Bill Sublette took 450 gallons to the annual rendezvous at Pierre's Hole.

When Congress moved against the liquor trade with a bill for absolute prohibition, John Jacob Astor protested to one congressman: "If the Hudson's Bay Company did not employ ardent spirits against us, we would not ask for a single drop. But without it, competition is hopeless; for the attraction is irresistible. . . ." In 1834 Congress overrode such objections and passed the law prohibiting any liquor in the Indian country. But the American Fur Company built a distillery at Fort Union on the upper Missouri and operated it until it was discovered and dismantled. After that the company, as well as the other traders, continued to smuggle alcohol up the river. Despite inspections of every boatload by troops at Fort Leavenworth and surveillance by two civilian agents at Westport on the bend of the Missouri, enormous quantities went upstream by steamboat and over the plains by mule train. At Council Bluffs in 1839, Father Pierre-Jean de Smet noted barrel upon barrel of whiskey being landed and sold to the Potawatomi. An employee of the American Fur Company later wrote of trading in liquor as a matter of course. More than one traveler with the trader's caravans to the Rockies reported kegs of alcohol among the cargo. And a number of observers told of the influx of strong drink from the Mexican provinces to the south.

Among Indians in close contact with whites along the settlers' frontier, the liquor traffic had gone on long enough to bring about the most hideous degradation. The situation was aggravated by the annuity payments that the government gave to displaced tribes as compensation for land taken from them. Whiskey traders congregated about the villages when the annuities were due to be paid. As the *Missouri Republican* reported in 1835:

It is no unusual thing, just after an annuity has been paid, to find the guns, blankets, powder, horses, in short everything necessary to the comfort of the Indians, transferred to the hands of the whiskey trader; and the wretched savages rioting in bestial intoxication.

The practice was made easier in cases where tribes were paid annuities in money rather than in goods. At Council Bluffs the Potawatomi were given $50,000 a year.

"All this money goes for liquor," observed Father De Smet in 1839. "As long as it lasts they neither work nor hunt."

When the money ran out the Potawatomi would offer their belongings. Wrote Father De Smet, "Indians are selling horses, blankets, guns, their all, to have a lick at the cannon." One squaw offered her four-year-old boy for a few bottles. Often the Indians would buy whiskey or other goods on credit against the following year's annuities, so that, when the government money arrived, most of it was automatically turned over to the traders.

As long as the American Fur Company had a monopoly on trade with the Indians of the upper Platte country, liquor remained relatively minor at Fort William. But in 1836 Lt. Lancaster P. Lupton, who had come west with Colonel Dodge's dragoons the year before, built Fort Lupton on the South Platte in the present State of Colorado. Within two years, three more trading posts had been built on the South Platte. Then in 1841 Lupton moved north and established a second post on the North Platte above the mouth of the Laramie—about a mile and a half from Fort William—and called it "Fort Platte."

With this competition, the American Fur Company began to set its own house in order. As the log walls at Fort William were rotting, an entirely new adobe structure was built nearby, its walls whitewashed, its parapets fixed with wooden pickets and the usual bastions erected at the entrance and two of the corners.

But more important than the reconstruction of the fort was the introduction of liquor as the principal item of trade. Apparently the aggressor was Lupton, whose business was conducted with no restraint on the use of alcohol. When he sold Fort Platte a year or two after founding it, the new owners were no less diligent in the use of liquor. At Fort William, the American Fur Company had to follow suit if it intended to keep its trade and was soon bringing in liquor from Mexican territory south of the Arkansas River.

For the Indian, the acts of trading and drinking were inseparable. The trading itself, usually conducted after dark, quickly degenerated into frightful debauches in which the white trader— who remained sober—fleeced the Indian, and the Indian sometimes ended by robbing or threatening the life of the trader. The standard price at the forts on the Laramie was three cupfuls of drink (watered down to three parts water and one part whiskey) for one buffalo robe. But the more the Indian drank, the more eagerly did he bargain for still more—finally offering anything he had for another cupful.

In 1841 a Brulé chief named "Bull Tail" came in to see the trader at Fort Platte. A dandy in dress, the proud chief wore long locks of hair colored with vermilion; a long green frock coat with epaulettes; a cap of grizzly fur decked with a red feather, and a United States government medal, bearing the image of President James Madison, around his neck. He was, in short, the picture of savage elegance. With him to the trader's room he brought his only daughter Chintzille, the prototype of the shy and beautiful Indian princess. She followed him, sobbing.

"Bull Tail would give his daughter to the Yellow-hair," began the old warrior, "—for who like him is so worthy to take her to his lodge? Bull Tail has for a long time called the paleface his brother, and now he would claim the Yellow-hair as his son. Loves he not Chintzille?"

"Were I to deny my joy at the words of Bull Tail, my tongue would lie!" responded the gallant trader. "The Yellow-hair has no wife. . . . How could he ever show his gratitude to her noble father!"

"The gift is free," answered the chief, "and Bull Tail will be honored in its acceptance,—his friends will all be glad with him. But, that they may bless the Yellow-hair, let him fill up the keg with fire-water, and Bull Tail will take it to his lodge . . ."

"But Chintzille grieves . . . !"

"Chintzille is foolish. Let the Yellow-hair measure the fire-water and she shall be thine!"

Even a trader's thin conscience balked at such a bargain, and the chief departed in defeat. But offering a daughter or a wife for liquor was by no means uncommon.

As the Indian grew drunk during the bargaining, the trader would be occupied in cheating him—by only partly filling the measuring cup, by holding the thumb or two fingers inside the cup while measuring, by switching to a smaller cup, by using one that had the bottom filled with tallow or by watering down the mixture. Through such unintended mercies the Indian was spared quantities of alcohol that could have killed him. Sometimes, when he was too drunk to taste the difference, he would be drinking pure water.

Even so, the effect of liquor on the Indian was hardly controllable, and many a trader's life suddenly became part of the bargain. One American Fur Company trader on the upper Missouri was dealing out liquor at an Assiniboin village when he was abruptly confronted by a wild-eyed, drunken warrior.

"You are the meanest white man I ever saw!" the Indian shouted, then reeled off a string of personal grievances that were completely unfamiliar to the trader. "I will kill you tonight!"

Shortly afterward the warrior rushed in again with bow and arrow and would have shot the trader had not a more sober Indian whipped out his knife and cut the bow string. Later the assailant reappeared with a cocked gun, only to have it wrested from him and the priming cap taken. A third time he came in with live coals, apparently intending to burn down the lodge. Not until the Indian had passed out from too much drink was the trader's life out of danger.

On the White River in the Dakotas, a Brulé was in a trader's house and demanded a free keg of liquor. When it was refused he tried to stab the trader with a butcher knife, but a bystander caught his arm. After being thrown out, he fired bullets through the door, killed a mule and an ox belonging to the trader and rode off with all the man's horses and mules.

There were numerous other instances of traders being robbed, shot at, stabbed, attacked by incendiaries and made to stand on live coals while the trading goods were rifled—all by drunken Indians. One intoxicated Sioux chief tried to attack a trader and precipitated two successive battles between the trader's Indian friends and enemies. While the trader wisely kept out of the fight, the Indians on both sides kept trying to snatch his weapons from him in order to murder each other. The night's fray ended with two dead and a considerable number wounded.

The explosive effect of the trade liquor upon Indians may be partly explained by its abominable quality. Often it was pure alcohol, which was the most potent form that could be packed on muleback. From drinking this and other raw beverages the mountain men themselves often lost all control when on a spree and were soon rolling about, crowing like roosters. Unless their weapons were sensibly cached ahead of time, they were apt to begin shooting or knifing one another. Trade liquor was, in artist Charlie Russell's words, "the kind that makes a jackrabbit spit in a rattlesnake's eye."

But it must also be noted that the American Indian had no intoxicant of his own; when it was introduced by the white man, Indian society was totally unprepared for it culturally, morally or psychologically. The Indian had not been exposed to centuries of Christian strictures against it and was not protected by all the social precautions that the white man had created to promote moderation. Nor had the Indian been indoctrinated with the Puritan notion that all physical pleasure must be sinful. He therefore embraced alcohol as a mysterious happy water that made him feel good all over; he bartered for it, begged for it, stole it, drank it till he could no longer stand and gave it freely to his squaw and children. A new arrival reported a scene at Fort Platte in 1841:

> Men, women and children were seen running from lodge to lodge with vessels of liquor, inviting their friends and relatives to drink; while whooping, singing, drunkenness, and trading for fresh supplies had evidently become the order of the day. Soon, individuals were noticed passing from one to another, with mouths full of the coveted fire-water, drawing the lips of favored friends in close contact, as if to kiss, and ejecting the contents of their own into the eager mouths of others—thus affording the delighted recipients tests of their fervent esteem . . .

Over on the Missouri, Father De Smet recorded thirteen deaths among local Indians in a three-week period—all from liquor. Witnessing one orgy among the Potawatomi, he wrote:

> In all directions, men, women and children were seen tottering and falling; the war-whoop, the merry Indian's song, cries, savage roarings, formed a chorus. Quarrel succeeded quarrel. Blows followed blows. The club, the tomahawk, spears, butcher knives, brandished together in the air . . . only one man, in this dreadful

affray, was drowned in the Missouri, another severely stabbed, and several noses lost.

At one of the forts on the South Platte, a traveler wrote of the arrival of a keg of spirits in a village of Arapaho:

> The men began to hurrah and fight with each other, the women to reel about, and belabour their half tipsy husbands with tongue and fist, and be in turn, well pummelled themselves. The very dogs assisted in the general confusion by their loud yelpings. . . . Most of the Indians are passionately fond of the fire water, and when it is growing scarce you will frequently see a man take a cup of the liquor, and after holding it in his mouth a few moments empty it into the mouth of his next neighbor and so on for a dozen others as long as any of the precious liquid remains. Those who have had it in their mouths will breathe upon the less fortunate ones, that they may at least share its delightful fragrance.

It is hardly surprising that such scenes could end in sobering tragedy. During one orgy late in October 1841, a drunken Brulé chief was riding at a headlong pace from Fort William to Fort Platte when he fell from his horse and broke his neck. Around the dead chieftain, half-drunk braves and squaws gathered to wail their sorrow and to blame the whites for giving firewater to the chief.

More than riot and death stalked in the path of the liquor trade. For the Indians who drank the white man's firewater were wasting their one source of wealth—the buffalo—with no material return. Rather than killing the animals for their own use or to trade for necessities, they slaughtered them for their hides or tongues alone, which they laid at the traders' feet for alcohol. In 1832 a party of several hundred Sioux were camped at Fort Union when they spied a huge band of buffalo across the Missouri River. Gathering their horses and weapons, they splashed across to the other shore and fell upon the herd with their usual proficiency. A few hours later they rode back into the fort and threw down 1,400 buffalo tongues. For this load they received several gallons of whiskey, which they fell upon with the same deadly purpose that they had shown with the buffalo.

With such scenes being repeated throughout the Great Plains, it was no surprise that observers predicted an end to the buffalo within a decade. Numbering perhaps 40,000,000 in 1830, the red man's cattle would survive considerably longer, but their eventual fate was sealed. With an artist's indignation, George Catlin cried out: "Oh insatiable man, is thy avarice such! Wouldst thou tear the skin from the back of the last animal of this noble race, and rob thy fellow-man of his meat, and for it give him poison!"

Less poetic was the U.S. Superintendent of Indian Affairs as he commissioned a new Indian agent for the Great Plains in 1842. The main duty of the office, he declared, was to suppress the liquor traffic: "The prevention of the use of strong drink has almost been considered the one thing needful to insure the prosperity of the Indian race and its advancement in civilization. The use of it has tended more to the demoralization of the Indians than all other causes combined . . ."

Little wonder that wiser Indians were already begging the whites to keep their whiskey. For many years the Pawnee, having seen its effects, refused it. "We are crazy enough already," they declared. According to one story, when white traders introduced it among the Crow at a feast, some of the chiefs became drunk and acted foolishly in front of their people. Later ridiculed, they refused to permit it in their nation. Whenever alcohol was discovered in their vicinity, they took it and poured it on the ground. Among the Crow, alcohol was called "fool's water." It was said that a party of their warriors was a magnificent sight, proudly dressed in rich costumes and equipment, for they traded their buffalo hides for the tangibles of life instead of impoverishing themselves on alcohol.

But, despite good intentions, not every tribe was able to resist the white man's firewater. When one Indian agent arrived at Council Bluffs in 1839, some of the Potawatomi pleaded with him to halt the liquor traffic, but within two months liquor was being sold to them under his very eyes, and they were again knifing and mutilating one another.

In 1841, when a supply party heading for Fort Platte was greeted by a band of Sioux on the North Fork, one of the chiefs was courageous enough to warn his own people away from the liquor.

> Brothers: Why would you drink the fire-water, and become fools? Would it not be better that the Long-knife no more bring it to us? We give for it our robes and our horses;—it does us no good. It makes us poor. We fight our own brothers and kill those we love, because the fire-water is in us and makes our hearts bad! The fire-water is the red man's enemy.

Yet a few days later the same chief, Bull Tail, was trying to trade his daughter Chintzille for a keg of whiskey. Thus the most appalling effect of the liquor trade, even beyond debauchery and poverty, was the destruction of the Indian's character. At the height of the whiskey traffic, one veteran westerner described the debasement of the Plains Indians under the blight of alcohol:

> They were gay and lighthearted, but they are now moody and melancholy; they were confiding, they are now jealous and sullen; they were athletic and active, they are now impotent and inert; they were just though implacable, they are now malignant and vindictive; they were honorable and dignified, they are now mean and abased; integrity and fidelity were their characteristics, now they are both dishonest and unfaithful; they were brave and courteous, they are now cowardly and abusive. They are melting away before the curse of the white man's friendship, and will soon be known as *"The nations"* that *have been.*

His prophesy was as premature as were those of the imminent end of the buffalo but the error was in timing, not in substance. As for his estimate of the Indian's loss of character, it may have been overdrawn, but it was not ill drawn.

• 5 •

Such was the condition that the Oglala and Brulé Sioux had reached within only a few years after Bull Bear had led them to the North Platte and Fort William. They had found a better supply of buffalo, but they were wasting it in trade for the white man's firewater. They had invaded the lands of enemy tribes and were therefore continually at war. And unwittingly they had placed themselves athwart the line of the white man's migration to the Pacific. This position was later to be the greatest test they faced; against it they would have to summon all their character and their leadership.

But meanwhile the councils of the Oglala were disrupted by ancient resentments against Bull Bear. Bad blood had risen anew between the old warrior and his main rival, Chief Smoke. One day in 1841 Bull Bear marched up to Smoke's lodge bristling for battle.

"Come out, if you are a man, and fight!" he roared. Fearing Bull

Bear's prowess, Smoke cowered in his tent and said nothing. Bull Bear was furious. "You are a coward and an old woman!"

So saying he stepped up to Smoke's favorite horse, which was tied by the lodge, and sank his knife in its side. With this ultimate insult Bull Bear stalked out of the camp as Smoke's people stood back to let him pass.

A battle had been averted, but Bull Bear had opened old wounds. In November 1841 he and some of his people were south of Fort William in the camp of Chief Smoke on the Chugwater River, trading with white men representing the Laramie forts. From Fort William the American Fur Company brought in a large amount of liquor as a gift, in order to pre-empt the liquor trade from the Fort Platte people. The scene turned into a drunken bacchanale and then to riot and murder. Seizing upon the confusion as an opportunity for vengeance, Smoke's warriors started war-whooping and fighting with Bull Bear's men. There was a rush for weapons; the camp was terrorized with gunfire and a barrage of arrows.

Bull Bear had been lying in his tent, but on hearing the racket he went rushing out and shouted angrily for the battlers to stop. Smoke's men were ready for him. Showered with bullets and arrows, Bull Bear sprawled at their feet.

When silence fell upon the camp, Bull Bear and seven other Indians lay dead, and fourteen were wounded. The Oglala had lost their leader. Chief Smoke and the white man's whiskey had won another triumph.

THREE ♦ *We Are Few, and You Are Many*

♦ 1 ♦

In May 1841 Thomas Fitzpatrick rode into the rendezvous point at Sapling Grove just outside Independence, Missouri. With him was a small party of Catholic missionaries under Father Pierre-Jean de Smet, which was heading for the northern Rockies to establish an Indian mission. Already camped at the grove were more than sixty settlers, mostly bound for California and Oregon.

As no settlers' party had ever crossed the continent before, they were in some confusion. Local Missourians had tried to dissuade them from going on what they called "the most unheard-of, foolish, wild-goose chase that ever entered into the brain of man . . ." And, when members of the party had started from the settlements to the rendezvous at Sapling Grove, many Missourians had followed them, some for five or six miles, wishing them well on their perilous journey.

As the group assembled and elected one John Bartleson their captain, it discovered that no one knew the route to the Pacific Coast. It was at that moment of hesitation that Tom Fitzpatrick arrived to guide the missionary party. Finding at last a man who knew how to reach the Columbia Basin, they threw in with the missionaries and headed west. Out of Sapling Grove plodded 77 men, women and children—most of them riding horses—and fourteen wagons, some drawn by oxen and some by mules. Wrote one of the pioneers, "I doubt whether there was one hundred dollars in the entire party. . . ."

From that time on, the Far West was never to be the same. Nor would Fort William—now being called "Fort Laramie" by many frontiersmen. For this group was the first emigrant party

43

to cross the central plains—the first tiny thrust of the American farm frontier beyond the great bend of the Missouri. From this trickle, a tide would rise to flood proportions through the decade of the 1840s.

On moved the little band of pioneers, lurching through gullies and struggling through sandy washes, shoveling out a road where none had existed before. It experienced stifling heat, a hailstorm, a cyclone, a buffalo stampede, a brush with Cheyenne Indians. Near Ash Hollow, several days' march below Fort Laramie, the party made the treacherous crossing of the South Platte where it was running high with spring snow water. One wagon was overturned and another swept downstream in the swift current. Horses and men disappeared under the water, to reappear separated and swimming frantically. Those not struggling for their lives plunged in to help the others. When all had been pulled out of the water dripping and bedraggled, the total casualty list was only one mule.

Forward they pressed, past Fort Laramie, up the Sweetwater and over the South Pass. At the Bear River in present-day Utah half the emigrant party broke off for California. Encountering unimaginable hardships in the salt desert, they first abandoned their wagons, then killed and ate their oxen for food and finally, while crossing the Sierra Nevada, had to turn for sustenance to some of their horses. The rest of the party went to Fort Hall, where Fitzpatrick and the missionaries left it, and finally to Oregon.

Both before and after the settlers split up, Indians stalked their trail. At the Green River, Fitzpatrick had found his old friend Henry Fraeb and had camped with him and his party of trappers a night or two before pushing on. A month later Fraeb's party was on the Little Snake River when a band of Sioux and their Cheyenne allies surrounded and attacked it; in a two-day battle the Indians killed five whites, including Fraeb himself, and finally left with several of their own dead.

This was the state of affairs when the emigration of 1842 rolled up to Fort Laramie in late June. Composed of settlers bound for Oregon, the party was not much larger than the earlier emigration —105 souls. Trader Joseph Bissonette of Fort Platte had told them they could not go on: "It is not safe."

At such news some of the women wanted to turn back, but, footsore and overloaded, the emigrants prepared to meet the hazards and hardships ahead. Wagons and more than one hundred cattle were sold at the two Laramie forts at sacrifice prices, in exchange for horses in poor condition and coffee and sugar at premium prices. Then the settlers rolled on up the North Platte.

Scarcely a mile or two beyond the Laramie they encountered a party of mountain men heading back for the settlements, their animals packed with buffalo robes. Leading them were Fitzpatrick and Jim Bridger, and they included some who had been in the Fraeb battle. To the innocent emigrants, who had yet had little trouble with Indians, the tales told by the mountaineers were sheer terror. To provide some kind of insurance as they penetrated into the teeth of Indian hostility, they hired Fitzpatrick to guide them. Turning in the trail and bidding goodbye to Bridger and his men, he began retracing his steps to the distant peaks.

But, as the settlers moved on, a party of some 350 young Sioux warriors left the vicinity of Fort Laramie and took their trail. Leading them was a chief who had lost relatives in the Fraeb battle on the Little Snake. According to reports, he had sworn to "kill the first whites on my path."

• 2 •

At the same time another westward party was laboring through the sands of the North Platte Valley. Heading the column of some 25 frontiersman was 2nd Lt. John Charles Frémont. Handsome in appearance and courtly in bearing, young Frémont was every inch the French chevalier. But he was also the resourceful American who could talk to his *engagés* not only in their own language but also at their own level. Ambitious, he had also married ambition in the daughter of Senator Thomas Hart Benton of Missouri. As an instrument of his father-in-law's expansionist aims, he was launched on his first command and his first expedition.

Frémont's assigned goal was momentous enough. As the American frontier had been halted at the Missouri River by the obstacles of the Indian country, he was to determine how settlers might get through to Oregon. He was also to locate possible sites for army forts along the way. But for Frémont the expedition could also be the springboard to his own larger aspirations. With Kit Carson as a guide, he would penetrate this wilderness and return to tell the nation.

Early in July Frémont, with several men, veered off to explore the South Platte, planning to rejoin the main party when it reached Fort Laramie. His expedition was therefore without him as it proceeded near Chimney Rock on the evening of July 8, where it encountered the same party of mountain men that had been encountered above Laramie by the second party of emigrants. Camping with the Frémont party, Jim Bridger announced that the Sioux had gone hostile. The news threw the newcomers a scare that persisted after the Bridger party had left the next morning. Most of them favored going back, but one of Frémont's lieutenants and a few others declared that they would "follow Mr. Frémont to the uttermost limits of his journey." Shamed by the admonitions of these stalwarts, the rest finally agreed to go at least as far as Fort Laramie. With foreboding they harnessed up and swung into the trail.

Such was the state of his men when Frémont met them in camp beside the Laramie on July 15. Their alarm was confirmed when he walked over to the fort and, in the shade of the entrance, listened to the warnings of the superintendent, James Bordeau. As a crowning blow, Kit Carson himself made out his will—a rare and serious act for a mountain man.

For the next five days, while his men repaired equipment, Frémont brooded on the situation in the shadow of Fort Laramie and Fort Platte. If he were turned back by an Indian scare, he would fail to achieve the goal of his expedition. Without reaching the South Pass, the gateway through the Rockies, he could hardly report on the practicality of the Oregon route. Besides, could he leave the emigrant party to face the Indians without help? But most important, returning in failure would add no luster to the Frémont name.

His deliberations were hardly aided by conditions on the Laramie. Clustered hard against the walls of the fort were the lodges of the Oglala and Brulé Sioux. With their young braves all on the warpath, the village was populated by women, children, old men and some elder chiefs including the renowned Bull Tail. On July 18 another party of Sioux—also without its young men—arrived and raised its lodges near the fort. Into Frémont's camp the Sioux crowded, examining his scientific instruments, asking for presents, offering to trade and undoubtedly looking for objects to pilfer. Wrote Frémont's surveyor, an educated and fastidious German named Charles Preuss: "They come into the tent, sit down, and smoke their pipes as if they were at home. I would not mind it so much if one could converse with them."

By the 20th Frémont had resolved to go ahead despite the hostile Indians. That evening he called his men around him and, with his Gallic flare for drama, made a little speech announcing his determination to proceed.

The next morning they struck their tents, packed the mules and saddled their horses. When the column was formed and ready to move, Frémont and most of his men strode into Fort Laramie. In one of the rooms, cool and pleasant after the morning sun, James Bordeau was ready with some home-brewed liquor to serve the travelers as their "stirrup cup." After days of almost suffocating fellowship with the Sioux, Frémont was happy to have a few moments of relaxation with his own kind. A man was placed at the door to keep any Indians out, and the company lounged about enjoying a last moment of Bordeau's hospitality.

Abruptly Bull Tail and several Sioux chiefs appeared at the door demanding entrance. The guard, aided by others, tried to block them. But the intruders pushed violently into the room. One of them gave Frémont a letter from Bissonette of Fort Platte. It warned against the proposed trek. To support Bissonette, one of the chiefs spoke up: "Our young men are bad, and, if they meet you, they . . . will fire upon you."

Frémont was hardly receptive to these warnings, and in the discussion that followed, using Bordeau as interpreter, worked himself into a rage: "We are few, and you are many, and may kill us all; but there will be much crying in your villages, for many of your young men will stay behind . . ."

So saying, Frémont abruptly took his men out of the room and stalked from the fort. "In a few minutes," as he later wrote, "we were among the hills, and this last habitation of whites shut out from our view."

♦ 3 ♦

By that time Fitzpatrick had guided his emigrant party up the North Fork, then up the Sweetwater toward South Pass. They saw Indians, but they were unaware that the large war party was on their trail. On July 15 they rested near Independence Rock, which rose like the back of a great whale from the grassy sea. On it a generation of mountain guests had already registered their names. As the party moved out next morning, several men remained to pay their respects to the rock and then caught up with the main party. The two leaders, Lansford W. Hastings and his lieutenant, Asa L. Lovejoy, remained behind to perform a more careful job. They were captured by Indians, who returned them to the wagon train and received a ransom of tobacco and ammunition. At the same time the Indian leaders told Fitzpatrick that the route was thenceforth closed: "Any party of whites which should hereafter be found upon it would meet with certain destruction."

Onward toward Oregon moved Fitzpatrick and the settlers—encountering more Indians, losing horses in night raids but pushing toward their destination. A few days after they had left the Sweetwater, Frémont and his men were laboring along the same river, encountering more Oglala but no trouble. To the Great Divide they marched, climbing a mountain that they mistakenly believed to be the highest in the Rockies. Then they considered their work done. Turning back, they reached the North Platte, built a boat and started to navigate homeward. After all their Indian scares, they now suffered an upset in which much of their provisions and equipment were lost—the worst mishap on their trip.

On August 31 they came within sight of Fort Laramie. The Indians around the palisade first discovered the flag of the travelers as it approached. A hubbub immediately seized the fort, and its lone cannon was fired and refired to salute the adventurers. Sensing the drama of the moment, Frémont halted his men, opened his pack and took out the crumpled uniform that had been preserved for such an occasion. Dressing himself in it, he drew himself up in front of his little party, had them present arms and gave the command, "Fire!" The brave little volley echoed across the Laramie plain, and the explorers resumed their march.

"Frémont was really at his finest," wrote Preuss. "A young lieutenant is always a strange creature . . ."

The first big Indian scare of the Oregon emigration was over. For all his bluster, Frémont had been little more than a belated spectator in securing the Oregon Trail. Fitzpatrick, with his unflinching demeanor in the face of Indian spears, had launched the first two parties across the mountains. Even Frémont, writing of the guide's service to the pioneers of 1842, acknowledged, "I have no doubt that the emigrants owe their lives to Mr. Fitzpatrick."

Back in the states, Frémont was received as a hero. In Congress he was eulogized by a Missouri senator who was pressing for the settlement of Oregon. Frémont had proved, he said, that the pass over the Rockies "is as easy as the hill on which this Capitol stands . . ." Shortly afterward, Frémont's report—a detailed and dramatic account—was published. Widely reprinted and as widely read, it gave the first thorough account of conditions on the route to Oregon—the terrain, the grass and water, the obstacles to be overcome and the dangers to be heeded. Frémont was also the first to advocate a step that would lend support to future emigrants: "If it is in contemplation to keep open the communications with Oregon Territory, a show of military force in this country is absolutely necessary; and a combination of advantages renders the neighborhood of Fort Laramie the most suitable place, on the line of the Platte, for the establishment of a military post."

On the strength of Frémont's report, as well as of other new information about the Far West, fresh wagon parties began assembling each spring at the bend of the Missouri for the westward trek. Starting with 1843 the emigrations were much bigger; though they sometimes started together, they were really too large to stay in single parties. Wagons, once numbering in the tens, now numbered in the hundreds. And, although the Sioux had warned Fitzpatrick that the route was closed, the great numbers of people and wagons using it were awesome. In 1843 one of the Oglala chiefs near Fort Laramie watched for several days as the wagons rolled past. Finally addressing one traveler, he pointed to the east and inquired, "Are there still any whites remaining there?"

The invasion soon became more than a matter of curiosity. As early as 1843 the loss of grass and game was evident. Beyond Fort Laramie, a member of a white hunting party complained of the Oregon emigrant trains passing ahead of it: "The great quantity of cattle these people took with them made the grazing very scarce and bad for us, besides that buffalo were hunted away all out of our path." By 1845 the Indian superintendent at St. Louis was reporting that the Plains tribes, "who subsist on game, complain that the buffalo are wantonly killed and scared off, which renders their only means of subsistence every year more precarious." The next year he reported that emigrants were killing buffalo for the sport of it, or simply for the tongues, and that Indian complaints were mounting: "The buffalo is already greatly diminished in number, and . . . must, in process of time, be entirely destroyed." One Sioux chief, attending a formal feast with a

50

party of emigrants camped at Fort Laramie, told them through an interpreter: "This country belongs to the red man, but his white brethren travel through, shooting the game and scaring it away. Thus the Indian loses all that he depends upon to support his wives and children. The children of the red man cry for food, but there is no food."

For a time the Indians were kept in check by fear of the Great Father's soldiers. Word of the prowess of the uniformed warriors must certainly have drifted westward after the Indian wars east of the Mississippi. In 1829 Col. Bennet Riley had taken a battalion from Fort Leavenworth to police the Santa Fe Trail against Indian depredations; at Chouteau's Island in the Arkansas River he had been attacked by some five hundred Iowa and Comanche and had killed eight of them at long range with grape and round shot from a six-pound cannon. News of his terrifying feat had spread throughout the plains; Indians, as one officer put it, "object to being shot at by a wagon." This awe of the Long Knife's soldiers was reinforced by Col. Henry Dodge's tour de force in the central plains in 1835. To Frémont at Laramie, the Sioux chiefs had acknowledged: "We know that our Great Father has many soldiers and big guns, and we are anxious to have our lives. We love the whites, and are desirous of peace."

But, although they refrained from any wholesale onslaught, they nevertheless harassed the emigrants in smaller ways. Nearly every wagon train experienced at least one terrible moment in which a party of Osage, Pawnee, Cheyenne or Sioux came thundering down upon them, only to stop just out of rifle range, parley with the leaders and then come into camp to trade. Then some of them might return a night or two later, sneak up to the circle of wagons and suddenly scare the animals into headlong flight. The emigrants would awake to the pounding of hooves as the Indians ran the horses off into the night. The men would hurriedly saddle any horses remaining and rush out in pursuit. A whole night of hard riding and sometimes all the next day might be required to overtake the marauders, who would often abandon the animals without a fight.

Occasionally the Indians would take prisoners from among the outriders. But this behavior was usually in jest or for trading advantage. In 1842 a large Crow war party swooped down upon the North Platte country as part of the hostilities then rampant be-

tween themselves and the Sioux. Just above Fort Laramie they
overtook a single French tradesman who worked at Fort Platte
and asked him through sign language whether or not he had seen
any Sioux. In their system of gestures, the term "Sioux" was made
by passing the hand across the throat. Thinking they meant to cut
his own, the Frenchman set up such a fearful howl that the Crow
decided to have some fun with him. They tied him on a horse, rode
into Fort Laramie and announced that they wanted to trade.
Bordeau was ready.

"What would you buy?"

"Tobacco."

"What have you brought to pay for it?"

"A white man."

Bordeau's interest turned to astonishment. "A white man?" he
gasped. "At what price?"

"Oh, he is not worth much," ventured one of the warriors. "A
plug of tobacco is his full value!"

Bordeau recognized the frightened Frenchman as a Fort Platte
employee and, going along with the joke, declined to buy.

"You might find a market for him at the next post."

With a chorus of whoops the Crow raced their ponies and their
prisoner down to Fort Platte. There they sold him to Bissonette for
a plug of tobacco and left in pursuit of more serious business with
the Sioux.

But by 1844 the Indian opposition was becoming formidable.
That summer a large war party of several hundred Sioux was en-
camped at Fort Platte. In that season, Joseph Bissonette believed,
they would normally be off on the fringes of the Crow or Blackfoot
country, looking for a fight. When an emigrant train of sixty wagons approached from the east, Bissonette sent out a messenger
ordering it to "come forward no further."

"There is a war party of Sioux Indians here," he warned. ". . . I
fear they mean some mischief to the train."

While the wagons were halted, several leaders of the train rode
forward to the fort, walking through the Indian camp. With the
travelers was a French mountaineer who understood the Sioux
language. As they passed one of the lodges, he overheard a young
brave declare, "It always makes me itch to see an American horse;
I want to ride it so bad."

"Wait a few days until the emigrants come up," answered another, "and we shall have all their horses."

When this exchange was repeated to Bissonette his fears were confirmed. Ordering the wagon train to wait in its place, he called the Sioux leaders together in the fort. With grave expressions, they sat down and passed the pipe. After it had gone round, Bissonette spoke, "I have lived with you now many years and have always dealt honorably." They agreed that it was true.

"I have never told you a lie."

"Never."

"And have been a brother."

"You have been our white brother."

Then Bissonette revealed his message. "Well, I have just heard news that is of utmost importance to you. The emigrants who come from the sunrise and will soon be here have been delayed; a man died; they buried him; he had the smallpox."

Instantly, the chiefs—horror written on their faces—scurried back to their camp. Within fifteen minutes the entire party had struck the lodges and was in the saddle, hurrying north to the Crow country. The wagon train came on and rolled safely to Oregon.

The following year the Indians showed new hostility. After being struck with four Indian stampedes, one wagon train of 1845 had two of its men killed and scalped while they were separated from the train. On the other side of the Continental Divide they had a sharp skirmish in which many shots were exchanged, though without injuries.

· 2 ·

While the red man's opposition was rising, so was the white man's resolve. The tide to Oregon was set not only in the minds of the emigrants but also in national policy. In the heated election of 1844, westward expansion had been the overriding issue. Demanding an end to the joint occupancy of Oregon by the United States and Great Britain, James K. Polk had swept into the presidency and his Democrats into the Capitol. Short of military action, it was widely believed that the issue would be settled on American terms through occupation of Oregon by American settlers.

Polk therefore had no intention of letting wild Indians interrupt the stream of emigrants to the Pacific. He had scarcely settled himself in office before an army expedition was ordered west to cow the Indians and secure the Oregon Trail. In command was Col. Stephen W. Kearny, a veteran frontier soldier who knew both hardship and the Indians. Possessed of a towering but usually controlled egotism, he was mellow with his friends and implacable with his enemies. But he was a soldier to his toes, and he brought hard experience and stanch discipline to this first army venture in the Rocky Mountains.

For his guide Kearny hired Thomas Fitzpatrick, freshly returned from Frémont's second western expedition, which had taken him all the way to Oregon and California. Having helped to launch the Oregon migration by piloting the pioneer expeditions of 1841 and 1842, Fitzpatrick was now helping to protect it. Of Fitzpatrick's powers as a wilderness guide, the hard-bitten Kearny would soon express the most open admiration: "an excellent woodsman . . . who has as good, if not a better knowledge of that country than any other man in existence." Together the two Irishmen—both with all the courage but little of the blarney of that irrepressible people—represented the American frontiersman at his best.

On May 18 five companies of crack dragoons (a kind of heavily armed cavalry) jogged stiffly out of Fort Leavenworth. Numbering nearly three hundred officers and men, they carried carbines, pistols, and sabers. Behind them lumbered two mountain howitzers, calculated to offer the final touch of fear to the red man. Of a caliber using a twelve-pound ball, they were actually accompanied by more impressive ammunition—exploding shells. Also emigrating westward were a few military rockets, which at night could provide the most awe-inspiring fireworks. Kearny was preparing not only a show of force but also a show of magic.

Behind the howitzers and in the rear flanks of the column, dust was raised by some thirty head of cattle and sheep. These animals, plus a store of flour and some eighteen barrels of salt pork and bacon, were the sole edibles brought along for three hundred mouths in a march of 2,200 miles and 99 days. Kearny was traveling light; he would prove his fleetness to the Indians, and for many of the rations he would rely on buffalo, antelope and deer.

Through Pawnee country the men marched, building their own bridges for the wagons, moving with a precision and expertness unknown to the plains. From the time they struck the Oregon

Trail along the Little Blue, they played leapfrog with emigrant trains. Admiring the resolute line of canvases, one of Kearny's officers wrote that those farm families would do more to conquer Oregon than "the active operations of thrice their numbers of soldiery."

Traveling an average of 21 miles a day, Kearny had passed up the entire emigration of 1845 by the time he camped on the North Platte below Scotts Bluff on the afternoon of June 11. He was only two days' march from Fort Laramie and had that morning sent a rider ahead to arrange for a council with the Oglala. But already, across on the north side of the river, the expedition saw a large village of Brulé Sioux. Fitzpatrick made haste to ride across the river—his horse splashing through the shallow water without having to swim—with an invitation from Kearny. He arrived to find the Indians fearful of the alien cavalcade that had suddenly arrived and pitched its tents across the river. They had never seen uniformed soldiers before; Col. Henry Dodge's troops had not penetrated so far as the Sioux country a decade earlier. Fitzpatrick's persuasive powers, however, not only quieted them but also induced them to accept Kearny's invitation to visit him.

Donning their finest ornaments—down to bear-claw necklaces and some enemy scalps—fifty or more braves leaped to their ponies and plunged into the river. From the south side the dragoons watched them come, their decorations glittering in the late afternoon sun, their horses rising and dropping as they clambered over sand bars and sank chest deep into channels, their dogs and even a few colts scurrying and splashing in their wake.

In the soldiers' camp they were greeted by Kearny, who talked to them of peace and proceeded to show them his weapons of war. Some soldiers demonstrated how swiftly their new breech-loading carbines could be loaded and fired. The Sioux saw the sabers, the pistols, and the two howitzers. Probably most important of all, they saw the tall and powerful army horses, examined their points with experts' eyes and calculated whether or not they might be able to outdistance the Indian mustangs. By all these things the Brulé were visibly affected; one officer wrote that they "trembled like aspen leaves all the time they remained in camp."

Still, the Brulé could also make their own show. While they were assembled at the edge of the camp, a young antelope leaped up from the grass nearby and bounded off in panic. Springing to horse, a dozen braves gave pursuit. While the frightened creature dodged its way across the prairie, the Indian ponies pounded close behind, turning sharply with every twist of the antelope, responding instantly to every command from the knees and feet of their riders. So sharply and steeply did they veer with each change of direction that the Indians could have reached down and touched the ground. All the while they kept their hands free for wielding bows and arrows, which they loosed from time to time without effect. Finally exhausted, the antelope dropped to the grass, where it was caught in an Indian's arms to be carried back to the camp.

Witnessing the whole display, the troopers were astounded.

"We thought we had seen some beautiful horsemanship in our day," wrote one, "—but it had all been riding an old hack to mill, with three bushels and a half of corn, compared to this."

It was the first silent comparison of mettle—cautious but still peaceable in this early hour—between the two great armies of the plains. In this first encounter there was no doubt that the Brulé were impressed. Kearny followed up his advantage by inviting them to attend the council he had called with the Oglala at Fort Laramie.

Next morning, when the soldiers rose, the entire Brulé village across the river had disappeared, leaving no sign except a few plumes of smoke from dying fires of buffalo chips. But up the river the Indians were winding slowly westward—the warriors riding, the squaws and children walking, the pack animals including the dogs dragging the lodgepole travois piled high with belongings.

Arriving at Fort Laramie on the 15th, Kearny found the Oglala and Brulé assembling for his conference. Next morning, in the midst of cold wind and occasional snow flurries, he took most of his officers and his two howitzers and rode in dress-parade fashion to the council meeting. On flat ground between the two forts was erected a frame of lodgepoles, covered with robes to shield the council from the elements. In front of this shelter the grass was covered with buffalo robes, and benches and chairs had been provided for the officers from Fort Platte.

To give official color to the occasion, the Indians had raised three banners, which were whipping fiercely in the wind. Two were American flags, and the third was supposed to be their own ensign. It had two bands crossing diagonally, signifying the four winds; clasped hands beneath to represent friendship and peace, and, in a curve above, nine stars, possibly representing nine bands of the Sioux nation.

As Kearny rode up he was greeted by some 1,200 men, women and children—mostly Brulé, with a smaller number of Oglala and, according to one account, some Arapaho. Heading them all was Bull Tail, chief of the Brulé—arrayed, like the rest, in his finest accouterments. After the initial handshakes, the chiefs and warriors sat on the ground in a large semicircle facing the seated army officers. Behind them and extending in a complete circle around the entire council were the Indian women and children. Apparently without the formality of the peace pipe, which may have been eliminated because of the chilly weather, Kearny shook hands with the chiefs. Then, using Joseph Bissonette as interpreter, he gave his speech:

> Sioux: . . . Your Great Father . . . has sent me with a handful of braves to visit you. . . . I am opening a road for your white brethren, and your Great Father directs that his red children shall not attempt to close it up. There are many whites now coming on this road, moving to the other side of the mountains. . . . You must not disturb them. . . . Should you do so, your Great Father would be angry with you; although he is the enemy of all bad Indians, he is the friend of those who are good.

Then, after warning them against whiskey and entreating them to "spill it all upon the ground," he closed with a reference to "a few things" that the Great Father had sent them as gifts. When he had finished, Chief Bull Tail rose and gave reply:

> My father: what you have told my people is right, and it pleases me. I know now if they are good to their white brethren, they will be well treated in return; and will find that such presents as those they are about to receive, will often come. Now I have found a father: my people will no longer think of dying—but will live.

Afterward the presents were placed in the open space between the two sides and were distributed by chosen warriors to all the Indians—cloth and beads to the women, looking glasses, knives and tobacco to the men. During the process, a squaw began to chant a song and was soon joined by other women and some of the men. It was a hymn of thanks, not only for the presents, but also for relief from the fear that they had all felt since they first saw the Great Father's strong and disciplined soldiers.

As the council was breaking up and the vast crowd beginning

to disperse, Kearny ordered one of the howitzers fired as a demonstration. Accordingly, three rounds were shot into the air, exploding as they struck the earth. At this frightening show, the red men were filled again with terror. Kearny then announced further, "At night I will send up stars to the heavens, which will tell the Great Spirit that you have listened to my words."

Later he fired a rocket into the sky—its roar and its showery tail shattering the night. According to one account, some of the Indians dropped to the ground for protection, while others ran off shrieking in horror.

Kearny had done his work well, providing the right mixture of greetings and warnings, of gift-giving and saber rattling. Wrote one of his officers, "There can be no doubt [of] the impressions they have received of our prowess . . ."

That same night, as if to claim the protection Kearny had won, the first parties of the 1845 Oregon emigration reached Fort Laramie and rolled their wagons into a circle on the grounds nearby. As on every other night of their exodus, they gathered themselves at bedtime for what one of Kearny's hardened soldiers wistfully called, "an earnest and heartfelt prayer . . ."

Next morning, still in a drizzling rain with traces of snow, Kearny left one company at Fort Laramie and swung his column again into the Oregon Trail heading west. According to orders he was to carry the flag as far as the Continental Divide. He arrived there on June 30; with a dramatic sense equal to the occasion, he stood just beyond the summit, mustered his command before him and congratulated the men on their conduct in the campaign.

Two weeks later Kearny's troops returned to Laramie, then marched south to the Chugwater, where they discovered a village of some two hundred Cheyenne. It was Kearny's second chance to deliver his message. Camped in a delightful meadow, the Cheyenne presented a kind of Elysian scene that touched the heart of more than one soldier. Warriors were just returning from a hunt, their horses laden with meat, and women were seated before a stretched buffalo skin, painting it with the colorful figures so familiar in the robe trade.

Finding a white trader among them, Kearny drafted him as an interpreter and, after due ceremonials of greeting, gave the Cheyenne chief the same message he had delivered to the Laramie council. During the parley the rest of the command was standing idly in the camp, taking in the scene. One officer, with the rather unusual features of a red beard and thick spectacles, was bending over the shoulder of a young squaw to view her handiwork, when she suddenly turned and saw him. Shriek followed upon shriek, and wherever the poor officer turned other Cheyenne maidens joined the chorus—some of them running, hiding and laughing. At length it was understood that they believed glasses enabled the wearer to see through clothing and that their red-bearded guest was violating their modesty.

With this incident the Chugwater council ended; Kearny swung his column southward to Bent's Fort and the Mexican border on the Arkansas. Then on September 24 his troopers dragged wearily into Fort Leavenworth. Despite moments of biting hardship, punishment from the weather and near starvation in barren country, they had averaged twenty miles a day for more than three months in absolute wilderness without the loss of a man.

Kearny was aware that Frémont, in his report of the 1842 expedition, had recommended a military post at Laramie to protect the Oregon Trail. But with this judgment he completely disagreed. In his report he insisted, "In lieu of the establishment of a military post in that upper country, I would suggest that a military expedition, similar to the one of this season, be made every two or three years."

By this means, wrote Kearny, "the Indians would be kept quiet through the reminder that the dragoons, who were mounted on superior horses, could overtake them no matter where they might flee."

• 3 •

But, although the Sioux made no serious attacks on the emigrants, their harassment continued. During the large emigration of 1846, the Oglala and Brulé camped at Fort Laramie made a habit of demanding a feast from every emigrant party that passed. Seated in a semicircle with the chief and warriors in the central position, they would devour biscuits and gulp the coffee proferred by the travelers. As the summer wore on, they grew more insolent and overbearing in their demands. During one feast they drained their cups, then deliberately smashed them. At this behavior, the emigrants' condescension turned to wrath; many men snatched up their rifles and were only restrained by wiser comrades.

As if to flaunt their own power, hundreds of Sioux sometimes escorted the wagons for miles after they left Fort Laramie. Pouring over the grassy slopes, riders dressed in their handsomest finery would gallop alongside, shake hands with the emigrant leaders and take up double-file positions on either side of the caravan.

As previous emigrations had observed, it was generally the young braves who were arrogant, whereas the chiefs tried to hold them in check. When incidents did occur, they were usually outlaw acts in violation of tribal orders. The Donner party, which later endured unimaginable suffering while trying to cross the Sierra Nevada in winter, was passing a large Sioux encampment near Fort Laramie when some fifty warriors appeared and surrounded part of the train. As they rode alongside, some of them kept trying to pilfer things from the wagons and even to snatch them from the hands of the emigrants. Unable to stop them, one of the emigrant leaders rode off to the Sioux encampment and reported the goings-on to the chief. Embarrassed and enraged, the old man grabbed a flintlock shotgun and leaped to his horse. Pounding down upon the wagon train, he let out a thunderous war whoop that frightened his braves into confused retreat. As he chased the last of the offenders, the chief loosed a blast of buckshot that served to propel the scampering retreaters still faster. Then he wheeled and rode in dignity and splendor past the wagons back to his village.

That the situation grew no worse in the next two years was at least partly owing to the establishment of a new Indian agency for the Upper Platte and Arkansas and to the appointment of Thomas Fitzpatrick as the first agent in August 1846. Using his enormous influence among the Plains tribes, he began moving from village to village in the vast territory from Fort Laramie to Bent's Fort, talking with the chiefs and allaying their resentment of the annual migration.

During the emigrations of 1847 and 1848, the Indian depredations were confined principally to horse stealing. When Brigham

Young and the pioneer Mormon cavalcade came through in the early spring of 1847, the Pawnee demanded gifts as a toll for passage over their ground, and, when the payment seemed insufficient, told the emigrants to go back. The chief said he did not like to see them go west through his country, as he was afraid the buffalo would be killed or driven off. But the Mormons went ahead, without interference. The next year the second contingent was interrupted at Horn River, where Pawnee ran off with its stock. In the pursuit that followed, two men were wounded. But during both years the Sioux and Cheyenne held their fire. Fitzpatrick had done his work well.

• 4 •

Kearny's plan for an annual army expedition might have controlled the Indians for a while, but much bigger plans for the Far West were brewing in Washington. Since the Democratic victory of 1844, the expansionists were in the saddle and whooping to plant the flag on the Pacific Coast. To clinch the American claim to Oregon Territory, President James K. Polk was determined to protect the rising stream of emigration. A few weeks after Kearny's recommendation against forts, Polk contradicted him in the message to Congress: "I recommend that a suitable number of stockades and block house forts be erected along the usual route between our frontier settlement on the Missouri and the Rocky mountains . . ." In the spring of 1846 the expansionists in Congress, led by Senator Thomas Hart Benton of Missouri, pushed through a law "for establishing military stations on the route to Oregon."

But even while the law was being enacted, the United States was getting involved in the war with Mexico. All available army strength on the frontier was thrown into the invasion of Mexico and the conquest of California. The establishment of Polk's forts on the Oregon Trail was necessarily postponed.

When the war was over and the peace treaty signed early in 1848, California and the entire southwestern territory beyond the Rockies became American possessions. As for Oregon, everything up to the 49th parallel had become American territory by the treaty with Great Britain in 1846. The Far West was completely

Yankee, beckoning to new and larger waves of eastern emigrants. There was more reason than ever to protect the line of march with army posts.

In 1848 the first such fort was constructed at the west end of Grand Island, on the south side of the Platte. Named for General Stephen W. Kearny, who had become a hero in the conquest of California, it became one of the historic way stations of the plains. As for the other forts, the army had already written to Thomas Fitzpatrick for his advice. "My opinion," he answered, "is that a post at or in the vicinity of Laramie is much wanted."

Before the post could be established, the need for it became even. more obvious. News of the gold discovery in California in January 1848 had spread across the states and was confirmed in December in President Polk's message to Congress. Through the winter of 1848-1849 the nation was a scene of feverish preparation. Both as individuals and in hastily formed "California mining associations", an army of gold hunters gathered provisions for the great trek. By March of 1849 the overland army had begun assembling at the favorite jumping-off places on the Missouri River.

Up the valley of the Platte rolled the wagons. It was Indian country, and every argonaut expected to fight for his scalp. As usual, the most treacherous enemies were the Pawnee. By day they would look for opportunities to attack straggling riders; by night they would sneak up and try to stampede the animals. During the summer of 1849, two men isolated from the caravans along the trail were murdered by Pawnee. But the Sioux were generally the best-behaved Indians on the Gold Rush trail. One observer at Fort Laramie wrote, with only slight exaggeration, that they were "the best Indians on the prairies. . . . Of the vast emigration which rolled through the country this year, not a person was molested, not an article stolen."

"There can be no doubt of the friendliness of these people," a Forty-Niner wrote of the Sioux. "Without their aid in keeping off the Pawnees, Cheyennes and Arapahoes, no whites could get through this country without a big army."

Such behavior was all the more remarkable considering the effects of some thirty thousand Forty-Niners on the Sioux domain. They pounded the Oregon Trail into a permanent scar on the land. By the end of the summer, the emigrant cattle had devoured all the grass in a swath from one to several miles wide, extending from the Missouri starting points to the Continental Divide. Timber along the route was cut for firewood and rafts; some was accidentally burned. Buffalo carcasses lined the route—some killed for food, many more for sport.

Championing the Indians, the U.S. Commissioner of Indian Affairs wrote that year: "The great destruction of the buffalo by the emigrants has . . . more or less interfered with their success in the chase . . ." Frightened by the vast line of canvas-covered wagons and robbed of grass by the white man's cattle, the buffalo faded back to other ranges—north to the hunting ground of the Crow along the Powder River, south to the land of the Arapaho and Comanche on the South Platte, the Republican and the Arkansas. Although the separation of the buffalo into a northern and a southern herd has been attributed to the completion of the Union Pacific Railroad in 1869, it actually began much earlier with the rising traffic on the Overland Trail.

"It is admitted by everyone who has any knowledge of the buffalo regions," reported the Indian Superintendent at St. Louis, "that these useful animals are rapidly decreasing. . . . Should they continue to decrease, the time is not far distant when the Indians will be compelled to change their mode of living, or perish for want of subsistence."

Furthermore, the 1849 rush to California brought a veritable desecration of what had formerly been the virgin land of nature and nature's people. Badly overloaded with unnecessary goods, the argonauts began littering the trail with their belongings before they reached Fort Kearney. From there west, the trail was more and more paved with articles—stoves, anvils, forges, bellows, plows, trunks, rocking chairs—which should never have left the states. Among the most preposterous were a small stamp mill, a six-pound cannon and a diving bell.

Too late most of the argonauts began lightening their loads. Weakened from lack of grass and overtaxed with their impossible burdens, the oxen were dying along the trail. One traveler wrote that the road resembled a slaughterhouse. Another counted fifty dead oxen in one day's walk near Fort Laramie. Two others noted eight oxen lying in a double row—an entire team that had fallen and died as one.

With such casualties in motive power, wagons became useless. They were left by the road—some of them partially burnt, some missing the spokes of wheels that had been used to make pack

saddles, some in excellent shape but with no takers. By midsummer there were fifty abandoned wagons at Fort Laramie
alone.

The fort was, in fact, the main place along the trail for resting
and refitting; at that point the rigors of the trail forced changes in
the mode of travel. Many people switched from oxen to mules or
from wagons to pack saddles. The traders were thriving on the
distress of their visitors. Wagons, oxen and other items were purchased from the travelers at one-tenth their value; mules, buffalo
hides, coffee, sugar and other necessities were sold at four times
the price on the frontier.

A few of the emigrants, having lost everything and fearing that
their lives would be next, turned back at Fort Laramie. Still others
determined to winter there and to set up camp near the fort.
Their destruction of the countryside and their uncontrolled merry-
making were a nuisance.

"May Heaven never send us any more for the winter," wrote one
Fort Laramie resident.

• 5 •

While the Gold Rush was at its height, troops were finally
sent out from Fort Leavenworth to establish posts along the
Oregon Trail at Fort Laramie and at Fort Hall across the Rockies
on the Snake River. Heading one company of mounted riflemen
was Bvt. Maj. Winslow F. Sanderson, a native New Yorker who
had emigrated to Ohio, been graduated from West Point and won
his brevet rank for "gallant and meritorious conduct" in the Mexican war. On the morning of June 17 he and his men rode into
Fort Laramie and set about reconnoitering the surrounding country to make sure that the Laramie site was the most advantageous.

But old Bill Sublette had chosen well. Returning in a few days,
Sanderson gave orders for the purchase of the fort from the
American Fur Company. For $4,000, the old adobe structure that
had served as the marketplace for the central Rockies was turned
over to the U.S. Army on June 26. As for the fur company, it
pulled out its men and proceeded to start a new trading post a
few miles down the North Platte.

By mid-August a second company of mounted rifles and another of infantry, together with wagonloads of stores and equipment, had arrived at Fort Laramie. Also on the scene were eight howitzers of twelve-pound bore and, according to one observer, "ammunition enough to send all the red men of the Western Prairies to their happy hunting grounds forthwith . . ."

Up to the foothills of the Laramie Range went detachments to cut timber. Limestone and sandstone were quarried from the banks of the Platte and hauled up the Laramie to make foundation blocks for new buildings. From mesas far upstream, beyond the reach of emigrant teams, other details were cutting wild hay for winter storage.

While the first adobe and timber buildings were under construction, the post resembled a tent city. Completion of the new permanent buildings was delayed more than a year. In the fall of 1850 the infantry company moved into temporary quarters in a large new stable, whereas the two mounted rifle companies occupied a new barracks built to accommodate only one company. In December the first officers' quarters, soon to be affectionately known as "Old Bedlam," were almost completed. But at Christmas time the two-story edifice still needed pillars and a roof for its porch and balcony. Also still under construction were quartermaster and commissary storehouses, a hospital, and additional quarters for officers and enlisted men.

As for fighting equipment, it was little better than the post itself. The percussion cap gun primer had been in popular use since the 1820's, but on December 23, 1850, the post commander wrote to his superior at St. Louis, "I have to request authority to turn over my flint lock muskets & accoutrements, so soon as the percussion muskets & equipments shall arrive . . ."

But no matter how inauspicious its beginning, a military fort had been planted in the heart of the Sioux empire. The stars and stripes, which had formerly been hoisted only on special occasions, now floated every day over Laramie. On the parade ground, soldiers drilled—"neat as new pins," as one emigrant observed. They had, in fact, come to stay for the next forty years. And to red men who called it an invasion of their domain the reply was that the Long Knife's soldiers were there to protect the red men against the depredations of bad whites.

FIVE ◆ *The Big Talk*

In the spring of 1850 the flood of population swelled to still higher levels, as more than fifty thousand gold-seekers passed Fort Laramie. The same conditions—the disappearance of grass, the scourge of cholera, the deaths of men and beasts alike—plagued the trail. When the last of the annual emigration had passed by, some seven hundred people had been left behind in crude graves from the twin seasons of 1849 and 1850. Commenting on the scenes of waste and destruction, one observer at Fort Laramie wrote, "We frequently cook our suppers with the spokes of a better wagon than half the farmers in St. Louis county own."

To this headlong migration and its impact on their land the tribes had not been blind. Bitter complaints, particularly about the losses in buffalo, were repeatedly made to the Indian agents. Still, the Sioux kept their patience. As Fitzpatrick wrote after the 1850 migration, "I have had no reason to complain of the Indians or their conduct for the past two years; nor am I aware of any act of aggression committed by the Indians alluded to, on whites, during that time." But by the season of 1851 the Cheyenne, once among the friendliest nations on the plains, had become bold and surly enemies, harassing and robbing the emigrants.

"Stealing horses," observed one visitor at Fort Laramie, "they regard not only as proper, but as a duty."

Sitting on this powder keg, Agent Fitzpatrick had already decided that the Indians deserved compensation for white despoliation. What was needed, he recognized early in his term, was a general treaty with all the Plains Indians, providing annual payments for their losses in game and grass.

Such an annuity system would not be new; it had been used repeatedly in the states to pay for Indian land when tribes were being removed westward beyond the frontier. It had almost invariably tended to make the red man dependent on, and finally subservient to, the white man. Yet Fitzpatrick knew no other way to pay the Plains tribes for their losses and thus preserve the peace.

In the spring of 1849 he left the mountains with a plan for a great council of all the plains and mountain Indians. At St. Louis he laid his idea before Col. David D. Mitchell, Superintendent of all the western Indian country. A Virginian by birth, Mitchell was an old fur trader who had worked the upper Missouri. Except for his service in the Mexican war, when he had led the force that captured Chihuahua, he had been Indian Superintendent since 1841. Like Fitzpatrick, he had been advocating a general treaty with the Plains tribes, for the sake of both justice and peace. He urged the agent to go to Washington with his plan.

Fitzpatrick went. Both the Indian Commissioner and the Secretary of the newly formed Department of the Interior recommended a grand council in their annual reports transmitted to the White House. Fitzpatrick returned with orders to call the Indians to a conference in the summer of 1850, and a bill providing for the council passed the Senate. On the strength of those encouragements, the agent began stirring the interest of the Plains chiefs in what they called a "big talk." Mitchell instructed his agents and subagents, as well as the fur traders in his territory, to tell the Indians that "their Great Father would see that they were fairly dealt with, and that any injuries they might have sustained in consequence of the destruction of their game, timber, and grass, by the passage of the whites through their country, would be fairly paid for by the government of the United States." He hoped in this way to keep them pacified until the treaty council.

But in 1850 a bill authorizing funds for such an Indian conference was killed in the House of Representatives. Fitzpatrick was exasperated. To Mitchell he wrote in obvious passion that the "immense emigration" passing through the Indian country for the past two years had "desolated and impoverished" it.

"Under these circumstances," he argued, "would it not be just, as well as economical policy, for the government at this time to

show some little liberality, if not justice, to their passive submission?" If not, "what then will be the consequences should twenty
thousand Indians well armed, well mounted, and the most warlike
and expert in war of any Indians on this continent, turn out in
hostile array against all American travellers through their
country?"

Following this outburst, Fitzpatrick was relieved of his office
—possibly because of resentment in high places at his outspoken
criticisms. But the Missouri congressional delegation rallied to his
support, and he was reinstated early in 1851.

A further victory was the ultimate success of his treaty plan in
Congress, which authorized $100,000 in expenses for the council.
Elated, Fitzpatrick met with Mitchell at St. Louis. Between them
they set the date of the council for September 1, 1851, at Fort
Laramie. By April, Fitzpatrick was on his way from St. Louis to
the mountains, anxious to summon the tribes to his rendezvous.
With him rode the one real hope for peace on the plains.

• 2 •

Pressing first along the Santa Fe Trail, Fitzpatrick held a
meeting with the southern Plains Indians at Fort Atkinson on the
Arkansas River. After he had explained the purpose of the grand
council, the Cheyenne and Arapaho agreed to go. But the Comanche, Kiowa and Apache refused to travel so far and camp
among such "notorious horse thieves" as the Sioux and the Crow.

Then Fitzpatrick rode northward to Laramie. From the fort he
sent messengers to all the northern Indians—to the Oglala and
Brulé Sioux; to their enemies the Crow, and to the other Indians
of the upper Missouri, the Assiniboin, the Gros Ventre, the Mandan, the Arikara and certain other Sioux tribes. He could not be
sure that they would all attend, especially as most of them would
have to camp with traditional foes. But within a few days they
had begun to gather around the fort—first the Plains Sioux and
then those from farther hunting grounds.

At that time there arrived Maj. John A. Holeman, newly appointed agent to the Indians of Utah Territory. Energetic, impetuous and eager to enter on his new duties, Holeman had
already talked to the Indian Commissioner in Washington about

the importance of having the Snake (also called "Shoshone") Indians attend the council. The Commissioner had answered that he wished that "as many of the tribes as could be got" would attend.

Seeing that preparations at Laramie were well advanced, Holeman hurried to the mountains; through an interpreter he talked with some of the Snake chiefs about the grand council. Then he went on to Salt Lake, where he relieved Brigham Young, who had been acting as ex officio agent, and received his support for sending the Snake delegation. Then he retraced his steps and met the village of assembled Snake some fifty miles west of South Pass. Sixty of their chiefs and head warriors were selected to go and act for the entire nation, but the chiefs were wary of moving into the territory of their hated enemies, the Sioux, let alone sitting down to council with them.

Decked in their feathered finery and armed to the hilt with rifles and ammunition, the band of delegates rode eastward with Agent Holeman. Hardly had the men started when they were set upon by the Cheyenne, who were driven off after the loss of two Snake. Enraged but still determined to risk a council with the white man, the intrepid band of Snake moved on for Laramie. Hearing of their approach, the Fort Laramie commander sent out a small detachment, including four musicians, to meet them.

At the same time Col. David Mitchell had been moving west with a retinue of civilian observers to the grand council. Before he left St. Louis late in July he arranged to have a long wagon train of gifts loaded from steamboats at the bend of the Missouri. But when he arrived there the goods were still being packed. He was especially exasperated because he knew that presents were the indispensable preface to any Indian powwow. As one of his party members explained, "Without these, no man living—not even the President of the United States—would have any influence with them, nor could he get them into council, or keep them together a day." But the tribes were already assembling at Fitzpatrick's call, and for Mitchell to be late for his rendezvous would compound the offense. On he pushed, leaving the wagon train to follow.

At the end of August, scarcely a day before the appointed date, Mitchell and his party rode into Fort Laramie. The plains above and below the fort were covered with people, horses, dogs. From

their campfires and their lodges curled a thousand fingers of
smoke. The chatter of the squaws at work, the laughter of the
children rolling about the camps, the incessant barking of dogs
filled the Laramie Valley with a cacaphony that exceeded even
that of the emigrant cavalcades. Also on hand for the council was
Jim Bridger, frontier scout extraordinary and an old partner of
Fitzpatrick. Now owner of his own fort in the country of the Snake
Indians, he had arrived early to serve as interpreter for that tribe.

On September 1, word reached the fort that the Snake party
had been sighted to the west. Then, down the trail along the
North Platte came a column of riders, decked in the finest array,
with bows and quivers on their backs and rifles in their hands. At
their head, riding a little distance in the front, was the imposing
Snake Chief Washakie.

When Jim Bridger reported the approach of the Snake to the
fort commander, the bugler was immediately ordered to sound
"Boots and Saddles." Racing across the parade ground for their
mounts, the troopers were ready for anything as the Snake approached. In the camp of the Sioux, which was spread below the
fort and along the Laramie, all other activity stopped. People
came running to look at their traditional enemies. Some of the
women began moaning aloud for loved ones who had fallen before
Snake arrows.

On they came, filing over the last hill and descending to the
stream less than a mile from the Sioux lodges. Soldiers, interpreters and white civilians watched nervously for any hostile
movement.

In that electric moment a Sioux brave, clutching bow and
arrows, leaped astride his horse and bolted headlong toward the
Snake chief. Alert for such a move, the Snake halted and loosed a
savage yell—a kind of welcome to battle. In the same instant one
of the French interpreters vaulted to his own horse and raced
after the Sioux.

The Snake chief, who had continued walking his horse ahead
despite the threat, lifted his rifle and aimed at his attacker. Before
he could fire, the interpreter caught up with the Sioux and yanked
him from his horse. Quickly the Frenchman snatched the other's
weapons, then stood by to halt any further move. The Snake,
braced for battle, stood motionless and impassive.

A general melee had been averted and the peace council saved.
For had the Snake chief shot his impetuous enemy, the entire

Sioux camp would have raised the war cry. And the Snake, though desperately outnumbered, were ready for any kind of battle. As Jim Bridger commented, "there wouldn't have been room to camp round here for dead Sioux."

As it was, Sioux and Snake chiefs were immediately on the spot and wrangling with each other through the interpreters. It turned out that the Snake chief had killed the father of the Sioux brave. Emotions were ablaze on both sides. But the Sioux warrior was taken back to his camp. And from this encounter, proving both the courage and the self-restraint of the Snake, the Sioux gained new respect for their guests. The Snake were invited to camp next to the army troopers, who kept themselves between the newcomers and the rest of the Indians.

Through the night the soldiers kept a heavy guard. From each post, every half-hour, came such calls as "Number Two, Twelve o'clock! All's well!" Meanwhile, the Snake posted their own sentinels on every prominent knoll; there, wrapped in their blankets, each man gripped his rifle and kept a vigilant watch.

"Uncle Sam told 'um to come down here and they'd be safe," Jim Bridger explained, "but they ain't takin' his word for it altogether."

◆ 3 ◆

For the next three days, Colonel Mitchell delayed his council, ostensibly to allow far-away Indian delegations to arrive. Actually he was waiting in silent fury for the freight contractors to come along with the gifts—the indispensable gesture in any Indian parley. On September 4 he learned that they had gotten well under way from the settlements some eighteen days before. They would take at least two more weeks to arrive, but he could hardly keep ten thousand Indians waiting that long. Already their horses had eaten all the grass along Laramie Creek. Obviously, the assemblage would have to move to better foraging ground. With a shrewd eye, Mitchell picked Horse Creek 35 miles downstream on the North Platte—a location that would cut two days' march for the supply caravan. On the 4th the entire host—three troops of cavalry and one of infantry, together with an army of Indians—pulled stakes and started moving east.

It was a painful exodus. The September days and evenings were hot and sultry. Among the Indians, all the work of breaking camp and packing the animals fell to the women, according to custom. Traveling in single file, they raised dust down the Oregon Trail in a train several miles long. Some of the horses were packed in the white man's style, but most of them pulled the Indian travois, consisting of two lodgepoles fastened over the animals' back and dragging on the ground behind. Across these poles were packed buffalo robes, blankets, cooking ware, children and small dogs. Sometimes a canopy was fastened over the travois to shade a squaw as she rode on the pack.

Many of the dogs—which to white men looked like plain wolves—also drew travois. The equipment was piled so high that sometimes the poor canine's head alone showed in front (indeed, the travois had been invented for dog power before the Plains Indians had horses). Each lodge had its own family of pack animals, and if a stranger temporarily cut into the line of march so as to separate a dog from the rest of his lodgemates, the offended animal would raise a mournful howl until the interloper moved out of the way.

Ahead of this solemn cavalcade rode the uniformed troopers. But though they were in the saddle by 6 A.M. several hundred mounted braves insisted on accompanying them. Wrote one traveler, "They were particularly useful in kicking up the dust, as they kept galloping about us all day."

On the afternoon of the 5th the exodus began drawing up at Horse Creek. Colonel Mitchell was on the ground assigning each tribe its camp spot. The Snake he placed east of the creek and south of the Platte, with both those streams and the company of soldiers between them and most of their enemies.

Through the 6th the Indians were still arriving. As the next day was Sunday, Mitchell gained more time by announcing that it was the "White Man's Medicine Day," in which no business could be transacted. The Indian women improved the Sabbath by laying out the conference ground and erecting a near-circle of shelters to protect the Indian participants from the sun, with a kind of arbor for the white delegation in the center. In the evening the Sioux staged dog feasts for their neighboring tribes—the Arapaho, the Cheyenne and, most astounding of all, the Snake—though the last did not observe the custom of dining on dogs. According to the Sioux and Cheyenne method, the fattest dogs were rounded up, executed, cleaned, singed and boiled in kettles until the bones could be pulled out.

"I found the meat really delicate," wrote one white guest, "and I can vouch that it is preferable to suckling pig, which it nearly resembles in taste."

Accompanying the dog feasts were dancing and singing, as well as incessant drumming and whooping throughout the night. For the whites as well as for the red men there was little sleep the night before the great council.

• 4 •

Next morning, September 8, the tribes drew themselves up in readiness for the summons, which Colonel Mitchell had announced would be the firing of a cannon. At 9 A.M. the booming report echoed and re-echoed across the Platte. The mesas came alive with people—the tribes moving in vast phalanxes to the appointed council ground. They came in order of rank—the chiefs walking ahead, the braves following on foot or horseback and the squaws and children plodding in the rear. In the morning sun they fairly glittered with their gaudiest attire—glass beads and pieces of mirror; necklaces of small bones, teeth and claws; feathers, furs and skin brightly painted with various figures. Even the children, ordinarily in scanty dress during the heat of summer, were wearing skins, beads, colored cloth and strings of porcupine quills. From each tribe rose its own song, adding to the discordant serenade that filled the morning air.

At length the tribes took their places in the great circle, leaving about a third of it open to the east. First to the north of the opening were the Sioux, then the Cheyenne, Assiniboin, Snake, Arikara, Gros Ventre, Mandan and Arapaho. As in Kearny's council of 1845, the chiefs sat in front, backed by their warriors, with the women and children completing the outer ring. It was, indeed, the greatest gathering of Indians ever held before or since, causing one awe-stricken observer to regret the absence of any "painter or daguerreotypist."

The Crow—also traditional enemies of the Sioux and Cheyenne —had not yet arrived, but Mitchell could not delay matters any longer. Accompanying him and Fitzpatrick in the center was perhaps a score of whites—army officers and civilian observers. Among them were Robert Campbell, one of the first owners of Fort Laramie; Maj. John H. Holeman of the Utah agency, and Father Pierre-Jean de Smet, the celebrated Catholic missionary to Indians of the upper Missouri and the northern Rockies. While the vast assemblage listened in silence, Mitchell rose and opened the ceremonies by proposing to "smoke all around with you." To the Indian, smoking together was like swearing an oath to tell nothing but the truth.

"Now," continued Mitchell, "I do not wish any Indian to smoke with me that has any deceit or lies in his heart. . . . All such will let the pipe pass. I don't want them to touch it."

With that he brought out a three-foot stone pipe, colored red and decorated along its length with hair and beads. Into the bowl was tamped a mixture of tobacco and kinnikinick, the red man's traditional smoke of leaves and bark. Mitchell and Fitzpatrick took the first puffs, then had the pipe passed to the chiefs, beginning with the Sioux. With great solemnity they took it by turns, smoked and passed it through the interpreter to the next. The pipe was so long that the interpreter generally had to hold the bowl. Nearly everyone would first run his right hand from the bowl along the stem to his body, some repeating the gesture more than once, in an ultimate pledge of truth. Many would, before smoking, point the pipe to the four directions of the compass, lift it upward in honor of the Great Spirit and hold it downward to recognize the "bad spirit." After each tribe's leaders had smoked, the pipe was refilled, returned to Mitchell and Fitzpatrick and then passed to the next tribe.

During this long and reverential process, the wife of an officer from the fort entered the circle and sat in an assigned seat under the arbor. Her entrance, apparently prearranged, gave Mitchell the opportunity to make a point. "In her presence," he told the multitude, "the white men give you an evidence of their peaceful intentions . . ."

Just after this incident a Cheyenne woman came forward leading a horse on which rode a young boy. In front of the white delegation she began chanting a mournful song. In a moment it was explained that a few years before one of the Snake chiefs now attending the council had killed her husband and orphaned her boy. According to Indian custom the Snake chief was obliged to adopt the fatherless boy as one of his own, and the mother was now presenting him for this purpose. But the Cheyenne chiefs soon came forward and took her away; it was not the proper time, they said.

After the pipe had been smoked all around, Mitchell again rose. Delivering a sentence at a time and waiting for it to be translated by the interpreters, he told the purpose of the "Great Father at Washington." "He has heard and is aware that your buffalo and game are driven off, and your grass and timber consumed by the opening of roads and the passing of emigrants through your countries. For these losses he desires to compensate you."

Mitchell then proposed that, as a first requirement, the nations cease warring among themselves:

> Your condition is now changed. . . . In times past you had plenty of buffalo and game to subsist upon, and your Great Father well knows that war has always been your favorite amusement and pursuit. . . . Disease, famine, and the vices of bad white men are carrying your people off fast enough without the aid of war.

To help prevent war, Mitchell said that the nations must agree upon the boundaries of their territories, in which each tribe would be responsible for peace and order. And, to promote discipline within the tribes, he asked that each of them elect one chief, "who shall be recognized as the head of the nation or tribe, and through whom your Great Father will transact all Government business."

If these proposals were accepted in a treaty, Mitchell told them, their Great Father would give to them $50,000 a year for fifty years. "It is not proposed to give you this sum in money, so that white men may cheat you out of it, but to give it to you in goods, merchandise and provisions."

But if the people of one nation were to "make war on another nation, take scalps, steal horses, carry off women, or do any bad act," their annuity would be withheld until the wrong was compensated. The same would hold true for injuries to "any white person lawfully passing through your countries."

As for the presents, which would ordinarily be a first order of business in such a meeting, Mitchell could only promise that they were on the way, and "I hope will be here in a few days."

Finally, he asked them to think over the proposals and return day after tomorrow "at the firing of the cannon and hoisting the flag" to give their views.

After Mitchell's address, Fitzpatrick rose and urged the tribes to follow Mitchell's request. Starting with a chief of the Brulé Sioux, several Indian leaders responded and agreed to discuss the plan. Then the first session of the grand council ended.

Clearly, Mitchell's proposal was more than a treaty; it was the death knell for a way of life. Should the tribes accept and honor it, peace would supplant war. To this much their actions at the council proved they were anxious to agree. But the plan left interpretation to the "Great Father." He alone would determine whether or not the treaty was being honored; he alone would choose how to enforce it; he alone would decide the form and valuation of the annuity. The treaty required of the tribes a thoroughgoing trust in the good faith of the whites; it demanded little or no risk by the Great Father, who could punish offenders at his own discretion.

Such terms presupposed a father-child relationship between the white government and the red men. That this relationship was assumed by Mitchell is shown in the tone of his remarks—as if a stern father were speaking to a wayward son. His last words to the Indians, in asking them to give their answer two days later, were, "I desire that each Nation select one or two to speak for it, that I may not have to listen to all who may desire to speak."

That the Indians thus allowed him to talk down to them—especially as they placed such importance on dignity and "face"—is almost incomprehensible. When Mitchell proposed his treaty they were still independent nations and the lords of the Indian Territory. Although the United States could not tolerate their negotiating treaties with foreign powers, it did recognize their sovereignty by making treaties with them, treaties that had to be ratified by the Senate. Yet since the first tour de force of Col. Henry Dodge in 1835, white officials had talked to them from positions of superiority and, what was worse, with condescension. And the Indians had accepted it with apparent approval. "What you have said is good," their chiefs would say. "We will make our people obey."

Were the Indians afraid of the white soldiers? Except for Colonel Riley's battle on the Arkansas more than a generation earlier the Long Knife's troops had shown no interest in fighting but had contented themselves with marching up and down the country while their officers called councils and talked. In numbers they constituted a mere island of blue in a sea of brown warriors. They had established one fort on the Arkansas and two on the

Platte, but these insignificant garrisons were, in the words of Thomas Hart Benton, "the sport of the Indians."

The basic reason for the Indians' passivity must have been that they were poor. If they were not poor to begin with, they had become so, almost imperceptibly, as the white man had debauched them, ruined their grasslands, driven off their game and killed them with disease. Nearly every spokesman at the council acknowledged this truth. Said the Arikara chief, in response to Mitchell's oration, "We came hungry for we are very poor and could find no buffalo . . ."

Indeed, since the gold rush of 1849, the red man had been living on promises. He believed the white men when they said he would be repaid for his losses. Compared to him, the Long Knives appeared rich. He saw them throw away goods, littering the California Trail with valuables. His main concern at the treaty council was to receive treasure from them. The strings attached to this treasure seemed vague and remote. They were as nothing compared to the gnawing in his stomach.

• 5 •

Until the next council meeting the grand pageant of Indian ritual continued. The evening after the first session, the Cheyenne sought to make peace with the Snake, which required making restitution for the two Snake they had killed en route to the council. In the ceremony prescribed for such occasions, the warriors of the two nations assembled in a circle, with the brothers of the victims seated between two Snake chiefs. The head men of both tribes exchanged orations, and all feasted together on boiled corn. Then the Cheyenne placed gifts—blankets, knives, colored cloth and tobacco—on the ground before the brothers. The two scalps were also produced and given to them; visibly grieved at the sight, they controlled their impulses and continued with the ceremony, distributing most of the gifts to the other Snake braves. Then children, apparently those orphaned in these and previous slayings, were exchanged for adoption. The rites were crowned by further orations, in which peace and good will were pledged by both sides. And on the following evening the Cheyenne visited the Snake at their lodges, joining in dancing and singing through the night.

This ritual was only one of many that punctuated the days and nights of the grand council. All the tribes—some old and bitter enemies of one another—feasted among themselves, gave orations, sang and danced and smoked the calumet. As provisions were low and the buffalo nowhere in sight, the dogs of the encampment were decimated. Father De Smet, an alert observer of all that happened, wrote of the council Indians: "They seemed all to form but a single nation. Polite and kindly to each other, they spent their leisure hours in visits, banquets and dances; spoke of their once interminable wars and divisions as past things, to be absolutely forgotten, or buried, according to their expression."

Peace was complete when the delegation of Crow, arriving late after a long journey from the Powder River country, appeared in the distance. The deadliest enemies of the Sioux and Cheyenne, they rode in a military column, displaying their weapons and chanting their songs, with a profusion of feathers in their head-dresses. They called forth the entire encampment to admire their proud appearance. From every direction, masses of Indians converged to watch them pass. After the chiefs and head men were seated in the council circle, the other tribal chiefs came to them and smoked the calumet. The circle of peace among the Plains tribes was at last closed.

Then Colonel Mitchell opened the new session and called for the answers of the chiefs. One by one, beginning with a chief of the Brulé Sioux, they stood up and replied. Some were ready to agree, but others gave what one observer called "begging speeches."

"We are a poor people, and want very much to see the presents you told us were coming."

"The game is going away, and I should like to see the time when you will give us horses, cattle and fowls as the white men have."

"We have heard all you have said; your words are very good, but we think we should have a hundred wagon loads of goods every year, and more buffalo. . . . We want to see the goods."

In the next few days, while Mitchell and Fitzpatrick waited angrily for the arrival of the supply wagons, they continued to meet with the tribes to refine the points of the treaty. On the 12th they met with interpreters and representatives of each nation to make a map defining the tribal boundaries. Father De Smet, Jim

Bridger and other mountain men helped to mark off the streams and mountains. By the end of the day the boundaries had been agreed upon, except that the Sioux insisted on the right to hunt below the North Platte in the territory of the Cheyenne and Arapaho. In the end the concession was made, so that all tribes were free to hunt throughout the entire region covered by the treaty.

In response to Mitchell's demand, each tribe selected a head chief to be responsible for enforcing the treaty, except the Sioux. They constituted by far the largest tribe on the plains and were split into several bands, which had never recognized a head chief.

"Father," reported one Sioux chief to Mitchell, "we cannot make one chief."

But Mitchell pressed the point by nominating his own candidate—a chief of the Wazhazha branch of the Brulé band, with a name pronounced "Mato-wa-yo-way." The appellation meant "the bear who is so formidable that his enemies scatter before him." This name was variously translated as "Scattering Bear," "Bear-That-Scatters," "Frightening Bear," "Conquering Bear," "Stirring Bear" and "Brave Bear." Probably because of the difficulty of translation, many contemporary accounts referred to him simply as "the Bear." In his youth he had been a bold warrior who had led his tribesmen in many raids against the Pawnee. But in his mature years he had learned moderation and wisdom. He was known as a chief who believed in the need to cooperate with the whites. One of them called him "brave and gentle and kind—a much wise ruler, a skillful warrior, and respected chieftain."

But the Bear had no ambition to be chief of all the Sioux. He knew that to accept such an office would be to ride the whirlwind. When Mitchell proposed his name, it was the Bear who protested the loudest. There were other chiefs, older and wiser, who were better qualified.

"Father," he told Mitchell, "I am not afraid to die, but to be chief of all the nation, I must be a *big chief*, or in a few moons I shall be sleeping on the prairie. . . . If I am not a *powerful chief*, my enemies will be on my trail all the time." But, he finally concluded, "if you and the Grandfather [President] insist that I become chief I will take this office. I will try to do right to the whites, and hope they will do so to my people . . ."

To formalize the choice, Mitchell placed the Bear in the center of a circle of 24 Sioux delegates. To each he gave a little stick, telling him to put it into the Bear's hand if he favored him; if the majority did not want him, Mitchell would propose another.

For an hour the delegates parleyed among themselves and with their own people. Finally two of them came forward and put their sticks into the Bear's hand. The rest followed, making the vote unanimous. But in reality they considered him no more than a formal voice in dealing with the whites—a "paper chief."

• 6 •

The encampment of ten thousand Indians and about three hundred whites had not lasted more than a few days before the vicinity of Horse Creek was almost unbearable; the grass was all consumed, the air was laden with dust and the lack of any sanitary facilities made the whole region an offense to the nostrils. The soldiers moved downstream two miles to better grass and clearer air, but the commissioners and their party mustered the fortitude to stay among their guests.

By the 17th Mitchell and Fitzpatrick had succeeded in framing a treaty agreeable to all the tribes. With the firing of the cannon and the raising of the flag, the tribes were summoned once again to the council circle. Pausing to permit interpretation and answer questions, Mitchell read the treaty to them sentence by sentence. In general it embodied the points that he had originally outlined, except that it permitted all Indians to hunt and fish throughout the Territory, and it also bound the United States "to protect the Indians from depredations of whites . . ."

After the reading, Mitchell and Fitzpatrick signed for the government, and each chief made an X opposite his name. Because the lands of the Snake lay outside his superintendency, Colonel Mitchell refused to permit them to sign the treaty—a stand that gave much embarrassment to their agent, John H. Holeman.

"I regret," he wrote to the Indian Commission in Washington, "that Col. Mitchell so construes his powers and instructions as to exclude them from being parties to the treaty . . ."

Possibly Mitchell's punctilio was a punishment to Holeman for taking it on himself to interfere with the council program by inviting the Snake. But they apparently took the decision in good grace and waited with the rest for their share of the gifts coming in the supply train.

Three days afterward, late in the evening of the 20th, the long-awaited wagon train arrived and was immediately formed into the customary corral. Quickly word raced through the villages, and a large crowd of eager men, women and children gathered to inspect the wagons. Next day Mitchell's cannon called the tribes to receive their presents. Decked once again in their brightest ornaments, they converged on the immense pile of goods; around it they made a great circle, taking in several acres of ground. One by one, each chief was called to Mitchell's tent and after a few moments reappeared before the assemblage in a general's uniform, complete with epaulettes and a shining saber.

For most of them, it was the first time they had ever put their legs into trousers. But the officers' boots were too much for their untrained feet, and they stood before their tribesmen in the full dress of generals, except for their moccasins. Each carried a certificate, whose value was emphasized by a large seal and ribbon, by which the Great Father (President) recognized his participation in the treaty council and his trustworthiness in future dealings. From each chief's neck hung a medal commemorating the event, with the head of President Millard Fillmore embossed on one side and, on the other, the clasped hands signifying peace and mutual trust. All these items were the essential exhibits of faith—Mitchell's shrewd appeal to the vanity and pride of the chiefs in honoring the treaty.

Then the lesser leaders and head warriors received their presents—the appropriate uniforms of brigadiers, colonels and other officers down to the numerous lieutenants.

After that the other gifts were given to the tribes—tobacco, cloth, beads, kettles, knives, paints, blankets and various foodstuffs. Braves of each tribe were employed to distribute the goods fairly, and there was no observable expression of jealousy or dissatisfaction. These presents, it was understood all around, were to compensate for the losses in game and grass suffered by the Indians up to that time.

The whole process of presentation occupied more than two days. At length on September 23 the last gift was delivered, the last assurance given, the last hand shaken. Across the fields the encampment was abustle again—this time in the confusion of

departure. It was a joyful instant—word had come that the buffalo
were plentiful on the South Platte, scarcely three days' ride away.
The Cheyenne, the Arapaho and many of the Sioux turned their
ponies southward. Snake and Crow—former enemies turned
friends—headed west. Still other delegations rode northward to
the upper Missouri with their medals, their certificates and their
uniforms.

As they broke camp and moved off, they left the ground strewn
with soda and flour given to them by the whites; all they had
really wanted—or knew how to use—were the containers. Cotton
cloth, thread and bed ticking were left behind as of no under-
standable use. And many of the heavy copper kettles were left
stacked in piles. There was a limit to what the dogs and horses
could carry on their travois.

It was the end of the greatest Indian council in history. Father
De Smet watched them go with magnificent hopes. "It will be," he
wrote, "the commencement of a new era for the Indians—an era
of peace. In future, peaceable citizens may cross the desert un-
molested, and the Indian will have little to dread from the bad
white man, for justice will be rendered to him."

Colonel Mitchell, reporting to Washington, was equally hopeful
that the treaty would "save the country from the ruinous and useless expenses of a war against the prairie tribes" by "gradually
turning their attention to agricultural pursuits."

"Fifty years it was thought would be time sufficient to give the
experiment a fair trial," he wrote to the Indian Commissioner,
"and solve the great problem whether or not an Indian can be
made a civilized man." The good faith of the Indian was amply
demonstrated at the council; "nothing but bad management, or
some untoward misfortune, can ever break it."

SIX ◆ *First To Bloody the Ground*

• 1 •

Mitchell's final warning—almost an afterthought—soon loomed large enough. Following the signing of the treaty, eleven leaders of the Sioux, Cheyenne, and Arapaho were escorted to Washington, D.C., to meet the President and to witness the strength of the white man's empire. But when they returned to their people they found that their report of the Long Knife's cities and railroads seemed too fantastic to be believed. By persisting in it they only made themselves appear to be fools or liars. The Plains Indians still had no real conception of the white man's power.

At the same time, when the Senate took up the Fort Laramie Treaty, it refused to accept Mitchell's fifty-year annuity period. Indeed, preserving the plains and mountains for the Indians for half a century against the pressure of the white frontier would have been impossible. The Senate reduced the time limit to fifteen years and gave the President discretionary power to reduce it to ten. But the annual payments were increased to $70,000 as at least partial compensation.

It fell to Thomas Fitzpatrick to present this amendment to the tribes of the central plains. Traveling among them in the summer of 1853, he secured the approval of the Arapaho and Cheyenne, then pushed on to see the Sioux at Fort Laramie. In his report of these operations he warned of the serious troubles that had overtaken the Plains tribes in the two years since the treaty, owing to their mounting contacts with the white man:

> The fact, startling as it may appear, was made manifest in my recent visit, that the Cheyennes and Arapahoes, and many of the

83

Sioux, are actually in a starving state. They are in abject want of food half the year, and their reliance for that scanty supply, in the rapid decrease of the buffalo, is fast disappearing. The travel upon the roads drives them off, or else confines them to a narrow path during the period of emigration; and the different tribes are forced to contend with hostile nations in seeking support for their villages. Their women are pinched with want and their children constantly crying out with hunger. . . . Already, under the pressure of such hardship, they are beginning to gather around the few licensed traders of that country, acting as herdsmen, runners and interpreters, living upon their bounty; while others adopt most immoral methods with their females to eke out an existence.

One other development, unreported by Fitzpatrick, had an impact on the Cheyenne and Sioux. This was the army's entrenchment at Fort Laramie. For the first time a body of whites, having little knowledge of Indian ways, had been put down permanently among them. The post was manned by regulars who had not come there by choice and had no special love for the West. To the easterner, Laramie was an isolated, Godforsaken outpost. The location was uninspiring, the post itself plain and dull. One California gold-seeker, stopping at the fort only a few days after it became a military post, wrote, "This is anything but an enticing place to live at." Another, stranded there for a week by heavy rains, grumbled, "I wish we were anywhere but at Fort Laramie." In the 1850s, another traveler said Laramie was a fort only "by courtesy, or rather by order . . ."

In such a place, located far from normal army discipline, boredom led to indulgence in elemental human pleasures. The sutler's store was the center of social life. A visitor of 1850, arriving on Sunday, wrote in his diary: "Went up the Fort with the intention of going to church, but called on the Quartermaster, and found the majority of the congregation collected there, smoking and drinking champagne. We joined the party . . ."

Noting with pleasure the presence of one or two officers' wives, he observed that putting up with Fort Laramie was "the height of conjugal devotion. . . . The task of getting here is bad enough for most ladies, but being content to remain, is a piece of amiability that may serve as a model for all."

Years later a newly arrived officer's wife wrote: "I was never so disappointed in any place in my life as this. My heart sunk within me, when I saw the Ft., situated in a low valley, surrounded by high bluff, & everything desolate, & dreary looking."

Thus at Fort Laramie, fighting men naturally looked to their occupation for relief from slow death by boredom. Charged with protecting the Oregon-California Trail, officers and men trained in the military tradition tended to regard the Indians as their appointed foes.

In the absence of the Indian agent, any post commander located among the Indians was responsible for conducting all affairs with them. But there was widespread ignorance in the army of the provisions of the Indian treaties. In the Fort Laramie Treaty, for example, it was the tribe and not the individual Indian that was to be held responsible for a violation. The tribes were to keep control of their own members, and neither the civil nor the military authority of the United States had any jurisdiction over individual Plains Indians. Yet when an offense was committed the standard procedure at Fort Laramie was to arrest, or attempt to arrest, the supposed culprit.

Accustomed themselves to giving their enemies no quarter, the Indians believed that capture meant torture and death. To give one's self up was to lose one's freedom to fight, which was valued above all else. Both the individual and the tribe therefore resisted any attempt at personal capture by outsiders, including the army.

Nor did outpost officers pay much attention to the customs of the Indian country. For example, it was understood among Indians and mountain men alike that a stray animal, whether horse or cow, could be taken and used by anyone who found it. If the rightful owner appeared, the finder returned the animal or gave compensation. Everyone recognized that most wilderness travelers, whether white or red, were hungry. "Let you be as brave as you please," said one Sioux chief, "if you starve you will take what you meet with and live." But in such instances it was the practice at Fort Laramie to make arrests and ask questions afterward. As Thomas Hart Benton of Missouri described the army regulars at western outposts, "They know nothing about Indians, and have no interest in preserving peace."

Both these conditions—the growing desperation of the Plains Indians and the introduction of an unsympathetic police force—made the atmosphere explosive on the North Platte and the Laramie. The situation became still more precarious when, in the absence of any open hostilities, the importance of Fort Laramie was downgraded by the army commander at St. Louis. In its first four years, the fort's commander was changed four times—and each new commander was of lower rank than his predecessor—until by 1854 Fort Laramie was in the charge of a second lieutenant only two years out of West Point. To the shortcomings of ignorance and indifference in the post leadership was added another—inexperience.

• 2 •

Beginning in the year of the treaty council, part of the Miniconjou band of the Sioux came down from the Black Hills country to join the Oglala and Brulé. Having no tradition of friendship with the traders on the Laramie, they were soon showing hostility to the passing emigrant trains. In June 1853, they were camped on the north bank of the Platte near the mouth of the Laramie, in a village of from eighty to a hundred lodges. From this position they harassed the emigrants and demanded presents.

In mid-June the Miniconjou grabbed one emigrant, rifled his pockets and stamped on his papers. At about the same time they forcibly seized the Platte River ferry boat from its owner. On the afternoon of the 15th a sergeant from the fort had to take the boat from them in order to cross the river. But when he was out in the current one of the Miniconjou shot at him with a rifle. The ball plunked into the water next to the boat. Furious, the sergeant put back to shore, stalked up to the fort and notified the commander, 1st Lt. R. B. Garnett, a southern officer who would later fall on the Confederate side at Gettysburg. Garnett had little respect or patience for the Indians.

At this final exasperation, he ordered 2nd Lt. Hugh Fleming to "proceed to the village, and demand the individual who shot at the Sergeant, and in case he is not forthcoming, take two or three prisoners, by force, if necessary."

Fleming, a graduate of West Point the year before, was a brevet second lieutenant awaiting an opening in the U.S. Army officers' list in order to receive his regular commission. He had been stationed in the Indian country less than a year. As most of the garrison was away from the fort tending the cattle herd and performing other duties, the entire force available for Fleming's mission amounted to 23 enlisted men, the post surgeon and the post interpreter—a French civilian named Auguste Lucien.

Leaving the post just before dark that evening, the soldiers marched to the Platte. They crossed the river in two boats, which were so small that they had to make several trips. Arriving before the Miniconjou village, Fleming halted his men and told Lucien to go to the lodge of Little Brave, the chief. Lucien was to tell Little Brave that the one who shot at the sergeant must be given up and that if he was not, the Chief himself "is to be my prisoner, for the depredations of his people."

Lucien went to Little Brave's lodge and soon reported back that the Chief was not there. The interpreter then returned to the lodges and spoke to the group of curious Indians gathering around. He demanded either the offender or several prisoners. They refused, with rising agitation.

Lieutenant Fleming then called his sergeant (the one who had been shot at in the river) and four other men out of the ranks. He ordered the rest to form a circle "to prevent surprise by mounted Indians." With his little detachment he marched in among the lodges.

At the soldiers' approach the excited Miniconjou fell back to a ravine in the rear of the village. There they began shooting with guns and bows and arrows. With his whole command Fleming charged them, returning the fire, and drove them away.

In some thirty shots fired by both sides, three Indians were killed. The poor shooting was undoubtedly because of the darkness. Taking two prisoners, Fleming had them tied and escorted back to the fort inside a hollow square of guards. About dawn he reached Fort Laramie, reported the skirmish and observed proudly that his men "behaved creditably both to themselves, and the Regiment to which they belong."

As for the Miniconjou, they began breaking up their camp and moving northward the same night. By next morning they were all gone in the direction of the Black Hills. But from Fort Laramie soon came a messenger asking Chief Little Brave to bring as many of his warriors as possible and come back to "have a talk." Within a few days the chief rode up to the fort with some sixty men. Twenty or thirty of them sat down to parley with Lieutenant

Garnett. The officer told them why he had sent the soldiers into
their camp:

> I regret the necessity which obliged me to kill any of your people,
> but under similar circumstances I will always act precisely in the
> same manner. I am now willing to forget what has passed, and
> receive you as friends; provided, you promise to behave your-
> selves hereafter; otherwise, I shall regard you as enemies, and am
> ready and able to meet you as such . . .

Should they attack any more whites, he warned, "you might
escape at the time, and even for years, yet sooner or later, the day
of retribution would certainly come."

Then Little Brave answered for the Miniconjou: "What you
have done was perhaps right, according to the manner of the
Whites. We wish to live, and are willing 'to cover up' what has
happened, and be friends."

With that the Miniconjou asked Garnett to seal the understanding with a gift. But he refused. "It will be time enough to speak
of such matters, when you show by your future conduct that your
promises are sincere."

Garnett then released the two prisoners; the Miniconjou
mounted and rode off.

Soon afterward the commander talked also with the Bear, the
Brulé chief whom Mitchell had made head of the Platte Sioux at
the treaty council. The Bear assured Garnett that the Miniconjou
did not represent the rest of the Sioux, who were all friendly.
Nevertheless, the incident rankled in the Sioux breast—not only
among Little Brave's people but also among the Oglala and the
Brulé. Many of the Miniconjou threatened revenge.

About three months afterward, Thomas Fitzpatrick arrived at
Fort Laramie to give the Sioux their annuity goods and to present
to them the Senate amendment to the 1851 treaty. He found them
agitated and resentful. Their manner was so menacing that he
requested a troop of soldiers to camp adjacent to the council
grounds. While he was discussing the amendment, they repeatedly
interrupted him with a recital of their wrongs and demands for
satisfaction. Fort Laramie, they said, should be removed immediately. "When first placed here, we were told it was for our
protection," they said, bitterly, "but now the soldiers of the Great
Father are the first to make the ground bloody."

Abruptly one or two of the chiefs refused to consider any more treaties. But at that point Garnett came from the fort to explain once again the reasons for Fleming's skirmish. This explanation seemed to placate them, and the chiefs signed the treaty amendment. Fitzpatrick gave them their annuities and departed.

• 3 •

At about the time of the shooting incident there had arrived at Fort Laramie a young Irishman fresh from West Point. He was John L. Grattan, born in Vermont, appointed to the Academy from New Hampshire and given a brevet commission pending a vacancy among the regular army officers.

Like most young lieutenants in the days when war still had some aspects of chivalry, he was anxious to be a hero. It was said of him at the fort that he was "a young officer of much promise, full of military enthusiasm, ambitious of distinction in his profession, and of undoubted gallantry . . ." According to another associate, Grattan was "a brave young man, impetuous, bold, and daring." When Fleming came back from his foray with a victory and two prisoners, young Grattan's imagination was stirred. He begged the commander to send him in charge of the next such expedition.

But Grattan was also, in the words of one contemporary, "inexperienced, hot-headed, and a sort of blow-hard." He was friendly enough with the Sioux who frequented the fort and was said to be on close terms with the Bear. But he also thought the Indians were treated too softly when they did wrong. Possibly on the strength of Fleming's success, he is supposed to have stated often, "With thirty men, I can whip the combined force of all the Indians on the prairie." On many occasions he was said to have insulted Indians to their faces, even shaking his fist at them. A trader observed at the fort, "If ever Grattan gets into a difficulty with the Indians, I hope he may come out safe, but I doubt it."

Meanwhile, the Sioux were giving Grattan plenty of opportunity to speak his mind. After the Miniconjou fight, they were more and more surly with the emigrants along the trail. The usual procedure was for a party of young braves to ride into the road ahead of an emigrant train, brandishing their guns. When the wagons

halted they would surround them while their leaders demanded
"toll." The emigrants were in the habit of carrying extra sugar
and coffee for this purpose. But so hazardous had the trail become
that the emigration of 1854 was greatly reduced.

Throughout this period most of the posts garrisoned by the
army were understaffed. Fitzpatrick observed:

> So small is the force usually at their disposal, that they maintain
> their own position in the country more by the courtesy of the
> Indians than from any ability to cope with the numbers that
> surround them. Instead of serving to intimidate the red man, they
> rather create a belief in the feebleness of the white man.

At Fort Laramie there were two companies of cavalry and one
of infantry; only the cavalry outfits offered any challenge to Indian
warriors who were all mounted. But early in 1854 Brig. Gen. N. S.
Clarke, commanding the western forces from Jefferson Barracks,
Missouri, ordered the withdrawal of the two cavalry companies.
This left only infantrymen, who, in the words of the local Indian
agent, were of no more value in protecting emigrants "than so
many stumps." David D. Mitchell, the former Indian superintendent who had presided at the 1851 treaty council, wrote that
a company of infantry "could be of no more use in protecting
travelers, or chastising Indians, than so many head of sheep."

On May 18 this shortcoming was compounded when 1st Lt.
Garnett was transferred from Fort Laramie, leaving the post in
the charge of 2nd Lt. Fleming. Probably because of his youth
and inexperience, he was inclined to neglect some of the details
of military procedure and was apt to be persuaded by subordinates
to act against his better judgment. In the same year Thomas
Fitzpatrick took sick and died in Washington, and his stabilizing
influence over his Indian friends was lost.

Early in August a small band of Cheyenne rode up to a herd
of cows grazing two miles from the fort. They belonged to the
post interpreter, Auguste Lucien, who had made himself generally obnoxious to the local Indians. When the Cheyenne ran
off with some of the cattle, they were pursued by a posse of
traders. But the Cheyenne suddenly stopped and made ready to
fight, at which point the traders halted out of rifle range and let
the Indians go. With this performance Grattan was disgusted, and
he laughed in the traders' faces for such cowardice.

In the same month the Sioux gathered along the North Platte

below the fort to receive their 1854 annuities. The supply wagons had already arrived, and the gifts were stored in the trading post of the American Fur Company five miles below Fort Laramie. From this post eastward to the buildings of trader James Bordeau, the lodges of the Sioux stretched for three miles. First below the American Fur Company post were the Oglala, then a small village of Miniconjou and finally the Brulé.

The new Indian agent had not yet arrived to give out the presents, but it was understood on August 18 that he was coming and was about eight days away. Meanwhile, the Indians were hungry from lack of game and were getting impatient. The warriors had decided to leave camp for a while to hunt buffalo.

Past them on the Oregon-California Trail plodded the tail end of the emigration of 1854—mostly Mormons headed for Salt Lake. They had with them teams of oxen—the white man's buffalo. On the 18th a wagon train of Mormon converts from Denmark was moving slowly past the Sioux. Among the loose cattle was a lame cow that had fallen behind the rest. According to both the Mormons and the Indians, the cow took fright and bolted into the Brulé camp. The Mormons, possibly fearing the Indians, made no effort to retrieve her. She was killed by a Miniconjou named "High Forehead," who was temporarily camped with the Brulé, and the hungry Indians feasted on her.

According to plains custom, this act was no crime. As a Sioux chief of a different band observed in another case, "Whenever it happens that animals give out, it is better to kill them than leave them on the prairie." Nevertheless, when the Mormons reached Fort Laramie some four hours later, they reported the incident to the commander.

According to the 1851 treaty, any destruction by a tribe had to be compensated for before that tribe's annuities could be given out. Apparently to make sure that his Brulé were not blamed for the act of a visiting Miniconjou, the Bear rode up to the fort and notified Lieutenant Fleming of what had happened. Speaking of the Miniconjou, he said, "Their hearts are bad toward the whites." According to Lieutenant Fleming, the Bear also agreed to give up the Indian. This incident is curious, as the 1851 treaty made no provision for taking prisoners in such instances but only for withholding annuities until the tribe involved had made restitution.

At first, Fleming did not appear to take the incident seriously.

He did nothing about it on the day it happened and, according to two witnesses, had decided to let the issue wait until the arrival of the Indian agent. But young Lieutenant Grattan, considering this the opportunity he had long awaited, urged Fleming to send him with a detachment to capture the guilty Miniconjou.

By the next afternoon Grattan had persuaded Fleming to send the force. At the time a civilian named J. H. Reed, traveling from St. Louis to Salt Lake, was at the fort recovering from an accident and was rooming with Grattan. "Would you like to be sent against the Indians?" he asked the officer.

"I would like very well to go," answered Grattan, "But I won't go unless I have orders to bring in the offender anyhow."

"If you go after the Indian," advised Reed, melodramatically, "don't return to the post without him."

• 4 •

With what precise orders Grattan took charge of the detachment is a mystery. But the discussion between him and Fleming was loud and continuous in the early afternoon of the 19th. Finally, Fleming ordered out a detachment of 22 enlisted men, to be accompanied by an interpreter and two twelve-pound guns— a field howitzer and a small mountain howitzer.

Suddenly the garrison was in a frenzy of preparation. Soldiers hurried to the adobe fort and rolled out the two howitzers and their limbers, which were hitched to two teams of mules. A wagon was brought out to carry the infantrymen. The garrison was mustered, and Grattan called for "volunteers on perilous service." At that time 32 soldiers were away from the post minding the cattle herd and tending the government farm twelve miles to the north. The muster therefore consisted of approximately 39 men, of whom 29 volunteered. Without Fleming's realizing it, all 29 were accepted, rather than the 22 he had authorized. One who did not volunteer was the post's ordnance sergeant. He refused, believing that there would be trouble and that Grattan was too rash.

Standing near the store was an Oglala chieftain with the remarkable name "Man-Afraid-of-His-Horses." It was not unusual for well-known Indians to be lounging about the grounds, talking with the soldiers. Man-Afraid was a rising young leader, the son of a chief of the same name, and was respected by Indians and white men alike. He grew fearful that trouble was looming. "I will go," he volunteered to Fleming.

"No," returned the officer, "do not go. If you get there and tell the news, the Indian who killed the cow will run off. Let the soldiers go first and then go afterwards."

Out of the parade grounds rolled the detachment—the howitzers first, with the gunners perched on the limbers. Behind them, riding the wagon, went the infantrymen, holding their long-barreled Springfield muskets. Grattan evidently stayed behind to hurry the post interpreter, Auguste Lucien, who was late getting ready. It was he who nursed a feud with the Indians, and whose cattle had recently been stolen by the Cheyenne. Though he had a Sioux wife, he feared the Sioux tribesmen. With little stomach for the expedition, Lucien was in no hurry to start.

"It is my place to do as the officer tells me," he moaned to a by-stander, "and I suppose the Sioux will want to kill me or think hard of me."

The more the officers argued with one another about the Miniconjou, the more frightened became the interpreter, and the more slowly he moved.

"I believe I am going to die," he whimpered while his horse was being saddled for him. All the while Lieutenant Grattan was poking him with his sword and telling him to hurry.

"I am ready," protested Auguste, "but must have something to drink before I die."

Somebody gave him a flask of whiskey, which he sampled and placed in his hip pocket. Then he mounted and started to ride off with Lieutenant Grattan. Man-Afraid-of-His-Horses then stepped up and spoke to the officer.

"You had better not go tonight. There are a great many Sioux."

"Yes," replied Grattan, evidently relishing the odds, "that is good."

Man-Afraid, together with a white civilian, joined them and followed the marching column, which had already crossed the Laramie River. Down the Oregon-California Trail and along the Platte moved the little expedition—the interpreter taking nips from the flask. According to one account, the infantrymen in the wagon were passing around another bottle as they rode. When they topped the last hill before putting the fort out of sight, Man-Afraid made another plea.

"There are a heap of lodges," he warned Grattan.

"That is good, as I am going to war on them," he told the Oglala. "If any other Indians want to interfere, you tell them to stay to one side."

On they pushed, marching more than an hour down the Platte. Finally they came in sight of the Sioux villages strung out along the trail.

"Look, my friend," Man-Afraid-of-His-Horses said to Lieutenant Grattan. "Do you not see a heap of lodges?"

But it was no use. Onward they hurried, with the horses jogging at a trot. At the American Fur Company buildings they halted. There the French traders noted, as they afterward stated, "both Interpreter & Officer were much excited." Grattan ordered the men to load their muskets and fix their bayonets. Apparently Auguste Lucien secured another bottle from the trading post. Noticing for the first time that the interpreter was drunk, Grattan asked him for a drink from the flask. But, when Auguste passed him the bottle, the officer coolly smashed it against his saddle.

On past the village of the Oglala they jogged at double time. By then, his head swimming with alcohol, Auguste's fear of the Sioux had turned to bravado.

"The soldiers killed three Minniconjous last summer," he chided them in a loud voice as he rode past. This time they were coming "to eat your hearts raw."

Grattan himself does not seem to have realized what the interpreter was saying in the Sioux language. Obviously concerned that the Oglala stay out of the trouble, he told them, through Man-Afraid-of-His-Horses, "The Oglalas have nothing to do with this business. . . . Tell them not to leave their camp; if they do, I will crack into them."

As they left the Oglala village, the civilian accompanying Grattan pointed out that the Indians were rounding up their horses—a sign that they intended some action. But ignoring this move, Grattan pressed on with his column.

Two miles past the American Fur Company post they came alongside the Brulé village, which faced them with an open semicircle of lodges. Immediately behind it was a bluff fringed with bushes, which dropped off to the Platte. The Brulé saw them and stood about, watching their movements. Grattan halted the troops once again and told them the purpose of the expedition. Then he added theatrically: "The Indian I am about to demand must be taken, if not freely given up, at all hazards, even if I die in the effort. . . . When I give the order, you may fire as much as you damned please." Then he added, "I do not expect to be compelled to fire a single gun, but I hope to God we will have a fight."

With that he proceeded to put the gunners through a drill in unlimbering and dry-firing the howitzers. Dissatisfied with one man's performance, he took his place and said that if necessary he would serve as gunner himself. The prospect of a clash with the Indians and the sight of their numerous lodges were evidently making him nervous.

On they pushed for the last mile to Bordeau's house, where Grattan stopped them once again. He ordered the infantrymen to prime their muskets and the gunners to load the howitzers with grape and canister. Around the soldiers gathered a group of traders from Bordeau's household, together with a number of curious men, women and children from the Brulé camp.

Among them was a Brulé chief, Little Thunder, an imposing six-footer who commanded the respect of the warriors; Bordeau once called him the bravest and fairest of all the Sioux—a "high-minded friend of the whites."

Speaking to the traders, Grattan called for James Bordeau. In a moment the little Frenchman showed himself. While the Lieutenant was explaining his mission, Bordeau was distracted by the antics of the interpreter, Lucien, who was spurring his horse back and forth and loudly threatening the Sioux. The trader was quick to sense the danger. "He will make trouble," Bordeau warned Grattan. "If you will put him in my house, I will settle the difficulty in thirty minutes."

"I will stop him," responded Grattan.

Several times he told Lucien to halt his demonstrations but to no avail. The threats and insults continued during the Lieutenant's parley with Bordeau and the Indians.

Grattan next asked to see the Bear, Chief of the Sioux. Bordeau sent an Indian rider to fetch him, and the messenger returned in a few moments with the old chief riding double behind him. After the Bear had dismounted, Grattan greeted him with the words: "I and all the soldiers love you. I have been sent to get the Indian who killed the cow. I want to take him to the Fort, and keep him until your Father the agent comes, and then will send him back to you."

Bordeau translated this message to the Bear, who seemed to draw himself up in anger—either at Grattan's message or at Lucien's threats. He turned to Man-Afraid-of-His-Horses, who was standing in the little group.

"You are a brave," he declared, "what do you think of it?"

"You are the Chief," snapped Man-Afraid, refusing to be committed. "What do you think?"

Impatiently, Grattan asked the Bear to give up the Indian. But the Chief was evasive. "I must go and put on my dress-coat before I give an answer."

In a few moments he was back with three other Brulé chiefs. Grattan asked whether or not the Bear had been to the lodge of High Forehead, the Indian who had killed the cow. The Bear said he had not, but at this moment an Indian came up from the camp and announced that the Miniconjou would not give himself up. With rising impatience Grattan turned to Bordeau. "You tell the Bear that I have come down here for that man, and I'll have him or die."

The Bear then conferred with the other chiefs, who left the group and went back into the village. To Grattan, the Bear answered with another equivocation, "Go down to the lodge where the man is, and see what he will say."

Exasperated, Grattan demanded which was the lodge of High Forehead. The remaining Brulé standing about answered that he was with the Oglala. But one Indian of the Wazhazha band came forward.

"No," he declared, pointing his finger, "there is his lodge."

With that Grattan ordered his men to mount and moved them toward the village. With him went Bordeau, Man-Afraid and the Bear, who was mounted double behind Lucien. In a moment another Indian came from the village with the same message as before—that High Forehead would not give himself up—"he would rather die." Grattan then addressed his men: "I am going within sixty yards of the lodge. I must have him, dead or alive. When I give the word, you must fire upon every man who is not a white man."

At that order Bordeau's anxiety turned to fright. To the chiefs he gave quick warning, "You had better be in a hurry and get the man as quick as you can."

But the Bear was still calm: "It is our custom to make a demand four times, and if it is not agreed to then, then we act. I want the Lieutenant to observe this rule."

But Grattan, beside himself over the Indian defiance, simply answered that he was "determined to go to the lodge." Bordeau gave a last, frantic warning: "You are going into a very bad place. You had better prepare yourself well."

"I have two revolvers, with twelve shots," boasted Grattan.

"Take them out of your holsters and be ready," rasped Bordeau.

With that the Frenchman turned back to his house. From the rooftop he and several other civilians watched the proceedings, passing a spyglass among themselves. They could see the Brulé taking their women and children out of the camp. Several hundred braves, stripped for battle, hid themselves with their horses under the little bluff behind the lodges.

Ignoring Bordeau's warning, Grattan resumed his march, riding at the head of the column, followed by the howitzers and then the wagon with the infantrymen. When he was about thirty yards from High Forehead's lodge, Grattan halted and drew his troops into battle order—the howitzers in the middle facing the Miniconjou's lodge and the infantrymen divided in a line on either side of the guns. About fifty Sioux, including the chiefs, gathered around them. Lucien proceeded to insult the Indians with surly remarks. Man-Afraid came hurrying back to Bordeau. "My friend, come on," he cried, "the Interpreter is going to get us into a fight, and they are going to fight if you don't come."

Borrowing a horse, Bordeau started out but, on the excuse that the stirrups were too long for his short legs, stopped and went back. To one of the men at his house he confided, "I am afraid there is going to be a fight."

By that time Grattan had sent Man-Afraid to High Forehead's lodge. Then, Indian fashion, the Lieutenant sat on the ground with the other chiefs and parleyed. His men were permitted to sit down as well.

Entering the Miniconjou lodge, Man-Afraid found High Forehead and five other warriors stripped for battle, their hair tied up for action, and occupied in loading their rifles.

"Light the pipe," said Man-Afraid. "Let us smoke."

In a short parley, they told him that "the soldiers killed three of us . . . we want to die also."

Back to Grattan went Man-Afraid. "There are six of them. If you go they will shoot at you."

At this news, Grattan asked the Bear to go and speak to the Miniconjou. The Chief went to the door of the lodge and came back with the word that they "will not give themselves up."

In the face of Grattan's obvious agitation, the Bear tried to parley. According to one account, he offered to pay for the cow with one horse, then with two. But Grattan refused, and the Bear's manner began to change. The soldiers, he said, were making too much of a small thing. "It was a poor cow. Today the soldiers have made me ashamed. I was made chief by the whites and to-day you come to my village and plant your big guns."

Obviously, the Bear had been under criticism for collaborating with the whites. Grattan's demonstration in front of the whole tribe had placed him in an impossible position. He could not sub-mit without losing all its respect. As for Grattan, he had made too many boasts in front of the men to back down now.

Meanwhile, the excited tempo of the moment was kept up by Lucien, who was shouting insults to the Sioux. They realized that he was drunk, but he was their only means of communicating with Grattan, and they suspected that he was falsifying their words. Finally Grattan, realizing the folly of letting Lucien continue to dominate the scene, spoke to Man-Afraid. "Go after Bordeau, as the Interpreter talks so much I cannot understand him."

Back to Bordeau's house rode Man-Afraid. "Come quick," he pleaded. "I am afraid it will be bad."

Again Bordeau mounted up and started toward the lodges. Man-Afraid rode ahead. "Stop," he told the group. "Bordeau is coming."

By that time the argument had grown feverish. The Miniconjou were standing outside their lodge, holding their guns. Grattan had ordered his soldiers to stand on their feet. The Bear was shouting furiously:

> Today there is one lodge of the Minniconjous with us and if I give him up all the village will blame me for it. For all I tell you, you will not hear me. Today, you will meet something that will be very hard. I would strike you if I were not a chief, but as I am a chief and am made so by the whites [I] will not do it, but you will meet something very hard.

Desperately, Man-Afraid tried to save the situation. "You are talking very bad," he told the Bear. "The Brulés have a great many soldiers; why do you not get them together and do something that will be good. Today you are acting the fool."

Lucien spoke to Grattan—possibly giving an interpretation of Man-Afraid's words. "How! How!" Grattan answered, using the Indian term for "I understand and agree."

Immediately one of the soldiers stepped forward and aimed his musket at the Indians standing in front. Possibly he had understood Grattan to say "Now! Now!" He fired, and one of the Indians fell.

At that tragic blunder, one of the chiefs—probably Man-Afraid —shouted to the Indians: "Do not fire. They have killed one man, and might be satisfied." The Indians, aghast, moved back a little; the Miniconjou still did not shoot. Grattan was on his horse riding back and forth, talking to his men.

Apparently both sides knew the extreme danger point they had reached and did not know what to do. But Bordeau, who had come to within 25 yards of the group, knew what to do. He turned and rode off at a gallop. The interpreter rode after him to bring him back, but the trader got away. Then Lucien came and asked Man-Afraid to stop the Indians from returning the fire.

"Yes," retorted Man-Afraid, "but you have killed one of us."

Grattan got off his horse, gave the reins to a soldier and came up to the interpreter and Man-Afraid. An Indian stepped up and spoke to Man-Afraid: "Come away. The soldiers will kill you." What he evidently meant was for Man-Afraid to get out of the line of fire.

"If they kill me," said Man-Afraid, "it will be good. I will stay."

"Stop the Sioux," Lucien pleaded to Man-Afraid, "and I will give you a horse."

But it was too late. The Bear stalked off, watching the soldiers over his shoulder. It was a sign that the parley was over. He was getting out of the firing line.

The tension exploded. At Grattan's order, the troops leveled their rifles. At that moment, the Miniconjou fired their guns. Grattan pointed his arm at the Bear and ordered, "Fire!" The soldiers aimed at the retreating chief and fired. He fell, wounded in the arm, the knee and the body.

Grattan then ordered the gunners to fire, at the same time taking his place beside the mountain howitzer. The field howitzer boomed first, followed by Grattan's gun. Both rounds went high—clipping the tops of some lodge poles. In the next instant the Brulé warriors who had been standing all around the soldiers loosed a volley of arrows. Grattan and five soldiers—mostly cannoneers—fell, peppered with shafts. Their guns empty, the other soldiers scrambled to escape. A few clambered into the wagon—one of them driving the team. They lifted three wounded men into the wagon, but a fourth was shot dead by the Indians.

From the bluffs behind the lodges, the hundreds of Brulé who had hidden themselves rose on their horses and thundered down upon the soldiers. Lucien was already riding away on his horse; behind him dashed the soldier who had been holding Grattan's mount. The remaining cannoneers leaped on the limber of the field howitzer and whipped up the team to escape. The wagon and the limber dashed past the fallen troopers, wheeled to the right and retreated toward the road. The remaining soldiers who had not reached the wagon were running after it. Seeing that they could not catch it, they stopped and tried frantically to reload while the Brulé horsemen whirled down upon them. They fired a few shots before the Indians surrounded them. Then they fell against one another under a hail of arrows.

On toward the road raced the remaining fugitives. Their pursuers, pounding after them, overtook the limber in a quarter of a mile and dispatched the gunners with arrows. The wagon went half a mile—nearly back to the road—before it was surrounded and the soldiers slaughtered. Lucien and the other mounted trooper were intercepted by other Brulé who rose from the bluffs below Bordeau's house. One of them shot down Lucien's horse, then came after the interpreter with a tomahawk. Suddenly sobered, Lucien pleaded with his attacker that he was "a Sioux by marriage." But with one blow the Indian struck him dead.

During the first shooting, Man-Afraid-of-His-Horses was barely missed by a Brulé arrow. Mounting his horse, he rode toward his own tribesmen, the Oglala. By the time he arrived among them he could see, looking back, that the Brulé had stopped the fleeing wagon. The Oglala were all standing in a line—some six hundred paces long—watching the battle.

"They are killing all the soldiers!" Man-Afraid hollered to them, excitedly. "Have we no brave men?" he demanded. "Do you not see that they are killing all the soldiers? What do you stand look-

ing on for? Do you not see they are nearly all dead? Are you going
to let them all die?"

With that he started to ride back, but they stopped his horse
and held it till the last soldier had dropped. The Oglala were
obeying to the letter Grattan's order to stay in their places.

• 5 •

Then Man-Afraid rode back to the battlefield, accompanied
by many Oglala braves. They met the Brulé as they were returning from the chase. Man-Afraid rushed in among them and hit
three of them on the shoulders. The Brulé stopped in amazement
and fell into an angry exchange with the Oglala. "Why did you
do this?" they asked Man-Afraid.

"Because you shot at me, and had you wounded me I would
kill one of you."

By that time the traders, panic-stricken at the massacre of the
troops, had barricaded their buildings. When Bordeau had raced
back from the scene of the shooting, he had immediately run for
his gun, ordered his people to load all the weapons in the camp
and prepared for a siege. When they saw the last soldier fall, the
civilian who had accompanied Grattan from the fort as far as
Bordeau's sprang to his horse to ride off and notify the garrison.
But the road was already swarming with Oglala and Brulé.
Bordeau stopped him, warning that it would be foolhardy to try
and ride through. Groups of Sioux were already charging Bordeau's buildings, and the whites ran inside. An Indian followed
them into Bordeau's house, crying out, "Let us wipe out the
whites here!" Leaping into the breach was Antoine Reynaud, one
of Bordeau's lieutenants and a veteran Indian trader on the Platte.
For a moment Indian and Frenchman grappled in the doorway,
while other Sioux crowded about outside. Among them were
several who were related to Bordeau by marriage.

"If you intend to kill the whites," one of them hollered to others,
"commence on us first." One friendly Indian, wielding a rifle, tried
to aim it at the Indian wrestling with Reynaud. But the Frenchman, fearing any more bloodshed, reached out with one hand and
knocked the barrel upward just as the charge went off and blasted
a hole in the ceiling. Next instant he managed to shove his op-

ponent out the door, slamming and bolting it. But outside, the Brulé were still in a frenzy.

"Now we have wiped out all these soldiers," the young braves were saying, "let us go to the fort, and wipe them out there. The houses are of pine, and we can easily burn them."

Wiser than the warriors, Chief Little Thunder came into Bordeau's house and told him what was afoot. Bordeau begged him to stop them.

"If they do not do any more harm and do not disturb anybody on the river," he argued, "I think their Great Father will forgive them for what they have done."

Little Thunder hurried out and, with the help of other chiefs, tried to calm the braves. Helping the chiefs was the onset of darkness. Bordeau wrote later, "My opinion is, that if the sun had been two hours higher they could not have stopped it."

Not long after, the Brulé's attention turned back to Bordeau's store. The warriors came to his house demanding provisions. "We have been waiting on the agent two months," they told the trader. "Our children are starving, and we are bound to have what we want."

Little Thunder and the other chiefs then told Bordeau that the young braves were "trying to pick a quarrel with you to kill you all" and that he had better give them what they asked. The frantic Bordeau opened his store and handed out all that they demanded. Still, Little Thunder had to walk among them all night haranguing them to allay their frenzy.

About midnight some Indians friendly to Bordeau came into his house with an astonishing companion—Pvt. John Cuddy, who had been found still alive after the battle. "If his wounds do not kill him," said the Indian who was accompanying him, "nobody will hurt him."

But crowding about were a number of hostile Brulé making threatening signs toward the man. "If you kill this soldier," the friendly Indian told them, "you kill me, for I shall die with him."

Next the Brulé turned to Bordeau, menacingly. "You had better not keep the soldier in the house, or we will wipe out the whites."

One of the chiefs came and advised Bordeau to hide the man outside in the bushes, because if the warriors found him in the house it would be an excuse to kill them all. Intimidated, Bordeau asked Cuddy if he could walk to the fort—an eight-mile trek. The soldier answered that, if someone would go with him, he thought he could make it. Bordeau sent a Frenchman and two friendly Indians with him for more than a mile up the road. At that point Cuddy told them that he believed he could go on by himself, and they returned. About an hour later Bordeau sent a horseman into the dark to notify Fort Laramie of the disaster.

Throughout that night of terror, Bordeau and his people kept guard. Shortly after the fight, Brulé squaws had begun striking the lodges and moving the village across the North Platte. By daybreak the next morning they had finished the task, finally moving the wounded Chief Bear. Then about five hundred braves came back across the river to look at the battlefield and count the dead soldiers. At sight of their enemies the night's excitement returned; they mutilated and robbed the bodies, peppering them with arrows. Twenty-four shafts were driven into Grattan's body; according to one account, it could be identified only by his pocket watch.

Presenting themselves again at Bordeau's, the Brulé demanded and received more of his stores. Then they announced that they were going to the American Fur Company's warehouse to take the annuities that they had been waiting to receive. They knew that, according to the 1851 Treaty, the Indian agent would never give them the annuities after the atrocity just committed. But they were hungry, and they had to have the goods.

Back along the road went the tide of Brulé warriors. Joining them were the Oglala, who had decided that, as part of the annuity goods belonged to them, they had better get theirs before the Brulé did.

At the Company's headquarters the Indians demanded the key to the warehouse door. The clerk who held the key went out by another door. Undaunted, the Sioux broke the lock, poured into the building and made off with all the annuity goods.

Scarcely had the Brulé left Bordeau's on the way to seize their annuities than Private Cuddy appeared once again. Apparently he had been unable to go on to the fort. One of the remaining Indians warned Bordeau that the soldier would have to hide outside until the warriors had recrossed the Platte. Back to the bushes along the riverbank went the miserable infantryman, his wound still unattended. When the last of the Indians had gone, Cuddy showed himself again. Taking pity on him, Antoine Reynaud hid

him in the blacksmith shop. Next day, August 21, Bordeau sent
him to the fort in a buggy, but it broke down on the road. A white
trader carried him behind his saddle all the way to the fort, where
he died the same day.

That morning about two hundred Brulé were back again at the
American Fur Company post—this time demanding the company's own goods. While they were storming about the door, a
brother of the Bear made his way to the steps with a message
from the wounded chief. "I have always been friendly to the
whites," repeated the spokesman, "and the American Fur Company has often befriended me, and it is my wish that you shall
not break the door of the Fur Company's store, but will leave
the goods untouched."

But it was no use. The words of other leaders were also ignored.
The mob surged forward, those in front hacking at the latch with
their tomahawks. The latch broke, the door swung wide and the
crowd plunged through. Inside they stripped the shelves of goods.
In their haste, they spilled coffee, flour and sugar all over the
floor and on the ground outside. Then they rode off across the
river with the spoils.

• 6 •

Early the day before, Bordeau's messenger had arrived at
Fort Laramie. To Lieutenant Fleming he reported the tragedy,
warning that the Indians were threatening to attack the post. As
most of the other troops were out on various details, the garrison
was reduced to a skeleton. Fleming did not yet know that his
available force was as low as ten men, for he still believed that
Grattan had taken only 22 soldiers instead of 29. It had always
been understood that the security of the fort depended on the
peaceful intentions of the Sioux. As Fleming himself put it, "we
must remember that with so few troops as were stationed at Fort
Laramie, so far in the Indian country, surrounded by thousands
of Indians, it becomes absolutely necessary to rely on the good
faith of some of them even for the safety of the garrison itself."
If the Sioux chose to attack the fort, all the new buildings would
have to be abandoned and a stand made in the old adobe trader's
fort. Could a thousand warriors take a fort held by ten soldiers?

Wrote the Platte Indian agent, "I presume none will say they could not have done it."

In this extremity, Hugh Fleming hastily scribbled two messages. The first, to Bordeau, was an admission of his helplessness:

> I am unable to take further notice at present of this unfortunate transaction; and I wish you to speak to the Bear and other chiefs with reference to the matter. Make the best terms with them you can for the present, for your own safety, and the safety of others likewise unprotected in the country.

Then he closed by asking Bordeau to recover the bodies of the slain. The second message he wrote to the eastern headquarters of his military department. So quickly did he dispatch it that he reported the loss of only 24 men (including Grattan and Lucien) without knowing how many had actually gone with the party. Then he called for help: "The Indians are hostile, menacing the fort; but all my men are on duty, and I think we shall be able to keep possession of it. We stand much in need of more troops, and hope they will be sent as soon as possible."

With that note Fleming sent a rider pounding eastward to Fort Leavenworth, where there was a telegraph connection. Back down the Oregon-California Trail rode the messenger, averaging nearly forty miles a day. On September 7 he pulled up at Leavenworth, where the message was wired eastward.

Meanwhile, on the 23rd or 24th the Sioux had finally left the region. The Brulé headed for the Niobrara River over the route to the Black Hills. On the way they pillaged the government farm operated from Fort Laramie twelve miles away and destroyed the buildings and implements. On the Niobrara, Chief Bear finally died of his wounds a week after the fight.

As soon as the Indians left, Bordeau buried the bodies of the soldiers on the battlefield, except for that of Grattan, which was carried to Fort Laramie and later buried at Leavenworth. The common soldiers' grave was pathetically shallow; less than a month afterward, as a Mormon wagon train passed by, some of the heads were showing.

But the main activity along the North Platte was a feverish preparation for defense in case the Sioux returned. The American Fur Company's post was barricaded for siege. Some of the traders came into the fort for protection, and others sought sanctuary by living with the Cheyenne. Wrote one observer at Laramie ten days after the fight, "I have never seen such a general stampede in any country."

For their part, the soldiers ventured out of the fort long enough to recover the two howitzers and the wagon. Still fearing a general uprising, Fleming asked the Indian agent to prohibit traders from selling guns and ammunition to the Sioux. The soldiers on outlying duty were called in, raising the garrison strength to 42. A small blockhouse was built among the outbuildings to protect them from being set afire.

By the end of August, an army officer had reached Fort Laramie on a regular inspection tour of the department and had called for a report from Fleming. Repeating his initial message, the Lieutenant recommended that a force be sent out "to punish the offenders in an effectual manner."

"But should this not be done," he added, "then great sacrifice of life may be expected, as all of the surrounding tribes, stimulated by neglect of this bloody massacre, will join hand in hand and rush on to the slaughter."

After securing eyewitness accounts from Bordeau and others, the inspecting officer transmitted them to his superiors and drew up the severest indictment against the Brulé. He wrote:

> The time has now fully arrived for teaching these barbarians a lesson . . . that is, how to appreciate and respect the power, the justice, the generosity, and magnanimity of the United States. . . . Troops could, and should, be sent to reinforce Fort Laramie at once, and a strong force might be despatched up the Missouri next spring.

With these reports the army launched its first campaign—to vindicate itself. As Bordeau's statement had indicated that the soldiers were the aggressors and had fired the first shot, the inspecting officer passed it on with the observation that Bordeau was "an Indian trader, and has a Brulé wife with several Sioux connections. His interests, of course, are opposed to any rupture between the government and the Sioux. . . . When, therefore, he speaks so positively as to which party fired first, he evidently betrays a strong bias in the premises."

By the end of September the story was that the whole affair had been deliberately planned by the Sioux, that the cow had been shot to provoke the troops into leaving the fort and that the Bear had gone there to report it and lure them to their destruction. The adjutant at Jefferson Barracks, Missouri, forwarded a statement from a passerby at the fort. French traders told him, he wrote, that for several days before the massacre, the Sioux were boasting "that they were strong enough to destroy all the soldiers if they could only find them out of the fort. . . . I afterwards was told, it was said among the Indians that this had been prepared beforehand by the Bear, who had told them to be ready for the fight, the Bear having himself killed Lieutenant Grattan as he ordered 'fire.'"

Even the incident that brought on the encounter—the killing of the cow—took on a more provocative color. According to the story reported by the army, the Miniconjou shot first at a Mormon and, missing him, had then aimed at the cow, declaring, "I have missed you; you are protected by God; but I will kill your cow." This version (Fleming reported that the man "barely escaped with his life") contradicted the accounts of both the Mormons and the Indians.

At the same time, the slow machinery of the army was moving; in October two companies of infantry were sent marching westward to relieve the fort. Heading them was Brev. Lt. Col. William Hoffman, former commander of Fort Atkinson on the Arkansas— a veteran Indian campaigner and one of the officers who had publicly deplored the reduction in garrisons at the frontier posts. Arriving at Laramie on November 12, he relieved Lieutenant Fleming of his command and called upon him for a third report.

By then Fleming's story was framed for his personal defense. In his earlier versions he had said simply that he had sent Grattan "to receive the offender." Now he added "and in case of refusal to give him up, after ascertaining the disposition of the Indians, to act upon his own discretion, and to be careful not to hazard an engagement without certainty of success."

In the first two reports he had not specified that the offender was a Miniconjou but had stated, "The Indians have been committing depredations upon emigrants and traders in the country all summer . . ." And, when the cow incident had occurred, "I was compelled to take notice of it, or give up entirely all protection to those travelling on this route." But in the November report he distinguished the culprit as a Miniconjou: "Last year we had a skirmish with the Minniconjou band, but were on the best and most friendly terms with all the others; and the force sent was sent only to act, if necessary, against the few lodges of the above hostile band."

Thus in assuaging his feelings of guilt at the loss of 31 men, Fleming could not bring himself to charge an Indian conspiracy but was content to hint that Grattan had exceeded his orders. In fact, Colonel Hoffman was soon convinced that the tragedy had vindicated his own position against weakening the frontier posts and leaving them in the charge of fledgling second lieutenants. In his report he exonerated the Indians from any plot. "There is not doubt," he declared, "that Lieutenant Grattan left this post with a desire to have a fight with the Indians . . ."

Such a charge immediately raised the hackles of proud army professionals. In transmitting the papers in the case to Secretary of War Jefferson Davis, the Adjutant General declared curtly, "There is nothing in the accompanying papers which corroborates the statement of Lieutenant Colonel Hoffman . . ."

From that point on the issue became public, resounding in the frontier newspapers and on the floors of Congress. The Indian Bureau and the supporters of a compassionate policy toward the Indians blamed the army for the Grattan tragedy. Wrote the Platte Indian agent: "I regret that the demand for the offender had not been postponed until my arrival. If it had been, I could have settled the whole affair without the least trouble." As for the Brulés' seizure of the annuities: "The Indians knew I would not give them their goods after the fight, and that in all probability the Government might send troops after them. Believing this, it is reasonable to suppose they would take the goods." Joining the attack, the same David D. Mitchell who had presided over the 1851 Treaty Council wrote an editorial in the Missouri *Republican* blaming "the conduct of the inexperienced, rash young officer in command of the detachment" but even more the government's policy of garrisoning its frontier forts with "the fragments of a company of *infantry*," which the Indians regarded with "sovereign contempt."

The cruelest blast came from Thomas Hart Benton, the lion of Missouri, who was then serving a term in the House of Representatives after an election defeat had brought his long career in the Senate to a close. Like many westerners, he distrusted easterners, including West Point army officers. The Sioux, he told his colleagues in the House, had been our friends for fifty years—since their first meeting with Lewis and Clark. But what had turned them against us? One answer: "sending our school-house officers and pot-house soldiers to treat the Indians as beasts and dogs." The man who killed the cow was simply observing the custom of the Indian country, and the chief had offered compensation. "But no! West Point discipline must make it a criminal offense, to be militarily punished." Grattan, concluded Benton, simply marched into the Indian camp looking for a fight and, instead of trying to take the offender, fired into an innocent crowd. "It was murder!"

On the other side, official letters favorable to the army position were furnished to frontier congressmen, who used them in speeches demanding more protection for settlers. The whole furor caused both houses to demand the army correspondence on the subject; they received all but the one statement giving an Indian version of the affair. This statement was a deposition by Man-Afraid-of-His-Horses—the most complete and one of the most objective accounts of the episode but technically not "correspondence."

At Fort Laramie, Colonel Hoffman did not know what a storm he had raised until he read about it in border newspapers in the spring of 1855. Immediately he opened a furious correspondence with the Adjutant General in defense of his statement about Grattan. To support it he gathered other eyewitness accounts and showered them on Washington. One of them from the Fort Laramie chaplain testified that Grattan had "an unwarrantable contempt of Indian character," had been seen "thrusting his clenched fist in their faces, and threatening terrible things" and was said by one of Bordeau's traders to be "quite intoxicated" during the Brulé incident. The cause of the whole affair was, concluded the chaplain, "the fact of the garrison being left under the command of inexperienced and rash boys."

At this broadside, the Adjutant General unceremoniously retreated. To the Secretary of War he wrote that "the Service is not likely to be benefited, but may to some extent be prejudiced by continuing this controversy . . ." And Secretary of War Jeff Davis "concurred."

Actually, as far as the charge of drunkenness was concerned, there was ample testimony that Grattan was absolutely sober. One

of those who said so was Man-Afraid-of-His-Horses. But his
deposition could not be revealed without substantiating Hoffman's statement that "Lt. Grattan left this post with a desire to
have a fight with the Indians."

So the military stuck to its story that the Indians were the
aggressors. And on the strength of this position it determined
upon an expedition to punish the "guilty" tribes.

Had any one of the ingredients in this tragedy been missing—
had the frontier army been better schooled in Indian treatment,
had Fort Laramie been commanded by an experienced officer, had
the Platte Indian agent arrived in time to give out his annuities,
had Lieutenant Fleming demanded compensation instead of a
prisoner, had Lieutenant Grattan arrested his drunken interpreter,
had Bordeau had the courage to go with the soldiers into the
Brulé village, had Grattan been temperamentally capable of returning with compensation instead of a hostage, had he simply
held more respect for the Indians—the Grattan massacre might
not have happened. But each of these unhappy ingredients was
present. Two generations of peace with the Plains Sioux were
shattered, and a generation of hostility began.

SEVEN ◆ *The Sting of the Wasp*

◆ 1 ◆

Within days of the Grattan massacre, the Plains Indians were unwittingly playing into the army's hands. The Brulé and Miniconjou were preparing for a long war—collecting guns, ammunition and arrow points. When the Platte agent reached Fort Laramie a week after the massacre, he found the Cheyenne and Arapaho camped nearby, waiting for the annuities that he had brought. But at his council with them, the Cheyenne chief demanded, according to the agent's translation, "That the travel over the Platte road by emigrants should be stopped; the next year I must bring four thousand dollars in money; balance of their annuity in guns and ammunition, and one thousand white women for wives." That night about two hundred Cheyenne rode at top speed near the agent's horse corral, where they fired three shots. "I found this band of Cheyennes," he reported, "the sauciest Indians I have ever seen."

Although the Oglala Sioux made contact with Colonel Hoffman and gave evidence of their good intentions, the fury of the Brulé mounted still higher after the death of Chief Bear. From their camp on the Niobrara, his brothers and near relatives led forays against the Oregon-California Trail and broadcast threats to "kill all the whites we find on the road." They would, according to one Sioux who reported to Colonel Hoffman, "keep up the war on the road all winter, and in the spring they will meet the troops who are sent against them." On November 13 the monthly mail wagon to Salt Lake was proceeding westward about 22 miles below Fort Laramie, with three employees and a passenger aboard. Suddenly it was attacked by a small party of Brulé, who killed three, wounded the other and made off with $10,000 in gold.

111

By that time, the contagion had spread from the Platte to the Missouri. Brulé and Miniconjou who had been at the Grattan fight went north to urge other Sioux bands to join their war. They had easily killed off the Fort Laramie detachment, they argued, and could do the same to any expedition. By October they had won over the Hunkpapa, Sans Arc, Blackfoot Sioux and some of the Yankton. A sullen band of Hunkpapas and Blackfoot Sioux told their Indian agent, "We do not want any of our Great Father's presents; we prefer scalps and stealing horses to anything he could give us." On the Missouri River a band of Yankton Sioux was sitting in council with its agent, who had given the members presents of coffee, sugar, flour, tobacco, gunpowder and lead balls. Without warning a warrior jumped up with a huge knife, cut open all the sacks and scattered the goods to the winds. Then he threw the coffee and ammunition in the river. Instantly, his excited comrades fired forty or fifty rifles in the air—thoroughly frightening the agent.

In the face of such conduct, even the agents of the Indian Department joined in the army's cry for punishment. The upper Missouri agent urged the government to send a force to pursue and chastise the Indians who had massacred the Grattan party. A new Platte agent was even more adamant; he recommended "giving every band of Indians from Texas to Oregon a genteel drubbing." A former Indian agent wrote his senator that "A prompt and decisive blow on the Sioux in effect would be worth to us, for years to come, millions of dollars and many strong armies."

In January 1855, Jefferson Davis recommended to President Franklin Pierce an increase in the regular army and a temporary force of three thousand mounted volunteers to deal with the Sioux emergency. The next day Pierce transmitted the proposal to Congress. Without an emergency force, he argued, "the combination of predatory bands will be extended, and the difficulty of restoring order and security greatly magnified." And without a permanent increase in the size of the army, "it may be expected that hostilities will soon be renewed, and that years of border warfare will afflict the country, retarding the progress of settlement, exposing emigrant trains to savage barbarities, and consuming millions of the public money."

Quick to oppose these measures was old Thomas Hart Benton. On the floor of the House he thundered that an increase in the numbers of regular troops would be a plague on the frontier. Today's dragoons, he cried, "are a burlesque on the name, and the sport of Indians." They never learned to ride but "roll off like pumpkins, if the horse goes a little fast, the man falling one side, and the gun the other . . ." They antagonized the Indians and then retreated into their forts while the retaliation fell on the unprotected emigrants. The regulars, he charged, "can do no good, but harm. They bring on wars. . . . God defend the West from these four new regular regiments!"

Nevertheless, the increases were eventually authorized, and the army prepared its expedition. Needed for such a command was a veteran Indian fighter who could ensure success.

• 2 •

As early as October 1854, Chief of Staff Winfield Scott had settled upon Brev. Brig. Gen. William C. Harney, then commanding a regiment against Indian depredations in Texas. Born on the Tennessee frontier in 1800, Harney had soldiered for more than a quarter-century, had fought Indians from Florida to Wisconsin and had earned a reputation as a dogged and fearless commander. Standing six-feet-four, with a face round and pugnacious, he had been known as an athlete in his early service. One chronicler called him "the swiftest runner in the army," and one of his favorite sports when off duty was to engage in foot races. On a number of occasions he had outraced Indian champions and boasted that he "could beat any red rascal that wore moccasins." While at Fort Winnebago in Wisconsin, he had determined to flog a recalcitrant Indian, but in a spirit of fairness he had offered to give the offender a hundred yards start in a race on the frozen Fox River; if the Indian reached a prescribed point first he would go unpunished. Carrying a whip with him, Harney was about to overtake his opponent and lay the lash on his back when the Indian swerved toward some thin ice. His own light weight carried him over safely, but Harney broke through into the icy water and lost both his whip and the race.

Given to rough speech in the frontier tradition, he once insulted one of his teamsters, who retorted that he was "as good a man as you."

"Very well," snapped Harney, "we will test that proposition." With that the two fell upon each other in a rough-and-tumble brawl, which resulted in something of a draw. Though the teamster was chastised, Harney admitted that he was a "pretty good man, after all."

More than anything else, Harney was a man who believed in swift retribution. It was Harney who, as a colonel in 1840, had delivered the last blow in the Seminole war with an expedition into the Florida Everglades; there he had surprised and captured a band of Indians and summarily hanged nine braves. When he was later given command of the 1858 expedition against the Mormons, who had displeased the federal authorities, Harney's plan of action was simple: Take Salt Lake City and hang Brigham Young and his Twelve Apostles. As this scheme was considered somewhat extreme, Harney was relieved of command of the expedition and was put in charge of another to the Northwest. There he proceeded to take on Great Britain, which was disputing the American claim to San Juan Island in Puget Sound. Harney occupied the island and stood off any attempted British landing until Winfield Scott could arrive and negotiate a settlement.

Nor was Harney especially punctilious in his observance of army rules when he believed he was in the right. Commanding a regiment in Winfield Scott's expedition during the Mexican war, he had been at Medellín, outside Vera Cruz, when Scott ordered him to make a reconnaissance but not to engage the enemy. Harney reconnoitered so closely that the enemy fired on him; when he fell back and the enemy attacked, he wheeled on them and drove them from their position. To the incredulous Scott, Harney reported, "I have violated your orders, attacked the enemy and driven them from Medellín." Though Scott was enraged at his insubordination, Harney was unperturbed. At the crucial battle of Cerro Gordo, it was Harney who led the main charge up the hill to the Mexican fortifications. After that victory Scott rushed up to Harney, hugged him and forgave all.

Now, in the midst of the 1854 Indian crisis, it was time for Scott to call upon his old subordinate (or insubordinate) to save the situation on the central plains. No one in the service was better qualified than this hard-bitten, steel-fisted old warrior. It happened that Harney was on leave, visiting his wife and family in Paris, where they had gone to seek a change of climate for his

son's health. But on October 26 the Adjutant General wrote
Harney that Jefferson Davis wanted to put him in command of
the Sioux expedition the next spring "if you should be in position
in season." At this trumpet call the old warhorse left his family
on Christmas Eve. When he reached Washington, President Pierce
summoned him to the White House.

"General Harney," he said, "you have done so much that I will
not order you, but I do wish you would consent to assume the
command and whip the Indians for us."

• 3 •

Arriving in St. Louis on April 1, Harney immediately set
to work marshaling troops and supplies for his expedition. By
early July, he and part of his staff were gliding up the Missouri
on a steamboat for Fort Leavenworth. There he assembled his
force of some seven hundred cavalry, infantry and light artillery
soldiers. Commanding the mounted troops was another stalwart
frontier campaigner, Col. Philip St. George Cooke. As a young
officer ten years earlier, he had accompanied Kearny on his expedition to Fort Laramie. Since then, Cooke had distinguished himself
in the Mexican war by leading a column of volunteer Mormons on
an extraordinary trek from the frontier settlements all the way to
California and back to Salt Lake. A veteran Indian fighter, he
now served as Harney's strong right hand.

Early in August Harney was ready to march. To his headquarters he outlined his plans: "I hope to force the Indians to the
alternative of giving battle or of deserting their families just at
the opening of winter, when the latter, of necessity would be
obliged to surrender themselves or incur the risk of starving."

With that he and his column filed out of Fort Leavenworth. It
was by far the largest force that had ever penetrated the Indian
Territory. And, although Harney had complained that his command was too small, the Sioux were much too divided among
themselves to require a stronger punitive force. The Oglala had
already come into Fort Laramie begging for peace.

On August 10 there arrived at Fort Laramie a new Indian agent
for the upper Platte—a white-bearded, stern-jawed New Yorker
named Thomas W. Twiss. Believing that the whites would inevitably overrun the Indians, he held a paternalistic and con-

descending attitude toward what he called "poor, helpless, ignorant children." But he was quick to defend the rights of his
wards against attempted inroads by the army. Fearing that
Harney's expedition would punish the innocent with the guilty, he
met with some of the Brulé at Bordeau's post on the anniversary
of the Grattan massacre. General Harney, he warned, was on his
way to punish the "bad" Indians. Twiss promised to try and protect the "good" Indians if they would take themselves south of the
North Platte. The "bad" Indians would have to remain north of
the river and take their medicine, and, if any bands south of the
river harbored any of them, he would declare them all enemies.

Ten days later Twiss met with the Oglala at another post north
of Fort Laramie and followed this meeting by a conference with
part of the Wazhazha. By the first days of September they were
all concentrated south of the North Platte on the upper Laramie
in a village of some four hundred lodges and perhaps four thouss-
sand people.

On the day after the Brulé meeting, the agent sent word to
Harney describing how he had separated the friendly Sioux from
the line of march. And to the Secretary of the Interior he reported,
"There is not, as I can find, within this agency, a single hostile
Indian; on the contrary, all are friendly."

Those still unaccounted for were most of the Brulé, including
about half of the Wazhazha band, and the relatively few Miniconjou who had come down to the Platte. These groups included,
generally speaking, those who had massacred the Grattan party.
Most of them were camped north of the Oregon Trail on the
Niobrara, the Cheyenne, and the White Rivers—in country
around the Black Hills largely uncharted by the white man.
Harney did not really expect a fight until he moved into that
country from Fort Laramie, and he was afraid he could not get
there before the snow fell.

However, one Brulé band generally operated below the North
Platte. With it at that time were those who had attacked the mail
party, including Red Leaf, the brother of Chief Bear, and Spotted
Tail, his first cousin. Almost certainly it included some of those
who had helped to wipe out Grattan.

But the band was led by Little Thunder, one of the most in-
telligent and farsighted of the Brulé chiefs, who had taken the
lead in preventing the Sioux braves from attacking Fort Laramie.

In early February he had understood that the fort commander was demanding the return of the mules stolen from the mail wagon; in an effort to comply, he and some of his warriors had brought them to the American Fur Company post. But, finding that the commander had given no such order, he had taken the mules and departed.

Soon afterward, small parties were descending on trading houses along the Platte and driving off scores of horses. If those men were of Little Thunder's band, they were demonstrating how little control he or any chief had over the young braves.

By June many of the southern Brulé under Little Thunder were camped near the forks of the Platte, above the north branch. In mid-August a runner from the Indian agent at Laramie Fork arrived there to warn of Harney's approach and invite them to the council at Bordeau's. According to one Indian account, the hunters had just brought in fresh buffalo meat, and it could not be moved until the drying process was finished; the head men counciled and determined not to move.

Getting a few reinforcements at Fort Kearney, General Harney struck on westward from that post on August 24. While his column was marching up the South Platte, Harney learned of Little Thunder's encampment. Those Indians were, he was told, "the murderers of Lt. Grattan and his detachment—of the mail party—and the authors of much of the insolence and outrages committed on the emigrants . . ."

On September 2 Harney crossed from the South to the North Platte. By that time, the expedition had traveled nine days from Fort Kearney with scarcely any grass for the animals, several horses had collapsed and the men were growing exhausted from the march. About noon they encountered a party of Laramie traders who had precise intelligence of the Brulé. Forty lodges (about four hundred people) were grouped on Bluewater Creek, a tributary of the North Platte. The braves were supposed to have been "a party in the Grattan massacre." The previous night some braves from this village had been "very insolent" to some emigrants camped at the mouth of Ash Hollow. One of them had kicked over an emigrant's coffee pot. And Harney's informers also brought him a message from Little Thunder, calling for a parley: "If you wish peace, we are willing; if you wish to fight, we are also willing." Ignoring the invitation to parley, Harney prepared to attack.

• 4 •

After making camp at the mouth of Ash Hollow late in
the afternoon, the General sent scouts up on the bluffs of the
Platte. From there they could see the Brulé camp upstream and
across the river, about five or six miles away.

That night Harney gathered his officers in his tent and laid out
his order of battle. Philip St. George Cooke, commanding mounted
troops and artillery, would start at three in the morning, secretly
skirt the village to the south in a forced march and take up a
position behind the Indians. Harney and the infantry would follow at four o'clock, planning to show themselves in front of the
Brulé lodges at daybreak. At the sound of the infantry's first
volley, Cooke's force would ride down upon the camp from the
rear. Being outnumbered in fighting men by about four to one,
the Indians would retreat into Cooke's arms; he would surround
them with his cavalry and cut them down with his artillery. It
would be not so much a battle as a mass execution.

At the appointed hour Cooke's force was in the saddle. Guiding
it was a Frenchman, who had served as an interpreter at the
Laramie treaty council. He led the men safely across the North
Platte, which was full of quicksands, and then on a ten-mile ride
in the hills around the Brulé village. As they were looking for a
concealed position above it, they discovered another group of
eleven lodges about three miles upstream; it later turned out to
belong to a party of Oglala camped with the Brulé. Just after
sunrise the soldiers halted and hid themselves behind a ridge
about half a mile above the upper camp, where they could view
all the Indian movements in the canyon of the Bluewater. Dismounting, the troops lay down in the grass with their rifles peep-
ing over the whole length of the ridge. They could see, on the
bluffs nearer the mouth of the Bluewater, the lookouts of the Sioux,
who had not discovered them. The village below was still silent
and motionless in the gathering light.

From Harney's camp at the mouth of Ash Hollow the infantry
started on schedule. But the General decided to delay crossing the
river until it was light enough to see the Indian lodges upstream.
Fording the Platte, the column turned toward the Bluewater. The

Sioux discovered the soldiers early, and they had scarcely marched a mile up the river before a delegation rode up to meet them. Little Thunder was said to be among them, calling for a parley. But Harney refused to acknowledge him and kept up his line of march.

At this rebuff the Indians raced back to the village. By the time the troops had rounded the last bend and come in view of the campsite, the Brulé had struck most of their lodges and were retreating on horseback up the Bluewater—as Harney had planned.

But at that point the General grew apprehensive about Cooke's being in his position. An aide had already been sent into the hills east of the Indian village to see if he could see Cooke's force. He returned to Harney and reported that he thought "the ground is too hard for the mounted men to reach their position."

Harney knew that, if Cooke's force were not in place, the quarry would escape. Something must be done to hold the Indians in the trap until he could be more certain that Cooke was ready to spring it. Accordingly, he sent an interpreter to the fleeing Indians, proposing a talk.

Little Thunder agreed to parley with Harney if the troops would halt and come no closer. To this condition the General assented, and, while both the infantry and the Indians stopped in their places, Little Thunder rode out and met Harney at a spot just past the original site of the village.

In his first official report of this episode, Harney did not say who initiated this talk; in a later report he wrote that Little Thunder had asked a second time for a parley, coming out to meet him with a white flag: "I halted and awaited his approach." But, according to three other independent eyewitness accounts of this particular incident, Harney sent out a messenger or "gave the signal" for a talk in order "to gain time," or "to give the Dragoons time to show themselves" and "kept him in conversation till he could learn of his cavalry's whereabouts."

Such an unsoldierly ruse was hardly in character for the rough-and-tumble Harney, but this encounter was not a battle in the ordinary sense. Harney was resolved to force a fight on an unwilling foe—a fight that might be his only chance to chastise the Sioux. So he concluded to catch the bird with a little salt on its tail.

Little Thunder rode up and, upon several invitations from

Harney, finally dismounted. He was, as one admirer put it, of "massive and majestic frame." Among the trappings decorating his bright costume were several medals given by white leaders as tokens of friendship. He customarily exuded a quiet dignity and self-confidence—what one observer called "a cool, observing collectedness of manner." But now he was justifiably fearful for the lives of his people. He offered his hand, but Harney refused it. Speaking through the interpreter, the General began, "You sent for me to come and fight you, or have a talk, and now you are running away."

"I do not want to talk with so many soldiers," answered Little Thunder, suspiciously.

Harney then accused Little Thunder's band of massacring Grattan and the mail party. "Your warriors have been murdering the whites—stealing our property and committing the most atrocious outrages upon our emigrants . . ."

Little Thunder acknowledged that there were "bad" men in his village but that he had "done all I could for peace."

"If we were bad, why would we be here? Why not have gone off, like the other Indians?" He added that the Indian agent had asked them to come and talk in order to avoid being punished. Harney then accused the Brulé of camping by the Oregon Trail "to steal and plunder."

> Only the other day you went to some emigrant's camp and kicked over his coffee-pot. Your Great Father has paid you to keep off this road and let his children pass. As far as [what] the Indian agent said, I do not mind what he said more than the barking of a prairie dog. . . . You have fallen on thirty of our men at Laramie, hundreds at once, and wiped them out. Now I am ready to fight.

Little Thunder pleaded with the General to spare his people.

"You must fight!" roared Harney. ". . . I want you to come on. I have not come out for nothing."

During the talk a squaw and two children, who had retreated the farthest upstream, were making their way up the west bank of the Bluewater; suddenly she spied Cooke's force across the Canyon. Running back, she warned the other Indians nearest her. Two young warriors rode up within range and challenged the soldiers to fight.

Still Cooke kept his men quiet; he had not yet heard any infantry guns. Within a few minutes—about half an hour after the talk began—the whole Sioux host was aware of the trap and showed the most frantic confusion. Many of the Indians ran up a steep enbankment, pocked with small caves and overgrown with brush, on the west side of the stream. Harney realized that Cooke was in place and had been discovered. There was no more need for delay.

"Go," he told Little Thunder, "and tell your young men that they must fight."

The chief leaped to horse and bolted back to his people. Harney's bugler sounded the charge. Little Thunder had scarcely joined his band when the infantrymen loosed their first volley. Advancing up the valley and firing at the fleeing Sioux, the forward company swung to the left and plunged through the Bluewater to attack those who were climbing the embankment. On those unfortunates they poured a devastating fire.

At the first shot, Cooke and his men sprang to saddle and started jogging swiftly in a column of fours across the Bluewater to head off the Indians who had clambered up the cliff. On the way Cooke dispatched a company downstream to cut them off if they tried to escape back across the canyon to the east. Then his main force, gaining the western mesa, charged the Indians who had climbed to the top. Under a withering volley, the Sioux fell back down the cliff, some of them hiding in the caves, most of them catching their horses at the bottom and splashing through the creek to escape eastward through a gap in the hills.

The troops that Cooke had sent to block them were too few and in a poor position. They could only fire as the Sioux thundered past. Cooke rode down and ordered them into the saddle for the pursuit. They obeyed, only to flounder in boggy ground. But Cooke had already sent most of his force plunging down the west cliff in pursuit, while his artillery raked the retreating horsemen.

To the south, Harney's infantrymen were advancing up the valley, sending up an exultant cheer when they saw Cooke's cavalry come into view. "I never saw a more beautiful thing in my life," one participant later wrote. Those who had not crossed the water continued on up the canyon to join in the pursuit of the Indians as they crossed the stream and pounded eastward. But being afoot they were helpless to chase horsemen and could only fire after them at long range.

While most of Cooke's cavalry was sent in the pursuit, the artillerymen were left at the foot of the cave-marked hill, crouching in the open and shooting mostly with small arms at the enemy still entrenched there. From out of the caves, their mouths shielded with brush, came a desperate fire of bullets and arrows on the exposed soldiers. Between shots, the officer in charge heard the cry of a child. Instantly he had the bugler sound a cease-fire. When the soldiers put down their guns two warriors jumped out of a cave and ran away before anyone could stop them.

Then—in mid-morning—Harney gave orders for the recall. Most of the mounted troops were far beyond earshot, chasing Indians over the broken prairie. But those in the canyon turned to the task of tending the wounded on both sides. Climbing up the hill to the caves, they heard the agonized cries and moans of women and children who had taken refuge there among the warriors. Near one hole in the cliff seven women and three children— two in their mothers' arms—were dead. Some of the wounded were so mangled that a half-century later the officer who had commanded firing on the caves could not bring himself to describe the scene. In the grass near the foot of the embankment they found a baby girl holding a puppy; when a sergeant picked her up she bit and scratched him—the last blow in the Battle of Ash Hollow.

Shocked and shamed by their own deed, the soldiers outdid each other in caring for their pathetic prisoners. Gently they carried them down the hill, laid them on the bank of the stream, made awnings to shelter them from the sun, bathed their wounds and gave them water to drink. Later the wounded were carried to the army camp back across the Platte and were attended by the surgeon.

Meanwhile the mounted troops had cornered some of the fugitives in cliffs several miles away. But being unable to dislodge them, the soldiers returned to the Bluewater around noon. They rode past an array of bronzed bodies lying in the grass—86 were found, according to Harney's report. But those who had fled took some of their wounded and dying with them, as was customary among the Indians. Bloodstained saddles and clothing were found along their whole line of retreat. One of the soldiers later estimated that "of those who escaped, scarcely ten could have been unwounded." Days later the troops found two Indian bodies on the banks of the Platte.

Harney listed five Indians wounded, and, as no chronicler mentioned any adult male prisoners, the five may have been the wounded women and children. The General reported approximately seventy women and children prisoners. They were taken back to the army camp across the Platte that night in a miserable rainstorm and were later moved to Fort Kearney.

As for the soldiers, the toll included four killed, one missing and seven wounded—all in Cooke's mounted command, which had also inflicted most of the losses on the Indians.

In neither of his two reports did Harney specify any losses among the women and children, and no figure for them was ever published. But one civilian accompanying the troops wrote, "We, of necessity, killed a great many women and children." In later correspondence Harney wrote of killing "some 100 of their people"; the difference between this figure and 86 may be the approximate toll of women and children.

"The battle was fought," Harney proudly wrote in his first report, "and the result was what I anticipated and hoped for."

"I do not suppose the Indians in this country ever had such a perfect clearing out as upon this occasion," wrote a civilian participant, reflecting the frontier antagonism for the Indian. "They will have cause to remember Gen. Harney for some time. . . . It was the finest thing I ever saw."

To Harney and his command the Secretary of War later expressed "the approbation of the President and of the Department . . ."

As for Little Thunder, he apparently escaped without being hurt. Wrote one officer, "as he impressed us favorably, we felt glad he was not."

For the next two days the troops were engaged in looting the Indian campsite. In their terror the retreating Indians had dropped everything—lodges, robes, saddles, powder horns. "I have a great many trinkets taken on the battlefield which I shall bring with me," wrote one correspondent to a St. Louis newspaper. The drying buffalo meat served as the soldiers' main fare for days: "We put a piece in our pockets, and chew it all day; it answers very well in place of tobacco." Among the effects were papers that appeared to have been stolen in the murder of the Salt Lake mail employees, as well as bayonets and pieces of army uniforms presumed to have been taken from Grattan's dead soldiers. What goods could not be carried off were burned. As for the remains scattered on the battlefield, one soldier wrote, "we took with us the bodies of our own fallen and left those of the Indians to the wolves."

• 5 •

To cap his triumph, Harney had his men erect an earthwork fortification near the mouth of Ash Hollow during the next few days. When he marched on for Fort Laramie on September 9, he left a company of infantry in it to protect the Oregon Trail. And to put a grim signature to the action on the Bluewater, Harney called the post "Fort Grattan."

But while he marched on up the Platte some Sioux renegades— probably part of Little Thunder's scattered forces—preceded him. Three days after the Ash Hollow battle, they attacked three white men below Scotts Bluff and mortally wounded one named Gibson. On September 15, even while Harney's column was approaching Fort Laramie, a few warriors came toward the stockade as if to trade. They rode by the army's herd of horses and mules, which was grazing outside the fort, with the herdsmen lounging in the shade of the walls. When the red men were between the wranglers and the herd they suddenly raised an Indian war whoop and flapped some blankets. The animals stampeded, and the Indians ran off with fifty of them. When Harney arrived shortly afterward and found what had happened, he dispatched a large force of cavalry in pursuit. Two days later the soldiers returned empty-handed and threw the General into a fit of profanity.

At the same time two white men from Fort Pierre stumbled into Laramie; they had walked 24 miles from Rawhide Creek, where Sioux had attacked and robbed them of their horses and belongings. And while one party of emigrants was camping on the Laramie, Indians cut all their mules loose, stole two or three and got away unscathed under a volley of bullets.

Harney was thus in no mood to deal kindly with the Sioux, even though those camped on the upper Laramie were friendly Oglala. They had heard of Harney's blow at the southern Brulé by messenger from the Indian agent and were thrown into new fear at Harney's arrival in Laramie. Indeed, he had been preceded by rumors that he intended "to kill every Indian he could catch, whether Sioux or not." Already he had become a legend; the Sioux called him "the Wasp" and shied away from another sting like that at Ash Hollow.

To vouch for the character of the Oglala, Agent Twiss came to Harney's camp near the fort and solemnly declared, "I pledge my head as security for their good conduct and fidelity." Harney then sent for their chiefs and principal men, who came down and met with him on September 22. The General refused to shake their hands, and, in his own words, "I assumed all the austerity I could put on . . ."

> The only conditions on which you can expect peace [he told them] are the prompt delivery of the murderers of the mail party in November last, the restoration of all stolen animals, and a pledge on your part to keep the road through your country open and safe to travel. . . . You must remain south of the Platte and take no part in the affairs that might happen north of that river.

Speaking for the Oglala was Man-Afraid-of-His-Horses, who grumbled that his people had already waited three months south of the Platte and had "killed no buffalo." But he would try to conform. A Brulé chief answered that he would try to comply, but first he wanted to consult his tribe:

> You must do what I ask or fight [Harney warned them], and even if you killed us all, for every one ten more would come, and your Great Father is determined to make you give up. He was never angry with you before, but now he is aroused. Your buffalo will all be driven away.

As he was anxious to march on to the Black Hills stronghold of the remaining hostile Indians, Harney could not wait for the hostages to be assembled. But he told the chiefs to turn them over to the commander at Fort Laramie; he would return in the spring, and if they had not given up the offenders he would be very angry.

With that the chiefs and their head men departed the council to talk with their people up the Laramie Fork. Three days later they came back and agreed to "do all in our power to comply with General Harney's demands." Wrote the General, "This state of feeling on their part, was what I supposed could only have been brought about by many serious encounters with them . . ."

Within two weeks of Harney's departure, the Sioux brought in

three of the warriors who had attacked the mail wagon. They
proved to be two brothers of the Bear and one of his cousins,
Spotted Tail. Riding their best horses and arrayed in their brightest costumes, they were singing their death songs in anticipation
of the worst; the French traders had already warned that Harney
planned to hang them. They were ready, they said, to "throw
away our lives for the good of the tribe." Two young Sioux boys
supposed to have been participants in the mail raid were not
given up, and agent Twiss made excuses for them. In their places
two other braves later presented themselves. The five prisoners
were taken down the Platte trail to Fort Leavenworth. But, at the
request of Thomas Twiss and the Indian Bureau, they were par-
doned by President Pierce and returned to their people the following spring. Harney was, in the end, denied this particular
revenge. But why did he concentrate on the mail-wagon attack in
demanding his prisoners, while ignoring the far more serious
Grattan massacre?

Soon after his arrival, Harney must certainly have talked with
Colonel Hoffman, the post commander, who had investigated the
whole affair and sent to Washington so much testimony supporting his conclusion. All at once Harney's eyes were opened. The
Grattan massacre had been virtually forced upon the Indians by
a brash young officer who was looking for a fight and who did not
have enough presence of mind to silence an interpreter who was
dangerously drunk. That Harney may have heard a still worse
version, perhaps based on the post chaplain's story that Grattan
himself was intoxicated, is suggested by the account of the affair
in Harney's biography, which was written years later with the
evident help of the General himself. In this version, "The soldiers
were drunk," and "the drunken Lieutenant ordered his men to
fire."

Harney himself did not drink and was tolerant of it in others
only as long as it did not interfere with their duty. Thus the
Grattan affair, as it must have been related to him at Fort Laramie,
would have seemed an unforgivable blunder to an officer of
Harney's discipline. To a man who had been sent out to punish the
Sioux for this episode and who had just killed a hundred of them,
the shock of this revelation at Fort Laramie must have been pro-
found. In his report of the Indian council he held at Fort Laramie,
written the day the chiefs agreed to his terms, Harney explained,

"I felt warranted to granting these conditions, and overlooking in a measure the massacre of Lieut. Grattan and his party, from the fact that I had already inflicted a severe chastisement upon them in killing some 100 of their people . . ."

But before he dispatched the letter he crossed out the phrase referring to the Grattan massacre. And in the same report he announced that he had sent a detachment back down the trail for the purpose of "breaking up Fort Grattan."

• 6 •

Summer was over, and Harney was worried about continuing his campaign with the onset of winter. A trader at the fort wrote to the settlements: "Let one of our snow storms catch his command in that part of the country, and you would hear of such suffering and death as would make your blood run cold. His mounted force will all be dismounted by next Spring."

But Harney was determined to press into the Black Hills and the Badlands, where most of the Brulé and Miniconjou were still holding out. "I felt satisfied," he wrote, "that I would lose much of my prestige, by not doing so & that the results would more than compensate for any loss of Animals & the temporary exposure of my Men . . ."

Accordingly, on September 29 he and his column left Fort Laramie and forded the North Platte. Camping the first night in a light rain, they plodded for the next three weeks along the old traders' wagon road between Laramie and Fort Pierre on the upper Missouri. For most of the march the night temperatures were chilling and often below freezing. Snow blanketed the first camp on the White River, before they reached the Badlands, but melted the next day.

All along the route Harney found ample evidence that the land was a favorite resort of the red man. But, though he sent out scouts for miles on either side of his line of march, they found not a single Indian in the whole country. Signs indicated that the tribes had retreated before him to the Black Hills. They were, in fact, making sure to keep away from the Wasp.

But, though the General would have invaded this stronghold, his guides told him it was "impossible to penetrate that country at this late season of the year, without endangering the safety of the troops and animals . . ." He therefore decided to pass on and winter at Fort Pierre, which had just been purchased from the American Fur Company and occupied by the army.

With the loss of only one man on the entire trek, the column reached its destination on October 19. The fort, far from being a warm refuge after their hardships, was a dilapidated excuse for a shelter. Quickly Harney proceeded to disperse his companies in cantonments. But the Dakota winter was merciless. The army cattle were dying from exposure and starvation, and finally the rest were mercifully slaughtered. More than a third of the horses died, and others lost ears or tails from frostbite. By midwinter the lack of vegetables brought on scurvy among the troops, and a few of them died.

Even before he and his forces were settled in early November, Harney had been visited by 25 Miniconjou. They pleaded for peace, saying that they wanted only "to be allowed to live." To prove their good intentions they presented some of the animals stolen from Fort Laramie and also a boy who was said to have killed the man named Gibson on the Oregon Trail. But, while they were camping nearby overnight, the boy escaped; fearing that Harney would then hang them all, most of them vanished.

A few days later the General was confronted by some forty Sioux of various tribes. Their message was the same: They were suffering from want and asked only to live.

By that time Harney was convinced that he had punished them enough and that the time was ripe for a peace council. Accordingly, he met again with the Sioux representatives on November 9 and gave them copies of a paper summoning ten men from each tribe to a peace council at Fort Pierre on March 1, 1856—if they desired to know the terms for peace. Through freezing temperatures and snowstorms, whole tribes trekked to Fort Pierre. At midday on March 1 the Indian delegations met with Harney and his staff in front of the stockade. Prominent among them was Harney's old adversary, Little Thunder. Notably absent were the Oglala; their agent, Thomas Twiss, had opposed Harney's invitation and had told them not to go. But Harney, enraged at this defiance, had ordered Colonel Hoffman at Fort Laramie to arrest Twiss and 'send their delegation to me at once." Suspended from office, Twiss later had to go to Washington to have himself reinstated.

As Harney opened the Fort Pierre meeting, he refused once again to shake hands. Silently the Indians sat down in a circle on the cold ground, and the General outlined his terms: The Indians were to give up those who had committed outrages, return stolen property, keep away from the roads, stop fighting among themselves and stop trying to pay for the murder of whites by giving buffalo robes to the traders. If they did not, warned Harney, "We will have blood for blood."

For its part, the United States would agree "to protect the Sioux from impositions by the whites" and to allow the Indians to take up any white offenders and deliver them to the nearest post, to restore the annuities and to set free all prisoners not implicated in "high crime."

The General then dismissed them to think over his proposition. Next afternoon the Sioux came back to give their answer. Little Thunder rose first. "I came here to see you because you sent for me," he began. ". . . I don't wish to fight you. What I want with you is to shake hands with you and hold your hands hard."

Harney's response was surprisingly warm, once against substantiating the probability that he had learned the truth about the Grattan fight.

> Yours was the first band of the Sioux I met when I came to fight, but if I had met any other band it would have been the same. I am sorry it fell so hard upon Little Thunder. From what we had heard I expected to fight them everywhere. . . . I don't find them as I expected. . . . There are a great many good men among them, but some bad ones, like other people. . . . I feel like shaking hands with all the chiefs, particularly Little Thunder. . . . I have no doubt in a few days, when those men are brought in, I shall be able to do it.

But, Harney said, he would not wait till then to release the Brulé women and children captured at Ash Hollow but would immediately order them freed.

This announcement was met with joyous applause by the Indians. For his part, the Miniconjou chief said he would bring in "the man who killed Gibson" and "the man who killed the cow."

For three more days Harney and the Indians met and talked. On March 5, with the agreement duly approved, Harney gave Little Thunder an official document making him the principal chief of the Brulé. "Here is your commission," said Harney. "I give you my hand as a friend."

Winning their applause, Harney moved among the other chiefs and subchiefs, giving commissions to them all and shaking their hands. To close the council he gave a soldier's benediction: "I hope the Great Spirit will take care of you, and that He will put *good* in your hearts, and that you all may have plenty, and keep your hands and hearts clean, that you may not be afraid to meet that Great Spirit hereafter."

Amid what the council transcript called "tremendous applause," the conference broke up. Next day, in a parting gesture, two thousand Sioux filed up to the fort and, when Harney appeared at the gate, serenaded him with drums and horns.

In commending his compact to Secretary of War Jefferson Davis, Harney pleaded for the United States to try and regain the trust of the Indians:

> They have been deceived so often by the whites that they would never again give them their confidence. . . . It is not yet too late for us to requite, in some degree, this unfortunate race for their many sufferings. . . . With proper management a new era will dawn upon such of the Indians as yet remain.

Davis in turn approved the agreement, recommending to President Pierce that it be "regarded as a valid compact." As it was mainly a restatement of the Fort Laramie Treaty and did not require new funds, the Senate's consent was not needed.

For their part, the Indians moved early to seal the bargain. In April the Oglala arrived from Fort Laramie and agreed to the compact. And by May 15—the deadline set by Harney—the Miniconjou had given up the two offenders, including High Forehead, who had killed the Mormon's cow near Bordeau's two years before. At this show of good faith, Harney listened to the Indian pleas for the lives of the prisoners. A few days later—shortly before he was ordered to close the Sioux campaign and return to Fort Leavenworth—he released the prisoners. It was the last stone in his edifice of peace.

Yet it was a pathetic gesture to end two years of tragedy. Harney himself had tried to draw a moral for the red men:

> Who is the cause of all this trouble now? Just one bad man. "The man who killed the cow." The Great Father does not care about a

cow; but that fellow was a bad fellow, and was not given up, this caused all the difficulty.

It was a very little thing, yet see how it spread over the whole Sioux nation from one bad fellow. I hope all the red people will remember this . . .

But a different moral was drawn by Thomas Hart Benton on the floor of the House: "West Point discipline," he charged, "made a simple debt into a crime." He listed the men and equipment lost in the Grattan affair, the retaliation of the Indians against emigrants and mail messengers, the cost of reinforcements for the frontier posts, the financing of the Sioux expedition and the funds to raise and supply an enlarged regular army: "A heavy penalty for a nation to pay for a lame runaway Mormon cow, and for the folly and juvenile ambition of a West Point fledgling."

Then the old warrior called attention to the statuary in the Capitol rotunda: Over the east door were the Pilgrim fathers being met by friendly Indians; over the north door were white men buying land from Indians with trinkets and cloth; over the west door, white men were defeating Indians in battle. Benton thundered:

It is history! The history of our Indian intercourse! Hospitable reception, land taken, Indians killed. Is there not enough in this history to induce us to stop, and think, and try to settle with all possible gentleness, these calamitous Indian wars, of which our own dreadful misconduct has been too much the cause?

In 1853 it seemed that every white man coveted the Indian Territory. Led by Senator Stephen A. Douglas of Illinois, agitators for a Pacific railroad were demanding rights of way through the heart of the buffalo country. A government survey party was in the field exploring possible routes. A bill to form a huge Nebraska territory stretching from the Missouri River to the Rockies was introduced in Congress. Some three thousand prospective settlers gathered in Iowa along the Missouri River, waiting for legal permission to cross the water.

For a generation the frontier had been halted at the big river by the Indians' domain. There no whites were allowed except those licensed to deal with the Indians or those emigrants passing through to Oregon, California and Utah. Into that same country the government had been resettling other Indian tribes from the East, promising that it would be theirs "as long as grass grows and water runs."

But, as a Missouri senator told a frontier audience, "the green hills of Nebraska are in sight." And around campfires on the Iowa and Missouri side of the river land-hungry men sat and waited.

At that juncture the main obstacle to the land-seekers was the Indian title. But in 1853 President Franklin Pierce ordered the Commissioner of Indian Affairs to visit the border tribes and urge them to sell their land. The newly appointed commissioner was Col. George W. Manypenny, an Ohioan whose sincerity and honesty were almost unique in a government bureau notorious for corruption. Probably no Indian Commissioner of the nineteenth century was more emotionally committed to Indian welfare than

132

was Manypenny. Undoubtedly against his own desires, he journeyed west from Washington to talk the frontier tribes out of their birthright.

Then in 1854, at the Administration's insistence, he returned west to negotiate the treaties. Fourteen tribes sold more than thirteen million acres, reserving some 1,300,000 acres to themselves. As soon as his treaties were ratified by the Senate, Manypenny admonished the government to keep its promises. "It should fulfil, with the greatest promptness and fidelity, every treaty stipulation with these Indians; frown down, at the first dawning, any and every attempt to corrupt them; see that their ample annuities are directed faithfully to their education and improvement, and not made the means of their destruction . . ."

Meanwhile the Nebraska Bill had been changed to create two new territories, Kansas and Nebraska. In June, Congress passed the Preemption Law to enable farmers to take up lands in the new territories at nominal prices.

The road was clear at last. Across the Missouri streamed the thousands. For the next three years—by horseback, wagon, stagecoach, train and steamboat—they surged west across Iowa and Missouri to the promised lands. Wrote one Nebraska traveler, "They are covering the territories like a swarm of locusts."

By 1857 the land mania had reached its peak; lot prices in the towns of Kansas City, Atchison, Leavenworth and Omaha had advanced several thousand percent. In the first few years the white population of Kansas and Nebraska had jumped from a few hundred to 136,000. One new arrival in Omaha wrote in 1857, "It would seem at this rate that the entire east would become depopulated."

From the beginning the flood tide washed into the Indians' domain. Many Kansas settlers invaded the lands reserved by the border Indians and built houses for themselves. Manypenny's agents were kept busy ordering them off the reservations. When many of them ignored the Indian agents, Manypenny appealed to the army to throw them out, but the military did nothing.

"Trespasses and depredations of every conceivable kind have been committed on the Indians," he wrote of the Kansas land rush. "They have been personally maltreated, their property stolen, their timber destroyed, their possessions encroached upon, and divers other wrongs and injuries done them."

Knowing that a host of border whites were waiting to trade the Indians out of their land payments, Manypenny had made every effort to write safeguards into the treaties. But too often the Indians themselves, whom Manypenny believed to be influenced by pretended white friends desiring only to fleece them, had demanded immediate payment in cash. As soon as it was in their hands many of them traded it for whiskey and other indulgences. As for the land reserved for themselves, much of it was divided into small farms owned by individual Indians. These farms were often sold quickly to white traders for liquor, and the Indians were left with nothing. Years later Manypenny wrote pathetically, "Had I known then, as I now know, what would result from these treaties, I would be compelled to admit that I had committed a high crime."

• 2 •

So far these movements had little effect on the so-called "wild" Indians of the Plains—the Sioux, Cheyenne and Arapaho. But the new territories of Kansas and Nebraska extended all the way to the crest of the Rockies, taking in their hunting grounds, including Fort Laramie. And, despite Manypenny's admonitions, the incoming settlers did not acknowledge that the Plains Indians held formal title to their lands. Speaking in the House, the Congressman from Iowa had simply said it was "owned by the United States, and ready for settlement—all 70,000,000 acres of it!" From the frontier town of Lawrence, Kansas, a pioneer settler wrote in 1854, "The buffalo before the onward march of civilization has retreated toward the setting sun, and the red man is destined to follow in the trail of the buffalo, until at last both will be extinct."

But could this uncharted wilderness, held by savages, really be invaded by the farmer? Along the Platte River, Fort Kearney and Fort Laramie could offer protection against the Indians. On the Kansas River, construction was started on Fort Riley in 1854. And, beginning the next year, the Army Engineers and the Department of the Interior started building roads westward to the Rockies. Close behind the road builders came the settlers; by the end of 1856 they were staking claims along the Loup Fork of the Platte, halfway to Kearney.

The red man resisted these advances. Hostility was so intense that most surveying and road-building crews had to be protected by cavalry escorts. On Rock Creek, near the Kansas-Nebraska border, one detachment was jumped by the Cheyenne, who respectfully withdrew when they saw the escort. At Fort Kearney a huge body of Pawnee opposed the road along the north bank of the Platte, but the work still continued.

To help protect the Oregon Trail, a detachment of troops from Fort Laramie was stationed at Platte Bridge near the present Casper, Wyoming. There in April 1856 the commander seized three Cheyenne for a minor offense. When they attempted to escape, one was killed and another wounded. In revenge the Cheyenne took the warpath, killing a trapper on his way to Fort Laramie, then shifting their attacks to the Oregon Trail near Fort Kearney.

Equally adamant were the Sioux, who gathered in a "grand council" in the Black Hills during the summer of 1856 to determine how to stop the white advance. Before they departed, they had pledged to one another that they would allow no white men to enter that country.

In 1857 a pack train of army topographical engineers left Fort Laramie to reconnoiter the Black Hills region. Heading it was Lt. Gouverneur Kemble Warren, a young explorer and map-maker who had accompanied Harney on his Sioux expedition. In mid-September he was intercepted near the Black Hills by a large band of Sioux. A party of headmen came into the army camp; seated under a canvas shelter in the midst of a rainstorm, Warren listened while Chief Black Shield spoke for the others:

> The Great Father asked us for a road along the Platte, and we gave it to him—we gave him one along the White River, and another along the Missouri. . . . This is the last place left to us, and if we give it up we must die, and we had better die fighting like men.

"I did not come to look for a road," protested the officer, "but only to see what is in your country . . ."

But the Indians made it plain to Warren that they intended to kill his whole party if he continued. "We have been told before that roads would not be made," declared another chief, "but still you keep making new ones."

To this theme, Warren himself commented that night in his

diary: "How true was all he said! The only security these Indians can have in the possession of their country would be its utter worthlessness to the whites."

The next day the Indians left, with an ultimatum to keep out. Warren decided to turn around and leave the Black Hills "for a future expedition."

But, though the Sioux successfully held onto their sacred Black Hills, the roads built through other parts of their domain were quickly lined with wagons. Throughout the 1850s the western army posts were supplied by growing columns of freight wagons. Among the leading pioneers were William H. Russell, Alexander Majors and William B. Waddell. Forming their partnership in 1855, they secured the contract to deliver all military goods west of the Missouri. Two years later they undertook to supply the army's vast Utah expedition, and within a year they had increased their wagons and teams from 350 to 3,500. Through the late 1850s the growing Mormon colony at Salt Lake and the addition of new mining camps in the Rockies kept the wagons rolling.

From this mounting traffic, the buffalo grass suffered more damage. Adding to the desolation were the large herds of cattle and sheep driven along the Overland Trail to supply the rising population in California.

Such traffic was too tempting to escape the attention of the Plains Indians, even though they were on comparatively good behavior in the late 1850s. Many a trail herd had to forfeit some cattle as "toll." Other drafts were levied at night, when Indian riders would suddenly swoop down on a herd and scare it into a stampede. Nor were freighters like Russell, Majors & Waddell immune from the theft of mules. The Indians had adopted a profitable means of protesting the white invasion.

• 3 •

By April 1858, more than freight and emigrant wagons was rolling past Fort Laramie. Road improvements had made possible a regular scheduled transportation line. For the first time since the pioneer mail carriers had first crossed the Plains in 1850, the postal service on the central route was increased from a monthly to a weekly schedule.

At that time the main California mail and passenger line, operated by John Butterfield, swung southward through Texas and New Mexico. But the weekly schedule on the central route soon proved itself, despite the snows and storms of the Rockies and Sierras. In 1859 Russell, Majors & Waddell purchased the mail line to Salt Lake and later the remaining link to California. Bringing new efficiency to the route, they built stations every ten to fifteen miles along the old Oregon Trail; their stages were soon running from the Missouri frontier to California in 23 days—cutting the former time in half.

Along this continental highway, "road ranches" sprang up near the stage stations, catering to the dry throats of the travelers. Between the stations and the ranches, a private traveler could go the whole route without carrying bed or provisions. The Overland Trail had become a thin spear of white civilization bisecting the Indian country.

Although most of the emigrants had tried to shoot buffalo for food, the stage passengers were soon taking their toll simply for the sport. For the first time, travelers with leisure time were being carried across the Plains. All were armed, and, to break the insufferable monotony of the stage ride, they would shoot out the window at buffalo as they passed. When stopping near a herd, they would stretch their legs by stalking the animals and shooting at them. When Horace Greeley took the stage through western Kansas in 1859 he reported, "Eight were killed yesterday at the next station west of this by simply stampeding a herd and driving them over a high creek bank." One factor in the buffalo's favor was that so many passengers were abominable shots. The driver of Greeley's stage stopped while one of them fired over and over without effect at different buffalo who approached within easy range. Greeley, who otherwise disapproved of shooting at buffalo for sport, told his companion to keep it up. "It amuses you and does not hurt the buffalo."

By that time Russell, Majors & Waddell were launching a project to dramatize the superiority of the central route over the southern. Early in 1860 the firm began stocking its line with ponies and riders; on April 3, 1860, the first Pony Express rider pounded out of St. Joseph, Missouri, with the United States mail. Ten and a half days later—half the stage's time—the last man in the relay flew into Sacramento, where he was hoisted to the shoulders of the waiting crowds. Soon, as the riders and station crews perfected their system, the time was reduced to nine days—considered the pinnacle of Yankee achievement.

Against the fleet, well-fed horses of the Expressmen, it was almost impossible for Indians to make good an attack. So heavily did the riders rely on escape, rather than on firepower, that they soon discarded their carbines and armed themselves only with Colt's revolvers. But, through most of the pony mail's one and a half years, there were almost no attacks by Indians east of the Rockies.

Within a year the pony mail had succeeded in its main purpose. Regular mail traveling by stage over the central route was increased to a daily schedule. Because of the secession of the Confederate states, the southern Butterfield line was discontinued. The central route through the heart of the Cheyenne and Sioux country was restored as the course of empire.

To clinch the issue, Western Union began building the first transcontinental telegraph, using the central route. By the spring of 1861, the singing wire had already been strung past Omaha as far as Fort Kearney; at the other end, the Californians had carried it over the Sierras to Nevada Territory. Spurred by special inducements for the winner, two rival construction companies from east and west began racing each other to reach Salt Lake first.

Early in July 1861 the westbound crew started with wagons and poles out of Fort Kearney. It had gone scarcely twelve miles when the Indians began building fires around the poles to burn them down. The telegrapher at the end of the line wired the post; within an hour, cavalrymen arrived to surprise some of the Indians while they were still at their work.

Most observers had thought the California crew would reach Salt Lake first, because of the shorter distance. But by early September the westbound poles had been strung ninety miles beyond Fort Laramie. On October 17 the line reached the Mormon capital, and six days later the first wire message from Salt Lake reached San Francisco: "Line is just completed." A month afterward the pony rider finally gave way to the telegrapher.

The continent was now spanned, not only by a road, a string of stations, and a continuing procession of animals and men, but also by a thin band of metal that carried the white man's words in an

instant. The domain of the Plains Indian had been slashed in two
by the cutting edge of white civilization.

• 4 •

In the spring of 1857, Indians came into Fort Laramie
from country far to the south. When they showed gold dust and
nuggets and wanted to trade, the whites around the fort gathered
in high excitement. Would the Indians show them where the gold
came from? The red men assented, for a consideration of sugar,
coffee, flour, tobacco, blankets and horses. The whites agreed to a
price and started south with the Indians.

Whether or not this party discovered gold in the Pike's Peak
region is not known for sure, but several parties were prospecting
the ground from there north to the South Platte in the summer
of 1857. By the spring of 1858 rumors of gold had caused several
parties to leave the settlements for the Rockies. In the summer a
real strike was made on Cherry Creek, creating the town of
Denver and precipitating one of the tumultuous gold rushes of
western history.

The first news of this gold discovery reached Fort Laramie
early in July. By the 23rd a party composed of James Bordeau,
Joseph Bissonette and other veteran traders had hurried south to
Cherry Creek. There, digging with an ax and other crude instruments and washing out the gold with a frying pan, they took
enough to satisfy themselves that the place was rich. Then they
rushed to the settlements for better tools and equipment.

On the morning of August 26 the Fort Laramie party arrived
in Kansas City with gold dust and quartz specimens. Instantly the
news spread all over town. While fresh parties were forming for
the mines, the Kansas City *Journal of Commerce* published the
news under the headlines: "The New El Dorado!!! Gold in Kansas
Territory!!"

By telegraph the word reached St. Louis the same day and was
soon trumpeted by newspapers all over the country. As confirma-
tion came from the mines, the gold fever seized the settlements.
The find was, ran the claims, a second California!

The vanguard of gold-seekers pressed westward in the fall of
1858. But the main horde waited through the winter—stirred week
after week by more exciting dispatches. In the early spring, from

as far east as New England and Georgia, the Fifty-Niners rolled west. Of those traveling up the north side of the Platte, many failed to cross it at the earliest opportunities and, because of the unusual high water, had to go clear to Fort Laramie before they could turn south.

In May 1859 the Pike's Peak frenzy was further intensified when a rich new strike was made on a fork of Clear Creek, stirring Denver to new excitement and launching several more towns higher in the mountains.

Almost forgotten in the rush were the owners of the land. The gold strikes had been made deep in country occupied by the Cheyenne and Arapaho, whose title to it had been confirmed in the Fort Laramie Treaty of 1851. Now it was swarming with gold-hunters. William Bent of Bent's Fort, who had become Indian agent to the Cheyenne and Arapaho, warned the Indian Bureau, ". . . A desperate war of starvation and extinction is therefore imminent and inevitable, unless prompt measures shall prevent it."

To save the situation Bent urged a new treaty that would put the Cheyenne and Arapaho out of the path of the whites. As early as the summer of 1858, some of their chiefs had acknowledged to him that the white man "would soon with his villages occupy the whole prairie" and that the buffalo "would soon disappear entirely." They hoped that the Great Father would give them a home where they would be protected from invasion until they could learn to be farmers like the whites.

In September 1860 the Arapaho and two chiefs of the southern Cheyenne, Black Kettle and White Antelope, met with the Indian Commissioner at Bent's Fort. There they ceded all the land given to them in 1851 at Fort Laramie, except for a tract lying generally between Sand Creek and the Arkansas River. For this vast grant, comprising all of eastern Colorado, western Kansas, and part of Nebraska Territory, they were given an annuity of $30,000 for the next fifteen years. But if they did not make satisfactory efforts to improve themselves by becoming farmers, "Their annuities may, at the discretion of the President of the United States, be discontinued entirely . . ."

Little wonder that many of the Cheyenne warriors refused to acknowledge such a treaty. But in February 18, 1861, the rest of the southern Cheyenne chiefs signed. Ten days later, having "extinguished the Indian title," the whites organized the Territory of Colorado.

• 5 •

Thus in the seven years from 1854 to 1861 the vast domain of the Plains Indian, stretching from the Missouri to the Rockies, was invaded and carved up by the white man. Only the plains above the North Platte Valley and west of the Nebraska frontier were relatively untouched. This land was the empire of the Sioux and the northern Arapaho and Cheyenne—the remaining "wild Indians" of the plains. Despite the bitter massacres of 1854 and 1855, they still made Fort Laramie their headquarters.

But events were stirring to challenge even their rights to their homeland. Nebraska Territory had opened the vast domain from Kansas to the Canadian border, without settling the question of the Indian title. By 1857 land promoters from St. Paul and Dubuque had founded Sioux Falls and other towns on the Big Sioux River east of the Missouri. Treaties were soon made with the Ponca and Yankton Sioux for some 16,000,000 acres extending as far west as the Niobrara River Valley. From the Missouri River towns, settlers looked westward across the green plains and began agitating for a new territory. In 1858 they convened a provisional legislature at Sioux Falls; by March of 1861 Dakota Territory, covering all the northern Indian country to the Rockies and Canada, was carved from Nebraska. Once again the white man was pounding on the red man's door.

No one was more aware of these rumblings in the east than were the wild Sioux Indians themselves. From his outpost on Deer Creek near Fort Laramie Agent Thomas Twiss reported, "These wild tribes have heard that all of the Indian tribes to the eastward of them have ceded their lands to the United States, except small reservations . . ."

Their fears were heightened in the spring of 1859, when the Army Engineers sent a party of topographers up the Missouri to explore the valley of the Yellowstone River. In charge of the expedition was Capt. William F. Raynolds, a veteran Indian campaigner who had been at Fort Pierre with General Harney in 1856. A man of stern and uncompromising standards, he was thoroughly convinced of the incorrigible savagery of the red man. Lending wisdom and stability to the enterprise was old Jim Bridger, one of the few whites who could guide Raynolds through the Sioux country.

Late in June Raynolds and his men marched out of Fort Pierre on the old traders' road to Fort Laramie. For days, as they passed on the north edge of the Black Hills, the Indians dogged their flanks and revealed their presence by their night fires. A detachment boating up the Yellowstone was stopped by a Sioux war party, which took the horses and gave them back only after a confrontation that threatened to erupt into a fight. On October 11 they reached the North Platte near Red Buttes. A week later, leaving his party in winter quarters near the Indian agency at Deer Creek, Captain Raynolds rode to Fort Laramie for supplies. After mingling with fellow officers for a few days, he returned to his men and prepared for new explorations to the north.

But, about two hundred miles in that direction, a large Sioux contingent had camped for the winter. Hearing of the white expedition, the Indians sent a chief of the Miniconjou, One Horn, southward to parley with Raynolds. A noted warrior, One Horn was also persuasive; the Sioux hoped he would be able to divert the white soldiers. Arriving at Raynolds' quarters, he announced his purpose: "I have been sent to notify you that you must not pass through our country."

Raynolds reminded him of the Harney treaty and its provision against molesting travelers. "We cannot restrain our young men," warned One Horn; "they will kill you."

"Then," answered Raynolds, "your tribe will be held responsible."

At this answer One Horn began to hedge. "Are any more parties coming?" he inquired.

"Not that I know of," answered Raynolds, "unless my party does not get home at the right time. . . . If we do not get there at the right time they will go for us, and if you want soldiers in your country that is the way to get them. Kill my party and then you will have enough."

The situation had been reversed since the day, eighteen years earlier, when Frémont had admitted to the Sioux chiefs at Fort Laramie, "We are few, and you are many." Now the white man was saying, "We are many, and you are few."

With some food and a few gifts, One Horn left the soldiers without accomplishing his assignment. And on May 10, 1860, the resolute Captain and his party struck out northwest, marching through a hostile wilderness that was sometimes unfamiliar even to Jim Bridger. Soon they realized that they had started too early in the spring. The streams were swollen, the mountains covered with deep snow. They lost wagons and one man trying to cross the rivers. On a fork of the Snake River the men grew mutinous and threatened to leave behind some of the equipment.

But still greater dangers awaited them in their descent of the Missouri. On Big Dry Creek, a small detachment was set upon by some 250 Crow, who charged the camp and fired their guns in a vain effort to stampede the mules. At the American Fur Company's Fort Berthold another detachment found a surly band of Hunkpapa and Blackfoot Sioux, who demanded presents and threatened to take whatever they wanted. But Raynolds refused without provoking retaliation.

The main body of his party reached Omaha safely on October 4 after one of the most remarkable expeditions in army annals. Despite the most terrible warnings of the Sioux, Raynolds had crossed and recrossed their country from Fort Laramie to the sources of the Missouri. And, in his report, he gave encouragement to white settlement. His band had found, he said, evidence of gold in the Black Hills and the valley of the Madison River, thus foreshadowing two of the West's most tumultuous gold rushes. Much of the vast domain, comprising what is now five states, was suitable for roads or railroads. As for the soil, probably more than three-fourths of it was good for farming.

The white man's eyes were upon the last redoubt, and the red man knew it. In a meeting with some of the Sioux chiefs at Deer Creek near Fort Laramie, Agent Twiss told them that the whites would not invade their country. But one of them corrected him in unanswerable terms. As a young man, he said, he had traveled east as far as Lake Michigan before finding any white people.

> And now our "father" tells us the white man will never settle on our lands and kill our game; but see! the whites cover all these lands that I have just described; and also the lands of the Poncas, Omahas, and Pawnees. On the south fork of the Platte the white people are finding gold, and the Arapahoes and Cheyennes have no longer any hunting grounds. Our country has become very small, and, before our children are grown up, we shall have no more game.

Reporting this exchange to Washington, the agent could not help agreeing with the chief in his description of the situation. He reported too that the buffalo no longer "makes the prairie appear black . . . as far as the eye could scan the horizon." Now it was found only in small bands on half a dozen rivers from the Republican to the Yellowstone, "very far distant for the Indians of this agency." All these changes, he warned, had a "tendency to irritate, excite, and exasperate the Indian mind." Hostilities, concluded Twiss, "may occur at any moment."

• 6 •

To meet the crisis, Twiss proposed a new treaty with the Plains tribes to put them on reservations and teach them to be farmers. Accordingly, on September 18, 1859, his agency at Deer Creek was the scene of still another council of the Sioux, northern Cheyenne, and northern Arapaho. When they were assembled, Twiss began:

> My Children, your Great Father directs me to say to you that as the buffalo and small game also are rapidly diminishing what do you propose to do to gain subsistence, when there is no longer any game for food, and prevent your old people and little children from dying by starvation? Will you labor like the white man, plant, hoe, and raise corn for food? Or will you die with hunger?

When Twiss had finished, the chiefs conferred with one another and then designated Medicine Man, an Arapaho chief, to answer for them:

> Our country for hunting game has become very small. We see the white men everywhere; their rifles kill some of the game, and we are no longer able to find any game; our little children are crying for food. We are obliged to travel many days before we can find Buffalo; and this too, when the snow is deep, and the weather cold. It is but a few years ago, where we encamped here, in this valley of Deer Creek, and remained many moons, for the Buffalo were plenty, and made the Prairie look black all around us. Now, none are to be seen, and we are obliged to go to the Yellow Stone, ten days travel, and then find only a few, for the Crow Tribe of Indians show hostile feelings towards us when we hunt there; oftentimes scaring away the game and stealing our horses. Our old people and little Children are hungry for many days, and some die; for our hunters caught no meat. Our sufferings are increasing every winter. Our horses, too, are dying, because we ride them so far to get a little game for our Lodges. We wish to live.

With that, Medicine Man announced that the Indians were willing to "settle on small farms and live in Cabins." He outlined the reservations which each tribe would accept—the Arapaho on the Cache la Poudre River, the Cheyenne on the Laramie, the Oglala on Horse and Deer Creeks and the Brulé and Wazhazha on the White River east of the Black Hills.

"Father, we give all the rest of our Country to our Great Father. . . . It is no longer of any use to us as nearly all the game has disappeared."

This proposal, he concluded, was "the only one that will preserve us from extinction, and permit us to dwell for a long time on these beautiful Prairie lands."

Twiss then went over a proposed treaty with them, incorporating the terms they proposed and providing for an annuity of $115,000 in goods, implements and assistance "for a period of time at the discretion of the President of the United States . . ." The chiefs signed the same day.

That treaty seemed to seal the history of the "wild tribes" of the plains. Reading their doom in the downfall of neighboring nations, the Sioux and their allies were ready to give up their ancient life before it was too late. In their contacts with the whites, the other tribes of the Missouri River and the southern plains had been dragged into debauchery, prostitution and utter abandon. Squalor, filth, exposure, starvation, tuberculosis and venereal disease were consuming them. But the northern tribesmen—though touched with the white man's vices—were not yet his slaves. By remarkable foresight and an extraordinary display of character, they meant to change their lives and save them.

Despite all this effort, the United States Senate rejected the treaty. In that act it threw away the last real chance to meet its obligation to the Plains Indians and to avoid an all-out war. The alternative was simple military power against the tribes. This alternative required, above all, more troops at the western posts.

But the Civil War was soon draining the Indian country of soldiers. Southerners were resigning or deserting to fight the North. Loyal troops were recalled to fight the South. For a time Fort Laramie was kept at a strength of 250 to protect the overland mail, which had just been increased to a daily service. But as neither the Sioux nor the Cheyenne attacked the stages, the Fort Laramie garrison was cut nearly in half by November 1861. Frustrated in making peace, the red man now saw his chance for war.

1

Two stagecoaches, carrying nine passengers and company employees, were rolling westward past Fort Laramie in mid-April 1862. On the 17th they were rocking through the sagebrush beyond Split Rock Station, on the Sweetwater River. A few days earlier Indians had attacked Split Rock itself, killing two operators and running off all the animals. Through this dangerous country the travelers were proceeding cautiously, eyes alert and guns in hand. All at once someone on the box of the front coach shouted, "The Indians are coming!"

A war party of Arapaho thundered along the road. Shots were fired by other Indians hiding in the brush. In an instant the coaches were surrounded. A driver was wounded in the chest. One of the mules was hit in the mouth. Frantically, both drivers urged their panic-stricken teams to a slight knoll above the road. Then they released the mules while everybody threw mail sacks, buffalo robes and other cargo out of the coach. With these objects they tried to barricade themselves under and between the two wagons.

Concealed in the brush, the Indians showered arrows and bullets on the defenders. According to one participant, bullets thudded "like hail" into the sacks. One man standing by a rear wheel was shot in the face. Two others were each wounded twice. A man shooting his rifle from the coach was hit in the leg. Twice the Indians rose out of the brush and charged the wagons. Each time the defenders turned them back with revolver fire.

Robbed of an easy victory, the Indians withdrew late in the afternoon. When they were out of sight the four able-bodied men helped the five wounded comrades along the road. At that point, the Indians returned and set fire to the coaches. But somehow

146

the party of whites stumbled on eight miles to the shelter of Three Crossings Station.

At this attack the Overland Road west of Fort Laramie was thrown into panic. The stage company drew its coaches and teams off the line for two hundred miles. With mail and passenger service abandoned and the telegraph line repeatedly destroyed, overland communication with California was cut. For the moment, at least, Indians ruled the continental crossing.

Such a predicament was hardly surprising. Beside withdrawing regular troops from Fort Laramie and other stations to fight the southern rebellion, the government had also withheld powder and lead from its 1861 annuity payments to the Plains Indians. This measure was apparently motivated by the desperate need for ammunition in the Civil War, but it had the effect of antagonizing the Indians at a time when United States troops had been reduced on the plains. To the Indians, ammunition was essential in hunting buffalo; withholding it in violation of the 1851 Treaty was considered a cruel breach of faith.

As rumblings of their discontent were heard, it had been feared that they would endanger the transcontinental stage and telegraph lines. Accordingly, Union volunteers from California had been sent to patrol the western half of the line. From the east, other troops had been sent to guard the Overland Trail as far as the crest of the Rockies; the commanding general had taken up headquarters at Fort Laramie:

> I am satisfied [he had written] that unless the Government is ready to abandon this route both for mails and emigrants an Indian war is inevitable. All the tribes in these mountains . . . are in bad humor; [they] charge the Government with bad faith and breaches of promise in failing to send them an agent and presents.

This had been the situation when the Indians struck the trail at Split Rock Station in April 1862. Now, moving swiftly to repossess the transcontinental passage, the army dispatched another regiment of volunteer Ohio cavalry to Fort Laramie. The slow-moving column raising dust out of Fort Leavenworth in early May was commanded by Lt. Col. William O. Collins, an Ohio lawyer who had raised several companies of volunteers. Originally sent to Missouri to fight Confederates, Collins and his troops were shunted instead to the Overland Trail to fight Indians.

Noble and commanding in appearance, with a dark beard and piercing brown eyes, the Colonel became the idol of his men on the rugged march to Fort Laramie. He quickly earned a reputation for fairness and humane decisions in the troubles that inevitably arose on the trail. Wrote one soldier, "He was a fine old gentleman, rather old for military service [he was only in his fifties], but finely preserved, energetic and soldierly."

With the Colonel was his only son, Lt. Caspar W. Collins. As a youth he had been his father's companion on hunting and fishing trips in the Ohio woods. But he was not a robust lad and had left Ohio with a persistent cough. On the Overland Road he came into his own, becoming tanned in the sun and losing his cough; in his father's words, he "eats like an Indian." Against the rigors of the trail he seemed to grow from a boy to a man almost before his father's eyes. The Colonel wrote home to his wife, "I have great hopes that the necessities of our situation will teach him industry and self-reliance."

Indeed, as they probed farther into Indian country, young Caspar played to the hilt his role of debonair young officer. One soldier wrote of him, "He seemed to dash into things without much premeditation, played a strong and magnificent game of poker, took one drink too much, once in a while, but was apparently a young man entirely devoid of fear and with an ambition to have military success and renown . . ."

In mid-May, as the column pushed into Sioux territory along the Platte, some two hundred Indians rode up and wanted to parley. Colonel Collins invited them to his tent; in front of it they formed in a circle and opened their talk. The chief, speaking first, said that they were concerned about the advance of this long body of soldiers. Collins could see that they feared that he had been sent to fight them and take their land.

But the Colonel assured them of his peaceful intentions. If they were good Indians, he said, they would be protected. They answered with a chorus of "How, how!" After sending them away with gifts of clothing, Collins noted that they had not stolen anything from his command, as the traders had warned that they would. In fact, one warrior found two stray army horses and returned them to the column.

"I am sure," wrote the warmhearted Colonel, "that if the Indian character was better understood and justice done them by respecting their customs, protecting the worthy and only punishing the bad, they would give less trouble."

On May 30 the weary column plodded into Fort Laramie under a punishing rainstorm. For four days they camped on the field nearby. Then they marched on to South Pass, with the Colonel dropping off detachments at key points along the route.

A month later, Collins and his main force were camping in South Pass when Indians attacked wagons on the trail behind them, killing two emigrants and shooting at some soldiers standing nearby. The Colonel took a hundred men and pounded after them, without success. A few weeks later an army teamster herding some mules was shot, and the Indians ran off the animals. In early July they robbed a mail station only two hours after Colonel Collins had passed through with a body of soldiers.

Despite all the reinforcements, the army still could not control the Oregon Trail. Obviously the bluecoats could not be everywhere at once. With their hit-and-run tactics, the Indians still kept the initiative.

But even these raids were only preliminary attacks by impetuous young warriors. The real striking power of the Sioux was being marshaled silently under the direction of the chiefs. Guns and ammunition were bought or stolen. Beginning in May 1863 the Sioux held councils with the Cheyenne and Arapaho south of Fort Laramie. By November, according to one report, the three tribes had sworn to wage war on the whites. They would, promised the chiefs, "shake hands and be friendly with the whites until they procured ammunition and guns."

In the face of these ominous movements, the stage line over the top of the Rockies was shifted from the Fort Laramie route to a more defensible trail via the South Platte and Fort Bridger. But the shift was a tactical mistake that made *two* army forces necessary—one to patrol the new stage and mail route and the other to protect the telegraph line on the old road. As a result, Fort Halleck was built at the edge of the Medicine Bow Mountains to guard the new route.

In the fall of 1863 Colonel Collins went back to the settlements and secured twelve more companies to patrol the Oregon Trail. He stationed them at several new posts—from Camp Mitchell east of Fort Laramie to the Platte Bridge and Sweetwater Stations on the west. Impressed by this strength, the Sioux held their fire.

• 2 •

For a time, at least, the troops that had been rushed to the high plains settled down to routine garrison life. Rather than being confined to Fort Laramie, the cavalry squadrons were generally stationed at the various new outposts. Escorts were provided for many of the emigrant trains. Other troopers guarded the large herds of army cattle and horses. The infantry tended the vegetable garden outside the fort or gathered hay and wood.

In fact, though every man knew his duties in case of emergency, an Indian attack on the fort itself was hardly expected. Never constructed for defense, it consisted of a number of adobe and frame buildings surrounding and facing the parade ground. Even the old traders' fort had been torn down. So vulnerable was the post that, according to one account, a returning detachment of cavalry was allowing its unsaddled horses to roll on the parade ground when a band of Indians rode through the buildings, yelling and waving blankets. The animals were stampeded out of sight before anyone could fire a shot.

But against such Indian tactics the soldiers were supposed to be well schooled. Infantrymen performed battle maneuvers and practiced shooting at targets. Artillerymen went through their gun drills, and cavalrymen used vast areas of the landscape for exercises in mass movement—wheeling into line and charging imaginary enemies.

On patrols a long distance from the fort, strict orders prohibited shooting, in order to prevent discovery by Indians. But bagging game while on the march was permitted if the men used sabers—a practical impossibility. Many an antelope or buffalo brought down with a bullet was scored with the saber before being hauled into camp, and it was commonly said of the frontier cavalry, "their sabers are lethal at forty yards."

Of all assignments at the fort, the most disagreeable was night guard duty. For two hours at a time, the soldiers would march along their sentry paths with muskets on shoulders, calling out "All's well!" at regular intervals. Failure to give the signal at the expected time would bring the corporal of the guard on the double; if the offender was found asleep, the penalty was severe.

In winter the biggest enemy was not the Indian, but the weather. Snow and chilling winds made sentry duty a scourge. As the army did not issue overclothing, it was up to each soldier to provide his own protection from frostbite. Buffalo robes, Indian blankets—any makeshift covering—might be seen moving along the sentry line through the winter nights. Then, after the two bitter hours, the corporal would relieve the guard with new victims hauled unceremoniously from their sleep.

Indeed, even the shelter of room and bed was scarcely sufficient against the Rocky Mountain winters. Each barracks or officers' room had a single fireplace from which a frequently stoked blaze kept the immediate vicinity too hot and the rest of the space too cold. As the night drew on, the temperatures plunged to freezing and below. Even in late September, Caspar Collins wrote his mother, "When a person first goes to bed in this country he can hardly bear a single blanket over him, but towards morning he can bear two or three large buffalo robes."

This kind of severity helped make life at Fort Laramie less than appealing for the few women on the post. Some of the senior officers were married, and their wives lived at the fort. When volunteer companies arrived during the Civil War, their officers' wives sometimes visited for several months at a time. Also on the post was the wife of William G. Bullock, the agent for the post sutler, who mixed on a social level with the officers' wives.

For those sturdy women, the attractions of the fort and its surroundings were meager indeed. One of them, suffering through a hard winter, wrote of the springtime, "When the wind blows off the snow, one does not see the sprouting grass but barren sand . . ."

As their letters to relatives at home reveal, boredom was the chief enemy. In their tight little society—a total of eleven women lived in the fort in 1864—there were few cultural or social activities in which decent women could participate and little food for the small-town gossip that they had enjoyed in the states. When Colonel Collins' wife visited the fort she pleaded for her daughter in Ohio to write her even the most trivial details—"the 'on dits' of the town."

Travel outside the fort was considered too dangerous for women, and their arrivals and departures were major adventures. Mrs. Collins dreaded firearms. But on her way home in August 1864, right after a series of Indian massacres on the Platte route,

she rode for days in a wagon surrounded by loaded revolvers—
wishing all the while, as she wrote, "that I could load and fire a
pistol."

Of a different sort were the laundresses and seamstresses whom
each company was allotted. Mostly European immigrants with
little education, they lived in separate quarters known as "Soap-
suds Row" and were definitely outside the social circle of the
officers' wives. That the enlisted men sometimes paid them more
than a little attention is indicated by records of occasional mar-
riages at the post. And, at an enlisted men's party reported by one
disapproving chronicler, all five of the women were drunk.

At still another level of Fort Laramie society were the Indian
squaws, who lived with their children and some transient braves
in a nondescript community known as "Squaw Town," upstream
from the fort. It was part of the long-established community of
"tame" Oglala that, under Chief Smoke, had settled down to live
by the favors and the trade of Fort Laramie and the California
emigrants. Some of the women worked as servants for the officers'
wives; others simply existed on the scourings of the fort, degraded
to the roles of hangers-on in the white man's establishment.

To receive special gifts of food they sometimes organized
dances, lasting several hours at a time, in front of the officers
lounging on the porch and balcony of the bachelor officers'
quarters. One such gathering consisted of eight or ten old men
who beat drums while a large circle of squaws—mostly old crones
—danced slowly round and round, shaking rattles and tree
branches. The whole retinue was dressed in buffalo robes and
blankets; one woman had a wolfskin on her head, and a man wore
the coat of an artillery lieutenant—how he got it was not questioned. After two or three hours the performers mercifully closed
their show. The officers took up a collection and purchased flour,
meat and rice from the commissary. Rejoicing over this reward,
the entertainers returned to their lodges at Squaw Town.

The proximity of some young squaws outside the fort was, of
course, a matter of interest to soldiers many months and a thous-
and miles from home. In the tradition of the Indian country, some
officers sought to emulate the mountain men and take squaw
wives. As acquiring a squaw chiefly involved paying a horse or
two to the father of the intended, such unofficial arrangements
were against army regulations. Indeed, unmarried squaws often

objected to being purchased in this way; many were more virtuous than their suitors. After one volunteer officer had bought a bride, the father, the girl and the horse all decamped before the union could be consummated. Another officer took his bride into Old Bedlam, the bachelor officers' quarters, where she resisted his advances by scratching his face and fought her way out the back door. For several days he pretended sickness to hide his wounds, but he becaming the laughing stock of the post.

During 1864 three officers were discharged from the service because, according to rumor, they had been too active in Squaw Town. One officer, transferred to another frontier fort, left without saying goodbye to his Indian squaw and baby. At Bordeau's post he changed his mind, saying, "I am going to get onto my horse and ride back there." All night he rode back to Squaw Town, broke the news to his sweetheart, kissed his baby goodbye and joined his detachment again as it was starting from Bordeau's in the morning.

But Squaw Town was not so romantic as it was pathetic. In the Indian tradition, the male inhabitants believed themselves above menial work, and the women employed as servants at the fort could not afford the high prices at the sutler's store. Describing their plight in an angry letter to the Indian Commissioner, Mrs. Collins wrote:

> The consequence is that many of them are in almost a starving condition and they will gather up from the ground scraps that our very dog has left untouched. There is only one other way by which they can save themselves from sharp hunger, [and] that is too humiliating to a woman and a Christian to more than allude to.

In midsummer the soldiers found that the emigrant trains contained the kind of femininity that they wistfully recalled from their home towns. Escorting such trains was therefore a pleasant duty, if only for the chance to talk with pretty girls. Three enlisted men riding outside the post on a few hours' pass came upon a wagon train and became acquainted with some Missouri girls. So intent were they in the conversation that one of their horses broke loose. As their time was nearly up, they went back to the fort and got a new pass to look for the horse. Just before they started again the pony showed up at the post, but they rode back to the wagon train anyway. The military police found them fraternizing with the emigrants and reported them to the commanding officer, who confined them to quarters.

Beyond such occasional adventures, life at Fort Laramie held few diversions. At a wage of $13 a month, the private was limited in his purchases at the sutler's store. As the paymaster visited the post only two times a year, gambling was sporadic at most. Still, some officers and men always managed to have money, and a poker game was in almost continuous progress in the back room of the sutler's store. Many of the participants were mountain men who used the post as their headquarters; they were also joined by teamsters and other civilian employees of the quartermaster. These worthies had more spare time and higher wages to lay at the feet of Lady Luck.

Chief among the mountaineers at Fort Laramie in the 1860s was old Jim Bridger, the prince of them all, who was regularly engaged to guide scouting expeditions in the Indian country. Holding court on the bench outside the sutler's store, Bridger entertained the soldiers with marvelous tales of the West—fantastic stories of bears, buffalo, Indians and the incredible wonders of what later became Yellowstone National Park. He told the same stories over and over. "He had probably told them so often," observed one young officer, "that he got to believing them himself." One of the pet notions with which he regaled tenderfeet was how the mountains kept growing in size. In the spring of 1864 a group of passing emigrants gathered about him in front of the sutler's store and inquired about the route ahead. "Mr. Bridger," asked one awe-stricken pilgrim, "how long have you bin in this kentry?"

With a straight face, the old man pointed a gnarled finger at Laramie Peak shining in the distance. "Stranger," he drawled, "d'ye see that high mountain over in the range yonder? Well, when I first kem to this kentry, that mountain was a hole in the ground."

As usual on army posts, drinking often ran to excess and was the bane of the post commander. Whiskey, which was available from the sutler, was the source of repeated quarreling and noisy disturbances and caused more than one well-begun party to end in a near-riot. Various methods were tried to control it; at some frontier sutlers' stores boards were mounted behind the bars with the men's names listed on them; the number of drinks a man consumed was tallied with pegs, and three pegs were supposed to mean he was finished for the day. Despite such efforts, drunkenness was a frequent cause of disorderly conduct, insubordination, insulting language to officers and absence without leave.

For the milder misdemeanors, punishment varied from extra guard duty to loss of rank. For a more serious offense, the culprit might be tied for a period of time to one of the cannons on the parade ground or ducked several times in the Laramie River. In dead of winter when the ice had to be broken to reach the water, this punishment provided a most effective lesson.

For a crime requiring a court-martial board, the sentence often involved a number of months at hard labor under guard, with ball and chain attached to the leg. At the end of that time the offender might be drummed out of the service, have his insignia stripped from him in front of the whole command and be sent forlornly out of the fort while the band played "The Rogue's March."

To combat misconduct the post commander gave every encouragement to wholesome occupations. Every Sunday morning the post chaplain held church services. The post library had six hundred books and the most recent possible issues of magazines and newspapers. The latter were usually a month old by the time they reached Fort Laramie, but, as the post was located on the transcontinental telegraph line, the garrison received war news as quickly as any place in "the States."

In good weather the soldiers also passed the time with baseball, horseshoes and other sports. Day passes were often allowed to small parties going into the mountains to fish, hunt or gather berries. On a winter Sunday the whole garrison, including women and children, would go skating on the frozen Laramie River; ladies unable to skate were pushed around on chairs.

Although the official post band consisted of only three drummers and three fifers, instruments were secured for a much larger brass band, which practiced assiduously and at every opportunity serenaded officers, wives and visitors with such favorites as "Home Sweet Home" and "Soft in the Stilly Night." A large glee club, accompanied by instruments, was equally devoted to serenading.

With such a diversity of talent, variety shows were often presented on the balcony of Old Bedlam—sometimes organized under the name of "Laramie Minstrels." One such performance ended in chaos, however, because most of the players had been imbibing too freely backstage.

During the winter "theatrical season" some of the officers and

ladies also presented legitimate plays with such suggestive titles
as "Loan of a Lover," "Flies in the Web" and Lover by Proxy."
After the theater, it was customary for officers and their wives to
visit the sutler's agent, W. G. Bullock, for eggnogs—of which he
was an acknowledged master.

Still further amusement was provided by the myriad pets
maintained about the fort—cats, dogs and a tame antelope that
ate bread, and butted everybody within reach. The Indians of
Squaw Town made frequent drafts on the dog and cat population
for their soup pots but made no perceptible dent in the animal
roster of Fort Laramie.

In fact the officers and men became so friendly with the nearby
Indians that nearly all participated at one time or another in
dog feasts and often pronounced the meat surprisingly good. Apparently any novelty was acceptable, considering the usual army
fare of salt pork, jerked beef and dried vegetables (the latter
shipped from the frontier in hard bricks, which expanded into
passable greenery when soaked in water).

On special occasions, particularly Independence Day and
Christmas, the post made extraordinary preparations for banquets, hauling in delicacies for weeks beforehand. In 1863 the
Christmas dinner menu included "roast pig, roast beef, cold boiled
ham, jellies, pickles, coffee, tea, peaches, cake, mince pie, and
ice cream"! As the three long dining tables accommodated only
75 people, the officers and noncoms, as well as their families (five
ladies and a number of children), dined first and then made way
for the rank and file.

Despite all these attempts, the battle against boredom in this
isolated post and these unaccustomed surroundings was never
won. Colonel Collins and his son Caspar made the most of their
opportunity to become experts on Indians of the Great Plains
and Rocky Mountains. Irrepressible Caspar, who was perhaps
more enthusiastic than was any other officer at the post, wrote
an eloquent estimate of Fort Laramie: "This post is a very pleasant place when you get used to it." In the privacy of his diary, a
soldier was more blunt: "Feel lonesome, and almost have the
'blues.' Will read over some old letters as there are no new ones ..."

In such an atmosphere the disciplinary rate was high. In 1862
the provost marshal for the Laramie territory had a new case
almost daily. As at other frontier posts, desertion was common,
and, once the Civil War had ended, it reached the proportions

of mutiny. As early as November 1864 the men of two volunteer Ohio companies had sent a statement to Colonel Collins insisting on being sent home, "or we will take the matter into our own hands and go." In July 1865 a Kansas company threatened to mutiny; one man was executed and some others arrested. When the company soldiers rallied to free them, the post commander quieted them by ordering a battery of artillery into place before the guardhouse.

The one factor that could revive morale in quick time was a fight with the Indians. For volunteers anxious to crush the Rebellion and save the Union, this dismal frontier duty was a painful disappointment, and the attitude of John Grattan lived on in many young officers of the 1860s. One veteran post commander at Fort Laramie complained that many alarmist reports from outlying detachments "are highly colored and much exaggerated—and it seems to be the desire of some to hurry on hostile operations."

Nor were enlisted volunteers immune to the fever. In the spring of 1864 one of them, encountering an Indian near the Sweetwater, deliberately shot and killed his horse. In that period the local Indian agent reported "numerous instances where friendly Indians under my charge were shot and killed by soldiers . . ." During a temporary peace a soldier from the nearest neighboring fort boasted in a letter to his sister that he and his buddies had killed three Indians: "We took the scalps of the ones we killed and let them lay." In mid-1862 Caspar Collins observed of the new volunteer companies at Fort Laramie, "I never saw so many men so anxious in my life to have a fight with the Indians."

• 3 •

Through the early 1860s events were stirring in the West that would more than gratify their desire. Several hundred miles east of Fort Laramie, the Sioux tribes of Minnesota gathered at the Lower Agency near Redwood Falls in June 1862. They had come for their annuity payments, which were overdue. For years they had watched helplessly while Indian agents had taken their rightful goods, had conspired with traders to cheat them, had permitted flagrant violation of laws against selling whiskey to Indians.

Their degradation and decay had reached an end. After waiting two months in rising anger and being told by certain whites that the annuities were not coming, they stopped waiting and acted. On August 18, 1862, they drew their tomahawks, bows and fireguns. They began killing every white man, woman and child they found. For days the horror flamed across Minnesota. Settlers took refuge in the forts; soldiers were reinforced by volunteers to fight the Indians. Before the carnage was over more than seven hundred white settlers had been murdered—one of the most fearful atrocities in American history.

For their crimes three hundred Indians were captured and tried; 39 were sentenced and hanged. Then the army began wholesale removal of Indians from Minnesota. Refusing to be herded to still another frontier dumping ground, many Sioux hurried to join their brother tribes on the Missouri River. There they urged the Yankton Sioux to ride with them against their white tormentors.

Fearing an outbreak in Dakota Territory, Gov. William Jayne held a council with Strike-the-Ree and his headmen at the settlement of Yankton. At the climax of the talks, the Governor reminded the old Chief of his obligation to remain peaceful under the treaty and not to imitate the Minnesota Sioux. Stung by this admonition, Strike-the-Ree started up from his seat and grasped the Governor by the shoulder. Almost convulsively fighting back his rage, he slowly answered:

> You blame the Minnesota Indians. They did wrong, but you do not know the cause. We know it! We know it! You do not! For long winters and summers they had been cheated and robbed by the agents and traders. They complained, but the Great Father would not make it right. Their hearts became bad; they thirsted for blood; they got plenty.

Then, measuring every word, he added, "We have the same cause to kill as our friends in Minnesota."

Strike-the-Ree spoke for all the tribes of the western border. Almost from its inception in 1824, the Indian Bureau had been a political pork-barrel prize. With each new administration in Washington, Indian offices were the rewards for election supporters. Bishop Whipple of Minnesota wrote that Indian agents were chosen from among "whiskey sellers, bar-room loungers, debauchees . . ." In the early days of the republic, John Randolph of Virginia had warned, "To be an Indian agent would corrupt the angel Gabriel." And by the 1860s the Bureau's reputation was so unsavory that, when one crusader appealed to President Abraham Lincoln for reforms, Lincoln answered with resignation, "It would take at least one additional man to watch each Indian agent." As a congressman in the 1860s, James Garfield told the House of Representatives that the Indian Bureau "is a stench in the nostrils of all good men. . . . As carrion attracts crows, so this department attracts to itself all forms of official baseness."

The salary for an Indian agent's office was the least of its attractions. The Indians' annuity payments were the real plum. It was said on the frontier, "An Indian agent with $1,500 a year can retire upon an ample fortune in four years."

Among the favorite ways of defrauding the Indian was to store his annuity goods in the warehouse of the local trader (often a relative of the agent), where they would be mixed up with the trader's goods. He would then sell them to the Indians and split the payments with the agent.

In 1865 Col. William Bent of Bent's Fort in Colorado Territory gave some pertinent testimony about the operations of Col. Samuel G. Colley, Indian agent to the southern Cheyenne and Arapaho. At Colley's agency on the upper Arkansas, his son Dexter was the licensed Indian trader. One of Bent's men was in the trader's lodge and brought out as evidence a box top marked "U.S. Upper Arkansas Agency." Commented Bent, "From comparison of the goods traded and the annuity goods, I am satisfied they were identically the same goods." When Dexter Colley had first come to the Indian country after his father became agent, his wordly possessions had consisted of not more than $1,500 worth of cattle. But after two or three years he boasted to Bent that he had made $25,000 to $30,000 "trading with the Indians."

A Major Redfield had arrived as Indian agent among the Yankton Sioux in the 1850s and had brought his nephew as trader. As Strike-the-Ree described it:

> Goods have been stored upstairs in the warehouse, and have all disappeared. . . . If they bring any goods for the Indians to eat and put them in the warehouse, the agents live out of them . . . and pay has been taken by the agents, and they have put the money in their pockets and taken it away with them. I have seen them take the goods from the storehouse of the Indians and take them to the mess-house . . .

When Redfield left, he loaded fifteen boxes of Indian goods on the steamboat; not content with that he sent back for more.

"When I am gone," Redfield told Strike-the-Ree, "you will meet with a great many agents but you will never meet one like me."

"I think," the chief later agreed, "I never want to see one like him."

But Redfield was wrong. He was succeeded by Dr. Walter A. Burleigh, who arrived with nothing to his name but a single trunk of possessions. According to Indian testimony, he proceeded to outdo Redfield's art. Plows, calico cloth and other items delivered for the Indians disappeared. Boxes marked for the Indians were unloaded from the steamboat and left on the bank; at night somebody scratched off the marks and put on other marks, so that the Indians never received the goods. Strike-the-Ree asked Burleigh to show him the invoices, but the latter refused. With insufficient blankets and food, many of the Yankton froze or starved to death.

"I think the agents are all alike," growled the old Chief. "The agent puts his foot on me as though I were a skunk. And the agents are all getting rich and we are getting poor." As early as 1856 he had told General Harney, "When an agent comes here he is poor, but he gets rich, and after he gets rich he goes away and another poor one comes."

The result was the opposite of that intended by creation of the Indian Bureau. After selling his land, the Indian was then robbed of the payment due him. The money that did reach him was generally dissipated in whiskey, which the unsophisticated savage was unable to resist—whiskey sold illegally under the very eyes of the Indian agent. Often it was sold on credit against the next annuity, so that when the goods arrived (less the portion stolen by the agent) they were claimed by the trader for debts. The schools and agricultural instruction promised by the treaties were, with some exceptions, forgotten. As a frontier churchman described the situation in his diocese: "The school a sham; the supplies wasted; the improvement fund squandered by negligence, or curtailed by fraudulent contracts."

Shorn of his wild game by the white man's invasion, cheated of his chance to learn the farmer's occupation and robbed of his annuity payments, the Indian sank deeper in degradation. Near the military posts, Indian women garnered crumbs from the white man's table through prostitution, sometimes with the consent of their husbands. Complained Strike-the-Ree:

> Before the soldiers came along we had good health; but once the soldiers came along they go to my squaws and want to sleep with them, and the squaws being hungry will sleep with them in order to get something to eat, and will get a bad disease, and then the squaws turn to their husbands and give them the bad disease.

Starvation, exposure, disease, debauchery—these factors combined to strike down the Indian as the white man advanced. Submission to such a monstrous system led only to a dead end. Bishop Whipple of Minnesota, pleading to President Lincoln for reform, wrote, "The sale of whiskey, the open licentiousness, the neglect and want is fast dooming this people to death . . ."

· 4 ·

Through the 1850s the Plains Sioux, still roaming their own land with a part of their once-endless buffalo herd still alive, were not yet so inextricably caught in this net. But their looming decline was clear enough by the time of the Civil War. Col. William Hoffman, whose duty at frontier posts ranged from Florida to California over a third of a century, made no exception of his tour at Fort Laramie when he wrote, "I am unable to say what proportion of annuities actually reaches the hands of the Indians, but I have no doubt that they have little or no benefit from it." [3]

By 1863 the Plains agencies had become as rotten as those along the frontier. Robert Campbell, one of the first owners of Fort Laramie, wrote from St. Louis to his Congressman:

> A new crop of Indian agents, have recently been sent to the plains &c,—a majority of whom seem to think that instead of being a check on the traders, they should participate in the profits! . . . [They] have frankly stated that they did not accept the office of Indian Agt, for the paltry salary, and openly intimated that they *intended to make more out of it.*

One of this breed was John Loree, who had been a farmer near St. Joseph, Missouri, and an active Union campaigner in a state with predominantly southern sympathies. Appointed by Lincoln to the upper Platte agency in April 1862, he proceeded to antagonize the Sioux from the moment he arrived at Fort Laramie. As in the previous year, the 1862 annuities did not include powder and lead. Loree held a council with the "tame" Oglala at Fort Laramie and persuaded them to agree that farm implements would be substituted for the ammunition. Their consent was taken to represent all the upper Platte Sioux. When the "wild" Oglala and Brulé heard of this deal they were outraged. Ammunition to hunt buffalo was their first need for life itself. They had no intention of abandoning the chase and grubbing in the dirt for their food. They would not agree to receive farm tools, and they remained short of annuities in 1862, as they had in 1861.

But this trick was only the first and least of Loree's offenses. His grand scheme was to run the established Indian traders out of business and to do all the trading with the Indians himself, eventually selling them their own annuity goods. A more venal and audacious crook never struck the High Plains.

Soon after Loree arrived at Fort Laramie he caught a trader selling whiskey to an Indian, arrested him and had him imprisoned. He then refused to grant any licenses to trade, on the ground that "all the traders in this region" were selling liquor to the Indians. Then he brought out a friend, A. W. Adams, and licensed him to trade.

Adams soon found that the other traders—including James Bordeau and the Fort Laramie sutler, Seth Ward—were getting "permits" to trade from the post commander. Still worse, they were outpricing him for the Indian furs. As Loree complained, Adams had "no show."

The agent's answer was to give battle in earnest. Seeking out Bordeau, he told him, "The only way you could save your property from confiscation would be to get in with Mr. Adams." Expedient as ever, Bordeau did just that and even had to share with his new partner the profits he had previously made under his 1862 "permit" from the post commander. As the new operations began, Adams told Bordeau that they had to share with a third partner, John Loree. When the partnership was later dissolved, the robes and pelts received from the Indians were divided into three equal piles. Loree took his own and Adams' shares back to the states and sold them. Bordeau had not (at least knowingly) traded in annuity goods, but he had paid a heavy ransom to stay in business.

Meanwhile, when the time came to renew licenses in 1863, Loree brought in two more of his own traders, including his brother Samuel Loree. In August 1863, Seth Ward met him near Fort Laramie and asked to renew his license. Loree was ready for him. "I will not grant a license to you or any of the old traders of the country. . . . I have given permits to three old schoolmates and friends of my politics."

With the nation gripped by the Civil War, Ward took this remark as a challenge to his sympathies. "If you question my loyalty," he snapped, "I can satisfy you on that score."

"There is no use arguing the point," returned Loree. "My friends are able to trade all the peltries the Indians will have." Then, with disarming candor, he added, "If I should give the old traders permission to trade my friends will have a damned bad show."

Ward was outraged. "I have layed over other agents," he thundered, "and I will over you."

"Do so," snapped Loree, unimpressed. "Pitch in."

The sutler stamped away from Loree and returned to St. Louis. There he exerted all his political influence to unseat the upper Platte agent.

It was the same story with G. P. Beauvais, Joseph Turgeon and other traders near Fort Laramie. One of them was told that he would have to see Loree's brother for arrangements to trade with the Indians, another that he could trade if he bought all his goods from the same brother.

Within weeks the Indians around Fort Laramie were enraged at the new trading deals. Loree's traders were offering paltry prices for furs and asking exorbitant prices for their own goods. More than forty Indians called on Beauvais and asked him to trade with them.

According to one report, Beauvais and Turgeon urged the Indians to destroy all the goods brought into the country until they received their licenses. They were said to be bragging that they "will make it too hot for Loree or his traders, without he has more Soldiers . . ."!

But Loree was just beginning to fight. In November he posted notices around Fort Laramie reminding residents of the intercourse laws in the Indian Territory and promising strict enforcement. He demanded that the post commander at Cottonwood

Springs arrest Beauvais and Turgeon for "plotting insurrection with the Indians against the constituted authorities." He wrote the Indian Commissioner in Washington asking for more force to control his enemies, charging them with trading liquor to the Indians and accepting stolen money from them. To take the Indians farther from the influence of the old settlers and the military, he removed his agency down the North Platte—sixteen miles east of the old place near Bordeau's post. In the fall of 1863 he journeyed to Denver; possibly through his urging, Colonel J. M. Chivington of the Colorado Department prohibited Indians on any military reservation and foreclosed any post sutlers from trading with them without special permits. Loree, it appeared, had allies in his battle with the old Laramie hands.

At the same time he was swelling his own pockets with the Indian trade. In November 1863 he licensed the trader at Cottonwood Springs, Jack A. Morrow, who took in Samuel Loree as partner. But, as Morrow himself later declared, "Samuel Loree was the nominal partner and John the real one who really done all the business . . ." To this enterprise John Loree contributed about $6,000 in merchandise—most of it annuity goods and plainly marked "To the Superintendent of Indian Affairs . . ." Among these goods were nearly one-half the 1863 annuities, which Loree had withheld from the Indians, stored in Bordeau's warehouse, later transferred to his own new agency down the river and finally turned over to Morrow for sale to the Indians. When the next year's annuities arrived in February 1864, a large part of them was also withheld from the Indians and sold for Loree's own benefit.

By that time the regular traders had won the outright support of the Fort Laramie officers. In January 1864 nearly all of them, including young Caspar Collins (but not his father), signed a petition calling for Loree's removal. Even Colonel Collins took up the feud with a letter to the Indian Commissioner reporting that Loree had left the agency without issuing any trading licenses and had been living at St. Joseph all winter. With it he enclosed a message he had received from an Oglala chief: "We have a large amount of Robes and are suffering. . . . We humbly ask you to take pity on us, and have our traders allowed us again if possible."

Against such countermoves, Loree acted swiftly. Seth Ward, he wrote Washington, was plotting his destruction. The post sutler had won over the Fort Laramie officers with "the Influence of hot whiskey punch." For their part, the "officers felt angry over the removal of the Indians from here as they cannot enjoy the company of the squaws."

But at that point, the Indian agent, for all his moral protestations, found himself on the defensive. One of his brother's employees was discovered taking a keg of whiskey to trade with the Indians. Moving fast to clear their skirts, Samuel Loree fired the man, and John Loree reported the incident to Washington.

But late in February 1864 the Lorees stepped onto shakier ground. Since 1861 the Indians had been denied the lead and powder promised in their annuities. Complaining that they needed these items for the buffalo hunt, Agent Loree reported that some of the Indians had starved to death during the winter of 1863-1864. When no change of policy was forthcoming from Washington, Loree and his trader associates decided to sell gunpowder to the Indians. To test the intentions of the military, Loree first went to Colonel Collins at Fort Laramie. "Do you have any orders connected with traders?" he inquired, without disclosing his plans.

Collins could only recall the regulation governing the sale of poor-quality goods that had been condemned for army use. "Only as to condemned provisions," he answered.

This reply was enough for John Loree. He told Samuel Loree and his partner that the road was clear. With a staff of clerks and a long train of wagons they started for the stronghold of the wild Oglala and Brulé with a large consigment of powder and balls. But they had not gone far when a troop of bluecoats from Fort Laramie rode up and arrested them—the charge: taking ammunition to the Indians.

When the traders were brought into the fort as prisoners, Agent Loree was thunderstruck. The arrest was, he wrote Washington, a "Great outrage." But Collins was adamant; if he had not led Loree into a trap, he had at least sprung the one that Loree had unwittingly laid for himself. In serious trouble at last, the agent took a sixty-day leave in order to explain his case in Washington.

The old traders took advantage of his absence to gather evidence that Loree himself had been defrauding the Indians. His former partners, Bordeau and Morrow, came forward to testify against him, as did some of his interpreters and other associates. Not only had he withheld annuities from the Indians in order to sell them through "blinds," but he had also personally traded government horses, blankets and other property to the Indians for buffalo robes. So voracious had been his appetite for personal profit that on one visit to an Indian village he had sold his gun, blankets, horse and the coat off his back.

Loree returned in time to start building a backfire with affidavits of his own. But by that time his two years' handiwork on the North Platte had completely disrupted Indian relations. Deprived of their regular traders and shorted in their annuities, the high plains Sioux realized at last how far they were dependent on the white man. The white trade that had begun with the founding of Fort Laramie in 1834 and the annuities granted in the Fort Laramie Treaty of 1851 had been their undoing. The corruption of the Indian Bureau that had sped the destruction of their brothers along the frontier had caught up with them. They had either to submit to the evil system or to make a last, bold try for their former freedom.

So in the summer of 1864 they listened to the pleas of the northern Sioux, who had fought the white men in Minnesota and Dakota. They listened again to their friends the Cheyenne and the Arapaho, who were battling the whites in Colorado and Kansas. By July 1864, Agent Loree was warning Colonel Collins that Sioux of the Miniconjou and Two Kettle bands were planning to attack Fort Laramie. In response, Collins ordered all local settlers including Loree to take refuge in the fort. In mid-August the 1864 annuities arrived; not only the ammunition but also flour, bacon, bread and other food were missing. The whole annuity payment consisted of sugar and coffee.

"They are without either provisions or ammunition," Loree wrote the Fort Laramie commander, "and therefore their case is most desperate."

In the face of the rising Sioux anger, Loree's own life was in danger. Fleeing from his agency for the last time, he forwarded his resignation from Missouri on September 30, 1864. With him he took at least one wagon and a team belonging to the Indian Bureau. When his successor brought this and other evidence to light, the Indian Superintendent at Omaha wrote angrily to Washington of Loree's "fraudulent transactions." "I am aware, myself," he charged, "of some of the acts of Loree which are in the highest degree reprehensible."

Seth Ward and the other old traders had done their work well. They had discredited Loree with Indians and whites alike; in doing so, some of them had not stopped at firing the old flames of resentment among the chiefs. Though Loree was a crook and a hypocrite, the whirlwind he reaped had been strengthened by the frantic countermoves of his enemies.

· 5 ·

Thoroughly disillusioned with the white man, the Sioux now gave up any hope of living side by side with him. They had given up the heart of their hunting ground in return for annual gifts, but now they had neither. They believed that their only choice was war.

Since late 1863 their old allies—the Cheyenne and the Arapaho—had been on the warpath in Colorado Territory. Led by Black Kettle and White Antelope, these two tribes claimed that they had been cheated in the treaty of 1861 and that they could never give up their buffalo range on the Republican and Smoky Hill Rivers. Parties of young warriors jumped the Cheyenne reservation below Sand Creek and began attacking isolated stations and ranches on the roads to Denver.

Governor John Evans of Colorado Territory called frantically for troops to protect Denver amd the mining settlements. Told that none could be spared from the war against the Confederacy, he was authorized to raise militia in Colorado. With feeling running high in Denver, the boys marched out to kill Indians.

The big question remaining was, what would the Sioux do? If they really meant to keep the peace, the Overland Trail could be kept open without diverting troops badly needed in Civil War campaigns.

At Camp Cottonwood on the South Platte, Maj. George M. O'Brien held a council with the Brulé and Oglala on June 8, 1864. Representing the Brulé was Spotted Tail, the same man who had led the attack on the mail party in 1855 and had delivered himself up to General Harney as a hostage. Since then he had continued to distinguish himself in battle against the Pawnee and was renowned as the greatest warrior among the Brulé. As their war leader, he was second in command to Little Thunder, the chief whose party Harney had mauled at Ash Hollow. As Little Thunder was ill, he had asked Spotted Tail to represent him. Though Spotted Tail was not yet a chief and not even much of an orator, he apparently took the lead in speaking for the Sioux.

"The white brother has sent for us," he began, through the interpreter. "What does the white brother want?"

Major O'Brien's response was abrupt and pointed: "Do you propose to remain peaceable?"

"We have been peaceable since our treaty," answered Spotted Tail, "and want to remain so. We will not fight with our white brothers."

"In case you had to fight," pressed the major, "which side would you take, Cheyenne or white?"

"We cannot be forced to fight on either side," answered Spotted Tail, cautiously. "We want to be permitted to live and hunt our game where we can find it, as was stipulated with us in the treaty . . ."

O'Brien then demanded that the Sioux keep off the Overland Trail, except in small numbers; stop buying whiskey; stop attacking the Pawnee, and report any hostile Indian movements against the white man's road. If they did not comply, O'Brien concluded, "You will be considered as enemies, like the Cheyennes, and treated accordingly; but if you comply you will be considered as friends."

Spotted Tail was a proud Sioux, but he was also discreet. During his confinement at Fort Kearney, he had seen some of the strength of the white man. He believed that his people should avoid battle with the whites, "as the whites could kill all of us." To O'Brien's ultimatum he agreed.

Then the council ended in general handshaking and another round of the pipe. But, though Spotted Tail was promising peace, he was speaking only for his own Brulé and not for the Oglala. Possibly still preparing secretly to join the Cheyenne, the Oglala may have only pretended peace. If so, O'Brien and the whites were taken in. "What do you think of the Cheyennes in making war on the whites?" was O'Brien's last question to Spotted Tail.

"We think they are fools, and will all be killed."

• 6 •

It appeared that, despite all the grievances of the Sioux, the concerted attack of all the Plains Indians would never come off. In Colorado the Cheyenne continued their raids through most of 1864, but by fall even they had opened peace talks with the commander at Fort Lyon. He told them that he had no authority to conclude a treaty but would send for those who did. Meanwhile, they could go and camp on Sand Creek, under the protection of the post. Assuring him of their peaceful intentions, Black Kettle and White Antelope took their tribe of some six hundred to the appointed spot and waited. It looked as though the bloody Plains war might end before it could engulf the Sioux.

But at that point the bellicose attitude of many western soldiers and civilians interfered. If the volunteer troops at Fort Laramie were "itching for a fight," so were those at most of the Rocky Mountain posts and settlements. Manifest Destiny was nowhere more forcibly at work than in those isolated American islands beyond the frontier. God's will, ran the argument, clearly called for American settlement across the entire continent. The primitive Indians stood in the way of civilization; they must either submit, and confine themselves to farming on reservations, or die.

The Cheyenne atrocities against isolated Colorado settlements in 1864 had simply confirmed what the whites already believed— that the Indian was the natural enemy of the white man and little higher than the beast of prey that stalked the mountains. "The only good Indian," they said, "is a dead Indian."

An exponent of this philosophy was the commander of the Colorado Department, Col. J. M. Chivington, a great bull of a man whose formidable appearance and belligerent attitude belied his former profession as minister of the Gospel. "I believe," he thundered, "it is right and just for white men to kill Indians." And in November 1864 he took a thousand troops out of Denver to attack the Cheyenne camped on Sand Creek. Sent there by the commander at Fort Lyon, the Indians were still waiting for a peace council when Chivington came upon them on the morning of November 29.

When the firing began, White Antelope went out alone and stood with folded arms to signify his refusal to fight. They shot him down, then scalped and castrated him. Black Kettle hoisted an American flag and a white flag but had to run from a hail of bullets. The whole village fled in panic, with the soldiers closing in on several sides. Many Indians, unable to escape, tried frantically to dig holes for protection. The soldiers came upon them and slaughtered them. Men, women and children were killed, scalped and hideously mutilated.

Chivington proudly claimed later that his men had bagged four or five hundred. It was the boast of a monster trying to exaggerate his crime. Between 130 (according to Indian estimates) and 175 (according to the body count of white observers) were massacred in the most revolting attack in the annals of Indian fighting.

On hearing of the atrocity, the nation was outraged. Military and congressional investigations castigated Chivington and his foul crew, but they went unpunished. Far more important was the reaction of the Indians, who resolved on a war to the knife. The Cheyenne sent the war pipe to their allies, the Brulé Sioux and the northern Arapaho, who were then camped in the buffalo country on the headwaters of the Republican. On hearing the awful details of Sand Creek, the friends of the Cheyenne were aroused as never before. Even Spotted Tail, the Brulé who had always counseled against fighting the whites, was overcome with a thirst for revenge.

Early in December the three tribes held a war council of more than one thousand lodges on Cherry Creek. On the principle that all whites were their enemies, they resolved to leave the country of the vicious Colorado troops, raid the vulnerable stations on the Overland Trail and then move north to the fastnesses of the Black Hills and the Powder River. There they would prepare to mount three thousand warriors in a war to the death. As one Sioux chief later told the whites, "You have set the prairie on fire."

TEN ♦ *The Bloody Year*

As the Sioux had been the first to smoke the war pipe, they were allowed the honor of leading the expedition northward. Heading them was Spotted Tail, who was soon to take over as chief of the Brulé in place of the aging Little Thunder.

To survive a northern winter without their regular annuities they would need other provisions, and they agreed first on a major blow at the settlement and fort of Julesburg, Colorado Territory, where the old Oregon Trail branched off from the new Overland mail route. On the morning of January 7, 1865, a small decoy party was sent forward to lure the troops out of the fort—a favorite Indian trick. Most of the garrison charged out and were attacked by some one thousand warriors. Fifteen soldiers, according to army reports, were killed before they could fight their way back into the stockade. At the same time the Denver stage rolled in from the east. As it reached the station, about a mile east of the fort, the passengers saw the Indians coming. Everyone, including the station crew, raced for the fort and made it through the gate just ahead of the retreating soldiers.

While the whites manned the palisades, the Indians contented themselves with plundering the settlement. They carried off so much food and goods on their ponies that they were three days returning to the camp on Cherry Creek. Scalp dances were held at night, and the chiefs made plans for the next descent on the Platte River route.

After the Julesburg attack, the white strongholds panicked. From Fort Kearney the post commander called for support. "The Indians," he wrote, "are masters of the Overland road . . ." For a

171

week troops from the isolated posts along the South Platte were collected at Camp Cottonwood west of Julesburg. Then they marched out five hundred strong on January 16 in pursuit of the raiders. But by the time they found the campground on Cherry Creek the Indians had already gone north for their next campaign. After ten days the soldiers dragged back to Cottonwood to find that a hundred miles of road had been ravaged by Indians. On the 14th and 15th, the raiders had descended on stations and ranches west of Julesburg—killing the settlers, pillaging and firing the buildings. Beginning on the 24th they struck the road again—running off cattle, burning buildings and tons of army hay and attacking any wagon trains they found. Six stations and ranches, including Julesburg again, were attacked on the 28th alone. Isolated bodies of troops sent after the Indians were in turn struck and forced to retreat.

After five days of regrouping, the tribes concentrated all their force for still another descent on Julesburg. On February 2 at least 1,500 braves surrounded the fort, looted and burned the stage station and other buildings, then moved northward up Lodgepole Creek toward the North Platte.

These raids in the winter of 1865 were the most savage and persistent in the history of the Overland Trail. They were the classic depredation by the Plains Indians against stations, forts, stores and isolated settlements. For a month the smoke of burning buildings marked the Indians' path. From the raids they gained an enormous store of loot—fresh beef, corn and plenty of cattle on the hoof for future needs.

With the taste of victory in their mouths, they moved northward to the stronghold of the Sioux in the Black Hills. On the way they vented their excitement on the telegraph line—destroying the poles and tangling the wire in thorough confusion for 38 miles on the transcontinental line. With a hundred miles of road devastated, the whole route in panic, wagons and stages paralyzed and even the troops arriving too late with too little at each point of attack, the Indians were indeed masters of the Overland Trail.

Until their latest northward movement across the North Platte, the garrison at Fort Laramie and its outlying posts had been only indirectly affected by the Plains war of 1864-1865. But on February 4 the grand column of Indians descended upon Mud Springs, a station about halfway between Lodgepole Creek and the North

Platte, where there were five civilians and nine soldiers—a pitiful force in the face of the Cheyenne, Brulé, and Arapaho nations. While the Indians at first contented themselves with driving off the stock, the telegraph operator wired for help to Fort Laramie, 105 miles west. There Col. William Collins reacted swiftly; he ordered the officer at Camp Mitchell, roughly halfway between Fort Laramie and Mud Springs, to hasten eastward with all his spare men. Within three hours after receiving the call for help, Collins himself was marching out of Fort Laramie with all the men that could be spared—about 120 cavalrymen.

The Camp Mitchell troops, traveling all night, reached Mud Springs before dawn the next morning—just in time to bolster the little station before the first real attack. Surprised at the reinforced garrison, the Indians backed off and counseled among themselves. During that time the Fort Laramie force was marching night and day through the bitter February cold. Early on the morning of the 6th, Collins reached Mud Springs with an advance contingent of 25 men, having covered the 105 miles from Fort Laramie in the remarkable time of thirty hours.

At daybreak several hundred warriors again poured over the hills surrounding the station and opened a new attack. The troops placed themselves in and around the buildings and returned the fire.

While the battle was raging, the main body of Fort Laramie troops rode in from the west. Many of the Indians tried to intercept the cavalry column, but the reinforcements rode safely into the station.

Then, while the troops fired from open ditches and log walls, the vast array of Indians tried to move closer through the approaching gulleys. Realizing that a charge against the station would mean heavy losses, the Indians settled down to a sniping duel with the defenders. From one concealed position scarcely 75 yards from the buildings, a force of two hundred warriors sent a high-angle shower of arrows against the defenders, wounding several soldiers and many animals. Collins sent some of his men to charge this point, and the Indians were driven off.

By mid-afternoon the whole force of warriors had begun pulling away. On the same day the Indians had broken their camp near Mud Springs and had moved up across the North Platte. On the morning of February 8 Colonel Collins followed them with some two hundred cavalrymen—a most dangerous mission. Reaching the North Platte near the mouth of Rush Creek, he and his men saw—across the river and considerably upstream—what appeared to be a forest of trees. It was an unusual sight in the plains country. Looking through his spyglass, the Colonel found the "trees" to be the main body of warriors. The Indians had already spotted his command and were charging toward him.

While the Indians swarmed over the ice of the North Platte, Collins dug in for defense. On a piece of level ground commanded by knolls, he corralled his wagons. Quickly the troops dug pits behind the knolls and braced themselves for the onslaught. At first the attackers rode boldly up to the troops but found them well entrenched and their fire dangerous. Then the Indians resorted to the same kind of shooting duel that they had practiced at Mud Springs—creeping up gulleys to fire at closer range.

By that time Collins had a howitzer that had been sent in haste from Fort Laramie. But the ammunition had been stored in the fort's powder house unused since the Grattan massacre more than ten years before. Many of the shells landed harmlessly without bursting; some, to the discomfiture of the soldiers, burst at the muzzle. For their part, most of the Indians were evidently using rifles to which they were unaccustomed. Not knowing how to sight them, they generally fired over the soldiers' heads.

During the shooting a small group of Indians, hidden under the bank of the river, rode past the wagons and took up a position behind the troops. From a vantage point beyond a small hill they dropped bullets into the wagons at long range. In response, Collins sent sixteen riders to charge his tormenters. Firing their revolvers, the troopers rode down upon the Indians and sent them leaping to horse. One Indian was shot while trying to mount.

But at that moment more than one hundred Indians swept upon the charging troopers. For a moment they battled hand to hand. One soldier fell, but his comrades took up his body. Another, apparently unable to halt his frightened horse, dashed into the Indians, who fell upon him immediately; later his mutilated body was found with no fewer than 97 arrows in it—another object of Indian vengeance for Sand Creek. The charging troops raced back to the pits with the Indians harassing their rear.

As night approached the battle subsided. While the attackers rode back across the ice on the river, Collins opened up once again with his howitzer. A lucky shot broke the ice under three of them, sinking them and their horses in the river. The next morning several hundred Indians returned and exchanged shots, but the main body had broken camp and moved north.

With two killed and sixteen wounded in the two clashes at Mud Springs and Rush Creek, Collins had escaped the complete massacre that the Indians might have accomplished had they not been determined to move on northward. To the Indians, life was too severe in winter to pursue the luxury of war. The February cold was ill suited for a long siege, and they were anxious to reach the buffalo country of the Powder and the Yellowstone before their spoils gave out. Collins was saved by the weather, but the whole of the plains had been mauled by the Indians in their most savage winter campaign. Back at Fort Laramie a week later, he sent a warning to his superiors: "They are well armed and mounted; have many rifled muskets and plenty of ammunition . . .; are full of venom and bent on revenge for the loss of their people south."

· 2 ·

While the Indians were holding high carnival on the plains, a new character entered the scene in the person of Maj. Gen. Grenville M. Dodge, one of the most famous division commanders in the Union army. After fighting with Grant through Tennessee and helping to take Atlanta, Dodge had been given command of the Department of the Missouri and had been ordered to proceed against the Indians. Even though temperatures were below zero, troops were commanded to march from outlying posts to the line of the Platte River. In one column from Fort Riley, Kansas, to Fort Kearney, Nebraska, thirteen men froze to death. Dodge himself rode stages as far west as they were running. Finding the troops afraid to venture out of their stockades, he lectured them about Indian fighting and ordered post commanders not to allow any troops back in the stockades until the telegraph and stage lines were opened.

Through the second week in February, Dodge's soldiers strung wire and fought Indians. By February 13 the telegraph was open again all the way to California, and stage operations were resumed soon after.

But, though the resolute Dodge had made the fur fly along the

Overland Trail, the Indians had actually had no intention of holding their grip on it through the winter of 1865. They were heading for their old hunting grounds on the Powder River and among the Black Hills, and they had simply despoiled the Overland Trail on the way. Without their loot they could not have sustained themselves through a winter trek.

For the time being, at least, they had their answer to the growing shortage of buffalo. Never before had they tried to live by pillaging the white man, but for two months in 1865 it had worked. As for the soldiers who had previously been so anxious to fight, they had more than enough. Through Fort Laramie went the frontier joke about the trooper who was ordered to go hunt Indians. His reply: "But I haven't *lost* any Indians."

Once in the buffalo country the Brulé under Spotted Tail determined to bury the war. But when the Cheyenne reached the villages of the Oglala on the Powder River in March, they began pressing these old allies to join the war. They recounted the atrocities of Sand Creek; they showed their herds of horses, mules and cattle and their stores of food stolen from the whites, and they offered the war pipe to the Oglala. Old Man-Afraid-of-His-Horses still stood for peace. But his son and some other war leaders, including the rising young subchief Red Cloud, took the pipe and smoked.

As early as April the Indians began attacking west of Fort Laramie. Through the spring of 1865 they kept up their forays— hitting where the whites were weak, running off the stock, destroying the telegraph line, killing isolated parties. When relief columns marched out from Fort Laramie, the Indians kept well out of their way, spied on their movements and then attacked the stations they had left behind. Thenceforth, 1865 was to be known as "the bloody year on the plains."

By that time Col. William O. Collins had completed his three-year tour of duty; in March he returned to the settlements with others of his command and was mustered out of the service. His rare perception and understanding in dealing with the Indians were lost to those who needed them. In his place as head of the forces policing the Overland Trail on the North Platte came Col. Thomas O. Moonlight, who had previously succeeded Chivington as commander of the Department of Colorado.

Hardly a statesman-soldier, Moonlight had the misfortune to be both naïve and impetuous. Furthermore, his military experience among the Colorado settlers had fixed him too with the notion that "the only good Indian is a dead Indian." Colonel Moonlight was not the one to curb the fierce attitude among the Laramie troops that came to the surface after Colonel Collins had departed. The several hundred Oglala who had made their homes in Squaw Town for a generation began to overhear awful maledictions voiced freely around the post: "None should be spared; all ought to be killed, men, women, and children, and no quarter given."

• 3 •

To help keep the peace when hostilities had broken out in the winter of 1864-1865, Colonel Collins had moved the Laramie Oglala some ten miles east, near Bordeau's old trading post on the North Platte. He put a squaw man, Capt. Charlie Elliston, in charge of the place, with a troop of Indian "soldiers" serving as policemen.

But the troops and officers who replaced Collins and his fellows in March 1865 were ignorant of the difference between friendlies and hostiles. Harboring the hatred of all Indians prevalent among frontiersmen, they regarded the encampment with suspicion. In the spring of 1865 Spotted Tail, Little Thunder and many of the Brulé came into the North Platte village, hoping to make peace at Fort Laramie. But they found the atmosphere so tense that they were afraid to appear at the fort.

"Affairs in this country have sadly changed since you left here," William G. Bullock, the sutler's agent, wrote to Colonel Collins, "and all the Indians have been forced to resort to hostilities for self-preservation. All of our friendly Indians have been driven off and those who rarely visited the Post have not been allowed to come in and make offerings of peace."

About May 18 a Sioux subchief, Two Face, arrived on the opposite side of the North Platte with a small party of followers. In the group was a white woman, a Mrs. Eubanks, and her daughter; they had been captured by the Cheyenne months before on the Little Blue River. Terribly mistreated by her captors, she had been purchased by Two Face for the price of three horses, and her daughter had accompanied her to the Sioux camp.

Now Two Face, expecting to win the favor of the officers, was
coming to turn them in at Fort Laramie.

From the Indian village a raft was sent across the river, and
Two Face and the two white captives were brought over. Mrs.
Eubanks was in wretched condition—scantily clothed, badly
frightened and bearing marks of great suffering. A white woman at
Bordeau's post gave her a dress and other attire. Then Charlie
Elliston took Two Face and his white captives up to Fort Laramie;
with them went trader George Beauvais and the Indian agent who
had suceeded Loree, in order to help explain the situation and
vouch for Two Face.

But when this group trudged into the fort the reaction was
unforeseen. Finally reunited with her own people, Mrs. Eubanks
told a frightful tale of torture. Not only the Cheyenne, but Two
Face himself, had abused her. So had another subchief, Blackfoot, who was then in a village on White River. Charlie Elliston
was sent with his Indian police to fetch Blackfoot. Both subchiefs
were put in irons at the Fort Laramie guardhouse.

At about that time Colonel Moonlight returned to the fort from
a scouting expedition. He heard Mrs. Eubanks' story and was outraged. Schooled in the attitude of Colonel Chivington, Moonlight
acted swiftly. He later reported, "Both of the chiefs openly boasted
that they had killed white men and that they would do it again if
let loose, so I concluded to tie them up by the neck with a trace
chain, suspended from a beam of wood, and leave them there
without any foothold."

At that point the sutler's agent at Fort Laramie, Col. W. G.
Bullock, learned of Moonlight's resolve. Hurrying to his office,
Bullock warned that hanging the subchiefs would "so aggravate
the combined hostile tribes" that they would "attack the garrison
of Fort Laramie and carry the place by assault . . ." Then they
would perform "a massacre of so barbarous and inhuman a character as had never been witnessed in the West."

But Moonlight was unimpressed. "Well, Colonel Bullock," he
answered, condescendingly, "you think there will be a massacre?
Let me tell you that there will be two Indians who will not take
part in it."

And with a "Good day, sir," he bowed Bullock out of his office.
Then he took the two prisoners to a hill overlooking Laramie
River, erected a gallows and hanged them on May 26. There he

In 1837, A. J. Miller painted this busy scene of the interior of Fort William (Fort Laramie), which had been founded as a fur post three years earlier by William Sublette.

After the army took over Fort Laramie in 1849, the adobe fur post (center) was used as a storehouse and magazine. At left, in this 1853 engraving is "Old Bedlam," the bachelor officers' quarters; to its right is the sutler's store.

Manager of the fur post in the late 1830s, James Bordeau remained an Indian trader in the Fort Laramie area for more than 30 years and played a role in some of its stormiest events.

Jim Bridger, "the prince of mountain men," was one of the fur post's early owners. In later years he was at Fort Laramie serving as guide for army expeditions against the Indians.

Fort Laramie National Historic Site

In 1851 the greatest Indian council in history was held near Fort Laramie to complete a treaty bringing peace to the plains. Afterward, some of the chiefs were escorted to Washington to meet President Millard Fillmore. Here the Arapaho and Cheyenne delegation, with interpreters, were photographed as they stopped on the way at St. Louis.

Sioux tribesmen are boarding the ferry boat across the North Platte River near Fort Laramie. In 1853, when a sergeant from Fort Laramie was crossing the river in the ferry, a Miniconjou warrior took a shot at him. This triggered a series of retaliations that led to a major Indian war.

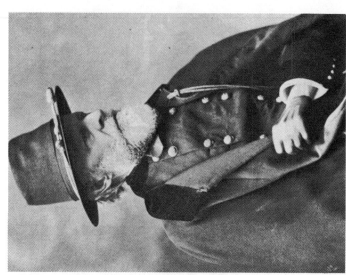

First visiting Fort Laramie with Col. Stephen W. Kearny's expedition of 1845, Philip St. George Cooke led the cavalry in the Battle of Ash Hollow and later commanded the Department of the Platte during the Sioux war of 1866.

Following the massacre of Lt. John Grattan and 29 Fort Laramie soldiers in 1854, Bvt. Brig. Gen. William S. Harney (above) led an expedition to punish the Sioux.

This rather imaginative sketch from Harney's biography shows his infantry driving the Sioux up the Blue Water into the arms of the cavalry. After losing 86 (not counting women and children), the Sioux called Harney "the Wasp."

Place of concealment of mounted men under Col. Cooke.

Gentle Slope.

Mounted Force

OGALALAS
11 Lodges

Capt. Steele's Co.

Direction of final flight. Buecured by all the available force

Gentle Slope

Lt. Robertson's Co.

Capt. Heth's Co.

Bad Slough

Place to which the Indians first fled many of whom were here killed or taken.

Maj Wood

Capt. Todd's Co.

Place where the "talk" was held with Little Thunder

SKETCH
of the
BLUE WATER CREEK
embracing the field of action of the force
under the command of
BVT. BRIG. GENL. W. S HARNEY
in the attack of the 3rd Sept. 1855,
on the "Brule" Band of the Indian Chief
LITTLE THUNDER

made by
Lieut. G. K. Warren.
Topl. Engr of the Expedition.
Sept. 3rd

BRULÉS
41 Lodges

Abandoned on the approach of the Inf. the Indians moving up the valley.

Magnetic Meridian Var⁰ about 14° East.

Mini To Wakpala or Blue Water Creek

Route of Infantry, commanded by the Inf. under Maj. Cady.

Route of Infantry

Gen! Harney's Camp. Sept. 4 5 & 6.

Route of Mounted Force

NORTH FORK OF PLATTE

Ft Grattan

Camp. Sept. 2 & 3

Note. Ash Hollow {Long 102° 02' 28 {Lat 41° 17' 18

Ash Hollow

SCALE OF MILES.
0   1   2 miles.
¾ inch to one mile

In the battle of Ash Hollow, or Bluewater Creek, General Harney caught Little Thunder's village of Brulé Sioux in a pincers between his cavalry (hidden to the north) and his infantry (approaching from the south).

Noted photographer William H. Jackson took this picture of Fort Laramie in its heyday (1868). Looking northwest across Laramie River, the two-story building is "Old Bedlam," while long buildings in center are enlisted men's barracks and mess hall.

A debonair group of officers of the Fourth Infantry Regiment lounges on the porch of "Old Bedlam", the bachelor officers' quarters, in this 1868 photograph. Informality of life at this remote post is indicated by variety of jackets worn.

Among the powerful Sioux chiefs in this 1868 photograph at Fort Laramie are: extreme left, Spotted Tail (Brulé); with pipe to mouth, Old Man-Afraid-of-his-Horses (Oglala); seated in center, One Horn (Miniconjou).

Distrust is evident in the face of Chief Red Cloud, photographed here in full Oglala regalia. At one peace council he tapped his rifle and said, "In this and the Great Spirit I trust for the right."

Some of the sadness in the face of his father, Man-Afraid-of-his-Horses, is traceable in the countenance of Young Man-Afraid-of-his-Horses. An Oglala, he is one of the few among the plains Sioux to succeed his father as chief.

After Col. Henry B. Carrington appeared at Fort Laramie with an army column in 1866, Oglala chieftains stalked out of a peace council. He marched into a hornet's nest to establish Fort Phil Kearny.

Bvt. Lt. Col. William Fetterman headed force of 81 men marching out of Fort Phil Kearny into ambush by nearly 2,000 Indians.

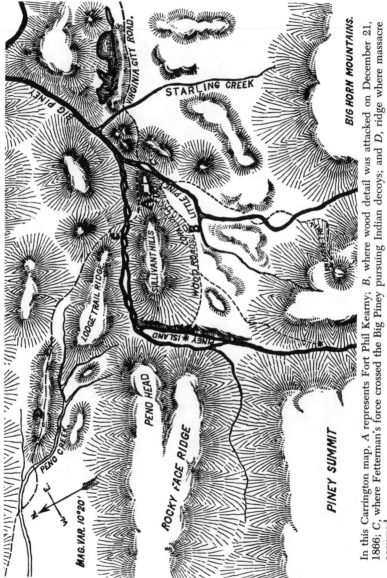

BIG HORN MOUNTAINS.

STARLING CREEK

VIRGINIA CITY ROAD.

BIG PINEY

LITTLE PINEY

LODGE TRAIL RIDGE

SULLIVANT HILLS

WOOD ROAD

PINEY ISLAND

PENO HEAD

PENO CREEK

ROCKY FACE RIDGE

MAG. VAR. 10°20'

N. E.

N. W.

PINEY SUMMIT

In this Carrington map, A represents Fort Phil Kearny; B, where wood detail was attacked on December 21, 1866; C, where Fetterman's force crossed the Big Piney pursuing Indian decoys; and D, ridge where massacre occurred.

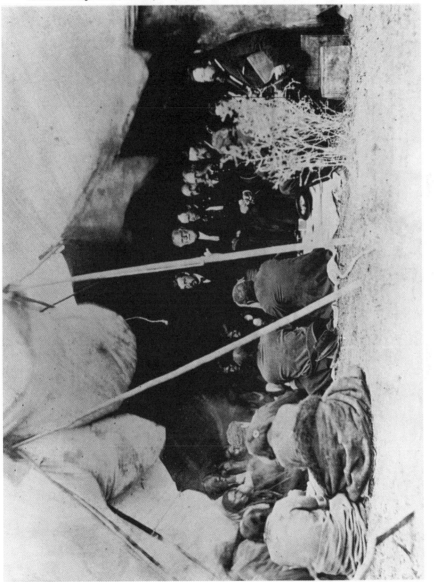

In one of several councils in 1867-1868, commissioners are seated on bench inside tent, while Indians sit on ground according to custom. Just right of center pole are Gen. W. S. Harney and Gen. W. T. Sherman.

A banner group of Fort Laramie personalities was gathered for this 1868 photograph. Standing in center are Col. W. G. Bullock, sutler's agent, and Man-Afraid-of-his-Horses, Oglala chief. At right, another chief shakes hands with trader James Bordeau.

In this oddly posed photograph, the peace commissioners of 1867-1868 stand with a Sioux squaw. Gen. William S. Harney stands at attention second from left. Gen. William Tecumseh Sherman and Indian Superintendent N. G. Taylor face the Indian girl.

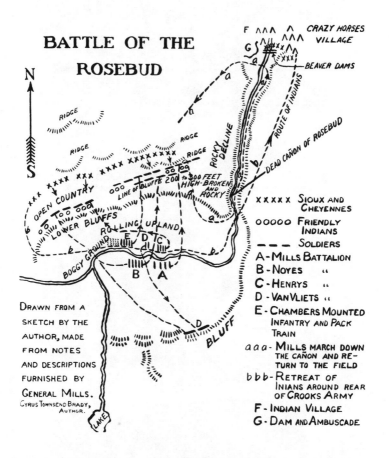

BATTLE OF THE ROSEBUD

N
S

F ∧∧∧ ∧ CRAZY HORSES VILLAGE
∧∧∧
G ∧∧∧
BEAVER DAMS

RIDGE
RIDGE
RIDGE
RIDGE
ROCKY DECLINE
ROUTE OF INDIANS
DEAD CAÑON OF ROSEBUD

OPEN COUNTRY
LINE OF BLUFFS 200 to 300 FEET HIGH-BROKEN AND ROCKY
LOWER BLUFFS
ROLLING UPLAND
E D C
B A
BOGGY GROUND

XXXXX SIOUX AND CHEYENNES
OOOOO FRIENDLY INDIANS
— — — SOLDIERS
A - MILLS BATTALION
B - NOYES "
C - HENRYS "
D - VAN VLIETS "
E - CHAMBERS MOUNTED INFANTRY AND PACK TRAIN
a a a - MILLS MARCH DOWN THE CAÑON AND RETURN TO THE FIELD
b b b - RETREAT OF INIANS AROUND REAR OF CROOKS ARMY
F - INDIAN VILLAGE
G - DAM AND AMBUSCADE

D
BLUFF

DRAWN FROM A SKETCH BY THE AUTHOR, MADE FROM NOTES AND DESCRIPTIONS FURNISHED BY GENERAL MILLS.
CYRUS TOWNSEND BRADY, AUTHOR.

LAKE

Crook's troops were resting on the Rosebud when Crazy Horse's force attacked from north on June 17, 1876. Col. Royall's cavalry (*B* and *C*) occupied bluffs at left and suffered heaviest casualties as Indians nearly surrounded them. Capt. Mills' force, recalled from march on supposed Sioux village down the Rosebud (upper right), attacked Indians in rear and ended battle.

Not necessarily accurate, since there was no hand-to-hand fighting in the Rosebud engagement, this artist's illustration still depicts the desperate spirit of one of history's few pitched battles on open ground between fairly equal forces of soldiers and western Indians.

A noted warrior in his youth, Spotted Tail succeeded Little Thunder as chief of the Brulé Sioux. He generally favored peace, but remained independent until his death by an Indian assassin in 1880.

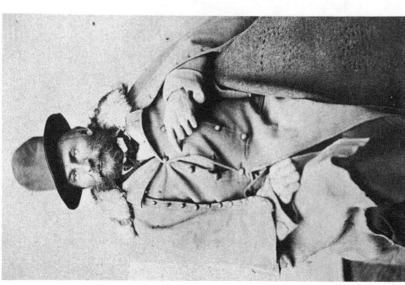

Conqueror of Indians from Oregon to Arizona, Brig. Gen. George Crook met his match in the Sioux and Cheyenne. Here he poses in familiar unsoldierly garb during his Big Horn and Yellowstone Expedition in 1876.

After the Rosebud and Little Big Horn battles, General Crook moved on to catch more Indians. Photograph shows part of his camp during the punishing "starvation march" from Heart River to the Black Hills.

Fort Laramie's finest—Captain James "Teddy" Egan's white horse company—led the attack on the Cheyenne village at Powder River, guarded the Black Hills road, and (in this picture) marched through Custer City, Dakota Territory, in 1876.

Full-dress uniforms, including spike helmets and knapsacks, are evident in this guard mount ceremony, Seventh Infantry Regiment, at Fort Laramie in 1883. Troops at left are standing at "parade rest" with Springfield rifles held in front.

Fort Laramie National Historic Site

White picket fence and school children symbolize the tame days that had overtaken Fort Laramie when this photograph was made in front of the officers quarters about 1889—a year before the post was abandoned.

left them swaying in the wind—a feast for scavengers and a warning to other "bad" Indians.

But, as Bullock had predicted, Moonlight's justice had the opposite effect. Knowing that Two Face had voluntarily brought in the white woman as an act of reconciliation, the Sioux recalled again Grattan's blind murder of Chief Bear and Harney's unjust attack at Ash Hollow. They no longer needed the Cheyenne experience at Sand Creek to arouse their hatred.

Indeed, Sioux anger was soon to be compounded. When news of the hanging reached General Dodge, he was surprised to learn of the Sioux camp located near Fort Laramie. As the Sioux were on the warpath, why didn't the Laramie troops attack the village? When told that these Sioux were friendlies, he ordered them removed to Fort Kearney, closer to the border settlements where they could be watched over more easily and be away from the influence of the hostile bands.

It was an order born of ignorance. The tame Oglala, known as the Laramie Loafers, had long since become dependent on the white man, but the Brulé under Spotted Tail's leadership had not. They wanted peace but not peace at the price of freedom. Most especially they did not want to forfeit that freedom while being removed to the land of their enemies, the Pawnee. They had not made a show of friendship in order to be herded along another Indian "trail of tears."

Nevertheless, Colonel Moonlight of Fort Laramie ordered the march early in June 1865. Down the North Platte on the 11th moved a disconsolate column of 1,500 Oglala and Brulé Sioux, their lodges packed on their travois, their dogs bounding and yelping alongside. In the lead rode some 140 cavalrymen commanded by Capt. W. D. Fouts. With them, too, went a number of wagons under the care of traders James Bordeau and George Beauvais, who were taking the opportunity to return, under military protection, to the settlements for merchandise. Also in the wagons were the families of Captain Fouts and one of his lieutenants, as well as Mrs. Eubanks and her child. Finally, a number of Indian police under the command of Capt. Charlie Elliston rode along to keep order among the Sioux.

Like Moonlight, Captain Fouts was contemptuous of Indian prowess and careless in the most elementary precautions. A bluff and somewhat coarse character, he had become a tired victim of

army routine. Believing that the Indians were willing to be removed, he considered his own troops to be more of an escort than
a guard. He had them march in the front with the wagons, while
the Indians ate dust behind.

Four Indian prisoners, guilty of certain offenses, were guarded
and fettered with balls and chains, but, as they complained about
walking, Captain Fouts let three of them ride horseback: the
fourth, nursing a swollen foot, was allowed to ride in a wagon.
Amazingly, all the other Indians were permitted to keep their
weapons—bows and arrows, guns and ammunition. And, most
remarkable of all, Fouts refused to issue ammunition to the rear-
guard troops marching nearest the Indians.

From the first, the incongruity of the two groups spelled trouble.
It was reported that many of the soldiers took squaws to their
tents at night. Although such behavior was hardly new to the
so-called "Laramie Loafers," it shocked and outraged Spotted
Tail and his Brulé. Then, as was customary on Indian treks, the
young braves spent the day racing their ponies back and forth
along the flanks of the column. Annoyed, Captain Fouts ordered
this racing stopped.

Beginning on the first day's march, Fouts and his men noticed
smoke signals from the bluffs north of the Platte. They heard
rumors that the Indians in their charge were visited secretly by
other Sioux tribesmen at night. But Fouts could not prove it and
took no precautions against it.

On the evening of the third day the weary column reached
Horse Creek, the scene of the Grand Council of 1851. There they
camped a couple of miles up the creek (south of the North Platte).
The troops and those in the wagon train settled down beyond the
east bank of the creek, leaving the Indians and their police behind
on the west bank. After the Indians had assembled in their camp,
Fouts took Charlie Elliston and addressed the chiefs, who were
sitting in a row near the campfire. Using Elliston as his interpreter, Fouts observed that the Indian boys were still running
their horses against his orders. "If there is any more racing during
the march," he warned, "I will tie the offenders to a wagon wheel
and give twenty-five lashes."

The chiefs and headmen said nothing. But among them passed
knowing looks. Later in the evening, long after Fouts had joined
the other soldiers east of the creek, the Sioux held a dog feast and
a secret council of all their warriors—nearly four hundred. Possibly

they had planned to escape from the soldiers even before the trek began—and were determined to wait only until they were several days' march from the troops at Fort Laramie. But in any case they now made final preparations. In the morning, while the soldiers and wagons pulled out ahead of them, they would make a dash for the North Platte River and escape northward to the Black Hills. The water was running high; their ponies were all trained to ford rivers, and their people could all swim. The army horses were not so trained, and many of the soldiers could not swim. If the Indians could get across the river before the troops could return and stop them, they could make good their escape.

Accordingly, an Oglala named "Black Wolf" was chosen to lead the crossing. That night, with the help of several young warriors, he rode to the Platte and picked a favorable crossing place, marking it with long sticks that showed above the water from one side to the other.

Next morning Captain Fouts ordered his troops to proceed two miles farther east, where they were to wait for the wagons and the Indians to close up. While the soldiers and teamsters were moving farther beyond Horse Creek, the Indians did not break camp as they had on the two previous mornings. Leaving their lodges in place, they mounted, and some of them started for the river.

Thinking that they had merely been delayed, Captain Fouts rode back across Horse Creek to get them under way. Charlie Elliston stayed behind, possibly knowing or sensing what was to follow.

The Sioux waited impassively while Fouts came well into their camp. Stopping among them, he demanded to know why they were not moving out. Rifles came up, and after two shots Fouts fell dead.

Immediately the Sioux stampeded for the river—the women and children riding into the water first while the warriors remained on the bank to protect them. Some ponies carried two riders across; others bore a brave and one or two children. All the while they were streaming into the water, Black Wolf rode up and down the bank shouting orders: "Throw away your heavy luggage. If your horse flounders, get off his back and hold to his tail or mane."

Finally, Black Wolf urged them on with a vow. Since it involved a torturous ordeal that included the puncturing and tear-ing of one's own flesh, it was recognized as the highest vow that an Indian could make: "If you all arrive safe on the other side I will dance the Sun Dance!"

At the first shots the three ball-and-chain prisoners with the main body of troops sprang to their horses and wheeled in the direction of the Sioux camp—as if by prearrangement. The soldiers near them hollered, "Come back!" But at that moment some other mounted Indians appeared to cover the retreat. In the exchange of fire, several soldiers fell before the prisoners made their escape. The lame Indian who had been riding in a wagon was led out and shot by the enraged soldiers.

The rear-guard troops, still at Horse Creek near the Indians, saw the fate of Captain Fouts but, being without ammunition, could do nothing. They immediately retreated to the main body of soldiers with the wagon train east of the creek.

Fouts' second in command was Capt. John Wilcox, a more prudent officer, who shared Fout's contempt for the Indians but had more respect for their fighting qualities. Hearing the shots, he feared that Fouts had been killed and expected the Indians to charge across Horse Creek and attack his train. Quickly he ordered the wagons corralled, the civilians gathered within and the troops deployed around the outside.

Instantly all was pandemonium. While the teamsters were swinging the animals into position, some of the civilians were rushing about in panic. At that moment a messenger rode up, telling of Fouts' death and of the Indian break across the river. Wilcox sent a rider ahead for reinforcements from Fort Mitchell eighteen miles away. A number of Indian horsemen raced after him, but he pounded down the road ahead of them.

Soon afterward, the rear guard pulled up at the wagons. Wilcox demanded why they had retreated and was told that they had not been allowed any ammunition. Exasperated, he quickly issued cartridges. Then, ordering half his force to dig rifle pits around the wagons, he took the rest and rode back to intercept the Indians. Near Horse Creek he saw the Sioux fording the river. Still unable to believe that all the Indians wanted to escape, he sent Charlie Elliston forward to parley with them. "Tell all who are our friends to return," he ordered, "and they shall not be harmed, but protected."

But, as Wilcox immediately discovered, "all were hostile." Filling the air with war whoops, the warriors charged Wilcox's detachment. According to his report, Wilcox ordered his men to dismount; the Indians, he knew, feared the marksmanship of soldiers on foot. At three hundred yards the Indians started shooting. The troopers returned the fire, momentarily stopping the attack. But other Indians came on around the flanks. From nearby high ground more Indians rose up and came thundering down upon them—in all, several hundred against seventy.

Overwhelmed, Wilcox ordered his men to mount and retreat. They wheeled and raced for the wagons, firing as they went, while the Sioux flankers tried to cut them off. The retreat became a rout as some of the troopers broke ranks and fled in panic. Wilcox reported that a few of his men had "behaved badly," but other eyewitnesses described the retreat as a headlong flight, with the Indians simply scaring the troops rather than trying to kill them. According to Wilcox, the Sioux were about to cut off any further retreat when they came within range of the troops stationed at the wagons. A fusillade from the pits sent them, in Wilcox's words, "howling to the rear." But one of the traders later wrote that the Indians were simply chasing the soldiers away from the river crossing, "yelling and swinging paraphernalia" much as they would stampede a herd of horses.

In any case, once the troopers rode into the safety of the rifle pits, the Indians exhibited their customary reluctance to storm protected works and rode off to the river. Soon Wilcox took another detachment and retrieved the mutilated bodies of Captain Fouts and the three privates killed in the fighting. Once again he was beset by an overwhelming force of warriors, who were intent only on chasing the soldiers back to the wagons and protecting the families still crossing the Platte.

By 9 A.M. Wilcox was reinforced by thirty troopers who had been repairing the telegraph line in the vicinity. They had been dispatched to the fighting after Wilcox's messenger had safely reached Camp Mitchell. Thus strengthened, Wilcox mounted another force against the Sioux.

But by then the last of the Indians, including the warriors, had crossed the Platte. Most had disappeared through the bushes and trees lining the river. Those remaining in sight made taunting signs, inviting the soldiers to follow. But Wilcox was wary of being caught helpless in midriver under the fire of a stronger enemy.

The troopers returned to the wagons in a fury over the day's debacle. Mrs. Fouts and her family were beside themselves with grief. All the dead had been terribly mutilated, and the whole command had been humiliated by a clever enemy. Into the body of the lame Indian the returning soldiers poured a fusillade of shots. Then in their wrath they cast eyes on the traders, many of them half-breeds and all of them allied to the Indians by marriage. There was a strong suspicion that the half-breeds and interpreters had known of the plot.

"The squaw men are as bad as the Indians," Captain Wilcox was heard to tell the soldiers, "and they ought to be killed."

Fearing for their lives, the trading men came to George Beauvais and asked him to intercede with Wilcox. A veteran companion of the Fort Laramie officers, Beauvais went to Wilcox and cooled his anger.

But Mrs. Fouts and her two daughters, screaming in anguish over their loss, were not placated. Among the party were several full-blooded Sioux—mostly the wives or relatives of traders. Mrs. Fouts pleaded with the soldiers to kill them all in revenge for her husband's death.

One of the Indians was an old brave named Green Plum, who had with him his four little grandchildren. Taking them all by the hand, he stepped through the crowd of hostile soldiers and presented himself in front of Mrs. Fouts. "I am a full-blooded Sioux," he declared. "I am alone in this world with these little orphans, who have neither father nor mother. If it is your wish to see us killed, now is your chance."

The distraught Mrs. Fouts relented; instead she begged the soldiers not to kill the Indians, and their lives were spared.

In the afternoon the bedraggled troopers and civilians—defeated and disconsolate—marched on for Fort Mitchell. The liberated Sioux moved north of the Platte in the direction of the White River, exultant over their deliverance. Every one of them had escaped across the river without mishap. True to his word, Black Wolf later danced the torturous Sun Dance, and the Sioux marveled at his courage in withstanding the ordeal.

· 4 ·

When Col. Thomas Moonlight at Fort Laramie heard of the outbreak, he made haste to clear himself of any blame for letting the Indians leave with all their arms. In a prompt report to his superior at Julesburg, Moonlight made serious insinuations against Fouts and Wilcox: ". . . how the command could make a march of over twenty-five miles with baggage by sundown that night . . . and give their undivided attention to fighting the Indians, is a mystery to me."

With appropriate flourish, Moonlight hurried to overtake the Sioux renegades. The morning after their escape he swung out of Fort Laramie at the head of more than 230 cavalrymen. After only two days of hard riding he was 120 miles northeast of the fort, pressing on the trail of the fugitives. But his headlong march of sixty miles a day had ruined many of his horses, and more than a hundred troopers had been forced to turn back.

At that moment the retreating Sioux were camped on Soldier Creek, near the headwaters of the White River. On the morning of June 17 their scouts discovered Moonlight's force marching down Deadman Creek. When the news was relayed to the village, the Indians broke camp and sent the women and children on northward with their goods. Then, agreeing on a plan with the scouts, the main body of warriors rode for the pass where Dead-man Creek runs into the White River. There they waited while the scouts followed Moonlight's column.

After marching some twenty miles before breakfast, the Colonel halted his men near the mouth of the creek. In the dry bed of the stream the soldiers took their ease while the horses grazed between the walls of the narrow canyon. When breakfast was over Moonlight ordered them herded into the camp. None of the animals was hobbled, and, as one company of California troops did not have picket ropes, its horses were standing completely loose. Some of the soldiers were starting to saddle up when someone called the alarm: "Indians!"

The troops sprang for their guns. The Sioux scouts—Moonlight claimed they numbered 200—were dashing down the hillside, shooting, yelling and waving blankets at the horses. Moonlight called it an attack and later reported that the Indians were "handsomely repulsed." In the shooting two soldiers were wounded and four Indians fell over, but, being tied to their horses in the customary fashion, were carried away.

The main result—and the Indian intent—was to panic the army horses. During the foray the animals reared and plunged in terror. Those that were picketed broke their ropes or pulled the pins. The Colonel's own horse had his head and feet tied with halter straps but still broke loose. By the time the Indians had ridden away almost all the horses were loose and stampeding in a body down the canyon. Colonel Moonlight and another officer ran in front and tried to stop them but had to fall as the horses thundered past. Another officer ran up, fired his pistols at the horses bringing up the rear and separated them from the rest. But 74 animals went rushing down Deadman Creek.

Saddling 25 of the remaining horses, a detachment rode off in pursuit. At the mouth of Deadman Creek it found the herd under the charge of several hundred warriors, who had been waiting there to catch them. This formidable band was in no hurry to leave. Using English words, several Indians shouted at the troops and taunted them to fight. Vastly outnumbered, Moonlight's remnant of cavalrymen turned back and left the Sioux in possession of the field and the horses.

Without their mounts, Moonlight's command was not only helpless against the Indians but also in serious danger. There was nothing to do but pack equipment on the remaining horses, destroy all extra baggage and trudge back on foot the 120 miles to Fort Laramie.

The Sioux, still interested only in escape, left the footmen alone and headed on for the Black Hills. Once again they had merely toyed with their enemy, had left him simply humiliated when they might have crushed him. The worst that Moonlight encountered on the road back was thirst, for water holes were 25 to 30 miles apart.

Less than four days after the encounter, the embarrassed cavalrymen walked into Fort Laramie. Unhorsed and almost unscathed, they suffered the supreme indignity that can befall a cavalry command. Moonlight put on a brave front in his report: "Every officer and soldier behaved throughout with great gallantry . . ." And he promised that he would never "attempt again to march a command, large or small," without providing hobbles for the horses.

But his resolve was too late. After that final debacle he was relieved of his command. His fate was considered terribly unjust by many of Moonlight's men, who admired his headstrong and cavalier style. Wrote one, "Colonel Moonlight was the peer of any officer that ever drew sword west of the Missouri River."

ELEVEN ◆ *The Battle of the Bridge*

◆ 1 ◆

After escaping from the Fort Laramie troops, the Oglala and Brulé journeyed northward to the Black Hills and then westward to the Powder River. There they joined the whole confederation of tribes—the wild Oglala, both northern and southern branches of the Cheyenne and Arapaho and part of at least two other Sioux tribes, the Miniconjou and the Sans Arc. Most of these tribes, after making the long hegira from the south in the winter of 1864-1865, had been resting, hunting buffalo and glorying in their victories over the Platte River soldiers.

Until now they had generally been fighting a defensive war. Their massive strikes in January and February against stations on the Overland Trail had been made on the run while they were migrating northward. Their purpose then had been to get enough plunder to last out a northern winter. The raids in the spring had been made by smaller, isolated war parties—not according to any stratagem of the chiefs.

But by June the grass was well up on the high plains. Their ponies could be sustained for a prolonged summer war. Never had they been stronger and more united. In the councils, the orators recounted the atrocities of Sand Creek. The Indian victories of the winter and spring were retold, and the white soldiers were ridiculed. Those chiefs preferring peace—Man-Afraid-of-His-Horses and Spotted Tail—were argued down. The war pipe made its rounds. Refusing to join, Spotted Tail moved out of the camp with his Brulé, but Man-Afraid-of-His-Horses bowed to the demands of his Oglala warriors and joined in plotting the campaign.

As before, the object was to clear the whites from the Platte

187

Valley. The Oregon Trail up the North Platte and the Overland mail route through Colorado along the South Platte ran through the heart of their territory. Travel on those roads had ruined the buffalo hunting on the central plains.

It was that same region over which the whites demanded exclusive control. Every Plains general from Harney to Dodge had demanded that the Indians stay out of the Platte area. The issue was clear, and the tribes meant to force it by nothing less than seizing and holding the Oregon Trail. For months they had kept it disrupted; for days at a time the stages had stood in the stations and the telegraph lines had been down. Communication between east and west coasts had been stalled. Now the Indians —little realizing how seriously the white man took his continental route—meant to make the break permanent.

The major obstacles to their plan were Fort Laramie and its satellite posts, from Camp Mitchell in the east to Sweetwater Station in the west. The most useful prize among them was the Platte Bridge Station, where Casper, Wyoming, now stands. There, on a bridge built a few years before, the Oregon Trail crossed the North Platte for the last time. Without that stronghold the Oregon Trail forces would be split and could then be pushed back in both directions.

• 2 •

Accordingly, the chiefs gave orders to prepare for battle. The sporadic raids that had lasted through June were halted. Warriors were forbidden to leave the main village. Weapons were made ready, and the medicine men went through their ceremonies to invoke victory.

In mid-July the entire village moved southwest to Crazy Woman Creek, a tributary of the Powder. From there the fighting men, numbering at least two thousand, rode south in a column about two miles long. Camping on the way, they arrived on the 24th at what is now Casper Creek, which opens into the North Platte a half-mile downstream from the Platte Bridge Station.

There they made final plans for a decoy tactic—the same that had almost worked at Julesburg. As the stockade was located on the south side of the river, it was first necessary to get the soldiers across the bridge, then prevent them from retreating over it before they could be annihilated.

On the morning of July 25 the chiefs sent ten warriors down the creek to the river, with orders to lure the troops out of the stockade and across the bridge. The main body then arrayed itself behind the large hill a few miles to the north of the bridge. There the chiefs, using white man's spyglasses, watched the progress of the decoys.

In the little station were 96 soldiers, mostly Kansas volunteers who had been anxious to go home ever since the Civil War had ended several months before. They and their fellows at numerous other stations along the North Platte route had clashed repeatedly with small bands of Indians. Hostile Cheyenne and Sioux were continually appearing along the route west of Fort Laramie; the road was considered unsafe for small parties of travelers, though army detachments were continually passing from one station to another. The soldiers considered duty at Platte Bridge to be dangerous, but they had no idea that the combined strength of the Oglala Sioux and the Cheyenne and Arapaho nations was looking down upon them.

In charge of the outlying posts west of Fort Laramie was Maj. Martin Anderson of the 11th Kansas Cavalry, who made his headquarters at Platte Bridge. A prudent officer, he respected Indian prowess and indulged in no theatrics.

On the morning of the 25th the Indian scouts who had been sent down Casper Creek showed themselves opposite the stockade and created some excitement among the troops. Several soldiers rolled a howitzer to the bridge and fired at them but did not cross the river. The scouts returned without having enticed the command out of the post. Early in the afternoon some more Indians showed themselves, and about a dozen troopers crossed the bridge and followed them some distance west. They could probably have been cut off and slaughtered by the main Indian force, but the chiefs did not want to show their hand on such small game. Although a number of Indians appeared and tried to surround the cavalrymen, the latter made their way back to the post without loss.

Late in the afternoon some other Indians were discovered east of the station trying to stampede the beef herd. A small detachment from the post routed them and killed one—a Cheyenne chief.

During the afternoon a few soldiers arrived from Fort Laramie with the mail. With them was Lt. Caspar Collins, son of Col.

William O. Collins. Having stayed on Oregon Trail duty after his father had returned home, young Collins was in charge of Sweet-water Station and was passing through to rejoin his command after a visit to Fort Laramie.

Late that night Capt. Henry C. Bretney also arrived with a detachment from the west, bringing the total Platte Bridge strength to 119 officers and men. Possibly Bretney had passed through undetected in the darkness, but more likely the chiefs did not want to spring their trap prematurely. In any case, he brought news that a supply train of 25 soldiers headed by Sgt. Amos Custard was also on its way to the post from the west and would arrive next day.

This news added an entirely new element to Major Anderson's worries. The number of Indians seen about the post—somewhere between fifty and ninety—was large enough to attack the wagon train when it came in sight. Anderson's first mistake was to neglect to send a night rider to warn the supply train that Indians were harassing the post.

Before daylight the chiefs drew their noose still tighter. The Cheyenne—numbering at least four hundred—were sent down to the river west of the station, where they hid in the bushes along the bank and waited for the decoys to do their work. At the same time, several hundred Sioux rode down and hid themselves in a dry wash near the river east of the bridge. The Arapaho crouched out of sight in nearby Casper Creek. According to plan, the troops would be lured across the bridge and westward along the road by decoys. As soon as the Cheyenne had attacked them, the Sioux and Arapaho would rise up and block any retreat to the bridge.

At the same time, the main body of Sioux moved from behind the large hill and took up positions in the canyons branching off the road to the west, ready to close the trap from the north. Obviously, the chiefs had far more strength than they needed; if the garrison fell for their ruse, it would surely be destroyed.

In fact, Anderson's forces were probably even weaker than the Indians believed. Only about two-thirds of the soldiers had rifles; the rest were either armed with revolvers or had no small arms at all. Partly because of the muddy condition of the roads, supply contractors had been very slow in bringing ammunition to this outlying post, and the riflemen had only about twenty rounds apiece.

• 3 •

The next morning, July 26, about the same number of Indians again showed themselves. In an officers' conference, Anderson was urged to send relief to Custard's wagon train. He then ordered the post commander of Platte Bridge, Capt. James Greer, to send out a detachment. Greer, in turn, ordered out between 20 and 25 cavalrymen under Sgt. Isaac B. "Jake" Pennock. When Sergeant Pennock had readied his detachment, he reported to Major Anderson and was told that Lt. Caspar Collins was "going along."

It has been charged that Major Anderson of the 11th Kansas Cavalry Regiment sent the young Ohioan in order to spare his fellow Kansas officers. However, the evidence is equivocal. It is also possible that Collins volunteered. Furthermore, the number of Indians in sight did not suggest that the mission was obviously suicidal, as some histories claim.[4] According to the diary of one eyewitness:

> The Indians in sight would be no hindrance at all, but their conduct was very singular and unusual and they appeared to be more calm and easy than usual, only a few "circus riding." Twenty-five men were, by the authorities, considered strong enough to travel in safety almost anywhere on the road from Laramie to South Pass.

In any case, the column jogged out of the stockade and pounded over the bridge; Lieutenant Collins, resplendent in a new uniform, rode in the lead. According to orders he took his men up to the edge of the bluff and followed it parallel to the road, in order to have a better view of Indian movements. Following him over the bridge and up the side of the bluff were Captain Bretney and ten troopers, in order to watch for Indians and to support Collins if necessary. Others, on foot, crossed the bridge to wait on the north side for any Indian actions. From the roof of the station, Lt. George Walker spotted some of the Cheyenne crouching among the bushes on the river bank. Calling down to Major Anderson, he reported the discovery.

"I have ordered twenty more men," returned Anderson. "They are now saddling their horses."

Before the reinforcements could leave the station, Collins had gone half a mile west. The Sioux, hiding in a draw below the bridge, and the Cheyenne, waiting under the river bank west of it, watched him pass. When he approached the road once again, Collins saw several Indians cutting the telegraph line. When they saw the bluecoats, they dropped down the poles to their ponies and rode north to the main body of Indians in the canyons of the bluff. Possibly to intercept them, Collins turned his troopers northward off the road, unknowingly moving directly toward the main body of warriors.

It was clear that, whether or not the Indians were ready to spring their trap, it would soon be discovered. No sooner had the last trooper turned northward than the Cheyenne rose from the river bank. With a chorus of whoops they rode headlong up the slope. Collins wheeled his cavalrymen into line to face them, but at that moment the main body of Sioux came thundering out of the little canyons. The thin line of cavalrymen was surrounded by two thousand charging Indians. Collins ordered the men into a column of twos facing east toward the post. Above the din of war whoops he shouted, "Retreat to the bridge!"

In an instant the Indians were upon them. For a moment the blue and the bronze closed in a writhing mass. For fear of hitting their comrades, the attackers used tomahawks and lances, rather than arrows and guns. Firing their single-shot carbines, the troops had no time to reload. They pulled out their revolvers and fired point blank, sometimes with the muzzles pressed against the bodies of the Indians. In the melee all the army horses were wounded, and four were killed. Most of the soldiers were hit; four were killed. They had returned to the edge of the bluff and were starting downhill when a wounded soldier who had fallen cried out for help. Already wounded in the hip, Collins wheeled and raced back in the teeth of the Indian fire. He was leaning over trying to pick up the wounded soldier when his frightened horse whirled and dashed into a body of Indians. An arrow hit Collins in the forehead and stuck there as he rode on, firing with both pistols. At the edge of the bluff he fell and rolled lifeless down the hill.

With the first Indian onslaught the infantrymen and Bretney's cavalrymen, who had followed up the ridge, hurried back to hold the bridge for Collins' retreat. Those already at the bridge could not fire the howitzer for fear of hitting Collins and his men. Led by Captain Greer, they ran forward, dropped to the grass in a skirmish line along the river bank and fired at the Cheyenne and Sioux who were pursuing the retreating column. With their repeating Spencer rifles—the only ones at the station—they dropped many Indians from their horses.

Some two hundred Arapaho hiding in Casper Creek to the east of the bridge now came howling into the open but were sent reeling back by fire from the bridge. The Sioux who had hidden in a draw near the river bank came scrambling out and attacked the bridge. Bretney's cavalry and infantry held fast and fired at them point blank.

At the same time the Cheyenne had disengaged from the Collins troopers and were pouring a heavy fire on them as they rode down the hill. Because of the deceptive terrain their shots went high, missing the retreating soldiers but striking full among the Sioux near the bridge.

"Stop firing!" they shouted angrily to the Cheyenne. "You are killing our own men!"

But so many of them were hit from the fire of the soldiers and the Cheyenne that they fell back to the river bank again. Meanwhile, the fire from the bridge and the skirmishers was taking such a toll among the Cheyenne and the main body of Sioux that they stopped pressing their pursuit. Most of Collins' cavalrymen pounded onto the bridge. One horse, having delivered its rider to safety, fell dead at the bridge. One wounded trooper, his horse downed on the slope, tried to crawl through the grass to the river. But he was followed and tomahawked by an Indian; while starting to mutilate the body the savage was shot by one of the sharpshooters near the river.

The Indians called off the attack. Picking up their dead from the battlefield, they gathered behind the main hill north of the station and fell into violent quarreling over the failure of their strategy. The Cheyenne charged the Sioux with cowardice in not capturing the bridge, which would have prevented the troopers from returning to safety. The Sioux retorted that the Cheyenne had shot at them and forced them back. The Cheyenne were so incensed that they swore never to fight again alongside the Sioux.

At the same time the bluecoats were quarreling. In an officers' conference Captain Bretney struck Captain Greer and was placed under temporary arrest.

Meanwhile, both sides were preparing for the next round. While the wounded soldiers were being cared for, the others were making cartridges for their carbines and digging a breastwork for the howitzer crew. Some Indians swam their ponies across the river and before Major Anderson could telegraph for reinforcements they cut the wire both east and west of the station. Others tried to decoy soldiers across the bridge by taunting, catcalling and even bringing Collins' horse near the bridge and whipping him.

But the trap had already been sprung, and the troops knew too well how badly they were outnumbered. Indeed, had the Indians known how low the ammunition was at the station, they probably would have attacked it outright—in which case the whole force would have been overwhelmed.

• 4 •

Desperate for help, Anderson had to get word to the nearest garrison eastward at Deer Creek Station. He sent Lieutenant Walker and seventeen men to repair the telegraph break. Seeing them, the Indians who had been cavorting north of the bridge gathered across the river and then forded it unobserved by the repair crew. At the station the howitzer was fired to warn the men, and most of them retreated. But a few of those farthest from the station were suddenly surrounded by Indians and had to fight their way through. Two were speared in the back—one fatally. A horse was killed, but his rider ran on to safety. The Indians chased the fleeing soldiers, but were turned back by others who ran out of the fort and covered the retreat with their guns. The telegraph was still broken; Anderson could get no reinforcements, and his ammunition was lower than ever.

In that fretful moment a soldier standing on top of the station shouted, "There comes the train."

Sure enough, Sgt. Amos Custard's five covered wagons and their drivers, together with an escort of some twenty cavalrymen, were sighted west of the station—about a mile and a quarter by line of sight, about two miles by road.

The Indians had also discovered the approach of the wagon train. Those who had been riding about in front of the post gathered to westward and made ready to surprise the train. Others of the main body, led by the Cheyenne Chief Roman Nose, pounded out of the hills to the attack.

To warn the wagoners and harass the Indians, Major Anderson ordered the howitzer fired. Two shells exploded in midair before they reached the Indians, but they served to alert Sergeant Custard. He sent five horsemen forward to see what the shooting was about. When they were about a quarter-mile in front, they ran headlong into the first Indians, who started to surround them. With no hope of turning back, they wheeled south and raced for the river. Some of the Indians followed, killing one soldier in the water and another on the south bank. The other three, seeing that they could not beat the Indians to the post, abandoned their horses and went on, half-hidden in the bushes along the river. Then they went into a dry ravine leading toward the station while the Indians tried to find them. Shooting back whenever they were discovered, the three soldiers made their way close enough to be covered by the guns from the post and dashed safely inside.

When Sergeant Custard first saw the Indians, he was moving across a level piece of ground near the river. At first he whipped up the teams to race for the post. But when the Indians descended upon him he tried instead to corral the wagons. The attackers came upon them before the maneuver could be finished, and the men all had to take shelter behind two of the wagons halted in a slight hollow. They cut loose the mules, took cover as best they could and sent a deadly fire into the Indians.

From the roof of the post the soldiers could see the battle. Some of them wanted to hurry out and rescue their comrades. But Anderson was now too well aware of the stakes. Outnumbered twenty to one, he could only hope to hold the stockade. Besides, he did not have enough uninjured horses left to mount an offensive. The Indians had played their trump against Collins, and the game with Anderson was up. The Major therefore refused to send any relief, holding that it would be suicidal and would fatally weaken the post itself. Wrote one officer, "At that time we thought the major was too cautious but since then . . . we were satisfied that the major's decision was a wise one, and that by it [alone] any of us are left to tell the tale."

After being repulsed in two frontal attacks on the wagons, the Indians settled down to a slow siege. Dismounting, many of them rolled logs and boulders before them for protection as they advanced toward the soldiers, shooting as they went. Some even dug trenches, relentlessly inching their way upon the beleaguered men. With the corral composed of only two wagons, the soldiers could protect themselves only with sacks of corn and other cargo. Three of them stayed in one of the wagons, shooting through holes in the canvas cover.

But, as the afternoon wore on, the shots grew less frequent. After a four-hour siege the Indians drew their circle close enough to prepare a final blow. Roman Nose led his Cheyenne in a mounted charge, feinting at the defenders to test their fire. When none came, the Indians rushed upon the wagons. The soldiers still remaining alive were tomahawked. At least one and perhaps more were tortured to death.

After scalping and mutilating the bodies of their victims, the Indians spent the rest of the day gathering up their own casualties. To haul them away they split telegraph poles and made travois. Judging from the number of poles and the travois tracks in the sand, their losses must have been shattering—estimates run as high as sixty killed by the doomed sharpshooters at the wagons.

At the station, the end of the shooting and the smoke rising from burning wagons told the soldiers that their comrades were all dead. That night, with the telegraph still down, Anderson sent two half-breed scouts through to Deer Creek Station for reinforcements. Starting immediately, fifty troops hurried up the trail and arrived at Platte Bridge Station the next afternoon. Notified by telegraph from Deer Creek on the 27th, the officers at Fort Laramie also sent nine squadrons of cavalry up the trail.

But the Indians had given up the attack on Platte Bridge. They knew from the number of the soldiers who had fought at the bridge in the Collins fight that the post had a formidable garrison. What they did not know was that the soldiers were desperately short of ammunition. They had seen in the wagon fight that the troops could in no case be lured into the open. Finally, they had no stomach for the further heavy losses they believed they would suffer in an assault on the stockade.

In all the fights and skirmishes on the 26th they had killed 28 men, but their grand plan to capture Platte Bridge Station and clear the Oregon Trail of bluecoats had failed. It had failed in that critical moment when the Cheyennes had unintentionally rained bullets on the Sioux attempting to seize the bridge. For, had the Indians been able to annihilate Collins' column and also to strike down those defending the bridge, they might have weakened the garrison enough to overwhelm the post. But they had actually assembled too many warriors. Their mission was smothered with masses of men who shot at one another in the confusion.

Stung by their losses and frustrated in their design, the Indians made a last show of defiance on the morning of the 27th. They gathered along the river before the post in what one soldier called a "grand parade." Then they began riding slowly away until the river bank was empty.

Some of them formed small raiding parties and attacked isolated stage stations for the rest of the year. Most of them rode back to their villages on the Powder River—spurred by reports that an army from Fort Laramie was invading the heart of their homeland.

At the same time the Platte Bridge soldiers ventured out to claim their dead. They found nearly all the bodies—most of them savagely mutilated and many of them peppered with arrows. The scalps taken at the wagon fight were scattered on the ground. Veteran fighters said it was a sure sign that the Indians considered Platte Bridge an empty victory.

A handful of volunteer soldiers—both those who died and those who lived—had held the Oregon Trail. In their grand offensive of 1865, the Sioux and the Cheyenne had won almost every battle but the last one. Never again would they come so close to winning back part of the ground they had lost since the founding of Fort Laramie.

TWELVE ♦ *The Treaty with Two Indians*

• 1 •

Beginning in 1862 the white man's frontier had thrust still more deeply into Indian territory, after gold had been discovered in the Montana country. A stampede reminiscent of the Pike's Peak gold rush of 1859 set in for the new settlements of Bannack and Virginia City.

At first the flood of gold hunters surged along the Oregon Trail to Utah Territory before turning northward for the diggings. But in 1864 John Bozeman carved a new road to Montana, leaving the Oregon Trail west of Fort Laramie and striking through the Powder River region—the very heart of the Sioux country. Indeed, the Powder River and the Yellowstone were the last hunting grounds north of the Oregon Trail where the Plains Indians could still exist on the buffalo.

The miners swarming over the Bozeman Trail added new fuel to Indian fury. It was against this tide of white men, as well as those still moving to California and Oregon on the Overland Trail, that the Sioux and Cheyenne had aimed their offensive early in 1865.

No sooner had the tribes struck the Platte roads than the white settlers began agitating for a counteroffensive. The Coloradans wanted protection for their supply roads and their outlying communities. The freighters supplying the new Montana diggings by the Oregon and Bozeman trails were clamoring for action against the Indians. The towns of the upper Missouri River—in Dakota and Iowa—were also reaching for the Montana trade. Through Judge A. W. Hubbard, congressman from Iowa, they secured an appropriation for a new and shorter wagon road along

198

the Niobrara River route in Nebraska. But the road builders were harassed by Indians; the Iowans—with real voting power in Congress—threw their weight behind the same demand for an Indian expedition that had previously been heard only from the western territories. Late in May 1865, Congressman Hubbard wrote pointedly to Gen. John Pope, the army commander at St. Louis, "I hope and believe you will be able to punish those Indians."

"General Dodge will attend to the whole business," Pope promptly replied. "I think you need have no concern about it. I will use all means at my command to secure safety to your wagon road parties and to keep peace on the plains."

Gen. Grenville M. Dodge not only had to keep open the Overland Road and the transcontinental telegraph. He also had to mount a major campaign against the Indian stronghold on the Powder River. The struggle for control of the continental crossing was nearing its Armageddon.

The best choice to lead such an expedition was Brig. Gen. Patrick E. Connor, a Californian who had won fame as an Indian fighter—the Harney of the 1860s. An Irish immigrant, he had joined the U.S. Army as a youth and had seen his first service in the West. In the Mexican War he had risen to the rank of captain and had been wounded in combat. At the beginning of the Civil War he was made colonel of the 3rd California Volunteer Infantry Regiment, which was sent out on the Overland Road to replace regular troops withdrawn to the main fronts. Snake and Bannock Indians were marauding the Mormon settlements and the Overland Road, but in January 1863 Connor and his troops killed an estimated three hundred of them in the battle of Bear River.

This victory made him the hero of the mountain settlers, and in March 1865 he was placed in charge of a new Department of the Plains. General Dodge began sending him troops for a spring and summer campaign to the Powder River. From Dodge's superior, Major General Pope at St. Louis, came an admonition. "You know how important these roads are and how deep the interest of Iowa in their completion. I have assured Judge Hubbard that you will clear out those Indians. Do not, therefore, fail to do it."

Never—not even in the Colorado gold rush—had economic

pressure been more openly directing the U.S. Army against the
Plains Indians. From Pope to Dodge to Connor, the military was
serving as the cutting edge of frontier commerce.

Late spring found Connor—a striking figure with deepset eyes
and dark muttonchop whiskers—in Denver making plans. Three
different columns were to leave the Oregon Trail at various
points, heading generally north to the Black Hills and the Powder
River. They were to attack any Indians on the way and to rendezvous finally on the Rosebud River in southeastern Montana Territory. At the same time Connor would build a fort to police the
Bozeman Trail in the Powder River country.

By the early summer Connor was at Fort Laramie superintend-
ing the final preparations. To commanders of the other columns
he gave the strictest orders: "You will not receive overtures of
peace or submission from Indians, but will attack and kill every
male Indian over twelve years of age."

When this barbarous command came to the attention of
General Pope in St. Louis, he was appalled. "These instructions
are atrocious," he wrote Dodge. ". . . If any such orders as General
Connor's are carried out it will be disgraceful to the Government
and will cost him his commission, if not worse."

Connor was already in the field when Pope's countermand was
sent, but it soon caught up with him by telegraph and courier.

Late in July, Connor's three columns, numbering 2,500 men,
left the various points on the Oregon Trail, moving north into the
Indian country.

From the beginning the operation was beset with trouble. The
supply contractors were inordinately slow in hauling up ammunition and provender. Waiting as long as he dared, Connor finally
started in midsummer, and even then he went without most of
the supplies he needed. The columns were harassed by storms,
disease, shortages of food, surprise Indian attacks and wholesale
loss of horses. Connor's own column, heading northward for the
Powder River, paused long enough to build a timber stockade
(which the commander modestly named "Fort Connor") and then
pressed on. Along the Tongue River on August 29, the soldiers
surprised an Arapaho village and killed 63 Indians (including
some women and children) in what was the biggest battle of the
expedition. When they returned to Fort Connor they found there
one of the other columns, which had arrived horseless and nearly

starved. Relieved of his command, Connor was sent back to his former post in Utah.

Though the General continued to be the hero of the mountain settlers, his expedition had failed to punish the Indians or to bring them to terms. The Sioux continued to harass emigrants along the Bozeman Trail, as well as the work crew building the road on the Niobrara route. Indeed, the latter road went unfinished, and the Iowa towns never won their share of the Montana trade. Despite pressure from Hubbard and the assurances of Pope and Dodge, the army had failed to smash the Indians. The Sioux still stood across the white man's path of empire.

* 2 *

Next the invaders tried another weapon—kindness. In April 1865 a new Indian agent for the Upper Platte had been appointed to replace Loree; the Bureau chose Vital Jarrot, who had lived for many years among the Plains Sioux. From his home in Illinois he journeyed to the Platte with orders to "induce the hostile Arapaho, Cheyenne, and Sioux of the plains to come in and accept terms of peace."

But, although the Indian Bureau was committed to peace, the army was not so disposed until after General Connor's fiasco on the Powder River. As the army's policy was never to make peace until after the Indian had been punished, Connor was said to have "accomplished all that could possibly be expected . . ." At the same time, the awful results of feuding between Indian agents and army officers—exemplified by the vendetta between Loree and the Laramie soldiers and traders—had brought a new policy out of Washington. Thenceforth, the army and the Indian Bureau were to cooperate with each other.

In October 1865 the commander of the Platte region determined to send peace messengers to the Sioux. But the Indians were still on the warpath and were raiding Platte River stations. No white man dared to go north and take a message to the chiefs.

Then commanding the Fort Laramie district was Col. Henry E. Maynadier, a seasoned veteran of five years on the high plains. One officer called him "a natural prince, a good soldier, and a judge of Indian character." He brought to the situation an understanding that had been missing since Colonel Collins had left the previous spring. He was just the man to carry out the army's new policy of cooperation with the Indian Bureau.

Maynadier sought out Big Ribs, a well-known friendly Sioux, who had done services for the whites before. With four other Indians, including Big Mouth of the Laramie Loafers, Big Ribs set out for the hostile villages of the Sioux. With them went an invitation from Colonel Maynadier to come in and make peace. They would, he promised, find Fort Laramie flying the white flag of truce.

It happened that the winter of 1865-1866 was one of the severest on record. November and December were extremely cold, and snow fell to great depths in the mountains and high plains. At the same time the Indians had been denied annuity rations of blankets and food because of the hostilities. They were also without sufficient dried buffalo meat because the young men had spent too much time fighting. Besides, the buffalo were still diminishing in numbers, and many bands had to travel long distances for a hunt that often proved disappointing.

Lacking food and exposed to the elements, the Indians were suffering unimaginable hardship. Many of the women and children died of cold and starvation. Most of the horses that did not starve to death were killed for food. As Chief Spotted Tail of the Brulé put it, "Our hearts were on the ground."

Such was their condition when Big Ribs and his party reached the villages of the Brulé and the Oglala. For the first time in nearly a year, they learned, they were welcome at Fort Laramie, their favorite trading post for more than a generation. They were ready for peace. Unbeaten by the army, they were beaten at last by nature.

On January 15, 1866, a large band of Indians approached Bordeau's post below Fort Laramie. But, after more than a year of war on the Platte, their intentions were feared. Responding to the alarm, Maynadier started to send troops to rescue Bordeau when a messenger came from the Indians. The group proved to be Big Ribs and his party, together with the Corn band of Brulé under Chief Swift Bear, who was ready to make peace. Overjoyed, Maynadier hoisted his white flag over the fort and was soon greeting the newcomers. He found them in pitiful condition— starving and half naked in the cold. After a council in which the

Chief promised no more depredations, Maynadier and Vital Jarrot handed out clothing and food.

Next came Man-Afraid-of-His-Horses with a large band of Oglala. Like the Brulé, they trudged in with utter resignation, cold and destitute and eager to promise peace and receive food. Maynadier had them camp with the Brulé and treated them with every solicitude. But early in February an old squaw went from the fort to the Indian village and gave a dark warning: "When the Indians are all assembled, the soldiers will bring up their big guns and destroy you."

Instantly the village was in a panic. The Indians were about to pull stakes and flee when Maynadier arrived with an interpreter. Assuring them of his good intentions, he prevailed upon them to stay.

Yet these two bands were the safest of the Brulé and Oglala. Spotted Tail, one of the Brulé leaders in the attacks on Julesburg and other Platte settlements, had not yet appeared; although he preferred peace he could not be called friendly. More dangerous was Red Cloud, who had figured in the Platte Bridge fight as head of the Bad Face band of Oglala. The most recalcitrant of all the Sioux leaders, Red Cloud had become the rallying point of resistance to the whites. Shrewd and suspicious, a strategist who saw beyond the limited tactics of most Indian leaders, he shared with Spotted Tail the greatest influence over the high plains Sioux.

But about 260 miles north in the Powder River country, Spotted Tail's Brulé had suffered with the rest. Among the stricken was his favorite daughter Ah-ho-appa, or Yellow Buckskin Girl. Since girlhood she had been accustomed to semicivilized life and had often stayed in villages near Fort Laramie when her father was leading war or hunting parties. Fascinated with the order and ceremony of army life, she had been used to watching the soldiers' activities for hours at a time. According to one account, she was determined to marry an army officer, and once, when a Brulé warrior had tried to carry her off, she had drawn a knife and cut herself free.

At seventeen, Ah-ho-appa was not hardened to severe winters in an Indian camp. In the terrible suffering of the 1865-1866 winter, she contracted either tuberculosis or pneumonia and was desperately ill when Spotted Tail started with his band for Fort

Laramie in February. On the way, carried on a travois, she realized
death was at hand and begged to be taken all the way to the fort
and buried in the white cemetery there. At least, Ah-ho-appa
believed, she could join the whites in the land of the Great Spirit.
Before she died on the trail, Spotted Tail promised that he would
carry out her wishes and sent a messenger to Maynadier asking
that she be permitted burial at Fort Laramie.

For his part, Maynadier was touched by this peaceful gesture.
A man of Spotted Tail's character, wrote the Colonel, "would
never have confided the remains of his child to the care of any
one but those with whom he intended to be friends always." He
sent back word to the Chief that he "would be glad to have
Spotted Tail bring his child here" and would help him and his
tribe.

Ah-ho-appa's body was wrapped in a smoked deerskin and
carried on to Fort Laramie. On March 8 the pathetic column,
hungry and shivering, reached the Platte. Hearing of their approach, Maynadier raised his white flag and rode out with several
officers to greet Spotted Tail. Back at the fort he invited the Chief,
together with some headmen and army officers, to his office.
Opening the "talk," Maynadier told Spotted Tail that the Great
Father would be sending peace commissioners for a council with
all the chiefs. But mostly he expressed sympathy for Spotted
Tail's loss:

> The Great Spirit has taken her, and he never did anything ex-
> cept for some good purpose. Everything will be prepared to have
> her funeral at sunset, and as the sun goes down it might remind
> you of the darkness left in your lodge when your beloved daugh-
> ter was taken away; but as the sun would surely rise again, so she
> will rise and some day we will all meet in the land of the Great
> Spirit.

In the privacy of the room, Spotted Tail was moved to tears
while the officer spoke. Then he took Maynadier's hand and
answered:

> This must be a dream for me to be in such a fine room and
> surrounded by such as you. Have I been asleep during the last
> four years of hardship and trial . . . ? We think we have been
> much wronged and are entitled to compensation for the damage
> and distress caused by making so many roads through our coun-

try, and driving off and destroying the buffalo and game. My heart is very sad, and I cannot talk on business; I will wait and see the counsellors the Great Father will send.

Strongly moved himself, Maynadier wrote that Spotted Tail's performance "satisfied some who had never before seemed to believe it, that an Indian has a human heart to work on and was not a wild animal."

Following Maynadier's promise, Ah-ho-appa's funeral was held at the white cemetery, where an Indian scaffold was erected. Before sunset a funeral procession, consisting of several hundred Indians and all the soldiers who were off duty, moved slowly to the burial ground. The Indians and soldiers assembled in concentric rings around the coffin. Next to it were Spotted Tail and the girl's mother; Colonel Maynadier; Maj. George O'Brien, by that time commander of Fort Laramie, and the post chaplain. While the chaplain offered a prayer, which was interpreted to the Indians, the mother and several aunts of the young girl were quietly weeping. Maynadier noted the "respectful behavior" of all the soldiers present ("as I was glad to see") and was deeply stirred by the event.

"The occurrence of such an incident," he wrote, "is regarded by the oldest settlers . . . as unprecedented, and as calculated to secure a certain and lasting peace."

• 3 •

Meanwhile, Red Cloud had also sent messengers to Fort Laramie asking about the peace talks, and Maynadier had sent them back with presents and his assurance of safe treatment. Three days after Ah-ho-appa's funeral, Red Cloud and his Bad Faces reached the Platte. Spotted Tail and some of his warriors joined Colonel Maynadier in riding to meet them; with appropriate ceremony they were accompanied to the fort. Another council was held, in which Red Cloud grumbled about the whites' overrunning the country "which the Great Spirit made for us." More reserved and wary than Spotted Tail, he complained of the bitter winter that had taken such toll among his people, as though the elements were the white man's doing. Spotted Tail was more conciliatory in recounting their troubles. He addressed Maynadier:

Our hearts were on the ground, my brother, and as you will see nearly all our women have cut off their hair in mourning for their children. But when we saw your white flag and smoked your tobacco, which we had not smoked for so long, our hearts were strong again, and if we had had to *swim* through the snow we would have come.

Fortunately, both Maynadier and the Indian agent, Vital Jarrot, had stores of provisions, which they handed out to Red Cloud's people, as they had to the others, and the council ended in a grand feast. "At present," reported Maynadier, "every prospect is favorable . . ."

At that moment still another character entered the drama of Fort Laramie. He was E. B. Taylor, publisher of the Omaha *Republican* and Superintendent of Indian Affairs for Nebraska, now chosen to head the peace commissioners. Optimistic, ambitious and resourceful, Taylor was determined to make a treaty with the Indians and to bring peace at last to the plains. "It cost the Government six millions of dollars to fight them last year," he wrote, "with no decisive result." Taylor was resolved to succeed where the army had failed.

After visiting Washington to discuss the terms to be offered, Taylor returned to the West early in March. From St. Louis he wired Maynadier to get the chiefs together for a "talk" with him by telegraph between Fort Laramie and Omaha to complete plans for the big council. By the 12th he was ready, together with the commanding general of the Platte, at the Omaha telegraph station. It was to be, declared Taylor, the first council by telegraph between Indians and white men.

At Fort Laramie, Colonel Maynadier gathered Swift Bear, Man-Afraid-of-His-Horses, Spotted Tail and a few other chiefs in the little telegraph office at the post. Most reluctant of all was Red Cloud, who was afraid of some trick in the lodge of the singing wire. But at length Maynadier succeeded and later wired Taylor that it was a "great triumph over prejudice and superstition to get Red Cloud into Telegraph office."

Then the key at Fort Laramie clicked out Taylor's first message from Omaha. It said that the Great Father had appointed commissioners to make peace. "He wants you all to be his friends and the friends of the white man. If you conclude a treaty of Peace he wishes to make presents to you and your people as a token of his friendship."

Within a few moments the chiefs had agreed to a peace council at Fort Laramie on June 1, 1866. Then the officials at Omaha bade the chiefs goodbye: "We shake hands by telegraph."

Maynadier and Jarrot grasped the chiefs by the hand and wired back: "Have shaken hands for you and part all well. . . . Indians much pleased."

For the next two months, Maynadier's optimism continued to rise. Red Cloud and Spotted Tail took their people to the Black Hills to trap beaver and to gather the other Sioux bands. Early in April, delegates from the northern Cheyenne arrived at Fort Laramie. Through another "council by telegraph" they also agreed to the June 1 date. About the same time, word reached Fort Laramie from the Black Hills that some young Sioux braves had tried to get up a war party against the whites; Red Cloud and the other chiefs had disciplined them by shooting their horses and ripping their lodges. As Maynadier reported, it was a good sign that the chiefs were serious about peace.

By the end of April the Indians had begun to assemble again at Fort Laramie, arriving early in the hope of getting more provisions. Even some Arapaho and a band of Miniconjou Sioux came in to get food. For a while it looked as though the supplies at Fort Laramie would be exhausted before the commissioners arrived. Jarrot wired Taylor to hurry: "There is danger of their dispersing and it would be difficult if not impossible to collect them."

Thus warned, Taylor speeded the plans of the other commissioners. On the morning of May 22 he and two others caught the Union Pacific train out of Omaha. From the end-of-track, eighty miles to the west, they bounced on to Fort Laramie by stagecoach. Arriving on May 30, they found many of the Sioux camped around the post and others arriving daily. Beside Big Mouth's Laramie Loafers and Spotted Tail's Brulé, the wild Oglala were represented by a small delegation, including their chiefs, Red Cloud and Man-Afraid-of-His-Horses.

Of the two, Red Cloud was the more recalcitrant. Getting him to attend at all was a triumph for Taylor.

Man-Afraid, who had tried to be a peacemaker among the Sioux ever since the Grattan fight in 1854, was getting old; already his authority was sometimes challenged by his son, "Young-Man-Afraid-of-His-Horses." But even "Old Man-Afraid" was unwilling to give up the last good hunting ground of the Sioux in return for some white man's presents. Such a move, he knew, would make the last of the wild Sioux completely dependent on their enemies for their food and shelter.

On June 5, Taylor and Maynadier, who had also been named a commissioner, called their first formal council with the chiefs. They assembled on the parade ground before one of the barracks, where Maynadier had placed crude pine benches decked with evergreen boughs. On these benches the commissioners and their attendants sat, whereas the Indians preferred their custom of sitting on the ground. After the usual ceremony of pipesmoking, Taylor made the first speech. "It is not the desire of the Government to purchase your country," he said, "but simply to . . . obtain from you a recognition of the right of the Government to make and use, through your Country, such roads as may be deemed necessary . . . for emigrants to the mining districts of the West."

Everyone knew that these words referred particularly to the Powder River road, as the Indians had already been compensated for the Oregon Trail under the Fort Laramie Treaty of 1851. According to one observer, Taylor promised the chiefs that "travel on said road would be confined strictly to the line thereof, and emigrants and travelers generally should not be allowed to molest or disturb the game . . ."

The chiefs knew from their experience on the Oregon Trail that such a promise could not be enforced. It was the westward pioneers, shooting game for the sport and bringing cattle that ate up the grass, who were helping to kill off the buffalo.

The next day the chiefs made their answering speeches. They showed "moderation and good feeling," according to Taylor's report. Possibly Spotted Tail did, for he was against war with the whites, and his Brulé had one more hunting ground on the Republican River to the south that they customarily shared with the southern Cheyenne and Arapaho. But that the wild Oglala showed such good feeling may be seriously doubted. In all his reports to his superiors, Taylor showed an unwarranted optimism. Like many Indian superintendents not living in close proximity to the wild tribes, he was naïve in his views on the Indians. Ambitious for recognition, he seemed determined to be the peacemaker of the plains. He wasted presents on the Laramie Loafers to help bind them to the treaty, when they could not have been goaded into a fight. The sizes of the recalcitrant bands he was quick to minimize. According to officers and others at Fort Laramie, he frequently declared, "I was sent here by the Government for the purpose of making a treaty, and it shall be accomplished if made with but two Indians."

Thus, when the wild chiefs told him that they would have to go and get the rest of their people before they could conclude a treaty, Taylor put the best possible interpretation on it. The commissioners believed, he reported, that "a treaty could and would be made . . ." But, according to another account, Red Cloud would not agree to the road, and when he left the council he put his hand on his rifle: "In this and the Great Spirit," he declared, "I trust for the right."

On June 8, Man-Afraid and Red Cloud left for the White River, where their tribes were camped east of the Black Hills. Taylor and Maynadier sent messengers, again inviting the Cheyenne and Arapaho to attend the council. Some more Indians came in but Red Cloud's Bad Faces refused to come. With his usual optimism, Taylor reported their strength as only 300 warriors and declared that "at least seven-eighths of the two bands (the Brulés and Ogalallahs) were present." The commissioners therefore renewed their councils with the Indians at Fort Laramie.

· 4 ·

Even though Colonel Maynadier was cooperating fully with the Indian Bureau, some of his superiors were not. As early as March 10, 1866, Maj. Gen. John Pope of the Department of the Missouri ordered two more forts built in the Powder River and Big Horn country. This order was given during the early efforts of Maynadier to bring in the tribes for a parley—in fact, the day before the celebrated council by telegraph between Fort Laramie and Omaha. The Indians had been rendered helpless by the severe winter, and all reports from Maynadier and Taylor indicated that peace could be had for the asking.

Indeed, had the Indian Bureau moved immediately for a peace conference when Red Cloud was at Fort Laramie in March, he might have signed. To the Indian struck down by a savage winter, survival itself was paramount; the rations at Fort Laramie and the promise of annuities meant life itself. But by June the snow was gone, the grass was up, the ponies were fattening and the braves were once again killing buffalo. No longer starving and freezing, Red Cloud and his fellows believed that they could cling to their immemorial way of life if they could keep the Powder River country. They would do so if they had to fight against the white man's rifle for every inch. "It is better for us to die of a ball," they told trader George Beauvais, "than starve to death."

Thus, by the time the expedition to establish two more forts on the Powder had been organized and dispatched, the Indian situation had changed, and peace was as far away as ever.

Leading the expedition was Col. Henry B. Carrington, a short but handsome Ohioan who had raised a volunteer regiment when the Civil War broke out. A teacher and lawyer by profession, he had been given various administrative tasks that had kept him from battle duty with his regiment throughout the war. When he finally joined the regiment a few months before it was ordered to the Indian country, his junior officers were aware that he was a desk commander. Slight and trim-bearded, sensitive and precise, Carrington did not seem the officer to command an outfit among hostile Indians.

Colonel Carrington's antithesis was his superior at the Omaha headquarters, Brig. Gen. Philip St. George Cooke, who had accompanied Stephen Kearny's expedition through Fort Laramie in 1845, had commanded the Mormon Battalion in its historic march across the plains to the Pacific and back during the Mexican war, had commanded Harney's cavalry in the battle of Ash Hollow and had led the horse column in the Utah expedition in 1857-1858. This grizzled frontiersman knew more about Indian fighting than about "soldier fighting" and had not made a dazzling mark in the Civil War. And, as he sent Carrington out to build posts on the Sioux hunting ground, he was not at all sure that the Little Ohio lawyer could handle the wild Oglala.

In mid-April, Cooke put Colonel Carrington in charge of the new Mountain District—north of the district for which Fort Laramie was headquarters. The new subdivision included Fort Reno, built on the Powder River by General Connor and originally named "Fort Connor." It was north of that post and at the foot of the Big Horn Mountains that Carrington was ordered to establish Fort Phil Kearny (not to be confused with old Fort Kearney on the Platte) and, farther north on the Big Horn River, Fort C. F. Smith.

On May 19, Carrington's column paraded out of old Fort

Kearney and raised dust up the Platte toward Fort Laramie. The long column of some seven hundred infantrymen and cavalrymen was soon dubbed "Carrington's Overland Circus." It was evidence of the army's naïveté that the wives and children of married officers were allowed to accompany the expedition all the way to Powder River. Serving as one of the expedition's two guides was the redoubtable Jim Bridger, who would be able to educate Carrington somewhat while they moved toward the Indian country.

As they rode up the Platte, Carrington's officers began to take his measure. They found him punctilious in observing army regulations, methodical in his attention to details of the march and, most obnoxious of all, wary and respectful of the Indians. His posted orders covered almost every possible contingency that might arise on the trail. He forbade hunting along the way and any departures from the guard limits "except for wood and water," required all mounted men to "carry their rifles by a uniform method," called for order and silence in camp after 9 P.M. and refused to march on the Sabbath. As they neared the Indian deliberations going on at Fort Laramie, he posted another onerous notice: "The pending treaty between the United States and the Sioux Indians at Fort Laramie renders it the duty of every soldier to treat all Indians with kindness. . . . Soldiers will attend to their own duties as soldiers, and all intercourse with Indian lodges or individual Indians . . . will be through headquarters."

Carrington was still en route when the chiefs at the Fort Laramie council heard of his coming. The approach of several hundred fighting men naturally aroused their suspicions. From the fort came Standing Elk, a chief of the Brulé, to determine where the long column of bluecoats was headed. On the evening of June 13, when Carrington was camped four miles below Fort Laramie, Standing Elk came to the Colonel's tent. After the amenities, which included a gift of tobacco from Carrington, the Chief came directly to the point: "Where are you going?"

Carrington told him just as forthrightly that he was going to establish two more forts along the road through the Powder River country. Then Standing Elk gave fair warning: "There is a treaty being made at Laramie with the Sioux that are in the country where you are going. The fighting men in that country have not come to Laramie, and you will have to fight them. They will not give you the road unless you whip them."

For the first time Carrington became aware that his business at Powder River might be more than merely cutting timber and building stockades. The next morning when the column moved out, Carrington himself rode ahead and was met at Fort Laramie by Maynadier and Taylor. But they apparently did not sense the strain his presence imposed on their negotiations. To each of the chiefs assembled in the council they introduced Carrington as the "White Chief going up to occupy Powder River, the Big Horn country, and the Yellowstone."

If Maynadier and Taylor had been making headway with the remaining wild Oglala, the advantage now vanished. Introducing Carrington was the same as saying that the council deliberations were a farce and that the white man was going to occupy Powder River anyway. Carrington noted the obvious recoil of the chiefs. Said one of them, "Great Father sends us presents and wants new road, but white chief goes with soldiers to *steal* road before Indian say yes or no."

In this moment the inexcusable clash of purposes between the Indian Bureau and the army caught up with the white negotiators. The whole mood of the wild Oglala changed. Within a few days, more of them left Fort Laramie for Powder River. They threatened to kill every man who crossed the North Platte. One spokesman warned, "In two moons the command will not have a hoof left." [5]

Taylor's treaty was in a shambles. The only Indians who had ever threatened the Powder River road had walked out on his council. The road was as unsafe as ever for travelers, and with the arrival of Carrington's column a full-scale war was almost inevitable.

But even this defeat did not daunt E. B. Taylor. Shortly after Carrington arrived, the long-awaited wagon train with presents drew into the fort. Part of these gifts Taylor distributed to the Laramie Loafers under Big Mouth and the Brulé under Spotted Tail, Standing Elk and Swift Bear. The rest he carefully reserved for the wild Oglala and other stubborn tribes when they should decide to come back.

Then he proceeded to finish the treaty with the chiefs attending and with a small delegation of Cheyenne. They solemnly agreed to permit travel through the Sioux country, just as though they were the Indians threatening such travel. On June 29, Taylor sent a jubilant telegram to the Commissioner of Indian Affairs in Washington: "Satisfactory Treaty concluded with Sioux & Cheyennes. Large Representation. Most cordial feeling prevails."

Having "given up" the Powder River route, Spotted Tail and his Brulé left Fort Laramie and headed south to hunt buffalo on the Republican. On the way, many of their young men—disgusted with the peace policy of their chiefs—slipped away and rode north to join the wild Oglala in warring on the whites. By the time Spotted Tail had crossed the South Platte, according to one report, his following consisted mostly of women, children and old men. To white friends they met along the way, the chiefs gave the warning. "Go prepared," they cautioned, "and look out for your hair."

To the whites the travesty was equally apparent. No sooner had the treaty been broadcast than frontier veterans began calling it worthless. Back at Omaha with the other commissioners, Taylor was furious. On July 16 he dispatched a telegram to President Andrew Johnson: "Satisfactory treaties of Peace have been concluded with upper Platte Sioux & Cheyennes at Fort Laramie. Contradictory reports are without foundation."

Taylor's claims were not only deceptive but also dangerous. At Fort Laramie, Maynadier's optimistic views led emigrants heading for Montana to take the Bozeman Trail in the belief that it was safe. In parties too small and too lightly armed, they rode unsuspecting into tragedy. Nor was Carrington warned that the treaty was a farce. With wives and children in his party, with enough soldiers for construction but not for battle, with most of them carrying outmoded muzzle-loaders and too little ammunition, the little Colonel rode on to the last hunting ground of the Oglala.

THIRTEEN ◆ *Red Cloud Hunts the Hounds*

◆ 1 ◆

For nearly a month after they left Fort Laramie, Carrington's troops did not see a single Indian. They began to think that the Indian warnings at Fort Laramie had been, as one of them put it, "just a bluff." At Fort Reno, Carrington sent troops in pursuit of warriors who had run off some stock, but they returned empty-handed. In mid-July, they arrived at the two branches of Piney Fork, a tributary of the Powder, and started building Fort Phil Kearny.

Early on the morning of the 17th, Red Cloud and his warriors whirled down upon the Bozeman Trail. They ran off more than 170 animals and tried to surround the troops that gave pursuit. But the soldiers got away with two killed and three wounded. The same day the Sioux killed a trader and five more people in nearby Peno Valley. That night a small wagon train of emigrants bound for the Montana gold fields was massacred.

From then on, the raids were almost continuous. In three weeks, 24 men were killed on the Bozeman Trail. On July 30, Colonel Carrington ordered that all emigrant trains be halted and inspected at Fort Reno and Fort Phil Kearny and allowed to proceed only if there were thirty or more armed men in each party. He sent a rider to Fort Laramie with a message calling for more officers, men and ammunition. From there the message was telegraphed to General Cooke in Omaha. But only a few reinforcements came, and the attacks mounted. As one soldier wrote: "The usual order of the day was to make a forced march to the relief of some immigrant or freight train. In most cases the Indians had taken their toll and gone before we arrived."

214

By the end of summer, every camping ground between Fort Reno and Fort C. F. Smith, the most northerly post established by Carrington on the Big Horn River, had been turned into a burial ground. In September the attacks were more frequent and were carried out by larger war parties. Many of Carrington's horses and mules were stolen, and his wood and hay details were often attacked. Established to protect travelers, Fort Phil Kearny was itself under siege. The foxes had turned on the hounds.

Throughout the summer of 1866, this situation was being under-estimated at Fort Laramie. Colonel Maynadier, who had helped make the treaty, was still convinced it would work. As a result, emigrants leaving Laramie were not sufficiently forewarned and often carried inadequate arms and ammunition. When Indians ran off horses belonging to local traders and even those of the post itself, the pursuing troops were under strict orders not to violate the treaty. "The object of your Expedition," one party was told, "is more to ascertain than to accomplish any good in chasing a few young Indians."

As late as September 10, the Fort Laramie Commander mis-takenly reported: "Col. Carrington is doing well. No trouble on Powder River Road since July. . . . All things are satisfactory on this route and at this Post."

But the situation was deteriorating rapidly as Red Cloud gained new Indian allies. Entrenched in the last buffalo country north of the Platte, he was giving the rest of the Sioux a hard choice: to join him or starve. Even the Brulé Sioux and the northern Cheyenne, who had gone south to hunt buffalo on the Republican, had found poor hunting. Their remaining young men began to break away and join Red Cloud's Bad Faces. Big Mouth of the Laramie Loafers reported that they had seen no buffalo south of the post. Wrote the Indian agent at the fort, "I am besieged on all sides by starving and importunate Indians."

The Post Commander realized the true situation when the treaty chiefs began to come into the fort with their people late in Sep-tember. Spotted Tail, with many lodges of Brulé, joined Big Mouth's Loafer band near Laramie, and asked for beef. He wanted peace and hoped he would not be forced to go into the hostile country. Next came the Cheyenne, who had only sent delegates to the treaty council in June. On October 12, they signed the treaty and were given their presents.

By that time Maynadier had been supplanted by a new post commander at Fort Laramie, Maj. James Van Voast, who shared the army's prevailing dislike of Indians. At first he sent Spotted Tail and Big Mouth away. But soon he was asking his superiors for permission to feed their people "to some extent" to prevent them from joining Red Cloud where the buffalo were abundant. Even hostile Red Leaf, who had been with Red Cloud and had refused to sign the treaty, brought in his Brulé band of Wazhazha to be fed.

From Omaha, E. B. Taylor took up the cry and called for food to be sent to Fort Laramie "as the only means of averting a general war upon the Plains." To these requests, the Indian Commissioner in Washington was initially hostile. At the bottom of one letter from the Fort Laramie commander he scrawled, "Not deemed necessary to be done." But by November, a new Indian Commissioner had taken over and, with winter approaching, he supported the Indians. Taking the case to Edwin M. Stanton, Secretary of War, he asked for provisions from the Commissary General. On November 23, Stanton discussed it with the Secretary of the Interior at a Cabinet meeting. By December 6, the red tape had been cleared away, and Stanton ordered a sizable ration distributed to "destitute Indians at Fort Laramie."

The relief came in time to save several bands from starvation but too late to fulfill Taylor's hope of averting war. When the Cheyenne had come into Fort Laramie in October, they had warned that Red Cloud would shift his attacks to the Oregon Trail during the winter. Almost immediately, the Sioux had descended on the Trail near Fort Laramie, harassing the telegraph stations, running off many horses and trying to burn army haystacks. The Commander strengthened the garrisons at outlying posts and promptly telegraphed Omaha for reinforcements.

"Give such aid as you can to the telegraph operators," he ordered all the noncoms in charge of small patrols on the Trail. ". . . Chastise the Indians if you can do so without too long a pursuit."

The same day—October 10—he telegraphed to Omaha again, asking that one company of relief troops march up each side of the North Platte: "This may save our hay." And again, "If it is possible to hurry up the troops for this Post, I ask that it may be done."

But Red Cloud himself had not actually left Powder River and was hurling his full fury at Fort Phil Kearny. So many young men had joined him from the southern Brulé and Oglala that his camp was said to number one thousand lodges. In addition, he had counseled with the bands of Sioux from the Black Hills and the tributaries of the upper Missouri—especially the Miniconjou and Hunkpapas—and some of them had smoked the war pipe. From their villages on the Tongue River to the north a number of the young men began to join Red Cloud's raiders.

Bolder and stronger war parties began to attack Carrington's post pickets. They were driven off only by howitzer shots from the fort—fired by Carrington himself, the only one in the command able to handle ordnance. Hay and wood parties were attacked and only rescued by relief columns from the fort. Late in September, the Indians drove off a herd of cattle and were pursued by a force of soldiers and civilians under Capt. Fred Brown.

A melodramatic type thirsting for battle with the "redskins," Brown soon had all he could handle. When he caught up with the Indians, they turned and nearly surrounded his party. After some close fighting, Brown's forces killed six of the enemy, whereas only one of his detachment was wounded. Brown returned triumphantly with all the stolen stock, and Carrington reported, "It has inspired my men with new courage."

But from Fort Reno to Fort C. F. Smith, the Bozeman Trail was under siege, and the troops were little more than prisoners in their own stockades. In less than five months, the Indians killed 16 soldiers and 56 civilians, drove off hundreds of animals and made a total of fifty hostile moves against Fort Phil Kearny. As one report stated, they "attacked nearly every train and person that attempted to pass over the Montana road." At Fort Laramie, Van Voast was having difficulty getting anybody to run messages to Carrington: "I don't suppose I could hire a citizen to go to Phil Kearny for any price. My Indians could not be induced to make the trip. The more money offered the more frightened they are."

At that time Carrington had still received only small reinforcements, and they were mostly ill-trained recruits with little or no target practice. At the fort, Carrington kept them so busy constructing buildings that they had no time to learn about fighting Indians. Cavalry troops had no saber practice and little training on horseback. Even at Fort Laramie, Van Voast complained that his cavalry recruits knew nothing about caring for horses: "It is the worst Cavalry I have ever seen . . ."

Despite this problem and a dangerous shortage of ammunition, Van Voast volunteered to lead an offensive against Red Cloud in the winter. As for Carrington, he talked of a winter campaign, and Cooke urged him to prepare for one. But, as Carrington's reports continued to complain of shortages and construction problems, Cooke's impatience mounted. Early in the fall he abolished Carrington's position as commander of the Mountain District and made him simply post commander at Fort Phil Kearny. Then Cooke determined, in his words, "as soon as I well could to relieve him of the command of the Post . . ." Not wanting to put him in charge of Fort Laramie, Cooke shifted Carrington's home regiment from there to Fort Caspar, formerly Platte Bridge Station, and waited for an occasion to transfer the Colonel to that post. On November 12, he again pressured Carrington to take the offensive:

> You are hereby instructed that as soon as the troops and stores are covered from the weather, to turn your earnest attention to the possibility of striking the hostile bands of Indians by surprise in their winter camps. . . . You have a large arrear of murderous and insulting attacks by the savages upon emigrant trains and troops to settle, and you are ordered, if there prove to be any promise of success, to conduct or to send under another officer such an expedition.

Then, to turn the screw tighter, he closed with, "Maj. James Van Voast has volunteered and has been instructed to make such a one in December from Fort Laramie, Dak."

Also pressing Carrington were several younger officers arriving as replacements. Among them was William J. Fetterman, a brevet lieutenant colonel, who arrived in November expecting to supersede Carrington if the latter should be transferred elsewhere. Anxious to win battle honors against the Indians, Fetterman was further inspired by Capt. Fred Brown in his yearning for Sioux scalps. Together they went to Carrington's office with an offer to take one hundred men and "wipe out" the hostile villages on Tongue River. Fetterman was said to have boasted that "a company of regulars could whip a thousand, and a regiment could whip the whole array of hostile tribes." To this boast old Jim Bridger, who was standing with Carrington at the time, gave curt answer: "Your men who fought down South are crazy! They don't know anything about fighting Indians."

When Carrington rejected this wild venture, the officers under him were more convinced than ever that he was too timid. Word reached General Cooke at Omaha that Carrington's officers had no confidence in him, that he was afraid or unable to attack Red Cloud, that he could not maintain discipline at his fort, that he was "jumpy" and took foolish precautions. Cooke's fears were confirmed.

Beside these rumors, Carrington's own reports to Cooke revealed an indecisive and erratic character. He leaped from one subject to another and back again with the air of a man nervous and distracted. One moment he was bombastic, the next cautious. He warned of the dangers along the Bozeman Trail, then declared how safe he had made it. He complained of his weak forces and boasted of his strength. He seemed preoccupied with justifying his every move.

Such reports could hardly inspire Cooke's confidence. Yet it was the very pressure from Omaha for an offensive, when Carrington knew he was too weak, that had helped to unnerve him. Carrington was caught between Red Cloud and Philip St. George Cooke, and his own officers were tightening the vise.

• 2 •

At the same time, Red Cloud was making his own offensive plans. In concert with the Miniconjou, Arapaho and some of the Cheyenne, he planned attacks on both Fort Phil Kearny and Fort C. F. Smith—using the old decoy technique. By this device the Indians meant to achieve a telling victory and drive the white man from their last and best hunting ground.

On December 6, Carrington's woodcutters were about four miles west of the post, inside the bend of Big Piney Creek, when they were attacked by Indians. The Colonel sent Fetterman with a company of infantry and another of cavalry to rescue them and drive the Indians across the creek. He himself took a small force of mounted men across the creek to cut off their retreat. Fetterman's main party attacked the Indians and pressed them back in a running fight. But the enemy had larger numbers and tried to surround the party. Most of the cavalry troops, many of them recruits, panicked and started to flee. Two officers called them back, and some returned when their superiors aimed their guns at them and threatened to shoot.

Meanwhile, Carrington had taken his force over a large hill known as "Lodge Trail Ridge" and had dropped down into Peno (now Prairie Dog) Creek. At that point nearly a hundred Indians suddenly appeared and tried to surround him. At the same time a cavalry officer from Fetterman's main body took some troopers and rode to join him. Together with Carrington's vanguard, part of the force had started to chase some retreating Indians when a larger body of them appeared and encircled the soldiers. An officer and a sergeant were killed; another officer cut his way out with his saber, and an enlisted man rode away only after killing two Indians at arm's length with his revolver.

Hurrying to the scene with the rest of his cavalry, Carrington kept the circling Indians at bay until Fetterman's main force joined him. The Indians then scattered, and the entire force finally returned to the fort with five men wounded. Carrington claimed ten Indians killed, and the engagement may be considered a victory. His wife later wrote, "It is of God's mercy that any one escaped." Fetterman was impressed but not satisfied.

"This Indian war," he acknowledged, "has become a hand-to-hand fight."

It has been claimed that in this skirmish of December 6, Red Cloud tried to spring his trap on Carrington but failed when the Colonel retreated and Fetterman came to his relief. If so, the ambush was poorly planned, for not more than three hundred Indians were engaged altogether—hardly enough for a decisive blow. Carrington's own detachment was never confronted by even a hundred at a time, and they were afraid to charge him. Although Carrington regarded the incident as a stern lesson, it may have added to the eagerness of his fellow officers for a fight. At the same time, it is likely that the December 6 engagement made Red Cloud realize that the decoy trick could work. He therefore tried to gather all the warriors from the Tongue River villages to join in a grand coup.

• 3 •

Up to that time, the "Missouri Sioux" camped with him on the Tongue River (mostly Miniconjou, Hunkpapa and Sans Arc) had not participated as tribes in the attacks, though some of their young men had joined as individuals. But in mid-December one of their old chiefs, White Swan, lay on his deathbed. He had been a principal force in keeping his people at peace, but he called them about him in his lodge and said: "I have tried to keep you from fighting the whites; but now I am going to die. If you want to fight the whites, collect together and go out and satisfy yourselves—fight them once more."

After that he died, and the drama made such an impression on the Missouri Sioux that many of them agreed to go with Red Cloud. Chief among them were the Miniconjou, headed by the war chief High Back Bone and accompanied by some Hunkpapa and Sans Arc. Beside them, in the force that marched south toward Fort Phil Kearny, were Red Cloud's Bad Faces and many other Oglala of Man-Afraid's band (though he, apparently, was not with them), Red Leaf's Wazhazha band and other Brulé who had deserted Spotted Tail, a number of Arapaho joining up without a chief and many northern Cheyenne who were thoroughly hostile since soldiers near the fort had shot at some of them a few days earlier.

On the 19th, Carrington's wood train was attacked again by a small decoy party. Carrington sent out a relief detachment under Capt. James W. Powell, a more cautious officer than his fellows. To Powell, Carrington gave strict orders not to cross Lodge Trail Ridge for fear of a trap. Powell chased the Indians across Piney Creek and escorted the train back to the post. He reported seeing between three hundred and five hundred Indians, but it is possible that the whole force of at least 1,500 was hiding behind Lodge Trail Ridge.

"If I had crossed," Powell observed, "I never would have come back with my command."

Two mornings later—December 21, 1866—the little drama was repeated. About mid-morning the Colonel's picket on a nearby hill reported the wood train under attack on the road that ran south of the creek. Those at the fort heard shots scarcely a mile and a half away. At the same time, other Indians showed themselves where the Bozeman Trail crossed the Big Piney north of the fort. From that distance—about a half-mile away—they shouted taunts to the garrison in English: "You sons of bitches, come out and fight us!"

Carrington shelled them with his howitzer and flushed more from the brush. But this second force was considered only a diversion to keep attention away from the attack on the wood train. Carrington again ordered Captain Powell to take a force and relieve the woodcutters. But, as the two men stood on the parade ground, William Fetterman stepped up and claimed the honor by right of seniority. "If anyone goes except the Colonel," he was heard to say, "I want to go myself."

Carrington agreed, letting him take 49 infantrymen. Lt. George Grummond, an officer whose ardor was scarcely restrained by the presence of his wife at the post, volunteered to command the force of 27 cavalrymen. Two civilians armed with repeating Henry rifles were allowed to go along for the adventure of killing Indians. Capt. Fred Brown, who the night before had declared that he had to have one more Indian scalp before leaving Phil Kearny, rode out of the gate ahead of the troops and later joined them without Carrington's knowledge. Aware of their eagerness for battle, the Colonel made a point of restraining Fetterman: "Under no circumstances pursue over the ridge . . ."

Just as the cavalry was riding out the gate a few minutes behind the infantry, Carrington strode across the parade ground and climbed to the sentry platform at the gate. Halting Lieutenant Grummond and his troopers as they were moving away from the stockade, he repeated his orders in a loud voice and demanded to know whether or not Grummond understood. "I do," came the response, and the column moved out once more.

Instead of taking the wood road south of the Piney toward the wagon train, Fetterman was moving north to the creek. Grummond and the cavalry caught up with him just before he descended into the creek bed. The force then headed northwest up the Piney, with the cavalry on the right flank as skirmishers along the side of Lodge Trail Ridge. Watching through his glass, Carrington thought Fetterman was simply trying to outflank the

Indians attacking the wood train in order to force a fight—"unless," he later wrote, "there was then a purpose to disobey orders."

Seeing the troop movement, the Indians left the wood train and forded the creek quickly enough to get ahead of the troops. Meanwhile, the other Indians at the Piney crossing had pulled back, exchanging a few shots with the passing soldiers. According to some Indian accounts, this party was led by the young Oglala warrior Crazy Horse. The Indians rode up and over the top of Lodge Trail Ridge, heading north toward Peno Valley.

At that point, Fetterman apparently realized that he could not catch the fleeing party that had left the wood train and decided to go after the other group led by Crazy Horse. Countermarching, he crossed Big Piney Creek at the regular ford of the Bozeman Trail and marched up the road, which led northward through a saddle just east of Lodge Trail Ridge. This movement was not noticed by Carrington, who had left his observation spot on the roof of his headquarters, but it was observed by others at the fort.

It is difficult to believe that Fetterman and his fellow officers did not recognize that Crazy Horse's party was a decoy. The encounters of December 6 and 19 had been of the same pattern and had been thoroughly discussed throughout the garrison. Fetterman, Grummond and Brown had all been involved in the engagement of the 6th. But the Indians they had seen on that day—numbering more than in any previous skirmish—had still not been strong enough to make a wholesale attack. When the officers marched out on the morning of the 21st they may have believed, as one of their fellows observed, "There are not enough Indians in the country to kill the men." Having failed for several months to force a real fight on their own terms, the officers may have decided to have one on Indian terms.

Still following the decoys, Fetterman took his command over the gap east of Lodge Trail, moving along a ridge to the north and exchanging scattered shots with the retreating Indians. Then he followed the road along the crest of the ridge that flanks the headwaters of Peno Creek on the east. The cavalry moved along the north end of this ridge, where Indian warriors were lying in the grass on both slopes—mounted Cheyenne and Arapaho on the west, dismounted Sioux in a little flatland on the east. Behind them, hidden by rocks, more mounted

Sioux were waiting. The Indian force was later estimated by Carrington to number three thousand, but eyewitness accounts put it at 1,500 to 1,800. Whether or not Red Cloud was among the warriors has been disputed even among the Indian accounts. However, two Indian reports made shortly afterward state that he was present, though he was probably not in over-all command.

The ridge along which Fetterman was pursuing the decoy party was in two sections, the more northerly being smaller and lower. As he crossed the gap between them with his infantry, Grummond's cavalrymen were about a mile ahead, where the ridge made its final descent to Peno Creek. At that moment, the Indian decoy party crossed the creek. The entire command was well within the trap.

At a signal, all the waiting Indians rose up and ran for the soldiers—the air resounding with their hideous war whoops. In that appalling moment Fetterman's infantry rushed to some nearby rocks. There, arraying themselves in a circle, they took what shelter they could and fired at their attackers.

The cavalry, caught so far from the main body, wheeled in panic. About half a dozen veterans, including the two civilians, recognized that retreat meant death. Dismounting, they threw themselves on the ground and fired at the oncoming horde. The cavalrymen were armed with seven-shot Spencers, the frontiersmen each with a sixteen-shot Henry—the forerunner of the Winchester. These new repeaters surprised the Indians with their fire power and drove back the first onslaught.

But the cavalrymen forfeited their own hopes for safety by retreating and were themselves the targets for hundreds of arrows. Half were cut down as they rode, their bodies strewn along the ridge road between the two beleaguered forces. Lieutenant Grummond was within two hundred yards of the infantry when he pitched from the saddle. Not more than fifteen cavalrymen reached the infantry.

Despite the overwhelming numbers against it, the main force at the rocks turned back the Indians in the first charge. According to one Indian account, two savages rode right through the troops and were killed. Others came in very close and were sent back by the fire. But the infantry was armed only with the single-shot, muzzle-loading Springfield rifled musket. To compensate for the slowness in loading and shooting, Fetterman used the Civil War tactic of firing by alternating ranks—one shooting while the other reloaded. But the terrible strength of the Indian numbers rattled the soldiers, some of whom were comparatively new recruits. Many shots were wasted at long range; others went wide of their marks.

At the beginning of the battle, just before noon, the sound of Fetterman's musketry was distinctly heard back at the fort four miles away. From a lookout post on a roof, Carrington searched with his glass but could see nothing. The assistant post surgeon, who had been sent out to join the command, returned and announced that Fetterman had gone beyond Lodge Trail Ridge.

From the rapid firing, Carrington knew that the command was in trouble. He called out the guard, ordered all unarmed soldiers to get guns from the magazine and had teams hitched to the wagons and ambulances. In a moment, the parade ground was in pandemonium—sergeants calling orders, men and horses running into positions. Carrington came down from the roof and inspected the men, rejecting those who had insufficient ammunition. In a few minutes, Capt. Tenodor Ten Eyck was on his way at the head of thirty cavalrymen with orders to find and reinforce Fetterman. Shortly afterward, he was followed by the wagons and ambulances, carrying rifle ammunition and forty more men—mostly civilians.

From beyond Lodge Trail Ridge the firing had died down for a short time (probably after the first repulses), then had flared again into what Carrington called "very brisk firing, apparently by file at first, and quite regular, and an occasional volley, followed by indiscriminate firing, gradually dying out in a few scattered shots." In his words, "I became apprehensive of disaster." But to those about him he could not confide his worst fears. When the shots faded he told them, "That means that Fetterman has killed or repulsed them all, or they are accumulating for a rush."

On the ridge near Peno Creek, Fetterman and his men were holding off their attackers with volleys of lead. Practically all the firing heard at the fort was by the soldiers; nearly all the Indians were armed with bows and arrows, spears and war clubs, though a few also had revolvers. The troops had only 2,800 rounds of ammunition, and some had fired all they had. Yet, with all the shooting, comparatively few warriors had been killed.

Indian accounts put their own battlefield losses at between seven and eleven (ten being the most likely), and a number of others later died of their wounds.[6]

As for the troops, the main body of about 65 soldiers was huddled behind rocks in a space not more than fifteen yards across. This made a mass target for clouds of arrows released by an enemy taking partial cover in the grass. Before they ran out of ammunition, almost all of the soldiers had been wounded and were nearly helpless. In separate rushes on the two clumps of defenders, the Indians overran their victims and killed them all with clubs. As they were finishing their bloody work, one of the soldiers' pet dogs ran away, barking. "All are dead but the dog," called one of the Indians. "Let him carry the news to the fort."

"No," answered another, "do not let even a dog get away." With that a young warrior dispatched it with an arrow.

Then they turned their attention to the mutilation that always accompanied an Indian victory—the purpose being to deprive the dead of limbs and organs that they would need in the land of the Great Spirit. Scalping was only the beginning; they stripped the bodies, shot more arrows into them, used the soldiers' own sabers to cut them up savagely and took the guns and again shot into the bodies. Carrington later reported that both Brown and Fetterman had been killed with bullets in the temples and assumed that they had committed double suicide to keep from being butchered by the Indians. But the post surgeon examining the bodies stated unequivocally that only Brown had died from a gunshot. Fetterman, he said, was terribly slashed: "I believe that mutilation caused his death."

Jogging in double-quick time, Captain Ten Eyck's relief soldiers hurried across Big Piney Creek. They were straggling up the Bozeman Trail beyond it when the sound of heavy firing died down. As they passed along the shallow divide on the way to the large ridge, one of them thought he heard screams and groans. From the top of the main ridge, they could see nothing of Fetterman's command. But at the point of rocks where the main Fetterman force actually lay, Ten Eyck saw at least a hundred Indians milling about.

At first the troops thought the scattered shots they heard were from Fetterman's men, still fighting somewhere out of sight. But the Indians were simply shooting the guns while finishing up their grisly work of mutilation. When they saw Ten Eyck's party, they began hollering and gesturing, taunting the soldiers to come down and fight. But the astounded Ten Eyck could see hundreds of other Indians—on the ridge beyond the first group, down in the valley of Peno Creek and across on the opposite buttes. Some of them were so excited from the heat of battle that they were dashing their horses over the Peno Valley, up and down the slopes, as though repeating the drama.

Ten Eyck had never seen so many Indians in his life. He estimated them at "not less than 1500 and I think over 2000." Back to Carrington he sent a messenger for reinforcements.

Riding past the wagon party already on its way with ammunition, the courier pounded into the fort and reported to the Colonel.

"The Captain says he can see or hear nothing of Fetterman but the Indians are on the road challenging him to come down, and large bodies are in all the valleys several miles around. He would like to have you send artillery, if you can." Then he added, "Captain is afraid Fetterman's party is all gone up."

Quickly writing an answer, Carrington gave his own thoroughbred horse to the messenger for the return trip. A while later the courier reached Ten Eyck with the message. Part of it read, "You must unite with Fetterman, fire slowly, and keep men in hand; you could have saved two miles towards the scene of action if you had taken Lodge Trail Ridge."

That Ten Eyck delayed his rescue by a roundabout route has since been the subject of controversy. But when Carrington wrote his message he did not know where the "scene of action" was and apparently believed it to be just over Lodge Trail Ridge. He thought that Fetterman had gone over or around the north end of Lodge Trail Ridge into Peno Valley, when actually Ten Eyck and others knew he had taken the Bozeman Trail. In following Fetterman's route, Ten Eyck certainly reached the actual scene as quickly by the road as if he had tried to flounder through the ravines and snow banks of Lodge Trail.

Technically, Fetterman had not disobeyed Carrington's order against going over Lodge Trail, but he had violated the spirit of it by going past Lodge Trail by the road to a point more than four miles from the post. At the same time, Carrington was wrong in ordering Ten Eyck out with thirty men to "unite with Fetterman."

Had Ten Eyck done so before the battle was over, he would have
met the same fate as his comrades.

As it was, he moved his command closer to the cluster of Indians, firing at them. Though most of them dispersed, he was expecting an attack momentarily from the others in Peno Valley.
Then, as he moved down the main ridge to the smaller one, Ten
Eyck discovered the terrible truth. One of the soldiers, scouting
ahead, reported, "There are the men down there, all dead."

Not until the forty men arrived with the wagonloads of ammunition did the Indians begin to leave the valley. Probably they believed that the wagons were artillery—the dreaded "guns that
shoot twice." As soon as the wagons came up, Ten Eyck ordered
them down to the battlefield. There the sickening sight awaited
them—not even a flicker of life except, lying in some bushes to the
right of the main pile of bodies, a gray horse whom the troopers
recognized as "Dapple Dave." Shot with arrow and bullet, he was
"not quite dead." [7]

• 4 •

Forty-nine bodies were piled on the wagons, and the pathetic procession returned to the fort about sundown. There the
consternation—among women, children and surviving soldiers—
was overwhelming. The worst fears were that the Indians would
invest the stockade. Carrington gave orders to build another stockade around the powder magazine; food and water were placed
inside, so that if the Indians invaded the fort the women and
children could be defended in the magazine. If the Indians entered
it as well, the magazine could be blown up, saving all from capture
and torture, at least.

Carrington next turned to the quest for reinforcements. The
garrison was desperately weakened and low on ammunition. If
he could get a message to General Cooke at Omaha, reinforcements could be sent from Fort Laramie. Certainly if Van Voast
had enough strength to talk of a winter offensive, he could spare
it now. Much closer was Fort Reno, under the command of Lt.
Col. (Bvt. Brig. Gen.) Henry W. Wessells, and he might spare
some troops. But orders for such movements could only come
from General Cooke, who in turn had to be reached by the tele-

graph at Horseshoe Creek Station, or failing that, at Fort Laramie. Somebody would have to ride nearly 200 miles to Horseshoe, or the full 236 miles to Fort Laramie, past hostile Indians, through snow, bitter cold and what would soon be a mountain blizzard.

In the emergency, Carrington hired two civilian couriers to take the message. All that we know of one of them—Daniel Dixon—is that he was later paid for his ride. The other was John "Portugee" Phillips, whose anglicized name seemed incongruous with his Portuguese accent. Born in the Azores, he had sailed to California and had joined the rush to the Montana gold fields in the mid-Sixties. He was now a wagon driver in Carrington's wood train—a tall, dark-bearded frontiersman who had seen plenty of Indian action around Fort Phil Kearny. His derring-do had been demonstrated earlier that day when he had accompanied the surgeon trying to catch up with Fetterman, and he also had gone out with Ten Eyck's relief party.

Hurriedly, Carrington scribbled his dispatch—a long and curious telegram, beginning not with news of the massacre but with distraught pleas showing his overwhelming concern at the pressures of his mission at Phil Kearny: "Do send me reinforcements forth with. Expedition now with my force is impossible. I risk everything but the post and its stores. I venture as much as any one can but I have today a fight unexampled in Indian warfare."

Then, without explaining how the fight had occurred, he gave details on the losses and the size of the Indian force. He jumped from determination ("This line so important can and must be held") to a plea for reinforcements and arms, finally ending:

Promptness will save the line but our killed show that any remissness will result in mutilation & butchery beyond precedent. No such mutilation as that today is on record. Depend upon it that this post will be held so long as a round or a man is left. Promptness is the vital thing. Give me Officers & men, only the new Spencer arms should be sent. The Indians are desperate—I spare none & they spare none.

With the telegram to Cooke he enclosed another to Gen. Ulysses S. Grant in Washington: "I want all my officers. I want men."

Late on the 21st, Phillips was ready to go. He wore a massive overcoat made of a buffalo robe, heavy gauntlets on his hands and a cap to cover his head in the biting cold. In his pockets he placed a few biscuits and on his saddle a small amount of grain for the horse.

One soldier at the fort later wrote, "We never expected to see him again . . ." According to another account, Carrington walked with Phillips to one of the gates, had it unlocked by the guard and stood talking for a minute or two. Then Phillips swung into the saddle. Carrington shook his hand and added a few more words, ending with "May God help you."

Horse and rider whirled and were away at a trot. For half a minute Carrington listened at the gate, then straightened and muttered, "Good—he has taken softer ground at the side of the trail."

That was the way Phillips rode south—off the road in the danger areas and away from the crossings where the enemy might lie in wait. He is supposed to have said later that he was as much as ten miles off the road. Phillips and Carrington both knew that the Indians would be waiting to ambush any messenger seeking outside help. As Carrington himself later wrote, "Previous mail parties and another party of expert border scouts which left later were scalped, and their bodies and the mails were found on the ground where they were overpowered."

Riding only at night, Phillips would break into a thicket just before dawn and rest during the day. Then by darkness he would press on through snow and sleet, with the temperature as low as 25 degrees below zero. It was in the night that he reached Fort Reno, rode up to the gate and was challenged by the sentry.

"Scout with message," shouted Phillips.

Once inside, he swung off his horse and showed the dispatch to the commanding officer, Brevet Brigadier General Wessells. To the questions raised by Carrington's obscure message, Phillips gave answers. Evidently realizing that the dispatch lacked adequate information about the tragedy, Wessells wrote another, stating among other things that Fetterman's command had been massacred to the last man. Phillips was ordered to carry this message beyond Horseshoe Creek Station another forty miles to Brigadier General Innis N. Palmer at Fort Laramie.

After he had rested and fed his horse, Phillips was pounding southward again, floundering through snow sometimes five feet deep. Crossing the frozen North Platte at Bridger's Ferry, he pulled up at Horse Shoe Creek Station. According to some accounts, two to four other men were with him when he arrived. Here he wired Carrington's messages to General Cooke in Omaha and to General Grant in Washington. Then he took the trail again to deliver Wessells' message to Palmer at Fort Laramie.

After a four-day ride from Fort Phil Kearny through a merciless blizzard, Phillips rode into Fort Laramie on Christmas night. A holiday ball was in full swing at the bachelor officers' quarters, "Old Bedlam," when his horse staggered into the parade ground at about 11 p.m. Challenged by the guard, Phillips asked to see the General and was informed that he was at the ball. There bright lights and music from the orchestra told of an evening's gaiety. Guided by a soldier, Phillips stomped into the party room—a huge specter bringing with him a blast of the cold outside. In his buffalo overcoat and his snow cap he was a rude intruder in that room full of smartly uniformed officers and their fashionable ladies. He asked for General Palmer and, upon finding him, handed him Wessells' message. The veteran officer, shocked by the magnitude of the tragedy at Phil Kearny, questioned Phillips for further details.[8]

The officers were about to choose partners for the next dance when the first of them received word that General Palmer wanted to see him. Soon the disaster was known to the guests and to all the garrison, casting a terrible gloom on the holiday season.

Early in the morning of December 26, a telegram from Palmer was wired from Fort Laramie to General Cooke in Omaha. There the old Indian fighter, apparently having received Carrington's message from Horseshoe as well, acted swiftly. To Palmer at Fort Laramie he wired orders to send two companies of cavalry and four of infantry to the relief of Fort Phil Kearny. When they reached Fort Reno, General Wessells was to "proceed with the reinforcements and assume command of Fort Phil Kearny." Carrington was to be relieved of the command and ordered to take charge of Fort Caspar. Cook had found his "occasion" to get Carrington out of the firing line.

Then next day Palmer wired back from Fort Laramie, "The most violent, blinding storm now raging; there would be nothing gained by moving in such a snow storm; meantime all preparations which can be made in-doors are going on."

For the next few days, while the storm paralyzed Indians and soldiers alike in the war zone, the rest of the nation heard the story through the newspapers. With no details yet from the Powder River country, the wildest exaggerations were credited from so-called "eyewitnesses." Fetterman's command was said to have been slaughtered while pounding at Carrington's gates pleading vainly to be admitted to the fort. Most astounding of all, the Indian Commissioner in Washington soon wrote that the Indians "were on a friendly visit to the fort" when Carrington sent out a force against them: "I regret the unfortunate death of so many brave soldiers, yet there can be no doubt that it is owing to the foolish and rash management of the officer in command at that post."

Carrington was, therefore, under fire for doing both too little and too much—by people hundreds of miles away who did not or would not understand his real predicament. Along the border and in pockets of settlement in Colorado and Montana, the massacre provided new ammunition for public clamor that the Indians be punished. The most radical reaction of all came from Gen. William Tecumseh Sherman, who wired General Grant from St. Louis: "We must act with vindictive earnestness against the Sioux, even to their extermination, men, women, and children. Nothing less will reach the root of the case."

At Fort Laramie, the snowstorm raged into the new year, with the temperature at 23.5 degrees below zero. As Palmer wrote, "No man or beast exposed to the storms could live." But on January 2, 1867, the weather subsided a little, and the next day part of the two cavalry companies plodded out of Fort Laramie into a world of white. It was followed by four companies of infantry, commanded by Maj. James Van Voast, and by the rest of the cavalry two days later—a total of more than four hundred well-armed troops. Reported General Palmer apologetically, "They left just as soon as intense cold and snow permitted."

The peaceful Oglala and Brulé camped outside the fort watched them go; at first, Palmer was afraid that his weakened garrison would be attacked. But at worst some of the Laramie Indians were simply spies for the hostiles and sent warnings that the expected rescue column was on its way. Indeed, messengers from the warring bands had arrived among the Laramie Indians before Portugee Phillips had come in, and rumors of a fight had been transmitted to the post through some half-breed interpreters. The Sioux messengers told the Indian agent near Fort Laramie that the hostiles expected an avenging army to come after them. They would be ready for them, was their boast, and they "will stake everything for one big fight. . . . a mighty last effort to keep one hunting ground."

"This is their last flicker," Palmer wrote Cooke as his relief column prepared to leave, "but they will take many a good fellow with them as their power goes out forever."

FOURTEEN ◆ *A Time for War . . .*

◆ 1 ◆

With the road completely covered in snow up to six feet deep, the march of the Phil Kearny relief was one of the most heroic in army annals. Taking the lead to break trail for the infantry, the cavalry would push through in file for a short distance, then turn and countermarch back over the same section to tramp down the snow. The infantry would follow after it to the next stopping place. In many spots the snow had to be shoveled to make a trail for the men and wagons.

Although the troops had hay enough for ten days, it gave out not long after they passed Fort Reno. With all forage covered by snow, the poor animals were frantic from hunger. Many broke their halter ropes at night and went in search of grass, and others ate the wood of wagon tongues and feed troughs or bit at the manes and tails of their fellows. Drinking water was almost impossible to find, as the streams were frozen to the bottoms except in the deeper holes. There the soldiers hacked through the ice and brought water in buckets to the mules and horses. Many of the men were frostbitten, and one froze to death. Through it all went two officers' wives accompaning their husbands on the expedition, facing not only cold and hunger but also possible Indian attack.

After a thirteen-day tramp, the miserable column staggered through the gates at Fort Phil Kearny. Lieutenant Grummond's widow later wrote, "I could have hugged every half-frozen man as he entered . . ."

At that time, the Indians were camped in their Tongue River stronghold and had no intention of making another winter sortie. Nor was Phil Kearny's new commander, General Wessells, ready

234

to mount an avenging campaign. He had, in fact, been ordered by Cooke to exercise "great caution." And he found the garrison in a pitiable condition—no wood for heat except green cottonwood branches and almost no vegetables to prevent the scurvy that was crowding the post hospital with victims. Wrote one officer, "it was almost a question with some of the soldiers whether it would be best to die by scurvy or be scalped by the Indians."

Nor did the relief column offer much help in these straits. As there was no feed for the horses or mules, the arrival of more animals simply compounded the problem. "Their arrival," wrote one soldier, "made our conditions, if anything, worse . . ." Desperate, Wessells had to turn the mules outside to forage as best they could. To save the cavalry horses, numbering some 150, he sent them back with a small detachment to Fort Laramie. The troops arrived safely but without the horses, whose carcasses marked the Bozeman Trail for years afterward.

As for Carrington, his orders directing him to take the command at Fort Caspar arrived with Wessells' relief column. In the teeth of another snowfall, he and his escort filed out of the fort he had built and defended. On the bitter march south the thermometer reached 38 degrees below zero, and in places the snow had to be cleared with shovels. Several soldiers had limbs or fingers frozen, and amputations had to be performed when the party trudged into Fort Reno. Among the women accompanying the column in a springless wagon was Mrs. Grummond, who was several months pregnant.

Carrington pulled into Fort Caspar only to find orders transferring him to Fort McPherson on the Oregon Trail east of Fort Laramie. And, while the forlorn caravan was retracing part of its route down the North Platte, Carrington accidentally shot himself in the thigh and had to be hospitalized at Fort Laramie for two weeks. Everything was going against him until February, when President Andrew Johnson appointed a six-man Special Commission to investigate the Fetterman massacre. Headed by Gen. Alfred Sully, who had conducted a campaign against the Sioux in the Yellowstone country, it consisted of three high-ranking officers and three civilians, including the veteran Indian trader, George Beauvais.

Starting in Omaha, they moved up the Oregon Trail to Fort Laramie, taking testimony from officers as they went. At Fort

McPherson they met with Colonel Carrington and received from him a wealth of evidence organized with his usual precision. From Fort Laramie one of the commissioners ventured up the Bozeman Trail to Fort Phil Kearny, escorted by troops and personally armed with several Winchester rifles. On the way, as he modestly reported, "nothing of importance occurred en route with the exception of the appearance of hostile Indians on two different occasions . . ." At Phil Kearny he took more testimony from officers. Although the commissioners disagreed on how to handle the Indians, there was apparently no disagreement on Carrington's conduct at Phil Kearny:

> The difficulty "in a nutshell" was that the commanding officer of the district was furnished no more troops or supplies for this state of war than had been provided and furnished him for a state of profound peace.
> In regions where all was peace, as at Laramie in November, twelve companies were stationed, while in regions where all was war, as at Phil Kearny, there were only five companies allowed.

Thus the blame really fell on General Cooke, who had been so quick to penalize Carrington. Cooke had, in fact, already been replaced as head of the Platte Department. Years later he wrote Carrington an apology: "I can do nothing more now than to express my deep pain at what transpired . . . you must take my regrets as sincere, and my congratulations, that in the end you were fully vindicated."

As for their other duty—to explore ways of bringing peace—the commissioners met with Indians at various points on the Oregon Trail as they journeyed to Fort Laramie in April 1867. The big prize was Red Cloud; from Fort McPherson they sent a message via telegraph to Fort Laramie and from there by Indian runner through the Powder River country. Drawn up in proper form according to the white man's ways, it is a classic example of the naïveté with which white peace commissioners approached the Indian problem:

> Chief Red Cloud
> Oglala Sioux
> Tongue River
> The Commission from the President of the United States, wish to learn from you why you are making war.
> Your course will compel him to Send his Soldiers into your

country in great numbers, and destroy your game, kill your warriors, and punish your people.

Do you wish to Send any word, or Say anything to us? Your
messenger will be Safe to return.

Send any answer you make, either to Fort Phil Kearny, or
C. F. Smith.

When the message and its accompanying present of tobacco
arrived among the Indians on the Tongue River, Red Cloud would
have nothing to do with it. But other leaders gathered in Red
Leaf's lodge and divided the tobacco. Old Man-Afraid-of-His
Horses announced that he would go and meet the commissioners.
"I now want to close the War," he said. "I want powder, lead, and
provisions."

Accordingly, Man-Afraid and Red Leaf brought some three
hundred Oglala and Brulé warriors into Fort Laramie on June 11.
There they met with the commission, as well as with Spotted Tail
of the southern Brulé and Big Mouth of the Laramie Loafers, who
next day gave speeches urging the others to make peace. In his
turn, Man-Afraid also spoke in favor of peace—and then asked
for provisions and ammunition. The former he was granted by the
whites, but they were shrewd enough to deny the Indians any
powder and lead. This denial hardly deterred old Man-Afraid,
who simply went back across the Platte and bartered with the
Fort Laramie traders for ammunition. Signing nothing, he returned to the camps on the Tongue in triumph.[9]

But, according to one source, Red Cloud and his irreconcilable
Bad Faces accused Man-Afraid of trafficking with the whites. The
two Oglala factions worked themselves into a fight in which
horses were killed, property destroyed and a few warriors
wounded. The result was to impress on the commissioners the
impossibility of making peace while the military forts remained
on the Bozeman Trail. As George Beauvais wrote, "they have
gone, and are now carrying on this war, for the purpose of averting
the death and destruction of their race by famine."

The commissioners therefore reported that the Powder River
should be given up to the Indians and that completion of the
Union Pacific Railroad would soon yield a shorter route to Montana anyway. Their recommendation was, in short, to let Red
Cloud win his war. To subdue the combined tribes, they wrote,
would require 25,000 men, five to ten years and $3-400,000,000.

• 2 •

For his part, Red Cloud was doing his best to prove them right. His warriors continued to harass Forts Reno, Phil Kearny, and C. F. Smith, bringing all travel to a halt on the Bozeman Trail. In a dozen engagements during 1867, they killed twenty men, wounded five and captured six.

In July the hostile Indians held their Sun Dance on Powder River and then made plans for another big attack on the order of the Fetterman battle. As they could not agree on which fort to strike, the Cheyenne and a few Sioux moved against Fort C. F. Smith, and Red Cloud's forces advanced on Fort Phil Kearny.

On August 1, citizens and soldiers were cutting hay near the northern fort when the Indians swept down upon them. The whites scurried to a willow-branch breastwork they had previously built for such an emergency. Firing breechloading and repeating rifles, they held off the attackers, with a loss of two soldiers and one civilian. The Cheyenne finally withdrew with the bodies of about eight killed and as many as thirty wounded.

Next day about one thousand Sioux gathered once again along the Little Piney. The woodcutting troops under Capt. James Powell were at work on the wood road. As at C. F. Smith, they were prepared with a little enclosure made of wagon boxes on the hillside. At first, the Indians decided to threaten the wood-cutters with a small force in order to decoy more troops out of the fort. But the braves were too eager and rushed out of their hiding places, exposing the real size of Red Cloud's force.

In the first charge, the Indians killed several men in the wood camp, but most of them escaped to the fort or to the wagon-box barricade. With little more than thirty men, Captain Powell faced about one thousand Sioux warriors. Expecting that the troops would have to reload muzzle-loaders after the first fire, the Indians charged headlong up the hill. But Powell's men had new single-shot breech-loaders; with boxes full of cartridges at firing positions inside the corral, they kept up a continuous volley.

Surprised at this murderous fire, the Indians fell back and dis-mounted. Then they tried again and again to attack the little barricade on foot. Powell's men repulsed them every time. Finally a rescue party came out of the fort. By that time, as in the Fetterman battle, the Indians were tired of fighting and withdrew. Powell—never a man to minimize his own accomplishments—reported about sixty Indians killed and twice that many wounded. But the Sioux later admitted only six dead and six injured. The whites lost six killed and two wounded—mostly in the first attack on the wood camp.

Although Red Cloud's plan had failed, he was substantiating the commissioners' report that a long and costly war would be necessary to clear the Powder River. From the Platte Valley came new evidence that war against the Indians was not bringing peace. Army campaigns south of the Platte were arousing retaliation by the Cheyenne, Sioux and Arapaho against the Union Pacific Railroad. Now almost across Nebraska, the U. P. was heading for a transcontinental connection at Salt Lake with the Central Pacific from California. But in two raids a hundred miles apart on May 25, 1867, the Indians killed nine railroad hands in western Nebraska.

In charge of U. P. construction was their old enemy, Gen. Grenville M. Dodge, who witnessed another attack the same day and roared, "We've got to clear the damn Indians out or give up building the Union Pacific Railroad." Cavalry, infantry and four companies of Pawnee scouts were rushed from Fort Kearny to the surveying parties beyond the end-of-track. But in June and July the Sioux jumped two isolated groups in what would soon be Wyoming Territory and killed their leaders. On August 6 a band of Cheyenne blocked the track beyond Plum Creek Station, Nebraska; killed five trainmen on a handcar; derailed a locomotive, and killed the engineer and fireman. Wrote Dodge, "I believe I shall get through to Salt Lake if Indians do not kill off all my party."

• 3 •

Such was the situation in the Sioux country when Congress took up the commission's recommendations for peace in the summer of 1867. In the stormy debate, frontier representatives called for a new campaign against the Indians. But Congress created still another commission "to establish peace with certain hostile Indian tribes." As a concession to the western war hawks, it added that, if the commission failed, the President could send four cavalry regiments against the Indians.

To fill the eight-man commission President Johnson appointed a banner group of notables, including Gen. W. T. Sherman, Gen. Alfred H. Terry and John B. Sanborn, who had also been on the earlier commission investigating the Fetterman massacre. The new group was headed by the Commissioner of Indian Affairs, N. G. Taylor, a former Methodist minister who was thoroughly sympathetic with the Indians' plight.

Surprisingly, he was joined in this attitude by the most colorful member of the commission, none other than Gen. William S. Harney, the wasp who had punished the Sioux so severely at Ash Hollow in 1855. After having spent most of his life on Indian frontiers north, south and west, Harney represented the true officer's sense of fair play. During the negotiations that followed, he agreed with a chief who said that "the palefaces have done wrong as well as the Indians." Declared the old General, "That's so, the Indians are a great deal better than we are."

On the same day that the Cheyenne wrecked the train near Plum Creek, the peace commission gathered at St. Louis and elected N. G. Taylor its president. Then it called upon the veteran trader, George Beauvais, to make contact with Red Cloud and Man-Afraid and to invite them to meet the commissioners at Fort Laramie. Three sets of couriers were sent from Fort Laramie to the Powder River, and three times they failed to attract more than a handful of leaderless Indians.

Nor was peace promoted when a new Laramie commander exhibited the same hostility toward Indians that other officers had been showing for years. When the largest group of 33 warriors came in on October 14, Beauvais invited them to his room and asked the commander to attend. But the latter replied, "I have nothing to say to them." Next morning three soldiers shot at two of the visiting Indians, though without hurting them. When Beauvais complained to the commanding officer, his words were ignored. Insulted by this treatment, the delegation was still prevailed upon by Beauvais to send three men back with presents to induce Man-Afraid and Red Leaf to come in (no one would promise to bring in Red Cloud).

While the wild Oglala stalled, the commissioners were busy

making peace with other tribes. On September 19, at the railroad town of North Platte, they met with some of the friendly Sioux chiefs—Big Mouth of the Oglala Loafer band and Spotted Tail, Standing Elk and Swift Bear of the Brulé. But also present were some wild Oglala headed by Man-Afraid-of-His-Horses. Swift Bear had promised the hostile Indians that, if they would come in and make peace, the commissioners would give them ammunition. But the commissioners had not authorized the promise; they had seen enough ammunition given to the Indians—ostensibly to hunt game—that had instead been used against the whites.

When the council began in a large lodge, all the chiefs demanded that the whites abandon the Powder River and Smoky Hill routes—the last good buffalo hunting grounds north and south of the Platte. At the same time Pawnee Killer, one of the most belligerent chiefs present, reminded the commissioners of Swift Bear's promise: "If you tell the truth you ought to be able to furnish us with ammunition."

Next day General Sherman answered for the commission. He refused the Indians any ammunition and instead told them to settle down on a reservation and become farmers. But, if they continued fighting, "we are ordered to make war upon you . . ."

When Sherman and the other commissioners had given their ultimatum, the chiefs responded with stony faces. Nothing was heard in the council lodge save the inhaling of the chiefs as they passed the peace pipe. Then they whispered among themselves. Swift Bear, embarrassed by the hard line of the commissioners, rose and replied: "I thought I brought the red men here to make peace. . . . You have made me tell a lie. . . . I thought you would take pity upon them, and give them powder and ball."

Another Oglala chief stood up and added: "I am poor. You are rich. When you come to our villages we always share with you. . . . I cannot make powder nor can I make ball. . . . I was raised upon buffalo meat. I want to live upon it."

Then the commissioners deliberated while the chiefs—partly ashamed for having begged—waited. Harney wanted to give the Indians ammunition, but Sherman objected. While they talked, Chief Pawnee Killer sickened at the degrading position of his fellows. Stepping to the flap of the lodge, he threw it back and went out. Then he stalked to his own lodge, where he daubed his face with war paint. Bursting out, he leaped to his horse and

rode off toward the Powder River country. Silently several other
chiefs followed him out of the lodge and out of North Platte.
There remained only the friendly Brulé and Laramie Oglala.
The commissioners agreed to give them ammunition.

• 4 •

After holding other councils with tribes south of the Platte,
the commissioners went to Fort Laramie, hoping that Red Cloud
and the other hostile chiefs would relent and meet them there.
But when the commissioners arrived on November 10, there were
only a few Sioux and a message from Red Cloud. Withdraw all
troops from the Bozeman Trail, he demanded, "and then only will
we make peace." The commissioners had to content themselves
with meeting a delegation of Crow Indians, who had always
been friendly with the white man.

With no hope of catching Red Cloud the commissioners ad-
journed to Washington and came back to Fort Laramie in April
1868 with the full text of a treaty. It agreed that the Powder River
country was "unceded Indian territory" where white men could
not settle or even pass without Indian permission. But it also
called upon the Sioux and Cheyenne to go on a huge reservation—
all of what is now South Dakota west of the Missouri River. On
April 29, Spotted Tail, Red Leaf and other Brulé chiefs "touched
the pen"; most of them then went south to hunt buffalo on the
Republican River. In May some chiefs of the northern Cheyenne
and Arapaho signed a similar treaty of their own. On May 25
Man-Afraid and other Oglala signed, followed by One Horn and
the Miniconjou next day. But Red Cloud sent word that the Bad
Faces and Hunkpapa would only come in "as soon as the posts in
the Powder river country are abandoned by the troops . . ."

By that time the commissioners were already on their way up
the Missouri River to Fort Rice, which had been built four years
before a few miles above the mouth of the Cannonball River.
Preceding them was Father Pierre-Jean de Smet, who had been
helping to promote Indian councils since the Fort Laramie treaty
of 1851. From Fort Rice he journeyed to the main camp of the
wild Sioux near the mouth of the Powder River. Then he returned
with a small delegation to Fort Rice. There on June 2 the council

was held with thousands of other upper Missouri Sioux, including the Yankton, Cuthead, Two Kettle, Sans Arc, Santee and Blackfeet Sioux. Father De Smet called it "the greatest council that had been held on the Missouri in fifty years."

But the delegation sent by the wild Sioux of the Powder River was not authorized to sign for the tribe. It returned and told the chiefs about the terms of the treaty, but, despite Father De Smet's remarkable peace mission, the Powder River Sioux were still at war. They would wait and see whether or not the whites really would abandon the hated forts on the road to Montana.

• 5 •

Actually, the white man's departure had already been set in motion. Gen. Christopher C. Augur, who had replaced General Cooke at Omaha, was also one of the peace commissioners. As early as May 19, 1868, while the commission was moving from Fort Laramie to Fort Rice, he had ordered abandonment of "the military posts of C. F. Smith, Phil Kearny and Reno . . ." By late August—some six weeks after the Fort Rice council—the last teams and horsemen had trooped out of the post on the Little Piney. According to one account, Little Wolf and a party of Cheyenne rode up to the fort while the last soldiers were still in sight down the Bozeman Trail. For miles, as the troopers plodded on, they could see the smoke from burning Phil Kearny.

Several times in the following months the commander of Fort Laramie, Bvt. Col. William M. Dye, sent messages to Red Cloud inviting him in to sign the treaty. This time the chief was amenable, and, after sending several replies that he would come, finally arrived at Fort Laramie on November 4, 1868. With him was a number of other chiefs and head men, with their families. Among the chiefs was Red Leaf, who had already signed the treaty with Spotted Tail and the other Brulé.

After so many other fishermen had failed, Colonel Dye was highly pleased with himself for landing Red Cloud. Allowing the Indians to pitch their lodges about two miles away, he opened negotiations at the fort with the chiefs.

Although the others seemed friendly, Red Cloud himself was sullen and suspicious, keeping his seat on the ground and hardly touching the officers' fingers when they came up to shake hands. Colonel Dye read the treaty to him, but, to the passages requiring the Indians to go on the reservation and become farmers, Red Cloud refused to listen. He and his people would not move, and they would not give up hunting the buffalo for their livelihoods. What he wanted most was powder and lead, and he declared that obtaining them was the main object of his visit. The first council broke up without result.

On the evening of their arrival the Indians were entertained at the house of their old friend, Col. William Bullock, the sutler's agent. Before they arrived he took all the furniture out of his dining room and covered the floor with oilcloth; as one observer put it, "they have no respect for carpets." At the appointed time the Indians walked in and sat on the floor—first around the sides and then filling in the rest of the room. In the center was a servant with four large boilers containing potatoes, soup, coffee and rice with sugar and raisins. Each Indian was given a tin plate and cup. After having two helpings of everything, they had the rest put in containers to take back to their villages.

The only Indian woman present was a wife of Red Cloud; when she had finished her dinner, she quietly stepped outside. The other Indians retired to Bullock's parlor, where they made themselves comfortable on his Victorian sofas and chairs.

At that point a number of the officers' wives were brought into the parlor and introduced to the chiefs. One of the women, Mrs. Ada Adelaide Vogdes, later described Red Cloud as tall, quiet, sedate and plainly dressed, with a buffalo robe thrown about him. By contrast, Red Leaf was short, decked in beads and other finery of all colors and wearing an old army hat. He wore a constant smile, she observed, adding, "his expression is rather fiendish, but still at the same time, it strikes you as a good fatherly looking countenance and one to whom you would go in trouble, were he in different circumstances." This remark, about the man rumored about the post to have killed Fetterman with his own hands, was an astounding compliment.

For their part, the Indians were pleased when the women shook hands and said, "Wash ta cola," which meant "We are good friends" in the Sioux language. Mrs. Vogdes wrote that their "little black eyes twinkled with delight."

After pipes and cigars, the Indians rose and made ready to

depart. Mrs. Vogdes, accustomed to the privileges accorded to
army rank, went onto the parade ground to see what ceremony
would attend Red Cloud's departure. But to her disappointment
he walked out and found his pony, threw a blanket on its back,
sprang astride without assistance, helped his wife to mount
behind and rode off with the others.

The result of Bullock's hospitality was to improve the chances
that the chiefs would sign the treaty by, in Dye's words, "gladden-
ing . . . their bellies with a feast." The next two mornings the
Colonel went over the document with them again. Red Cloud
asked about the boundaries of the Indian lands and the ban
against white trespass. Then, picking up dust and rubbing his
hands with it, he "touched the pen" to the paper. Among the five
other Oglala chiefs signing the treaty was Young-Man-Afraid, who
had assumed the chieftainship of most of the Oglala from his
father, Old-Man-Afraid-of-His-Horses.

After six years of bloodshed, peace had come to the high
plains. To Ada Adelaide Vogdes the blessing was simpler and
more personal: "Now I hope we will be able to enjoy a ride, or
walk, outside the garrison."

Yet trouble loomed from the moment Red Cloud touched the
pen. In his speech at the time, he declared—with utter disregard
of the treaty he had just signed—that he was not committing himself to go on the reservation and that he wanted to continue
trading at Fort Laramie.

Such a performance was typical of the Sioux, who had a way of
refusing to recognize or understand treaty provisions they did not
like, while at the same time signing the treaty in order to get
ammunition, food and other short-term benefits. That this behavior was at all inconsistent did not occur to them, and more
than once they later claimed—probably in good conscience—that
"bad" provisions had never been explained to them. Such an
approach to treaty-making the whites never understood.

In 1868 this situation was further clouded by inconsistencies
in the treaty itself. The Sioux had signed with their eyes on the
white man's promise to vacate the Powder River country. But this
clause had simply been inserted to catch Red Cloud and actually
contradicted the main object of the treaty—to put the Sioux and
northern Cheyenne on a permanent reservation. In 1867-1868 the
keystone of government policy toward the Indians of the high

plains was to get them away from the line of the Union Pacific Railroad and to tame them by teaching them to farm. The treaty set aside all the land in present South Dakota west of the Missouri as the Sioux and northern Cheyenne reservation, which the Indians "will regard" as "their permanent home, and they will make no permanent home elsewhere." They were allowed "to hunt on any lands north of the North Platte River, and on the Republican Fork of the Smoky Hill River, so long as the buffalo may range thereon in such numbers as to justify the chase." Other than this hunting right, they "will relinquish all right to occupy permanently the territory outside their reservation . . ."

Yet the treaty also stated that "the country north of the North Platte River and east of the summits of the Big Horn Mountains shall be held and considered to be unceded Indian territory" into which no white man could go without Indian consent and where the military posts would be abandoned and the road to Montana closed. The Indians' title to the Powder River country was thus recognized, but he could not use it except to hunt buffalo— certainly an illogical situation.

Little wonder that the Indians interpreted the treaty in their own favor. They maintained that the great Dakota reservation was simply a territory guaranteed to them and that they were still free to live elsewhere. The contradictions in the treaty of 1868 thus held the seeds of a still bloodier war. Fort Laramie, which had originally drawn the Oglala and Brulé south from the Black Hills in 1834 and 1835, had become the scene of their undoing.

FIFTEEN ♦ *The Peace That Was a Lie*

♦ 1 ♦

The ink was scarcely dry on the treaty signatures when the army moved to uproot the Indians. While still at the Fort Laramie council, General Sherman had written Gen. U. S. Grant that the Indians in the vicinity of the Union Pacific Railroad must be removed at once, "even at our own Military expense, without awaiting the lawful but slow action of Congress."

The first to be disciplined were the Laramie Loafers. Thenceforth, they were told, their Indian agent and their traders would be at Whetstone Creek on the Missouri River above Fort Randall in Dakota Territory. In June 1868 they were loaded into army wagons and began their sorrowful hegira to the country their ancestors had left in the westward migration of the late 1700s.

Next to be awakened were the Brulé, who were hunting buffalo on the Republican. Couriers were sent south to notify Spotted Tail and Swift Bear that they had to move north to the Missouri River and into the Dakota reservation. This demand was in violation of the treaty itself, which specifically permitted the Sioux to hunt on the Republican. But for some time Spotted Tail had been resigned to the superior strength of the whites. In spite of excited opposition from his young men, he moved his people across the Platte and into the reservation through the summer of 1868. The following year the army—again in violation of the treaty provisions—drove Oglala and Cheyenne bands out of the territory below the Platte and sent them fleeing northward to the reservation.

Also moving from Fort Laramie to the new Whetstone agency were the old traders who had been familiar figures on the North

247

Platte since the 1830s. Bordeau, Bissonette and the others found their business gone and their reason for staying at Fort Laramie ended. With their Indian wives and half-breed children, they joined the Sioux exodus to Whetstone. Never again would Fort Laramie sustain its fond place in the hearts of the Sioux.

Northward in the Powder River country, Red Cloud heard of these events and refused to comply with the order to move. Fort Laramie had been the trading center of his people for more than thirty years. As he later said, "The bones of the Oglalas are all around that fort." He had been told nothing about any change of trading location when he signed the treaty, he claimed, and he would not change now.

To force the issue Red Cloud, Man-Afraid and Red Leaf gathered all their strength for the next trading visit to Fort Laramie. With all their people—warriors, women and children—they moved southward to the North Platte. Early on the morning of March 25, 1869, they crossed the river and rode to the fort in a long column of twos. As they came they chanted a Sioux song —a thousand voices stirring the frosty air. Before the garrison knew what was afoot, the Indians fanned out in front of the post buildings, forming a long line in apparent battle array. The soldiers and civilians of Fort Laramie came running to see the commotion; the sight was enough to chill the hardiest veteran. There sat several hundred warriors on their ponies, the sunlight dancing on their bright feathers and the tips of their spears.

Taken off guard, Colonel Dye feared that Red Cloud was threatening to invest the fort. With many of the soldiers on detached service along the Oregon Trail, Dye was obviously out-numbered. But he determined to make his own show of strength. Quickly his orders were repeated across the parade ground. Rumbling into place were two artillery pieces, their crews stand-ing by with shells and ramrods, their black muzzles facing the intruders. Rushing forward with guns and cartridge boxes, two companies of infantry formed into ranks facing the Indians. The regular posting of guards was put off in order to bring every available man into the line.

Then while the two forces glared at each other within easy range of bullet and arrow, Colonel Dye secured an interpreter and shouted across the intervening space, "You have not had permission to come in such large numbers. If you do not go, you will be fired into."

The warriors sat their ponies, silent and immovable. Dye desperately hoped to keep from firing, for it would bring on a wholesale battle whose outcome he could not foresee. For a seemingly endless period the two sides sat facing each other. Wrote Ada Adelaide Vogdes, who was watching the whole spectacle with mixed terror and fascination, "every thing had a war-like appearance for hours."

A second time Dye repeated his threat. Still Red Cloud and his warriors sat unperturbed, as though daring the soldiers to fight. As time dragged on many of them dismounted from their ponies but kept their positions in line.

When Dye gave his ultimatum a third time, it was understood in the garrison that if it were not obeyed he would order his men to fire. The chiefs waited still longer. Then one of them gave a "singular noise." At this signal the Indians leaped astride their ponies, wheeled and rode off at a gallop. Separating, they spread out over the hills west of the fort in a grand display of their numbers. Sighed Ada Vogdes, "a more exciting day for a few hours, I never experienced."

But Red Cloud's object was to trade, and Colonel Dye was not ready to deny him. Next day the Indians were allowed into the parade ground in small numbers at a time. They congregated at the sutler's store but were happy to dicker with any of the whites who had something to trade. Among the latter was the redoubtable Ada Vogdes: "I rushed around all day to get a blanket worked with beads, which I succeeded in doing, for a bag of flour, 20 lbs of bacon . . . & some coffee and sugar." More remarkable, the irrepressible woman invited three chiefs, including Red Cloud, to her home for a meal. In the absence of her husband, who was apparently on duty away from the post, she coolly entertained three savages who had, little more than two years before, helped to massacre 81 whites at Fort Phil Kearny. When they left her home and returned to the sutler's store, they gave her an arrow as a memento.

• 2 •

Although Red Cloud was still having his way, he was doing so on borrowed time. Where the army had failed, civilization was succeeding. Already the Union Pacific Railroad had crossed southern Wyoming, and along its path new towns were rising. In

1867 and 1868, Cheyenne and Laramie City (not to be confused with Fort Laramie) were founded as railhead-construction centers, but they lived on as trading settlements for the new country. Near some of them, forts were established to protect the settlers—Fort D. A. Russell at Cheyenne, Fort Sanders near the site of Laramie City and Fort Fetterman (named for the commander of the Phil Kearny massacre victims) on the North Platte some eighty miles beyond Fort Laramie.

South in Kansas Territory, the Kansas Pacific Railroad was pushing westward toward the heart of the buffalo country. Where settlers had formerly arrived by the hundreds in wagon trains, they now arrived by the thousands under the power of the iron horse. Nebraska became a state in 1867, Wyoming a territory in 1869. In the same year the Union Pacific made its junction with the Central Pacific built from California, and the continent was girded with rails.

From the new Wyoming railroad towns, as well as from the older mining centers in Montana Territory, the settlers' frontier pressed against the near-vacuum of Red Cloud's Powder River empire. Led by the Cheyenne newspapers, the frontier press was clamoring to place the wild Sioux on the reservation.

As there was little chance of achieving this confinement without another war, Red Cloud was invited on a trip to Washington, where he might become so impressed with the white man's power that he would voluntarily submit. Accordingly, the chief and his party came into Fort Laramie in 1870. From there they were escorted with much solicitude to the railroad at Pine Bluff, carefully avoiding Cheyenne, where Red Cloud was hardly a popular figure among the boisterous citizens. Spotted Tail also journeyed to Washington with his own retinue, and the two took the opportunity to complain loudly of their grievances. On June 8 Red Cloud told the Secretary of the Interior: "The white children have surrounded me and have left me nothing but an island. When we first had this land we were strong; now we are melting like snow on a hill side, while you are grown like spring grass."

Two days later, after meeting President Grant and dining at the White House, the chiefs went back to the Interior Department. This time the Secretary urged them to settle on the Sioux reservation. He brought out a copy of the Fort Laramie treaty of 1868 and explained it to them.

Red Cloud flew into a rage. Shouting that the paper was nothing but lies, he demanded to go home. The next day the Secretary gave in, agreeing to put Red Cloud's Indian agent and trading post somewhere near Fort Laramie.

Then, after a detour through New York, Red Cloud returned to his people. In conferences at Fort Laramie, he secured the agency location about thirty miles east of the fort, near the site of the Upper Platte agency during the Civil War.

There Red Cloud settled his people in the summer of 1871. The location, well south of the Dakota reservation, actually violated both the spirit and the letter of the 1868 treaty. At that point, Red Cloud had won the peace as well as the war. As far as his own Oglala were concerned, the government had suspended its reservation policy.

Meanwhile, Spotted Tail had also won a major point for his Brulé during his Washington visit. Rejecting the Whetstone agency with its degrading effects on his people because of nearby whiskey peddlers, he secured a new agency on the White River southeast of the Black Hills. The site was about one hundred miles northeast of Fort Laramie and believed to be inside the reservation. When it came time to send Spotted Tail his annuity goods, Fort Laramie became the jumping-off place for the wagon train. But then Red Cloud's Oglala, as well as many Brulé, refused to let the wagons across the North Platte. Did not the 1868 treaty prohibit the white man from crossing the river? On the north bank of the Platte, angry warriors were riding their ponies back and forth, war-whooping and shooting their rifles in the air. The freight contractor asked the Fort Laramie commander for a military escort. But the Indian agent protested that the moment the troops crossed the river there would be a new Sioux war.

Finally, the Brulé annuities were delivered to Spotted Tail at the Red Cloud agency. When the Brulé warriors came down from the White River agency to get them, they pushed on south to hunt buffalo on the Republican Fork of the Smoky Hill River, where they had been expelled only three years before. With them went Red Cloud and the Oglala; after a successful hunt, the two bands wintered on the Republican. Without a war the Sioux had reasserted another provision of the 1868 treaty.

But while they were gone, their Indian agent was laying plans to move Red Cloud's agency northward near Spotted Tail's on the

White River. When Red Cloud returned he was furious and refused to be moved. The issue raged throughout the summer of
1872, and on at least two occasions the agent had to call for
troops from Fort Laramie to protect himself and his staff. In
August 1873, while Red Cloud was absent once more, the agency
was moved to the White River, about 70 miles northeast of Fort
Laramie and a comparatively short distance west of Spotted Tail's
agency. Once again Red Cloud was outraged but had to accept an
accomplished fact.

Although the Indian Bureau believed the two agencies were
now within the Sioux reservation, when the line was surveyed,
they were found to be in Nebraska. The Bureau let the matter
stand, and once more the 1868 treaty was ignored.

• 3 •

Up till then, the Oglala and Brulé Sioux had enjoyed better
lives than they had had before the 1868 treaty. They were receiving generous annuities, and, because so many other tribes had
been confined to reservations, they were having good buffalo
hunts on the Republican with little competition.

But that "Indian summer" could not last long on the white
man's frontier. In 1872 Spotted Tail and Red Cloud again took
their warriors to the Republican—and they found the white hunters there in droves. A market for buffalo hides—partly for use as
conveyor belts in factories—had developed in the East. The white
man's systematic assault on the buffalo, which had been opened
in the late 1860s by the hunters supplying meat for the railroad-
construction crews, had become wholesale slaughter.

Foregoing the excitement of the chase and the "surround" developed by the Indians, the hide hunter reverted to the earlier stalking method, except that his long Sharps rifle enabled him to
choose a spot at a safe distance and pick off one buffalo at a time
while the herd milled about in confusion. With two skinners, a
cook and a wagon, he could kill and haul away up to a hundred
buffalo a day. The harvest was hauled away on three western
railroads—Union Pacific, Kansas Pacific and Santa Fe—and is
supposed to have numbered about 1,250,000 hides and robes in
1872 and 1873.

It has been wrongly claimed, without evidence, that the United

States instigated the buffalo hunt in order to bring the Indian to his knees. But it is true that the Grant administration was not displeased with the results. Wrote the Secretary of the Interior in 1873, "I would not seriously regret the total disappearance of the buffalo from our western prairies, in its effect upon the Indians, regarding it rather as a means of hastening their sense of dependence upon the products of the soil and their own labors."

To this precious policy, a few voices in Washington objected. Said one congressman, "I am not in favor of civilizing the Indian by starving him to death . . ." Nevertheless, neither the administration nor Congress raised a hand to halt the buffalo massacre.

The inevitable result was felt by the Sioux as early as 1873, when they had a poor hunt on the Republican. Some Oglala clashed with white hide hunters, and a chief and two warriors were killed. To make up for their misfortune, the Sioux attacked a hunting party of their old enemies, the Pawnee, and killed about fifty men, women and children. Then they made off with the dried meat and hides of about eight hundred buffalo.

In the fall of 1874, the Brulé, with some Oglala and Cheyenne, again rode south for the chase. But they found the valley of the Republican littered with bones and foul with stench. That winter they killed about a hundred buffalo—among the last of the millions that once had roamed the central plains.

There was one more range left—the Yellowstone and its tributaries, including the Powder. That area was occupied by the Miniconjou under old Chief One Horn, the Hunkpapa under the medicine man Sitting Bull and a large number of wild Oglala who had not come in with Red Cloud. The last were led in their hunting and raiding expeditions by the young war chief, Crazy Horse.

Already this final hunting ground was threatened by another railroad. In 1871, Northern Pacific surveyors were planning their line along the south bank of the Yellowstone—into the heart of the northern buffalo country. Although the Hunkpapa Sioux loudly objected, the army escorted the survey parties and established three forts to protect the construction workers. The first was Fort McKeen (later Fort Abraham Lincoln) opposite Bismarck, where the Northern Pacific crossed the Missouri River.

At this new invasion the Bozeman Trail–Powder River drama was repeated. Beginning in 1872 the Hunkpapa and Miniconjou attacked parties of soldiers and made several assaults on Fort

Lincoln itself. In the summer of 1873 the 7th U.S. Cavalry regiment under Lt. Col. George A. Custer was transferred from the southern plains to Fort Lincoln. Custer soon led an expedition against the Sioux, who attacked his column on the Yellowstone River and killed four men. In the same summer about 150 frontiersmen from the Montana mining towns invaded the unceded Indian country on a prospecting expedition. They successfully defended themselves against Indian attacks but represented another treaty violation to send the Sioux into still greater rage.

So far, none of the Oglala—not even the wild bands that had stayed on Powder River—was involved. But when the Red Cloud and Spotted Tail agencies were removed to the White River in northwestern Nebraska, the tribes were close enough to the Powder for the wild Miniconjou warriors to visit as often as they pleased. Lining up with the agency Indians for rations and annuities, they bragged of their raiding exploits and excited the young agency braves into new resentment against the whites. For a time the suspicious Oglala would not allow their agent to leave the stockade for fear he was up to some trick.

In February 1874 a party of a hundred Miniconjou left the agencies and went raiding along the North Platte. Beyond Fort Laramie they came upon a wagon party hauling wood from Laramie Peak back to the fort. An officer and an enlisted man who had separated from the train were killed. The Indians then slew a civilian on Laramie Creek and another on the Niobrara. Soon a Miniconjou assassinated a white clerk at the Red Cloud agency. The agent then sent a rider eighty miles to Fort Laramie with a message calling for troops.

At the post the commanding officer had also had enough of Indian depredations. With fourteen companies of troops he hurried to White River in March 1874. When the wild Sioux heard of the army's approach, they went into new fits of excitement, threatening to kill the agency staff. But many of the treaty Indians protected the agency whites. Just before the troops arrived, the wild Sioux pulled down their lodges and fled the agencies. Red Cloud and some of his Oglala went with them to the Dakota Badlands. As for the troops, they went into camp on White River a mile and a half above the Red Cloud agency. There they built a permanent post, Fort Robinson, named after the lieutenant who had been killed with the wood train.

• 4 •

For some time, the Department of the Missouri had been commanded by Gen. Phil Sheridan, who firmly believed that the army's function was to clear the West of Indians for the benefit of white settlers. To support the advance of the Northern Pacific—itself a violation of the 1868 treaty—he determined to build a new fort in the Black Hills, which would have been still another violation. In the fall of 1873 he visited Fort Laramie to promote the plan but found both the wild Sioux and the agency Sioux in no mood for such trifling. Shifting to the north, he visited Fort Abraham Lincoln in the spring of 1874 and launched an exploratory expedition in the Black Hills. It was a flagrant violation of the treaty—born of the army's contempt for the Indian and Sheridan's disregard of the law when it interfered with his purposes.

Heading the expedition was Bvt. Maj. Gen. George Armstrong Custer, hero of sixty engagements in the Civil War—a flamboyant officer who had done his share of Indian chasing and killing on the southern plains. On July 1, 1874, he left Fort Lincoln with 1,200 soldiers, a contingent of civilian miners, some Arikaree and Santee scouts, a delegation of scientists and a battery of newspapermen. In the Black Hills he had one encounter with an Indian village. The inhabitants fled, and in the process a Santee scout had an altercation with one of the chiefs and apparently wounded him.

As if this encounter were not enough mischief, members of the expedition found gold on French Creek about eight miles south of Harney Peak. Custer was so pleased with the favorable conditions for settling the Black Hills that he could not wait until he returned to Fort Lincoln to make a report. On August 3, while camping on a fork of the Cheyenne River, he dispatched a messenger southward to Fort Laramie with a telegram to his superiors.

For the messenger, "Lonesome Charlie" Reynolds, it was a dangerous ride through territory teeming with Indians who resented Custer's invasion of their land. But he was a professional hunter and scout with years of experience among hostile Indians. Taking the best horse available, he muffled its hooves with cloth to avoid discovery and set out just before midnight. After riding by night and hiding by day, Reynolds reached Fort Laramie a few days later with Custer's dispatch.

While news of the expedition spread across the parade ground, the message was tapped out in the telegraph office. It proved to be more of a pastoral poem (eight printed pages) than a telegram. Custer was overflowing with superlatives on the Black Hills—the unsurpassed scenery, the profusion of wild fruit and game, the abundant timber and water, the rich soil. He wrote of the desirable building sites and the ideal winter ranges for cattle. The very air was laden with perfume. And finally: "Gold has been found at several places. . . . I have upon my table 40 or 50 small particles of pure gold . . . most of it obtained today from one panful of earth."

As if this news were not enough, Custer made stronger reference to gold in another dispatch on August 15 and again in his final report:

> Veins of what the geologists term gold-bearing quartz crop out on almost every hillside, but in one place . . . a hole was dug eight feet in depth; the miners report that they found gold among the roots of the grass, and from that point to the lowest point reached, gold was found in paying quantities. On some of the water courses almost every pan full of earth produced gold in small but paying quantities. . . . It has not required an expert to find gold in the Black Hills, as men without former experience in mining have discovered it at an expense of but little time or labor.

Custer had not returned from the Black Hills when his news was released to the press in mid-August. Naturally it created a sensation throughout the West and the Mississippi Valley. The closest settlements—Yankton, Dakota Territory; Sioux City, Iowa; Sidney, Nebraska; and Cheyenne, Wyoming Territory—prepared for a rush.

Swiftly General Sheridan moved to stop the storm he had sown. Within days after Custer's announcement, Sheridan sent a frantic wire to Gen. Alfred H. Terry, then commanding the Department of Dakota: "Should companies now organizing at Sioux City and Yankton trespass upon the Sioux reservations, you are hereby directed to use the force at your command to burn their wagon trains, destroy the outfits and arrest the leaders, confining them at the nearest military post in the Indian country."

Still, a number of miners got through in the fall of 1874, risking not only arrest by the soldiers but also death from the Indians.

In fact, the Sioux and Cheyenne—both the wild and the agency bands—were in a state of excitement. Some of them began collecting additional arms; the Brulé encountered one party and killed a miner. But generally they held their fire; they would see how well Terry's soldiers kept out the invaders before raising the hatchet.

It was in that hectic hour that another "peace" commission came to the agencies to see about taking still more Indian territory —this time the "unceded" lands that had been specified in the 1868 treaty in order to win Red Cloud's signature. As had become customary in this ugly business, part of the responsibility was given to men of the cloth—churchmen and missionaries who were believed to be trusted by the Indians. Bishop William H. Hare of New York was chairman, and, when illness forced him to return to civilization, the chairmanship fell to Samuel D. Hinman, a long-time missionary to the frontier Indians.

After reaching Cheyenne by the Union Pacific Railroad on July 28—while Custer was still on his expedition—the commissioners journeyed to Fort Laramie, pressed on with a military escort to the Indian agencies and then took an extended tour through the Black Hills. By the time they returned to the Spotted Tail agency on September 5, Custer's report had been trumpeted through the nation, and the Black Hills excitement was at its peak. The Sioux—especially Red Cloud and the Oglala—were in a frenzy, and the commissioners wisely decided not to broach the question of the Powder River country. They therefore fell back on a secondary purpose—persuading the Sioux to give up their right to hunt in "unceded Indian lands" between the Sioux Reservation and the North Platte (in Nebraska) and on the Republican Fork (in Kansas). As compensation, the commissioners offered them $25,000 worth of horses and guns. Spotted Tail agreed, but Red Cloud was adamant—even when told that the rights would be taken away anyway. On June 23, 1875, the Brulé and Oglala—all except Red Cloud—signed the agreement to give up their rights in Nebraska and Kansas south of the Niobrara Valley.

All this activity did nothing to calm the Sioux, who were already outraged by Custer's invasion of their reservation and the subsequent gold rush to the Black Hills. Although General Terry's soldiers caught one expedition out of Yankton and dealt with it according to Sheridan's orders, most of the miners eluded the army. Through their newspapers and their congressmen, the frontier settlers were clamoring for the Black Hills and the Powder River. One of the Hare Commission members wrote that the unceded territory "is of little advantage to the Indian," whereas the people of Wyoming Territory could make good use of it. "It is a great wrong to the citizens of this Territory that its domain should not be settled by a white enterprising population." As for the Black Hills, the Governor of Wyoming Territory went to Washington for a conference with President Grant and General Sherman, by then the army chief of staff. Troops should be used, the Governor declared, to protect the miners in the Hills from the Indians.

The reaction of the two soldiers was, first, that the miners were unlawfully trespassing and would be told to leave, and, second, that the United States would proceed to purchase mining rights in the Black Hills from the Indians so that the miners could go back. Grant thereupon ordered the Secretary of the Interior to appoint another commission to treat with the Sioux, including both agency and wild bands. And to western army headquarters came an order to clear the miners out of the Hills. It would be expedient, incidentally, to have them out before the wild bands gathered for the big council.

In early summer the job of dealing with the miners was turned over to Brig. Gen. George Crook, who had just been appointed to head the Department of the Platte. Probably the most celebrated Indian fighter in the country, Crook had already put down uprisings from Oregon to Arizona. Shrewd, single-minded, tough but fair, Crook arrived at just the right time to avert or to fight an Indian war. He had hardly settled in Omaha before he was ordered to get the miners out of the Black Hills by August 15, 1875.

Riding the rails to Cheyenne, Crook took several ambulances and a small military party northward through Fort Laramie. In the diggings he went among the miners and invited them to a "talk." Explaining that they were unlawfully trespassing on the Indian reservation, he told them that they would have to leave the country. At this news, most of the miners trudged out of the Hills on the trail south to Fort Laramie. The Sioux watched them go and waited to see how well they obeyed.

But Spotted Tail, notified of the forthcoming council with the new commissioners, journeyed to the Black Hills to see for himself the true richness of the gold discoveries. There he found some of the miners still on the ground busily digging gold. On his return he talked with his Indian agent and other white friends. They told him the Hills were worth between $30 million and $50 million —far above the price the commissioners were authorized to pay. When the Sioux learned the value of the region that had been invaded they were still more incensed. Red Cloud told a delegation of white men who visited him: "The people from the states are stealing our gold, digging it out, and taking it away, and I don't see why the Great Father don't bring them back."

• 5 •

This was the situation at the Indian agencies when the new commission arrived to obtain mining rights in the Black Hills. Heading the nine-man group was Sen. William B. Allison, a long-time Iowa politician. It included Gen. Alfred H. Terry of the Department of Dakota, the veteran trader George Beauvais and the usual complement of churchmen. Meeting first at Omaha, the commissioners rode the train to Cheyenne, picked up an escort of Capt. James "Teddy" Egan's famous company of white horses at Fort Laramie and arrived at Red Cloud agency on September 4, 1875.

Gathered there to meet the commissioners was a huge concourse of tribes. Beside the Oglala and Brulé, there were Hunkpapa and Miniconjou from the Powder River and Yellowstone "unceded territory"; Two Kettle, Sans Arc, Yankton, Santee and Blackfoot Sioux from the Missouri River and its northern tributaries, and finally northern Cheyenne and Arapaho who had been settled in the Sioux reservation. It was probably the largest convocation of Plains Indians since the Great Council of Fort Laramie in 1851.

Notably absent, however, was Sitting Bull of the Hunkpapa. To the messenger who had come to tell him about the council, he had replied that if God had sent for him he would have gone, "but the Big Chief for the white men must come see me."

For several days the commissioners met informally with the chiefs to discuss the issue; they found them divided between

those who would sell the Black Hills at an exorbitant price and
those—largely the wild Sioux from the unceded territory—who
would not sell at any price. There was, indeed, such a fearful
excitement among the wild Sioux that Spotted Tail was apprehensive for the lives of the commissioners. On September 20,
when the first formal council opened on the plain along the White
River, two companies of cavalry (including Captain Egan's white-
horse company from Fort Laramie) escorted the commissioners
to the spot. In case they were not enough, Spotted Tail and some
of his warriors rode alongside the wagon carrying the commissioners to help the soldiers protect them.

In a small grove of cottonwoods, a large tarpaulin was raised
as a cover over the commissioners; on each side of them the two
companies formed in lines and stood by their horses ready for
action. Then, after the chiefs had sat down facing the commissioners, Senator Allison made his opening speech. To the Indians
it was an old story:

> We have now to ask if you are willing to give our people the
> right to mine in the Black Hills. . . . The great object we have in
> making this agreement is to secure a lasting peace with you. It
> will be hard for our Government to keep the whites out of the
> Hills. . . . We do not wish to take from you any right or property
> you have without making a fair return for it. . . . There is another
> country lying toward the setting sun, over which you roam and
> hunt and which territory is yet unceded, extending to the summit
> of the Big Horn Mountains. . . . It does not seem to be of very
> great value or use to you, and our people think they would like
> to have the portion of it I have described.

Then the chiefs were asked to consult among themselves and
to decide what price they would ask. This move was a mistake,
for it left the issue open to the interminable wrangling that char-
acterized Sioux councils. Three days later they had not agreed on
a price, and a militant minority was opposed to any sale at all.

As the council gathered for its second meeting on the 23rd, it
was apparent that the Indians had worked themselves into a
feverish state. From among the thousands who covered the surrounding hillsides, every band sent its delegation to the council
with a headlong rush of horses, the riders brandishing their
repeating Winchester rifles. Each arriving group dashed around
the tent shooting into the air. To the shaken commissioners, the
interpreter gave assurance that this behavior was not unusual at an

important ceremony. But Senator Allison was disturbed: "Such a terrific display of firearms seems unnecessary at a peace council."

As the meeting opened the chiefs conferred excitedly among themselves. They were trying to choose a spokesman, and there was some reluctance among them to accept the honor, as they had been warned that some of the wild Sioux from the north had threatened to shoot the first chief who offered to sell out. While they were deliberating, the agitation swept among the warriors. One of them was Little Big Man, a Hunkpapa from Sitting Bull's wild band in the Yellowstone country. Already stripped for battle, he was stirring his warriors into a frenzy. Some of them were shouting threats to the chiefs and the commissioners.

Suddenly Little Big Man spurred his horse into the space between the commissioners and the chiefs. At his belt were two revolvers. In one hand he waved a rifle, in the other some cartridges. Shouting savagely to the Indians in their language, he warned, "I will kill the first Indian chief who speaks favorably to the selling of the Black Hills!"

At this threat, Captain Egan of the white-horse cavalry bellowed an order: "Stand to horse—mount." The soldiers swung astride their horses and held their carbines at the ready. In the same instant, as though by a signal, the wild Sioux pressed their own horses in front of the soldiers, matching them man for man. But Young Man-Afraid rode up to Little Big Man. Leave the council grounds, he told him, or you will be killed.

A clash between the Indians was imminent, and the shooting would surely involve the cavalry and commissioners. In that hectic moment Captain Egan stepped up to Alfred Terry. "General," he declared, "your party is surrounded and my men are shut out."

Even the interpreter agreed that this behavior was not customary: "It looks like hell will be to pay here in a few minutes."

In the next moment Young Man-Afraid plunged forward with his own wild Oglala and made a third ring inside that of the hostile Indians, covering them and protecting the commissioners and the chiefs. Then he stepped into the center of the council and shouted to all the warriors to go back to their lodges "till your heads are cool."

Immediately the Indians began to scatter. The council broke up in a tumult, and most of the warriors returned to their lodges. But the danger was far from over. Spotted Tail told the commander of the troops to take the commissioners back to the agency "as quickly as possible." Senator Allison and General Terry conferred and told the commissioners to climb back into the wagons. Then they hurried back to Red Cloud agency, the cavalry-men riding on both flanks and in the rear.

Even so, some of the warriors rode savagely around them, press-ing their ponies close to the troopers and threatening to kill one of the commissioners. One Indian rode his horse through the soldiers' ranks, shouting "I will have the blood of a commissioner." Still the troopers held their fire; one of the friendly Indians told the maddened warrior that he could take out his vengeance on a colt quietly grazing a short distance away. The brave thereupon rode over and killed the colt.

After that all the hostiles rode back to the main camp in the grove of trees. The commissioners were escorted safely back to Red Cloud agency, but a savage battle and possibly a total massacre had been averted by the narrowest means.

With fully half the Indians angrily departing for their homes, the commissioners still tried to salvage something from the council and called upon the remaining chiefs to state their de-mands. In a meeting at the agency on September 27, the chiefs poured out their feelings. They had agreed upon a price—$70 million—but there was still confusion over what form it would take. Some wanted it in the bank to earn interest; others cata-logued an enormous list of presents needed. Said Red Cloud:

> My Great Father has told me that there have been six genera-tions back of Indian tribes and I am the seventh. . . . For seven generations to come I want our Great Father to give us Texas steers for our meat. I want the Government to issue for me hereafter, flour and coffee, and sugar and tea, and bacon, the very best kind, and cracked corn and beans, and rice and dried apples, and saleratus and tobacco, and soap and salt, and pepper, for the old people. I want a wagon, a light wagon with a span of horses, and six yoke of working cattle for my people. I want a sow and a boar, and a cow and a bull, and a sheep and a ram, and a hen and a cock, for each family. . . . I want some white men's houses at this agency to be built for the Indians. I have been into white people's houses, and I have seen nice black bedsteads and chairs, and I want that kind of furniture given to my people.

And, as another chief put it:

> Our Great Father has asked me to give up the heart of this land where I was born and raised, and the heart of this land is

big and good, and I have camped all around it and watched and looked after it. . . . Even if our Great Father should give a hundred different kinds of livestock to each Indian house every year, it seems that that would not pay for the Black Hills.

The next day, when the commissioners balked at these ambitious demands, Spotted Tail asked them to submit their own proposition in writing. On the 29th they offered to buy the mining rights in the Black Hills for $400,000 a year or to purchase them outright for $6 million. These terms the Indians would not consider, and the council broke up in utter failure. In their final report the commissioners recommended sweeping reforms in the treatment of the Indians and proposed that Congress fix a fair sum for the Black Hills. Finally, the Indians "should be told that its rejection will have the effect to arrest all appropriations for their subsistence in the future, and all supplies not absolutely required by the treaty of 1868."

Such a high-handed solution would have brought war, at least from the wild tribes, but the Black Hills crisis had already slipped beyond further arbitration. The nontreaty Indians had ridden back to the Powder and the Yellowstone for the fall buffalo hunt. At the agencies the young men were furious at the white invasion of their lands and disgusted at their own chiefs for even proposing a price for the Black Hills. Many of them began stealing away to join the wild Sioux.

At the same time, the breakdown of the peace council was a signal for the army to throw up its hands and end all attempts to keep miners out of the Black Hills. It was as if the Indians had been obliged to accept the Great Father's offer, and they would have to take the consequences.

So by October 1875 the clandestine rush was on once more. The Cheyenne newspaper announced—perhaps with some exaggeration—that five men were leaving for the Black Hills "every minute." Through Fort Laramie surged the tide of rainbow hunters. In the goldfields the miners founded Custer City and other settlements. On December 1, the Wyoming territorial legislature authorized a road from Cheyenne through Fort Laramie to Custer City. A stage line was approved by the council of Laramie County, which at that time extended up the entire east side of Wyoming Territory. Announcing that operations would start in the spring, the stage owner added that General Sheridan had told him that the coaches "will not be interfered with by the soldiers."

In December the freight traffic was speeded northward by a new iron bridge over the North Platte at Fort Laramie, thus eliminating the need to ford the unpredictable river. Thenceforth wagons rolled past Fort Laramie under the very noses of the officers, with no opposition whatever. By the end of January 1876 another stage line—beating the first into actual operation—started running from Cheyenne through Fort Laramie and then to the diggings via the Red Cloud and Spotted Tail agencies, flouting not only the military men but also the Indians themselves.

The invasion of the Sioux reservation and the theft of the Black Hills were no longer covered up but were out in the open for all to see. Driven to a last refuge by successive Fort Laramie councils and broken Fort Laramie treaties, the Sioux faced this ultimate insult. The only question remaining was whether or not they would fight.

SIXTEEN ♦ *The Last War Whoop*

♦ 1 ♦

At first there was little reaction to the stampede—not even from the young warriors. The theft of the Black Hills might still have been accomplished without war, except that President Grant's administration could not commit such an enormity without finding a way to blame the Indians. The agency Sioux were sticking by their treaty rights, and they were also keeping the peace in the face of outrageous provocation. Their moral position was impregnable, but they had embarrassed the Indian Bureau by refusing to come to terms on the Black Hills. For the first time, both the Department of the Interior and the War Department had lost their patience with the Indians. Yet whom could they punish?

At that point it was noticed that, although the 1868 treaty was supposed to put all the Sioux on the reservation, the wild Sioux were still living in the unceded territories. Some of them wintered at the agencies to draw rations, but many Oglala under Crazy Horse, and Hunkpapa under Sitting Bull stayed on the Powder and the Yellowstone all year round. These Sioux were violating the treaty, the Grant administration decided, and must be called to account. Actually, neither of their principal leaders had signed the treaty, and they were not obliged to observe it.

An inspector in the Indian Bureau, E. C. Watkins, returned from a tour of Montana Territory and submitted a report on November 9, 1875. The Sioux, he wrote, were insolent and defiant, had recently attacked the Crow and were the terror of every traveler: "The true policy, in my judgment, is to send troops against them in the winter, the sooner the better, and *whip* them

265

into subjection. . . . The Government owes it . . . to civilization,
and the common cause of humanity."

Such high-minded material was just what was needed. The
Commissioner of Indian Affairs sent it to the Secretary of the
Interior, and the Secretary of the Interior sent it to the Secretary
of War. High-level consultations—including President Grant,
according to one account—followed. On December 6, 1875, the
Commissioner of Indian Affairs ordered his men at all the Sioux
agencies to send runners at once to the wild bands in the unceded
territory. They were to come into the reservation by January 31,
1876, or "they shall be deemed hostile and treated accordingly
by the military force." The Secretary of War was notified, "If said
Indians shall neglect or refuse to comply with said order, I have
the honor to request that the proper military officer be directed to
compel their removal to and residence within the boundaries of
the reservation."

As many of the treaty Indians were living outside the reservation at Red Cloud and Spotted Tail agencies, this order was
obviously contrived for another purpose. So was the time period
allotted, considering the slow pace of communications at that time.
Most of the agents did not receive the Indian Commissioner's
message until late in December; they immediately dispatched
runners, but it would have been impossible for the wild tribes to
come in by the deadline, and some of the messengers themselves
did not arrive back by January 31.

The evident reason for such haste was that the military wanted
time, once the deadline had been passed, to mount a winter campaign. From Philip St. George Cooke in 1866 to George Crook in
1876, the western commanders had been calling for an attack on
the Indian villages in the winter. Then the bands were divided
into small isolated villages because of the scarcity of feed for the
ponies and could be surprised and overpowered separately. In
December 1875, General Sheridan had ordered his department
commanders to prepare for such a campaign, should the Indians
fail to comply. In the same month, selling of ammunition to
Indians was prohibited at Standing Rock agency, and the other
agencies followed suit in January. Some of the young men left
the agencies for the nontreaty villages before their guns could be
confiscated.

Actually, the wild tribes had no intention of complying with the order. Some of them moved, but not in the direction of the reservation. Most of their leaders had not signed the Fort Laramie treaty of 1868, and there was no reason in law or equity why they should leave the unceded Indian lands.

In fact, as rations were low at the agencies and many treaty Indians were hungry, more of them left to join the wild bands during the winter of 1875-1876. The deadline of January 31 passed without any wild Sioux coming into the reservation.

Therefore, on February 7, 1876, the Secretary of the Interior notified the Secretary of War and "turned over" the non-treaty Sioux to the attention of the army. This move was precisely what Sheridan and his fellow officers had been wanting for years. For the first time since the Harney expedition of 1855-1856, they had a free hand to deal with the Sioux without restrictions from the Bureau of Indian Affairs. For twenty years they had been hampered by peace movements and equivocal government support. Often, before they could retaliate after an Indian victory, they were frustrated by the appearance of a peace commission. That would not happen this time.

• 2 •

Quickly Sheridan carried out his plan. General Crook was ordered to march from the south, Gen. John Gibbon from Montana and Gen. Alfred Terry from Fort Abraham Lincoln on the Missouri. But the same snow through which the army had expected the Indians to march on their way to the reservation was too much for Terry's column, which stayed at the fort. Gibbon's expedition proved inconclusive, and the main invasion was Crook's, which assembled at Fort Fetterman throughout February. To direct the over-all campaign, General Sheridan went to Fort Laramie, which contributed three companies of cavalry, including Captain Egan's white-horse outfit. They proceeded to march up the Oregon Trail along the south bank of the North Platte. Others from Fort D. A. Russell at Cheyenne marched north to the vicinity of Fort Laramie and then followed the Oregon Trail to Fort Fetterman.

In charge of the "Big Horn Expedition" was Col. (Bvt. Maj. Gen.) Joseph J. Reynolds, a veteran campaigner in his mid-fifties.

Though he had won battle honors in the Civil War, he had served a number of years as a professor of engineering and was hardly an experienced Indian campaigner.

When Reynolds' column of nearly nine hundred men marched out of Fort Fetterman on March 1, Crook went along as an observer. They were looking for the village of the wild Oglala under Crazy Horse, with the intention of attacking it and killing as many Indians as possible. This idea was a far cry from the object that the Interior Department had in mind—"to compel their removal to and residence within the boundaries of the reservation."

But this time the army was doing things its own way. In fighting the Sioux it had found by experience that the only way to insure a "victory" was to surprise and attack a village. With superior mobility and reconnaissance, the warriors could ordinarily avoid a fight until they could catch some soldiers in a trap and attack them with overwhelming numbers. For years the army's objective had been not so much to fight pitched battles with the warriors as to destroy villages, which involved combatants and non-combatants alike. Almost the only "victories" won by the army against the Sioux or their allies—Harney's at Ash Hollow, Chivington's at Sand Creek, Connor's at Tongue River, Custer's at the Washita—had been such surprise attacks on villages. Crook and Reynolds meant to strike another such blow at Crazy Horse's Oglala. Once they had been beaten, they would be compelled to go onto the reservation.

By March 16, Reynolds and three hundred cavalrymen were marching ahead of the main force to surprise what they believed was the Oglala village. Before daylight on March 17, two of Reynolds' scouts found a village of a hundred lodges on the bank of Powder River. Falling back, they reported the news to Reynolds. "Colonel," one of them announced, triumphantly, "here are the Indians. Now that I have found them, all you have to do is fight them."

Without going himself to see the village, Reynolds ordered out his battalions—one to attack the village, another to occupy it after the Indian retreat, a third to head off retreat.

As it turned out, the village was not on the other side of the hill, where the scout had said it was. When the battalions reached that point by their individual routes, they realized the error and had to move on in hopes of finding the village. When they did find it, there was no attempt to surround the village and prevent escape, as Harney had done at Ash Hollow.

The lead company was the white-horse outfit commanded by Captain Egan, who had orders to charge the village. As the troopers approached it through some broken timbers, they came upon an Indian youngster tending the pony herd. A lieutenant aimed at him with his revolver, but Egan was not ready to announce his presence and ordered the officer to "Let him alone." But after they had passed, the youth let out a whoop to warn the village. At this sound, the troopers charged at a trot, and the Indians came running out of their lodges. Realizing that they outnumbered the soldiers in sight, they threw themselves down behind brush and began shooting at Egan's men. The captain ordered his troops to dismount and advance slowly in a skirmish line through the fallen timber, leading their horses and firing their pistols.

After some time, one of the other companies approaching from a different direction began shooting at the Indians, who realized for the first time that the force against them might be too large to resist. Soon after, another battalion came riding in to support Egan. Facing this new force, the Indians abandoned the village and retreated among the trees on the river and into the hills to the northwest. The troops occupied themselves in rounding up the Indian pony herd and looting the lodges. Colonel Reynolds himself appeared and rode into the center of the village.

"What have you got?" he demanded of an officer.

"A very large village and the meat and everything."

At that moment the Indians in the hills began dropping bullets into the village, and the Colonel had to get off his horse to avoid being hit. After making a quick survey he ordered all the property, including buffalo robes and dried meat, destroyed. Though his men needed the food, he decided that he could not readily load it on pack animals while the village was under Indian counterfire and also that he had insufficient means to transport it. That he did not attack the Indians again was explained by his desire only to punish them and to convince them that they could not live off the reservation and defy the United States. But an additional reason was that his troops and horses were too exhausted and numbed with cold to make another charge.

Meanwhile, the lodges and all Indian property were fired, including kegs of gunpowder that sent lodgepoles somersaulting skyward. Pressed sharply by the Indians, some of the troops fell back, exposing those still in the process of destroying the village. Reynolds himself did not order his battalion commanders to hold their ground, and, although the troops fell back in an orderly manner, the truth was that they were driven out of the village by the Indians. The few dead soldiers were abandoned, and of course the bodies were mutilated. Even the band of some seven hundred Indian horses that Reynolds took with him was allowed to graze unattended at his first night's camp; Indian warriors who had followed Reynolds had no trouble running them off next morning.

With every advantage for victory, Reynolds accomplished only one success, that of destroying Indian property. On all other counts he suffered defeat. In fact, he had even attacked the wrong enemy; although the army long referred to it as "Crazy Horse's village of Oglalas," it was in fact a village of Cheyenne, who had not been ordered into the reservation and who were thus attacked without the least provocation.

On March 18, Reynolds joined the rest of the command at the appointed rendezvous on the Powder. Crook was furious at the outcome of the fight—not only at Reynolds' retreat but also at the destruction of blankets and food that the troops desperately needed. Out of supplies, the expedition fell back to Fort Fetterman. Crook ordered a court-martial of Reynolds and two other officers; Reynolds was found guilty of misbehavior before the enemy and was suspended for one year.

As for the Cheyenne, they were impoverished by the blow in severe winter weather and could only make their way to the village of their friends, the Oglala, three days' march to the north. In that bitter trek some women and children are supposed to have died before reaching the relief of Crazy Horse. Describing the surprise attack on their peaceful village, the Cheyenne won the alliance of the Oglala. When the two bands moved out to the Hunkpapa camp further north in the Powder River Valley, Sitting Bull was outraged at the news. All he and his people had asked was to be left alone, but now the soldiers were coming to fight them. To all the other villages of the Sioux and their allies—including the agency Indians within the reservation—he sent riders. Come to the big bend of the Rosebud, they said. "It is war."

• 3 •

At the agencies many of the chiefs tried to hold back the warriors. But they and their families left in great numbers. By May, Captain Egan had returned to Fort Laramie from an extensive patrol and had reported that "nearly all the young men have left" Red Cloud agency. Indians were all over the Powder River country, and he had seen seven hundred or eight hundred in one party going north. Another traveler reported at Fort Laramie that from eight hundred to one thousand had left for the hostile country on Powder River and that Red Cloud agency was "almost deserted."

Red Cloud himself, having seen the strength of the whites in two visits to the East, counseled his people against going. But even his own son left, taking with him his father's prize Winchester.

As for Spotted Tail, he was more successful in holding his Brulé, and he came into Fort Laramie declaring that they were "at peace and will not go out on warpath." Still, about fifty lodges left Spotted Tail agency for the hostile camps.

At the same time, Hunkpapa, Miniconjou, Sans Arc and other agency Indians joined the trek. In early June, word reached Fort Laramie that more than 1,800 lodges were camped on the Rosebud. At a grand council, Sitting Bull told the other chiefs: "We are an island of Indians in a lake of whites. We must stand together or they will rub us out separately."

Not all the Indians headed for the hostile camp. Many warriors from the agencies fell upon the gold adventurers who were invading their reservation along new roads to the Black Hills. Within days of Reynolds' attack on the Cheyenne camp, a pony expressman was killed and scalped below Hat Creek. In April, a party was attacked three miles above the Cheyenne River stage station in Red Canyon, and most of the people were killed, scalped and mutilated. From Fort Laramie the commander reported the road in a turmoil: "A good many miners are coming from the Black Hills through this Post in a destitute Condition, out of rations and money." Many of them, he added, had been wounded by Indian attackers.

With the entire road terrorized, Governor John Thayer of

Wyoming Territory traveled to Omaha late in April and asked General Crook for more troops. They were especially needed, he declared, in the dangerous and rugged country of Sage Creek and Red Canyon: "The Indians crawl up the sides of the canyon and shoot down or throw rocks upon travelers."

At this appeal, Crook hurried to Fort Laramie, where he ordered Captain Egan's white-horse cavalry to patrol the Black Hills road. The troops jogged northward to set up camps at the headwaters of Sage Creek, north of the Niobrara River, and at the mouth of Red Canyon, above the Cheyenne River. With those precautions, promoters at Cheyenne City now boasted that their route to the gold fields was the safest of all.

But the troops had scarcely settled on the route than a wagon train was attacked on Indian Creek. For three hours the teamsters held off the Indians. Fourteen animals were killed and one man was wounded before Egan's troopers arrived and chased off the attackers. When the stage driver from Fort Laramie to Red Cloud agency was scared off the run by Indian attacks, a stock tender employed at Fort Laramie volunteered. After his first trip his body was found ten miles from Red Cloud agency, and the stage company had to suspend operations. In early June the Indians even ventured south of Fort Laramie and ran off twenty horses from a ranch on the Chugwater. About the same time they attacked two separate couriers and burned three or four stage stations along the Black Hills roads.

With such actions Captain Egan's small force was kept on the run guarding the line. As early as the end of May, the patrolling force out of Fort Laramie was increased to two troops of cavalry and three companies of infantry. But at the beginning of June the road was so harassed that all travel was suspended except for one large train of 75 wagons, which was escorted all the way by two companies of cavalry.

Meanwhile Sheridan was organizing a spring campaign. This time he intended to make up for the Reynolds fiasco on Powder River and catch the Sioux in a giant trap. Once again Gen. John Gibbon took 450 men from Fort Ellis in Montana Territory and marched southeast to the Yellowstone. Gen. Alfred Terry, whose force had been unable to move in the winter, marched west from Fort Abraham Lincoln with 950 men, including the 7th Cavalry Regiment under Gen. George A. Custer. On June 8 the vanguards of both columns joined at Glendive Creek. Then they moved southward in two columns, Gibbon and Terry along the Yellowstone and Big Horn, Custer along the Rosebud.

In the south, Crook again organized his column at Fort Fetterman, drawing troops from several western posts. Late in May, seven companies of cavalry and three of infantry marched out of Fort Laramie to join the expedition at Fetterman. With two other companies already deployed on the Black Hills road and the Oregon Trail, Fort Laramie had only 25 infantrymen reporting for duty in late June. As Sheridan put it, "the post is down to bed rock."

• 4 •

On May 29, 1876, General Crook marched north from Fort Fetterman with one thousand men on what was officially termed the "Big Horn and Yellowstone Expedition." This time the veteran Indian fighter was in personal command to guard against any blunders.

By the second week in June the column had marched up the old Bozeman Trail past the abandoned forts and had reached the headwaters of the Tongue River. On the 9th about one hundred Sioux and Cheyenne appeared on the bluffs above and fired into the camp. But after two soldiers had been wounded the Indians were chased away by a cavalry charge.

Fearing that this encounter would cost him his chance to surprise Crazy Horse, General Crook pressed his column onward. In the next few days he was joined by some 260 Crow and Snake Indians as scouts and allies against their old enemies, the Sioux. Counting 65 Montana miners who had joined his column, Crook commanded 1,325 men.

According to the Crow, the great Sioux village was on the Rosebud a few miles north of the great bend. Therefore, Crook left his supplies in a base camp on Goose Creek and pushed northward at a faster pace. By the 16th he had reached the headwaters of the Rosebud's south fork. Early the next morning he marched north to the junction with the north fork. There, in an amphitheater just west of the big bend, he halted the column for a rest at about 8 A.M. To the northwest, after the Rosebud made its right-angle turn, it narrowed into a small canyon for several miles. Crook mistakenly believed that the Sioux village was on the other side of that canyon. After resting (he played cards with some of his officers), he would push on for a surprise attack.

Actually, the great village of several thousand Sioux and Cheyenne was 22 miles northwest, on Reno Creek, near its junction with the Little Big Horn. Late on the 16th, Cheyenne scouts who had seen Crook's column came riding into camp with the alarm. In a hurried council, Crazy Horse argued for an immediate attack before Crook could find and destroy the village. With luck the Indians could surprise the soldiers while they marched up the valley of the Rosebud.

Immediately, hundreds of warriors stripped for battle and donned their war paint. Then they leaped to their horses and, brandishing their guns, streamed over the hills in the darkness. Near daybreak they stopped and rested their horses, then pushed on. As they neared the Rosebud, Crazy Horse sent scouts ahead to look for Crook's column.

Meanwhile, the general's own Crow scouts had ridden up the largest hill North of the Big Bend. As they topped its crest—nine miles from the head of Crook's column—they met the Sioux scouts coming up from the other side. Both parties fired at each other. The Crow—one of them wounded—wheeled and raced back to the command shouting: "Sioux! Sioux!"

Robbed of their surprise, the main body of Sioux raised the war cry and swept up the hill. It was to be a free fight between soldiers and Indians of roughly equal strength—one of the very few such battles in history. It would be a fair test between red man and white.

Down on the Rosebud, the Crow and Snake allies were the first to respond. Grabbing their rifles and leaping to horse, they rushed whooping up the slope. Over the top streamed the Sioux and Cheyenne—war bonnets trailing in the wind, rifles gleaming. Straight into them spurred the Crow and Snake, clashing in the confusion, so that the soldiers below could not tell friend from foe.

Apparently the first white man to see the Sioux was Capt. Anson Mills, commanding a battalion of horse, who ran to a vantage point at the first alarm from the scouts. When he first saw the enemy it was so far away that it looked like a flock of crows swooping over the hill. But he could hear the war whoops. Quickly he ordered his own troops to saddle up and shouted down to Crook that the Sioux were coming. Moments later Mills and his men were splashing across the stream to Crook's side.

"March rapidly," ordered the General, "and as soon as you get to higher ground take the bluffs and hold them."

Then, while Mills and his force streamed up the slopes on the double, Crook himself mounted his black horse and rode to a hill-top where he could get a view of the enemy. So preoccupied was he with sizing up the attackers that his regimental commanders were left to deploy their own commands. For twenty minutes, while the Crow and Snake held off the spearhead of Crazy Horse's thrust, the troopers were saddling up, forming ranks and marching swiftly to positions on the northern slopes.

Still underestimating the enemy, Crook believed that the attack was little more than a harassing move to keep him from reaching and destroying the village that he believed lay a few miles up the Rosebud. Determined not to be taken in by this ruse, he quickly decided to ignore this attack and march on for the supposed village. But, by the time he had ridden back from his vantage point, his officers had already sent out the various commands to battle, hurrying to seize the nearest ridges and meet the enemy's charge. In an effort to regain control of the situation, Crook rode up to the infantry companies that had taken a position in the center. From there he sent out orders to the other commanders, trying to bring his forces together for the march up the Rosebud.

By that time the troops were already engaged with the enemy, and the roughness of the slope—cut by streams flowing down into the Rosebud—had the effect of splitting the command three ways. In the center the infantrymen were trying to stop the Sioux but were at first driven down the hillside—almost to the creek, according to some accounts. After regrouping they advanced up the slope again, and this time held their ground. On the right, Captain Mills' battalion made a series of charges, driving the Indians from one ridge and then another.

On the left, Col. William B. Royall's 3rd Cavalry Regiment was separated from the rest of the command by Kollmar Creek, largest of the canyons on the battlefield. Taking advantage of this separation, Crazy Horse soon concentrated most of his force there. The cavalrymen dismounted and left their horses in the ravines under the charge of a quarter of their men; then they fired as rapidly as they could with their single-shot Springfield carbines. But they were no match for the repeating Winchester, Henrys and Spencers carried by many of the Indians, who delivered a barrage of fire as they charged and recharged.

Crook sent orders for Royall to fall back across the hillsides and join the infantry in a continuous line. But apparently Crook's first two messages never reached Royall. When the Colonel finally did receive this message, he was forced to perform a maneuver—a retreat from superior Sioux forces—that he knew to be almost suicidal. To avoid exposing his men by having them mount their horses, he had the animals led along the south side of the canyon and covered their withdrawal with his men on foot.

Seeing this move, the Cheyenne and Sioux tried to break through and stampede the horses. Noticing the exposed position of the troops on the bluff, other Indians came to reinforce the attackers. When the troops reached the brink of Kollmar Canyon, where their horses were partially protected in the ravine, Royall wanted them to mount and retreat the rest of the distance on horseback. But the Indians were pressing so closely with such raking fire that that the soldiers could not show themselves in a run for the horses. Shouted one officer, "Better die here than back in the ravine!"

Once again the Indians tried to surround them by sweeping across their south end, toward the Rosebud. One company, commanded by Lt. Peter Vroom, was encircled for a few minutes, during which time five soldiers were killed and three wounded. Capt. Guy V. Henry of Royall's command was shot through the face. For a few minutes he tried to stay in the saddle but finally swayed and toppled to the ground. With him fell his orderly, who was also wounded. Then many Indians rushed up for the kill and were so eager to outdo one another that they rode over the stricken men. Seeing Henry's plight, Crook ordered the Crow and Snake Indians to save him. They raced southward across the slope and drove the enemy away long enough for Henry and his orderly to be carried away.

With new reinforcements, the Cheyenne and Sioux mounted still another charge against the bluff from the south. By that time the regiment's numbers had been somewhat depleted. The Indians outnumbered the troops perhaps ten to one and had the added advantage of repeating rifles. On they thundered, firing a continuous volley and yelling their frenzied war cries: "Yip, yip! Hi Yah! Hi Yah!"

As the Indians drove upon them, the soldiers in the middle wavered. Some turned, and the rest fell back. In that sickening instant, the noncoms and officers held firm.

"Face them, men!" shouted one sergeant. "God damn them, face them!"

"Great God, men!" yelled an officer, "Don't go back on the old Third!"

Cheering to give themselves spirit, the men turned back and shot another volley in the very faces of the enemy—"almost to burn the noses of their ponies," as one officer reported. Against murderous fire the Indians wheeled and ran back. The heartened soldiers chased them for nearly two hundred yards.

Still trying to get his men mounted in the ravine, Royall called for help from Crook, who sent two companies of infantry scurrying across the slopes. Royall's men were rushing down the bank for their horses when the Indians massed and charged again. But the rescuing infantrymen, with long barreled Springfields, fired a volley into their midst and halted the main attack. As it was, a group of Sioux horsemen plunged down the ravine and shot some of Royall's men while they were trying to mount their horses.

Up to that point, Crook had remained determined to disengage from the attacking force and destroy the supposed village down the Rosebud. The seriousness of the Sioux threat—his own horse had been shot from under him—still had not dawned on him. Impatient to unite his whole force, he had given peremptory orders to Capt. Anson Mills: "You must take your battalion and go for their village away down the canyon."

Mills then pulled his cavalry out of the line. Thinking this move meant a general retreat, the Indians mounted a charge at the right flank. But the soldiers, aided by the expert fire of the mule packers and miners, drove them back.

With eight troops of cavalry, Mills led his column down to the Rosebud and north into the narrows. The troops had gone several miles—some of them expecting an ambush at any moment—when they heard hoofbeats behind them. An officer and an orderly from Crook galloped their horses along the length of the column, on the other side of the stream, and called for Mills to halt. From across the water Crook's adjutant told Mills to turn back and rejoin the main force. It was a disappointment to all the officers of the column. When they hesitated, the adjutant splashed across the Rosebud.

"Are you sure he wants me to go back?" demanded Mills, when the other rode up.

"Mills," was the answer, "Royall is hard pressed and must be relieved. Henry is badly wounded, and Vroom's troop is all cut up. The General orders that you . . . defile by your left flank out of this canyon and fall on the rear of the Indians who are pressing Royall."

Leading their horses, they climbed up a side canyon and emerged onto a plateau. There they mounted and pounded back to the battle, arriving in the rear of the main Indian line which was preparing for another attack on Crook. The Indians, seeing Royall's troopers in full retreat, thought that the soldiers had been beaten. They promptly launched a new attack against the entire line. But at that critical moment Captain Mills' troopers appeared in their rear, charging down upon them with mock war whoops.

Fearing a trap, the Indians fell back, the dismounted ones running for their horses. Then they plunged down the slope to the west of Royall into the flatland along the Rosebud, rode downstream, crossed it near the mouth of the narrows and scrambled up the west side of the canyon. They retreated to the northwest abandoning the fight.

• 5 •

In his reports, Crook claimed that his cavalry and the scouts pursued them for several miles. But none of his other officers reported a pursuit; other first-hand accounts are vague on the subject, and Indian accounts do not mention it. At most the allied Indians scouts may have chased them as far as the mouth of the Rosebud narrows.

It has also been claimed that Crazy Horse had set a trap for Crook with the main body of his warriors in the narrows of the Rosebud, and a later newspaper interview with Crazy Horse was supposed to have supported this theory. But none of the other Indian accounts makes any mention of such a trap; they all agree only that Crazy Horse hurried all night from his camp and attacked Crook as soon as he could. Any effort on his part to set a trap had been foiled when the Crow scouts had discovered his advance forces and had brought on the battle immediately. The white man's claim that there was such an ambush rests on supposition of the same sort as the false assumption that Crazy Horse's village lay just beyond the Rosebud narrows. But the ambush story became a favorite in the army, possibly because it made Crook appear clever in avoiding it and mitigated the raw fact that the Rosebud was no victory.

In any case, the Battle of the Rosebud was over, and the enemy had been repulsed. As soon as he could, Captain Mills confronted Crook: "General, why did you recall me? . . ."

Crook was sick with disappointment. "Well," he drawled, ". . . I found it a more serious engagement than I thought. We have lost about fifty killed and wounded, and the doctors refused to remain with the wounded unless I left the infantry and one of the squadrons with them . . . I knew I could not keep my promise to support you with the remainder of the force."

Actually, the loss among the troops had been nine killed—all in Royall's 3rd Regiment, where the fighting had been fierce—and 21 wounded. One of the allied Indians had been killed and 27 wounded.

Among the worst injured was Capt. Guy V. Henry of Royall's regiment. As he lay in the field hospital along the Rosebud, his cheeks shattered and clotted with blood, he told a brother officer, "The doctors have just told me that I must die, but I will not."

With such resolve the gallant gentleman clung to life. To another friend he said, "It is for this we are soldiers."

As for the Sioux and Cheyenne, their losses were heavier. In contrast to their conduct in most battles, they did not recover all their dead and left thirteen on the battlefield. More than a year later Crazy Horse put the dead at 36—a number that may be considered credible.[10]

With such comparatively light losses, the Battle of the Rosebud could be regarded as a colorful display of fireworks and horsemanship, with a strange air of unreality. There was much charging, dashing and wheeling; much burning of gunpowder, and much noise. At times the air seemed almost filled with lead.

True, the concentrated attack upon Royall and the brave defense by his men constituted an encounter as desperate as any in Indian-fighting annals. Four men won the Congressional Medal of Honor in the clash. But outside Royall's command, the casualties among the soldiers totaled five wounded men.

Had Crook taken the battle more seriously from the beginning, rather than attempting to disengage and attack a supposed village downstream, could he have defeated Crazy Horse at the Rosebud? Possibly, but the mistakes he would have had to undo started before the battle really began—allowing himself to be caught unprepared when the Sioux first attacked and spending so much time reconnoitering the situation that he could not direct the deployment of his command.

The Rosebud was, in short, his only opportunity to smash the enemy he had marched out to find, and he failed to recognize it. On the other hand, Crazy Horse had at least succeeded in defending his village from a possible later attack by Crook. The General's command was so worn out in the fight that he fell back to his base of supplies forty miles away on Goose Creek—and for the time being did not rendezvous with Gibbon and Terry. As one of Crook's officers wrote, "we had been most humiliatingly defeated."

• 6 •

For the next few days Crook waited at Goose Creek for reinforcements and supplies. He tried to open communications with Gibbon, Terry and Custer, who were coming down from the north. Though frustrated by his setback at the Rosebud, he was still confident of beating the Sioux. As an aide wrote, "We shall hit them again in a week or two, as soon as the supplies come, and we expect to wind the whole matter up by the first of September."

But the country was swarming with hostiles, and it was impossible to get through to Terry. During those days there was an ominous lapse of war news from the entire Sioux country. On July 6 Fort Laramie received a telegram with the first authentic word of Custer's fate. A scout from Gibbon's column had arrived in Stillwater, Montana Territory, with news of a "fearful disaster" on the Little Big Horn.

Eight days after the Rosebud, Gen. George A. Custer had done what Crook had failed to do: He had discovered the main village of the Sioux. Dividing his command to surround the enemy, he had charged the camp. But the force of several thousand warriors had been too much for him. His own detachment of 261 men had retreated to higher ground, where it was surrounded by hordes under Sitting Bull and Crazy Horse. There the soldiers were slaughtered to the last man—an appalling loss that supplanted the Fetterman massacre as the worst tragedy in the Indian wars.

The news of Custer's fall, reaching the East in the midst of the centennial celebration of United States independence, shocked and angered the nation. Western spokesmen called for a volunteer army of frontiersmen to exterminate the redskins. Sheridan ordered a dozen more companies of infantry to join Terry in tracking down Sitting Bull and Crazy Horse. Under War Department pressure, the Interior Department temporarily turned the Sioux agencies over to the army, and Sheridan's troopers took control from the Indian agents. Red Cloud was so furious that he took his Oglala away from the agency to Chadron Creek, there hurling maledictions at the pony soldiers of Fort Robinson.

It was July 10 before couriers came into Crook's camp on Goose Creek with the first authentic account of the Custer fight. Two days later three soldiers staggered in from Terry's command with a longer message. When Crook read its awful details, another officer discerned in his countenance "a feeling that the country would realize that there were others who had underrated the valor and numbers of the Sioux."

But Crook might also have asked himself if the tragedy would have happened at all had he pressed on the heels of the Sioux after the Rosebud battle in an effort to squeeze them against Terry's forces. For not doing so he was severely chastised in the western press. His return to the base of supplies on Goose Creek is justifiable when it is understood that he was desperately short of rations and ammunition. But that he should have waited at Goose Creek for still more supplies, as well as for reinforcements, for a month and a half before moving again toward the planned junction with Terry is not so defensible.

Had he moved north as soon as possible after refitting from his base-camp supplies, he could have reached the vicinity of the main Sioux village (a two- to three-day march) before the Custer massacre. In that case he might either have joined up with Custer (had his scouts been able to make contact) or have run onto the village first and encountered the onslaught that felled Custer. That Crook's 1,300 men would have suffered the same fate as Custer's 261 is questionable, though certainly they would have been badly mauled. True, Crook did need reinforcements before leaving Goose Creek, but Custer needed them even more.

At any rate, by the time Gen. Wesley Merritt joined Crook with ten more cavalry companies on August 3, many of Crook's own men were referring to their cautious commander as "Rosebud George."

As if trying to make up for prior mistakes, Crook pushed ahead with renewed vigor. On August 11, he met Terry's column near the Yellowstone. Twelve days later they separated again in search of hostiles, Terry going north and Crook marching east. Believing that the Indians were heading for the reservation, Crook feared for the safety of the Black Hills miners. With only two and a half days' rations, he forbore to march on to Fort Abraham Lincoln and instead plunged south on a two hundred-mile trek from Heart River to the Black Hills settlements. On this famed "mud march" through rain and cold, prey to hunger and exhaustion, his men were reduced to eating their own horses. Wrote one officer, "I saw men who were very plucky sit down and cry like children because they could not hold out."

On September 8, the general sent an advanced detachment under Capt. Anson Mills to the Black Hills for help. A week later Mills attacked a Brulé village at Slim Buttes and killed some of the Indians, including the chief. After that, other Sioux parties harassed Crook for most of the remaining march into Custer City. He now had one small victory to his credit, but by the end of his torture march he had seen more hostiles than he had wanted.

Leaving his troops in the Dakota settlements, Crook rode back to Fort Laramie for a conference with Sheridan. He was so disgruntled with his own showing against the Sioux that he would hardly talk to anyone. The ladies of the post, who were anxious to know when their husbands would be back from the Black Hills, kept trying to trick him into revealing his plans. Late in September one of them ventured, "You will be coming in next Christmas to get some mince pie and turkey?"

But Crook was stoical: "We can't tell."

• 7 •

So far the Indians were winning the war of 1876. They had beaten Reynolds on the Powder and Crook at the Rosebud and had annihilated Custer on the Little Big Horn. But the Indians were almost out of ammunition. And by keeping the Sioux on the move the army had at least dealt an economic blow. As one of Crook's officers wrote, "The Sioux, though having lost but one small village, have been so kept on the move that they have been unable to lay up the stores of meat, etc., which will be indispensable to them this winter."

True to form, the hostiles drifted back to the agencies to be fed by Indian Bureau men who could not or would not distinguish them from the peaceful Indians. Sitting Bull refused to come in and, after an encounter with Gen. Nelson A. Miles near the Yellowstone, took some of his people north into the sanctuary of Canada.

"Our next objective point," Crook finally announced, "is Crazy Horse."

But Sheridan could not promise Crook that he would have all the supplies and men he needed. In this uncertain situation, with the Indians still unbeaten, Washington also acted true to form. At about the time Crook was beginning his march south from Heart River, Congress had approved a treaty securing the Black Hills and had authorized a new peace commission to wrest them from the Indians. This time, except for one general who declined to serve, the appointees were all civilians—mostly men who had long held the confidence of the western tribes. They included the usual church representative—this time the Episcopal Bishop of Minnesota, Henry B. Whipple, who had championed the Sioux even while his neighbors were recovering from the terrible massacre of 1862. Chairman of the eight-man group was George W. Manypenny, who had been Commissioner of Indian Affairs in the mid-Fifties, when he had been forced into the unpleasant task of talking the border tribes out of their lands along the Kansas and Nebraska frontiers.

These men went west in September 1876 with a ready-made agreement fixed by Congress. It was not a treaty, as the United States no longer recognized the tribes as sovereign nations; it was rather an amendment to the treaty of 1868. The Indians were to give up the Black Hills and all the other lands outside the reservation (including the Powder River country); permit three roads through their reservation to the Hills; receive their annuities at points on the Missouri River, rather than at the agencies that had been difficult for the white man to supply, and "use their best efforts to learn to cultivate" the soil.

For its part, the United States would furnish rations, agricultural assistance and schools. But the catch was that no rations would be given to Indians not farming or to children not going to school.

Finally, as it was admitted even by the United States that the Missouri River section of the Sioux reservation could not sustain the Indians as farmers, they would have the option of being removed south of Kansas to the Indian Territory (Oklahoma), which had become the final dumping ground for all the tribes east of the frontier. In a gesture of fair play, it was conceded that the Indians could send delegates south to the territory and decide for themselves whether or not they liked it better than the Missouri River. But if they did not like either and would not "touch the pen" to the document, they would receive no more rations beyond the annuities of the 1868 treaty.

Thus did the United States descend to the last infamy in its erosion of the Indian: the threat of starvation. For 1876 was not 1868. The buffalo that were still in existence in 1868 to supplement the annuities were now gone—either slaughtered by the hide hunters or made inaccessible to the Indians by agreeement. Even the northern herd in the valleys of the Powder and the Yellowstone would be denied the Indians when that territory was thrown open to white settlement, as provided for in the agreement now offered. The choice to be given the Indians by the pious commissioners of 1876 was simple: Sign or die.

By the end of August the commissioners had ridden the Union Pacific to Cheyenne and were heading by horse and wagon for Fort Laramie. Arriving there on September 2, they left a few days later with a company of cavalry as escort. This time they avoided a general council and instead met the tribes separately, starting with the Oglala at Red Cloud agency on September 7. When the commissioners went out to meet the Indians in the open near the agency, the commander at nearby Fort Robinson urged them to take a military guard, as had the commissioners of 1875. But they refused: "It would indicate that we had no confidence in the Indians." Unarmed, the commissioners met what Bishop Whipple described as "three hundred Indians, each with a Winchester rifle and a belt of cartridges."

From the commissioners Red Cloud and his warriors heard hard words: "Unless you decide to go to the Indian Territory next season, or to the Missouri River this fall, the Government will stop issuing rations here next month."

For nearly two weeks the Oglala were allowed to discuss the terms. When they met with the commissioners again Chief Little Wound was the spokesman: "The country upon which I am standing is the country upon which I was born, and upon which I heard that it was the wish of the Great Father and of the Great Council that I should be like a man without a country. I shed tears."

This time Red Cloud and his head men—once the terrors of the Bozeman Trail—were the first to sign the agreement. The commission moved on to the agency of Spotted Tail, whose people had already been given a copy of the document to consider. Meeting with them in the agency schoolhouse on September 20, the commissioners found them in a different mood from that of the Oglala. As he greeted one of the commissioners before the speeches began, Spotted Tail smiled wryly. "The white man wants another treaty," he sneered. "Why does not the Great Father put his red children on wheels, so that he can move them as he will?"

Disillusioned at last with his long role as peacemaker for the Sioux, Spotted Tail rose to make his speech, holding in his hand the pages of broken treaties. Relentlessly, he reviewed them one by one.

The Horse Creek Treaty of 1851: "These promises have not been kept. . . . All the words have proved to be false."

The Fort Laramie Treaty of 1868: General Sherman "didn't tell the truth."

Then he chronicled his present grievances: the new Sioux war, "brought upon us by the children of the Great Father who came to take our land from us without price"; the occupation soldiers, "who think only of our death"; the demand for a Missouri River agency—"I left . . . one hundred of my people buried there"; the ban against buying ammunition to kill game—"the result has been great suffering to my people. . . . It seems as if the wish of the Great Father was that my people should go into the ground . . ."

With the Brulé in a belligerent mood, the commissioners ended the session and met again three days later. The chiefs were still adamant. Spotted Tail made plain his fear that the whites would not fulfill their promises if he "touched the pen" to the treaty. "I have always found it full of deceit." As for the annuities and the rations, he wanted everything spelled out carefully so that there could be no trickery: "How many kinds of goods, how many kinds of cattle, and how many wagons, and for how many years . . ."

Bishop Whipple read aloud the provisions about increased rations. But Spotted Tail did not believe them: "From the former treaty I have not seen these things." Then he asked once again, with mounting anger: "You say we will receive them. . . . For how many years is that to last?"

"The provisions of the treaty," answered the Bishop, "are to last until you are self-supporting."

The Chief could see that this answer left the same kind of loophole that the whites had always used. Breaking off his talk, he turned and stalked out of the council room. Outside were Red Cloud and another Oglala chief, who had come over from the other agency. For a few minutes they exhorted Spotted Tail to sign, as they had already done. Then they went into the building with Spotted Tail and talked to the Brulé chiefs, urging them to "touch the pen." Spotted Tail himself, after another short wrangle with the Bishop, then addressed his people.

"If our friends above had not signed it," he said, gesturing toward the Oglala chiefs, "I would help them in holding out, but as our friends up there have signed it I ask all good men who are trustworthy to come up and sign it."

Then Spotted Tail and the others touched the pen to the paper. That they did not understand its meaning is shown by their comments. Said Spotted Tail, "I touch it with the thought that I am going to remain here without having to change to any other place." Another chief asked for his old friends as traders, "and the first kind of goods I wish them to sell is ammunition."

Through the rest of the Sioux agencies went the good commissioners, signing up the chiefs and headmen. By the end of October they had visited all the bands and concluded the agreement. It was actually invalid, as the 1868 treaty had specified that any amendments had to be approved by three-fourths of the adult males. But the Indians did not know of this clause.

Then the white negotiators reported back to the Commissioner of Indian Affairs, calling for immediate legislation to provide the rations and agricultural help stipulated in the treaty. They catalogued the wrongs done to the Indians since the Fort Laramie Treaty of 1851. They confessed their own shame upon hearing the woes of the Indian chiefs, and they concluded:

Unless immediate and appropriate legislation is made for the protection and government of the Indians, they must perish. Our country must forever bear the disgrace and suffer the retribution of its wrong-doing. Our children's children will tell the sad story in hushed tones, and wonder how their fathers dared so to trample on justice and trifle with God.

• 8 •

Still the wrongs of 1876 were not ended. Conferring at Fort Laramie, Sheridan and Crook agreed that the agencies were filled with former hostiles. Red Cloud's angry threats confirmed their suspicion that the agency Indians were still dangerous. Lacking a victory over the hostiles in the field, the generals determined to win a victory at the agencies. Take away the Indian's horses and guns, and he would be impotent.

The new agreement just signed by the Indians and the commissioners included the guarantee that "each individual shall be protected in his rights of property, person and life." Despite this provision—already created by Congress and agreed to by the commissioners—Sheridan's forces marched on the three most troublesome agencies, Red Cloud, Standing Rock and Cheyenne River. The commissioners were still signing up Indians at the Missouri River agencies when Crook sent orders from Fort Laramie to the commander at Fort Robinson. On October 23 a regiment of cavalry started for Red Cloud's camp on Chadron Creek. Before dawn on the 24th, Pawnee scouts sneaked among the lodges and stole all the ponies. When Red Cloud, Red Leaf and the rest awoke, they found themselves without mounts and surrounded by soldiers. There was nothing to do but obey orders to come out and lay down their guns—a miserable arsenal of only fifty rifles. Then the Indians were hauled back to the agency under guard and confined until the end of the Sioux war.

In a pretext at fairness, the horses were driven to Fort Laramie in order to sell them and give the Indians their market value. Many of the same horses had previously been turned over to the Indians in payment for their hunting rights in Nebraska at a value of $120 per head. They were now sold at Fort Laramie for $5.00 and less apiece. This was dutifully returned to the Oglala—a final insult in the great theft of 1876. The army was triumphant in robbery if not in battle. Wrote Crook to Sheridan, "I feel that this is the first gleam of daylight we have had in this business."

The Oglala—dismounted, disarmed and imprisoned—were humbled in the dust. From the golden days of the 1830s and 1840s, when they had ruled the Platte Valley from their headquarters by Fort Laramie, they had now fallen at the white man's feet. Beside himself with rage and shame, Red Cloud could only complain pathetically at this blow from the Great Father: "What have I done that I should receive such treatment from him whom I thought my friend?"

Among the high plains tribes, only the northern Cheyenne, the wild Oglala under Crazy Horse and some Miniconjou under Lame Deer remained to be whipped. In November 1876 Crook launched his third Powder River Expedition from Fort Fetterman. On the 25th a detachment under Col. Ronald S. Mackenzie attacked and routed Dull Knife's village of Cheyenne on the north fork of the Powder. Most of the Cheyenne joined Crazy Horse's camp on the Tongue River. Then in early January 1877 Gen. Nelson Miles struck at Crazy Horse's forces and sent them into retreat. Later in the year he attacked the Miniconjou and killed Chief Lame Deer. The war had turned in favor of the whites.

In February, Crook induced Spotted Tail to find Crazy Horse and offer terms of surrender. With both his Cheyenne and Oglala warriors slipping away and going into the agencies to be fed, Crazy Horse finally marched into Red Cloud agency on May 5, 1877. Within four months he was attempting to jump the reservation when he was stopped by agency Indians and brought to Fort Robinson.

As they took Crazy Horse into the guardhouse, he saw the barred windows and realized that he was to be imprisoned. Jumping back from the doorway, he pulled out a knife in each hand. Little Big Man—the same one who had threatened the peace commissioners in 1875—seized Crazy Horse from behind and held his arms. Swift Bear and others ran up and also grabbed him. The frantic Crazy Horse lunged about to get free, shouting: "Let me go! Let me go!" Around the door of the guardhouse all was confusion, with friendly Indians, including Red Cloud, trying to subdue Crazy Horse or even to shoot him. The officer of the day came up with his saber unsheathed, and the soldier guarding the door tried to use his bayonet. As Crazy Horse thrashed about, both his knives cut Little Big Man's left arm. According to one story, Little Big Man accidentally turned the knife so that it stuck into Crazy Horse's stomach. According to another, the sentry lunged with his bayonet and struck the door, then lunged again and stabbed Crazy Horse in the stomach. At any rate, Crazy Horse stopped fighting.

"Let me go, my friends," he cried, hoarsely. "You have got me hurt enough."

That night, with his father and mother by his side, the last of the fighting Sioux died. He had been born in the year that Fort Laramie was founded and had arrived there as an infant when his people had migrated to the Platte. A Miniconjou chief who was Crazy Horse's friend touched the dead warrior's breast. "It is good," he whispered. "He has looked for death, and it has come."

SEVENTEEN ◆ *The Last Trumpet*

◆ 1 ◆

On November 3, 1878, a Concord stagecoach rolled north out of Cheyenne, bound for the Black Hills on its regular run to the diggings. Inside, in the custody of sheriff's deputies, were two accused bandits, William Mansfield and Archie McLaughlin. Charged with participating in a stage robbery near Canyon Springs, they were being sent back to Deadwood City for trial.

The Canyon Springs holdup, complete with pitched battle and the death of a passenger, had been the culmination in a series of outrages on the Black Hills road through 1877 and 1878. The heavy gold shipments out of Deadwood and Custer City had attracted a host of road agents, who repeatedly stopped the stages and made off with the treasure boxes. For a time troops from Fort Laramie had escorted the treasure coaches, but the robberies had continued—sometimes within a few miles of the fort. With terror stalking the whole trail from Cheyenne to Deadwood, local editors were calling for vigilante action and suggesting a rope for those who were caught.

Scarcely a mile beyond Fort Laramie, the stage bearing the two accused robbers was approaching the North Platte Bridge through a stand of cottonwood trees. Suddenly the coach was halted at gunpoint by five masked men. They relieved the guards of their weapons and turned them out of the coach. At first it looked as though the intruders might be rescuing the prisoners. But they quickly set about tying the pair by the hands, placing them on top of the coach and putting ropes over their heads. Then they drove the coach under a large cottonwood near the river and fastened the ropes to a limb. When it was clear that the end was near, one of the victims cursed his captors, while the other pleaded for his life. But with a flurry and a shout the coach was driven from under them. They were left hanging with no support but the ropes around their necks. Wyoming justice had written an aftermath to the last stage robbery on the Black Hills line.

Violent as it was, the Fort Laramie lynching symbolized the end of one era and the beginning of another. The parties in the drama were neither Indians nor soldiers. A new force for public safety—the civil peace officer—had arrived. At the same time a new threat to the peace had appeared—the white outlaw. The western public itself, represented perhaps by the lynchers, was as insistent as ever upon severe and summary measures. Although the incident occurred within a mile of Fort Laramie, the army was a nonparticipant, its force inapplicable in the new reign of civilians.

Not that the western forts had all suddenly become impotent. Those near the Indian agencies—Fort Robinson at Red Cloud, Camp Sheridan at Spotted Tail—were keeping their garrisons in readiness for any signs of Indian unrest.

Action at such posts was not altogether unknown. Late in 1878, more than three hundred northern Cheyenne who had been sent southward to the Indian Territory after the Black Hills War, jumped the reservation and migrated north to join the Oglala Sioux. Hunted by the military throughout their exodus, they were brought into Fort Robinson in the middle of winter. Told that they would be returned to the hated Indian Territory, they refused to go. The commanding officer disciplined them by depriving all— men, women and children—of blankets, food, fire and water. On the night of January 9, 1879, they broke out of their prison and raced for the snow-covered prairie. The soldiers followed and shot them down, then for days hunted the survivors like wild game among the bluffs of the creeks. Of the 320 original renegades, 75 lived through the ministrations of the United States Army.

There was also the job of moving the Sioux to the Missouri River, the only home left them under the 1876 agreement after they had refused to settle in Indian Territory. Late in October 1877 the Oglala and Brulé left their agencies in Nebraska for the Missouri. Escorting them on their long march were several companies of cavalry from Fort Robinson and Camp Sheridan. But through the winter the Indians became so dissatisfied with the

Missouri location that they were allowed to resettle at the forks of the White River in the spring of 1878. They were now about as far from the Missouri as they could go and still remain in the Sioux reservation.

One of the objectives of the 1876 agreement—to place the Indians where their rations and annuities could be cheaply supplied by steamboat—was thus thwarted. Another objective—to make farmers out of the warriors and students out of the children—was also frustrated as long as Chiefs Spotted Tail and Red Cloud remained to oppose these "progressive" measures. Some of the bands tried agriculture, but their destitution was a clear disappointment to the eastern theorists who believed that Stone Age hunters could be made into civilized farmers in a single generation. Stock-raising was more to the liking of a nomadic and equestrian people, but once again there were limits on how far they could cultivate the arts of animal husbandry. Instead of becoming less dependent on government support, as the Indian Bureau had hoped, they became semipermanent wards.

In the Yellowstone Basin there still remained the old source of Sioux wealth—hundreds of thousands of buffalo. But the Sioux and Cheyenne were confined to the Dakota reservation and had given up their hunting rights elsewhere. They were prevented by law from attempting to escape into their old life.

By 1879 the white hunters who had cleaned out the southern herds on the Republican and the Cimarron were moving northward for the last hunt. With their wagons, their long Sharps rifles and their skinning knives, they pressed into the great triangle bounded by the Missouri, the Yellowstone and the Musselshell. The slaughter that began that year threw the buffalo into a panic. In the fall of 1880 they began migrating eastward—toward the Dakota reservation and into the arms of the Sioux.

At Cheyenne River Agency the Miniconjou and Hunkpapa heard with delight that the buffalo were coming back. Sixty braves—with their women, horses and dogs—rode northwest to meet them. As they jogged along their weapons gleamed in the sun, and for one precious moment the old life was theirs again. On the day before Christmas they swept down on the first herd and slaughtered fifty—only one got away. Through the winter they killed two thousand, returning to their agency with meat and robes to make their villages prosperous and warm through that one winter.

But after that the white hunters surrounded their quarry with professional care. Only a few escaped, and they broke northward into Canada. In the peak years of 1881-1882, the herd was reduced to 75,000. By October 1883 a remnant of some 1,100 remained in Dakota Territory east of the Black Hills. But Sitting Bull and his followers had just returned from their long exile in Canada. With other Sioux warriors they fell upon the pitiful stragglers. Helped by white hunters, they destroyed the last ones in a few days' time. Only about two or three hundred buffalo, protected from hunters by their remote refuge in the mountains, remained in the United States. Through earnest conservation, there are today more than 150,000 bison in the U.S. and Canada.

· 2 ·

Having taken the last of the Indian's cattle, the white man promptly arrived on the northern plains with some cattle of his own. In 1882 a new United States commission headed by Newton Edmunds, a former Dakota governor, went among the Sioux agencies offering 25,000 cows and 1,000 bulls if the people would sign a new agreement. The Indians were told that the paper would simply divide the big reservation into six reservations for the separate tribes, a change that some of them had requested.

According to the treaty of 1868, three-fourths of the adult males were required to sign before any such change could be made. But many of the leaders were suspicious and refused to "touch the pen." To swell the numbers on the roll, even boys scarcely out of puberty were allowed to sign. Others were told, according to their later testimony, that if they did not sign they would be sent to the Indian Territory. Red Cloud later claimed that he had been forced to sign on pain of imprisonment. Still others were told, according to their later statements, that the paper already had enough names and that if they did not join they would be "left out in the cold."

Despite these tactics, only about four hundred of a population of 25,000 Indians affixed their names. The commission returned the agreement to Washington with the recommendation that it be ratified by Congress without the required number of names. It argued that the agreement of 1876 had violated the treaty in this respect and had established a precedent for this new violation.

Buried within the 1882 agreement was a technicality that the Indians had not understood—that, in the process of dividing the reservation into six parts for the six tribes, nearly one-half of it would be outside the division and would be turned over to the United States.

This monstrous fraud had been perpetrated under pressure from two sources—the frontier settlers who coveted the Indian lands and supporters for the extension of two railroads, the Chicago and Northwestern and the Chicago, Milwaukee and St. Paul. Already their railheads stood at the Missouri on the edge of the reservation. It so happened that much of the area to be withheld from the Indians by the agreement was in a wide corridor across the reservation along the proposed lines of these railroads to the Black Hills.

When this phony document was submitted to Congress for ratification by President Chester A. Arthur in February 1883, the Senate turned it over to a select committee for investigation. The committee visited the Indians, held hearings at the agencies, discovered the colossal hoax and denounced it in a scathing report. At the same time it proposed another agreement. Although aimed at acquiring the same land, it at least had the virtues of offering the Indians more benefits and of telling them squarely its provisions.

This agreement Congress duly authorized, but when it was submitted to the tribes in 1885 they vehemently opposed it. One of the railroads then swung southward through Nebraska, passing through Fort Robinson on its way to the Black Hills.

The move had the side effect of threatening Fort Laramie's existence. Since the Indian War of 1876-1877, its abandonment had been proposed from time to time. But until the mid-Eighties its continued existence had been justified by its usefulness in supplying and reinforcing the other forts near Indian reservations. Indeed, a telegraph line had been strung between Fort Laramie and Fort Robinson during the winter of 1884-1885.

But in 1885 the post commander wrote that "it seems to me probable that the new line of railroad ascending the Niobrara reopens the question as to the need of retaining this as a permanent post." Urging an early decision, he pointed out the shopworn condition of the tired old fort. Thirty-six years of sheltering American soldiers had taken its toll. Disposal of human waste over this entire period had finally resulted in "saturation of the

ground to a degree that must in time prove injurious to health."
As for the fifty or more houses at the fort:

> The public buildings at this post are nearly all in a wretched
> state of dilapidation. They are a lot of very old structures, never
> good, either in plan or construction, and they have been disfigured
> and confused by unsightly additions and modifications, embracing
> every kind of material and every style of architecture, until the
> post presents a most unsightly appearance at all points.

Nor was there any justifiable activity for the troops beyond
maintaining their own subsistence through log-cutting and hay-
gathering details. Through 1885 and 1886 almost no field operations were conducted outside the post. In 1886 the commander
reported, "In view of new railroad construction and the conse-
quent change of condition governing the disposition of troops it
appears to me, this Post has lost its military significance as a location, and that no considerable expenditure on new or repair of old
buildings would be justified."

In the same year the army's Adjutant General agreed: "Even if
another railroad should hereafter be extended through the valley
of the North Platte to and beyond Fort Laramie, Fort Robinson
would still remain much the most important station because of
its closer proximity to the Sioux reservation."

In the fall of 1886 and again in the summer of 1887, two infantry companies stationed at Fort Laramie made practice marches
to Laramie Peak and up the North Platte River. But these
marches were isolated efforts that only served to emphasize Fort
Laramie's impotence. The garrison was reduced in 1887, and
repairs were delayed pending a decision on the fate of the post.

• 3 •

The decline of Fort Laramie's importance was actually a
symptom of the dynamic changes that had swept over the Fort
Laramie country. A few small stock ranches in support of the
Oregon Trail traffic had appeared on and near the North Platte
as early as the 1860s. By the 1870s other and larger spreads had
clustered near the settlements in southeastern Wyoming. Among
them was John "Portugee" Phillips' ranch on the Chugwater.

After the Sioux war ended in 1877, cattlemen took up land across Wyoming, Dakota and Montana territories, stocking their ranges with Texas longhorns. By the late 1880s the ranchers were finding themselves crowded by a new breed migrating from the mid-western plains—the sod-house farmers.

Thus by 1890 the Northwest was sufficiently populated so that the Census Bureau could no longer distinguish an American frontier. For decades the Bureau had been able to draw an arbitrary line along the farthest west points where the population reached one or more persons per square mile. But in 1890 a network of such populated areas extended across the West, and there was no more frontier line.

The passing of the "wild" Northwest became official in 1889-90 with admission of six new states, including Wyoming, both Dakotas, Montana, Idaho and Washington. Statehood came to North and South Dakota late in 1889 and to Wyoming in mid-1890.

The wild country in which William Sublette had first planted his pioneer outpost had been tamed by a cavalcade that had followed in his path. The buckskin-clad trapper, joined first by the soldier and then by the cowboy, had been supplanted at last by the farmer—a new kind of westerner in a new kind of West.

As for the Indian who had preceded the white man in the high plains, his prescribed domain was being narrowed still further. In 1888 another commission came to the Sioux with a new plan for getting part of the reservation; once again the chiefs refused. But next year, a few months before Dakota statehood, a fourth commission appeared. Once again it was after the approximate territory that Newton Edmunds's commission had tried unsuccessfully to acquire in 1882-1883. And among its members was the same Gen. George Crook who had fought the Sioux at the Rosebud in 1876.

Opposing these commissioners as they moved through the Sioux agencies were Red Cloud, Sitting Bull, Little Wound, Young Man-Afraid and other chiefs. But they had run out of allies. The Indian Bureau and the eastern reform groups who had stood up for Indian rights had been won over to the new proposal by the provision for eventually giving individual Indians their own private land and making them citizens. And, of course, statehood for the Dakotas was intensifying the pressure for land for western settlers. As Crook himself told the Indians:

It strikes me that you are in the position of a person who had his effects in the bed of a dry stream when there was a flood coming down, and instead of finding fault with the Creator for sending it down, you should try and save what you can. And that when you can't get what you like best you had better take what is the best for you.

At the same time the commissioners listened to the many grievances of the Indians and promised to do their best to find solutions. By this combination of threats and promises they finally secured the necessary signatures of three-fourths of the male tribesmen to an agreement by which the Indians would receive $1.25 per acre for all land sold to new settlers in the first year, with reduced payments down to fifty cents an acre thereafter.

But before the reforms recommended by the commissioners could be enacted by Congress, President Benjamin Harrison proclaimed acceptance of the new Sioux agreement and opened for settlement the land between the Cheyenne and White Rivers. Next the House of Representatives refused to approve the proposed reforms.

The Sioux had, of course, regarded the commissioners' promises to press for reforms as actual promises of reforms. They were now convinced that, once more, they had been double-crossed by the white man.

During the land negotiations, Red Cloud and Sitting Bull had argued that, with less territory, the tribes would be still more dependent on the whites, who could cut off their rations at any time. At the same time, the Indian Bureau had become impatient at the slow progress of the Sioux toward self-support through agriculture and had become convinced that they would never achieve it while they received full rations. According to the agreement of 1876 the Indians were to receive such rations until they became self-sufficient; the Bureau now violated this provision by starting to reduce the rations gradually in an effort to force the Indians to greater efforts in their own behalf.

This measure, introduced right after the land agreement of 1889, vindicated the warnings of the chiefs. It was presented in the face of the drought of 1889-1890, which ruined what limited crops the Indians were cultivating. Long since robbed of their own livelihood by the slaughter of the buffalo, unable to live by the white man's ways, the Sioux sank deeper into poverty and desperation. It appeared that even the Great Spirit had failed them.

• 4 •

At that moment a Paiute Indian near Pyramid Lake, Nevada, launched a new religious revival with himself as its messiah. Through a Ghost Dance that he taught his people, they were to be reunited with their dead loved ones. Quickly this awakening swept through all the western tribes and reached the Sioux in the summer of 1889.

At the Pine Ridge agency in South Dakota near the Nebraska border, the Oglala held a council in the fall and sent a delegation to witness the messiah craze in Nevada. Joined by Short Bull and Kicking Bear from two other agencies, the group traveled west of the Rockies and was gone all winter. When the delegates returned in the spring of 1890, they gave a twisted and exaggerated version of the messiah's teaching. He had come, they said, to destroy the white men for their treatment of the Indians; he would bring all the dead Indians back to life, restore the buffalo and give to the tribes their old life and power.

Thus, although the white man had encircled them and destroyed even their self-respect, they had left one avenue of escape—religious delusion. The Indians embraced it in a last pathetic spasm. From Standing Rock to Pine Ridge, the Sioux threw themselves into the Ghost Dance to bring on the Day of Armageddon.

Fearing that the Indians were working themselves into an uprising, the Indian Bureau tried to suppress the Ghost Dance. This effort only threw the Sioux into new religious fury. Short Bull declared that he himself was the messiah and that he would make the white soldiers powerless in a clash with the Sioux. With the Indian agents calling for help, fear of a new outbreak quickly spread to Washington. President Harrison ordered the War Department to move against the Indians. Under Gen. Nelson A. Miles, three thousand soldiers were rushed to the Sioux reservations. Troops from Fort Robinson near the old Red Cloud agency were the first to arrive at Pine Ridge.

At their coming the Oglala and Brulé were thrown into a panic. Led by Short Bull and Kicking Bear, about three thousand of them fled westward to the Dakota Badlands, where they hoped that the rugged terrain would make them safe from the troops.

Farther north, other bands removed themselves from the agencies so that they could continue the Ghost Dance.

So far the Indians had attacked no whites and had only retreated deeper into their own reservations to avoid the troops. But it was feared that Sitting Bull, camped with his Hunkpapa on the Grand River, was plotting an uprising. Indian police trained by the Standing Rock agent were sent to arrest him early on the morning of December 15. Before daylight they entered his cabin and roused him from his sleep. At first he was willing to go, but as they took him through the door and his people gathered outside to resist the police he changed his mind.

"I am not going," he shouted to the policemen. "Do with me what you like. I am not going." Then, to his own warriors: "Come on! Come on! Take action! Let's go!"

One of his braves fired his rifle and wounded the lieutenant of the police. The officers themselves immediately shot and killed Sitting Bull. Then the Indian police and the Hunkpapa warriors closed in a hand-to-hand scuffle. Six policemen and eight Hunkpapa were killed or mortally wounded. At length white troops arrived and halted the melee; the Hunkpapa braves retreated up the Grand River.

Sitting Bull's death threw the Sioux into still greater excitement. Three days later those in the Badlands attacked a party of whites; a detachment of troops went after them and were ambushed in two indecisive skirmishes. But by late December troop reinforcements had nearly surrounded the Badlands refugees and had forced them back to Pine Ridge Agency.

On December 28 another band of Miniconjou, fleeing from the Cheyenne River to the Badlands, was intercepted by troops of the 7th Cavalry, Custer's old regiment. Headed by Big Foot, an ailing chief, the group of several hundred was escorted to Wounded Knee Creek, about twenty miles northeast of Pine Ridge. There they camped overnight while the troops prepared to disarm them.

The next morning, with soldiers encircling the camp, the warriors came out of their tents and sat on the ground. Unknown to the troops surrounding them, they had revolvers, knives and Winchester rifles hidden under their blankets. At the same time, on a bluff overlooking the camp, the troops manned four Hotchkiss guns, which could fire fifty exploding shells a minute.

When the warriors were told to surrender their rifles, they

became obviously agitated. Some of them went to their lodges and returned with old, broken guns. The Chief declared that they had already given up all their rifles.

Next a detachment of soldiers was ordered into the lodges to search for weapons. At this invasion of their privacy, the Indians grew more edgy; women and children, turned out of the lodges, were showing great excitement. A medicine man began moving among the warriors, urging them to revolt.

The soldiers returned with about forty guns, most of them antiquated. It was obvious that the real arsenal was concealed under the blankets of the braves. They were ordered to come forward one by one and to give up their rifles. As this process began, one of them moved about, holding his rifle in the air and refusing to give it up. Two soldiers seized him, and the gun went off accidentally.

At that moment the medicine man took a handful of dust and threw it in the air. Several warriors thereupon jumped up, threw off their blankets, brought up their Winchesters and fired point blank at the troops. Instantly the soldiers answered with a devastating volley. The rest of the Indians jumped up and also began firing their repeaters, pumping the levers to make a continuous roar.

With their single-shot Springfields the soldiers were outgunned, but they outnumbered the Indians. When the warriors had emptied their magazines, they fell upon the nearest troops in savage hand-to-hand fighting. Thirty-one soldiers were killed and perhaps thirty more wounded. But, supported by others who rushed up to the scene, they overwhelmed the warriors and killed most of them—approximately a hundred, including Chief Big Foot.

As the surviving warriors broke out of the military circle in an effort to escape, the Hotchkiss guns on the bluff were fired at them with terrible effect. The exploding metal sent more dead and wounded to the ground, including women and children. The survivors leaped into the ravine behind the lodges and fled in panic, many mothers running with babies in their arms. With their blood up, the 7th Cavalry soldiers raced after the Indians, shooting them down as they ran. Although the officers cautioned against firing at women and children, a number of them were hit.

A few of the women were able to stagger all the way to Pine

Ridge agency, twenty miles away. There large numbers of Oglala and Brulé were camped after coming back from the Badlands. When the first survivors stumbled in, outraged Brulé warriors took their guns and, leaping to horse, raced for Wounded Knee Creek. After a two-hour ride they arrived to find the soldiers hunting and shooting the survivors. Some of the troops, after being driven back, threw up breastworks in order to repel the attackers.

Then the whole 7th Cavalry detachment took its own wounded and a group of prisoners to Pine Ridge agency, which they found under siege by other maddened Brulé. When the soldiers came, the large Sioux camp withdrew from the agency to White Clay Creek.

The fighting that had ended before the Wounded Knee massacre was reopened, with Indians attacking isolated settlers and detachments of troops. On December 30 they set fire to houses between Pine Ridge agency and a Catholic mission; when a large detachment of cavalry arrived, it was surrounded and besieged until reinforcements came.

But so many troops were in the reservation that the Indians knew that they were desperately outnumbered. After pleas from General Miles, they came in and surrendered early in January. The army replaced the civilian agents with its own officers and restored full rations to the Sioux. The pitiful Indian "war" of 1890 was over, and quiet reigned in the new State of South Dakota. The Sioux, their energies drained by religious fervor and the panic of mass murder, settled down to dress their wounds and mourn their dead.

Immediately following the "battle" of Wounded Knee, a snowstorm and blizzard raged through the reservation. Three days afterward, troops went back to Wounded Knee Creek to gather the dead and strip the bodies of clothing for souvenirs. Among the frozen forms scattered in the snow for two miles over the plains they found some women and children still living but terribly wounded and partly frozen. Four infants, covered with shawls, were found alive next to their dead mothers. Most of those brought back, including three of the four babies, soon died.

At the agency the soldiers dug a long trench; into it were tossed 146 naked and frozen bodies. Then the sickening evidence was covered with dirt. Said one of the men in the burial detail, "It was a thing to melt the heart of a man, if it was of stone, to see those little children, with their bodies shot to pieces, thrown naked into the pit."

Two generations after Bull Bear had led his people from the Black Hills southward to trade with the white man, the saga of the Sioux nation was over. Sioux contact with the western frontier, begun auspiciously with the opening of trade at Fort Laramie, had ended 55 years later and a hundred miles away in a frozen pool of blood. The red man had nowhere else to go, and not much left to do, in the white man's West.[11]

• 5 •

In a final touch of irony, the old fort itself fell with the Sioux. On August 31, 1889, Fort Laramie was ordered abandoned. The order would have been carried out in that year, but there were not enough barracks for the men at Fort Logan, Colorado, where the last two companies were to be transferred. While the accommodations were being built, the Fort Laramie garrison prepared for its final march.

On March 2, 1890, Capt. Levi F. Burnett and 57 enlisted men assembled on the parade ground to the last blast of the trumpet. With flags fluttering in the frosty air, the two infantry companies filed out of the fort and threaded their way the 22 miles to Bordeaux Station on the Cheyenne and Northern Railroad. There they boarded three cars and rattled southward by way of Cheyenne and Denver to their new home at Fort Logan.

Remaining behind were an officer and 24 men to ship the post records to Washington and otherwise complete the "funeral" of Fort Laramie. From Fort Robinson came Lt. Charles W. Taylor and a small detachment to handle the final auction of property. Although he advertised the event for April 9, he drew only a small crowd because of a severe storm that had struck the country the day before. For a total of $1,417 the buildings and appurtenances of Fort Laramie passed into private hands.

A major purchaser was John Hunton, long-time trader and rancher who had been the last post sutler of Fort Laramie. After the War Department turned over the military reservation to the

Interior Department "for disposition" in June 1890, John Hunton homesteaded most of the fort location. Expanding his holdings, he operated a ranch on the historic grounds he had occupied as a trader since 1867.

Until his death in 1928, Hunton did what he could by himself to preserve the ghostly shell of Fort Laramie. Later, historical societies and the state of Wyoming moved to secure the site. In 1937, 214 acres of land embracing the fort were acquired by the Wyoming Historical Landmark Commission. The Federal government designated the site as "Fort Laramie National Monument" and placed it under the care of the National Park Service in 1938.

Now termed a "national historic site", Fort Laramie has been expertly returned to its appearance in 1876. Eleven buildings have been restored and refurnished, and another is planned. The uniform—forest green instead of blue—is back on the parade ground. Once again laughter echoes through the sutler's store and Old Bedlam as a ranger, conducting a group of visitors, tells some anecdote of former days. But it has a milder ring than that of the stalwarts who once formed ranks at the bugle's blast on this same compacted ground. To Americans of a tamer generation, Fort Laramie has become a museum and a legend.

Notes

[1] Owing to an error in Anderson's date-keeping, as acknowledged in his journal of May 30, Fort Laramie's founding date should be May 31 instead of the previously accepted June 1.

Although Robert Campbell has been credited with founding and building Fort William (Laramie), he is not mentioned as a member of Sublette's 1834 expedition in any of Anderson's accounts. Apparently he was still at Sublette & Campbell's fort on the upper Missouri. Sublette's clerk, William Patton, was in charge of building the fort on the Laramie.

The name "Fort William" has been said to honor both William Sublette and William Anderson. But Anderson's first-hand journal mentions no honoree beside Sublette. When rewriting his narrative in ink after he returned to St. Louis, Anderson did not describe the naming of the fort, but afterward penciled in between the lines that it "is to be called Fort William, in honor of Sublette and myself." In his later newspaper account, he extended the honor to another, William Patton: "A friendly dispute arose between our leader and myself, as to the name. He proposed to call it Fort

Anderson, I insisted upon baptising it Fort Sublette, and holding the trump card in my hand (a bottle of champagne) was about to claim the trick. Sublette stood by, cup reversed, still objecting, when Patton offered a compromise which was accepted, and the foam flew, in honor of Fort William, which contained the triad prenames of clerk, leader and friend."

The fact that Sublette had also named Fort William on the Missouri River for himself would support the on-the-spot authenticity of Anderson's journal, in preference to his two later accounts.

[2] The spelling is generally rendered "Bordeaux," but National Archives documents of the 1850s and 1860s show his signature without the "x."

[3] Throughout this period, army officers argued that the care of Indian tribes be taken from the Department of the Interior and given to the War Department. But whether or not the Indians would have been better off under the ministrations of the U.S. Army is another question. That the War Department itself was scarcely immune to corruption became painfully clear in the 1870s, when the Grant administration turned its eyes on the political spoils latent in sutlerships at army posts. In 1870 the appointment of post sutlers was taken away from the post commanders and concentrated in the hands of the Secretary of War. Almost overnight, under the administration of Secretary William Belknap, the sale of sutlerships to applicants for sizable bribes became a common practice. Belknap received $6,000 a year from the sutlers at Fort Sill, Oklahoma, and two generals of impressive influence received thousands more for securing sutler appointments at a dozen posts, including Fort Abraham Lincoln and Fort Fetterman. Other favored parties, including the President's brother, Orville Grant, were given exclusive trading licenses at the Sioux agencies in the Dakotas, and the established traders were sent packing at great losses in investment.

An exception was Fort Laramie, which was nevertheless taken care of by an appointment dictated personally by President Grant. When a vacancy in the sutlership occurred in 1872, it was seized upon as an opportunity by John S. Collins, the son of a former business partner of Grant's in Galena, Illinois. Hurrying to Washington, Collins secured an interview with the President on December 19. The young man came directly to the point: "The post tradership at Fort Laramie, Wyoming, is vacant, and I came to make an application for it . . ."

"Well," answered Grant, "these matters properly belong to the Secretary of War, General Belknap. I will give you a note to him . . ."

Collins presented the letter to the Secretary, who told him that he was embarrassed over the many applications for the post, "and I regret that the President did not *order* me to make this appointment." Stalling Collins, the Secretary later told him, "A complaint has been lodged here that you are a Democrat." Collins then went back to Grant, who wrote another note to Belknap:

"If you see no special reason why John Collins should not receive the apt. of Sutler at Fort Laramie, or if you have no appointment which you wish specially to make yourself, I wish you would give it to him. The charge of Democracy against him ought not to be held as a reason for his non appointment. The family I have known from my infancy. They have always been Democrats. But I have had no stronger supporter than E. A. Collins and his two sons."

With that, Collins was appointed sutler at Fort Laramie—a post he held for ten years. For once Belknap had been controlled from above. In 1876, when the sale of sutlerships and other malpractices were exposed by a congressional investigation, Belknap resigned as Secretary of War and was promptly found guilty in an impeachment trial. The army's moral position in comparison to the Indian Bureau had received a serious blow.

⁴ The accepted explanation has been that Major Anderson ordered Collins to lead the detachment in order to spare the Kansas officers, who were expecting to be ordered home any day. They are charged with finding excuses to avoid an assignment that meant certain death.

The earliest document blaming the Kansans is a letter dated August 21, 1865, written by W. G. Bullock, the sutler's agent at Fort Laramie, to Col. William O. Collins. Beside giving a distorted account of the battle, he wrote that the Colonel's son "fell victim to the infamous cowardice of the officers of the 11th Kansas." The letter indicates that Bullock's informant was Capt. Henry C. Bretney, an Ohio officer. A Bretney account was also used in a later history of Fort Caspar (Platte Bridge Station).

A man of passionate opinions, Bretney had clashed with the post commander, the Kansan Capt. James E. Greer, two weeks before the battle. Bretney and some of his Ohio troops had actually drawn guns on some of Greer's Kansans. Subsequently, feeling had run high between the Kansas and Ohio troops, including the officers, and this animosity has been cited as the reason why Collins, an Ohioan, was sent out by Anderson, a Kansan. But the feud could just as easily be cited as the reason why Bretney made such charges against the Kansas officers, whom he hated violently.

The next account was the report "of the circumstances leading to and connected with the death of the late Lieutenant Caspar W. Collins," sent from Fort Laramie to the Adjutant General in Washington on April 7, 1866. This states that Collins was "ordered" to command the relief detachment, emphasizes the "vastly increased numbers" of Indians in evidence before his departure and blames Major Anderson for sending Collins "on this perilous duty" rather than any of the four Kansas officers "present at the post for duty." This report was written by an Ohio officer and based on testimony from Ohio enlisted men (the Kansas regiments had been sent home by the time of the investigation).

Another description of the episode in a biography of Caspar Collins was drawn many years later from the memory of John C. Friend, who was present as an Ohio enlisted man. This version states that the various Kansas officers pleaded that they were sick or otherwise excused themselves.

These three "Ohio" accounts were all written by persons who were not present at the battle, and they are not publicly documented with written statements by the eyewitnesses themselves. On the other hand, there are seven first-hand "Kansas" accounts by other eyewitnesses—several of them discovered in original research by Jesse W. Vaughn for his authoritative book, *The Battle of Platte Bridge*. Of these seven, five do not specify whether Collins volunteered or was ordered. The other two use the word "ordered," but refer both to Collins and the detachment together and do not make clear whether or not Collins himself was specifically ordered.

The fact that these accounts were by Kansas officers and enlisted men has been used to discredit them, on the ground that they would not be inclined to speak ill of themselves or their comrades. But one might as easily discredit the three "Ohio" accounts on the ground that they were prejudiced against the Kansans. As for the charge that the Kansas officers claimed to be "sick" or otherwise unable to serve, the fact is that on the same morning they commanded other troops in the encounters with the Indians.

Furthermore, there is some affirmative evidence that Collins actually volunteered. In his *History of Wyoming*, Charles Coutant clearly obtained his description of this episode from John C. Friend. According to this version, "Lieutenant Caspar W. Collins stepped forward and said he would go . . ." Another account (by a soldier who arrived at Platte Bridge the day after the battle and got his information from the other soldiers) also states that Collins volunteered.

One of the "Kansas" accounts, written on the same day as the event and therefore of prime historic worth, is Sergeant Pennock's diary. It indicates that Anderson had left it to Captain Greer to send the detachment and that Greer had placed Pennock in charge. Not until Pennock reported to Major Anderson before departing was it announced that Collins was "going along." Was this change of plans occasioned by Collins' asking to command the unit or by Anderson's deciding to order him? If Anderson simply wanted a commissioned officer to command the column, it would have been up to Captain Greer to choose one from among his Kansans. Yet Greer does not seem to have been involved in this particular matter, and it was Major Anderson who told the detachment at the last minute that Collins would command it.

Nor is it clear that Collins "knew that the order meant death . . ." Only one of the seven "Kansas" accounts indicates that a large or formidable number of Indians was in sight before Collins left the station. Five indicate a relatively small number, and one is silent on the subject.

Actually, the stations on the Oregon Trail had been harassed by small bands of Indians for months, and small detachments of troops had continued to pass back and forth. On the previous day the Platte Bridge soldiers had repulsed the Indians in three encounters without losing a man. There were more Indians seen around the station than usual (as many as ninety in some versions), but these odds were not considered impossible against the Collins detachment of 20 to 25. As a Fort Laramie commander of the period instructed one of his detachments: "With your party you are safe against three times your number of Indians in a fight. If you act on the defensive you are safe against ten times your number."

Despite the overwhelming force that actually attacked Collins' men, at least three-fourths of them escaped. That Collins actually was killed is not proof in itself that his death was a foregone conclusion.

In short, although Major Anderson made mistakes in judgment, the accepted story that he deliberately ordered Collins to the slaughter as a sacrifice to save the lives of cowardly Kansas officers is not justified by the evidence so far brought to light. It is an unwarranted reflection on the memory of the Kansas officers and in no way adds to the assured luster of Caspar Collins' name.

[5] It has generally been believed that Red Cloud was one of those who withdrew from the 1866 council at Carrington's appearance. Frances Carrington's reminiscences even have Red Cloud himself making the statement about the soldiers' stealing the road "before Indian say yes or no." She includes a second-hand account by Margaret Carrington (the Colonel's first wife) about a silent encounter Carrington had with Red Cloud after the council—the

Indian with his hand on his knife, the officer with his hand on his revolver. In a report made a year after the event, Comm. John B. Sanborn stated that Carrington arrived at Fort Laramie "while negotiations were going on with Red Cloud," but Sanborn had not been present at the time, and his statement is second-hand. Actually, the evidence indicates that Red Cloud was not present at Fort Laramie at the time. He left the post on June 8, according to a letter of Taylor's dated June 9 (in the National Archives), ostensibly to go and get his people on White River. Then, according to Taylor's annual report for 1865-1866, "A band numbering perhaps three hundred warriors, headed by Red Cloud, a prominent chief of the Ogalallahs, refused to come in." Neither Taylor in his correspondence and reports nor Carrington in his extensive testimony and other public statements ever claimed that Red Cloud was present when Carrington arrived at Fort Laramie in mid-June 1866.

[6] One Indian participant stated less than five months after the battle that the Indians had lost ten ("all leading warriors") and many wounded. Forty years later Red Cloud could not recall more than about ten killed on the battlefield, though others might have died of wounds. Only a few months after the battle a second-hand but otherwise creditable Indian account stated that "there were eight Indians killed on the battle ground, and about fifty wounded, and twenty-two of the wounded afterwards died of their wounds."

[7] The descriptions of the Fetterman massacre and of the circumstances leading up to it are drawn not only from generally known sources but more particularly from "Papers Relating to the Sanborn Commission Investigation of the Fetterman massacre," in the records of the Bureau of Indian Affairs in the National Archives.

The report of the commission had, of course, been printed with some other pertinent material in *U.S. Senate Documents*, 40th Congress, 1st Session, Ex. Doc. 13, Vol. Serial No. 1308. Colonel Carrington's own extensive testimony before the commission was published in *U.S. Senate Documents*, 50th Congress, 1st Session, Ex. Doc. 33, Vol. Serial No. 2504. But the rest of the supporting evidence and other material, consisting of 480 pages, includes the minutes of the commission and the speeches of commissioners and Indian chiefs meeting at various locations in 1867; the lengthy report of Comm. J. V. Kinney after visiting Fort Phil Kearny; the verbatim testimony taken by the commission at Omaha and Fort McPherson from Lt. A. H. Wands, Lt. W. F. Arnold, Bvt. Maj. Gen. Philip St. George Cooke, Capt. William H. Bisbee, George B. Mackey (an enlisted man), Dr. C. M. Hines (assistant post surgeon at Fort Phil Kearny) and Todd Randall, a trader; and the verbatim testimony taken by Commissioner Kinney at Fort Phil Kearny from Capt. Tenodor Ten Eyck, Capt. James Powell, Bvt. Maj. Samuel M. Horton (chief medical officer of the Mountain District and post surgeon at Fort Phil Kearny), J. B. Weston (a citizen), Raphael Gallegos (special Indian interpreter) and Michael Boyer (post guide and interpreter at Fort Phil Kearny). All of these men except General Cooke, Captain Bisbee, Randall and Gallegos had been at Fort Phil Kearny at the time of the massacre.

Much of this evidence is at variance with that of Colonel Carrington, and the testimony of Powell and Bisbee is clearly hostile to him. Powell's is so patently biased against Carrington and so contradictory in many particulars to the weight of other testimony as to be almost worthless. It was useful, however, in evoking a point-by-point refutation by Colonel Carrington in a long letter on November 5, 1867, to the Secretary of the Interior; this valuable letter is in the files for 1867 of the Upper Platte agency of the Bureau of Indian Affairs, National Archives.

Another useful source is the report of the military investigation of the massacre by Carrington's replacement, Bvt. Brig. Gen. H. W. Wessels, dated January 21, 1867. This four-page letter, "compiled from the statements of several officers and others, who were at the post at the time of the massacre," is also in the National Archives.

In general, this body of additional testimony differs from Carrington's in several particulars: (1) Fetterman did not march over Lodge Trail Ridge but instead took the Bozeman Trail, (2) none of his command was able to retreat from the spot where most of the bodies were found, and (3) Fetterman himself was killed by the Indians and not in a double suicide with Captain Brown.

[8] There has been considerable historical controversy over whether Phillips rode alone or with others. In his testimony before a special commission investigating the Fetterman massacre in the spring of 1867 (*U.S. Senate Documents*, 50th Congress, 1st Session, Ex. Doc. No. 33, Volume Serial No. 2504), Colonel Carrington stated, "I hired two citizens to take dispatches to Laramie." A sergeant writing from Fort Phil Kearny a week after the massacre stated that "the same evening Colonel Carrington sent citizen couriers to Laramie with despatches to department headquarters for reinforcements . . ." Many years later some other contemporaries stated that he had others with him. In 1917 John C. Friend stated in a letter that he had been the telegraph operator at Horse Shoe Creek Station at the time, and that two men were with Phillips.

However, in his *History of Wyoming* (1899), Charles Coutant (who had evidently consulted Friend) stated that Phillips had stopped at Horseshoe Station to send a dispatch to Brig. Gen. I. N. Palmer, commander of the Western District of the Platte, with headquarters at Fort Laramie. This Friend version does not mention any companions. In Carrington's testimony in which he said, "I hired two citizens," he also went on to speak of a single "courier" reaching Fort Reno, again, of the "courier" reaching Horse Shoe Creek telegraph station, and finally of the "courier" arriving at Fort Laramie. Thus, although he hired two couriers, Carrington does not state that they left together, and he refers to only one making the ride through to Fort Laramie.

In 1894 Carrington signed an affidavit supporting the application of Phillips' widow for $5,000 compensation on the strength of this ride (which she received by congressional appropriation). This affidavit indicates that Phillips left alone. He "volunteered his services as dispatch bearer to Fort Laramie"; "confidential dispatches were intrusted to his care"; "during the night after the battle he started on his dangerous mission." In none of his writings does Carrington tell of any other rider getting through; in his affidavit he states that others leaving about the same time did not get through. Another account by a soldier stationed at Phil Kearny at the time says that "The mail carrier, a man named 'Portugee' Phillips, volunteered to make the attempt." Still another soldier stationed at Fort Reno when Phillips came through declares that he was alone. A first-hand account of Phillips' arrival at Fort Laramie by Maj. David Gordon mentions only John "Portuguese" Phillips as the messenger.

That Phillips arrived alone is proven in a telegram from General Palmer at Laramie to Cooke at Omaha on December 26. After briefly outlining the Phil Kearny disaster, Palmer states, "My dispatch is from Wessells and particulars I get from messinger who brings dispatch." That this man was also Carrington's courier is shown by Palmer's next statement: "Col. Carrington sends nothing to me . . ."

In short, the very earliest sources, supported by some later reminiscent accounts, show that Phillips rode alone. Other reminiscences state that he arrived at Horseshoe Station accompanied by from two to four others. Actually, Portugee Phillips and Daniel Dixon were both later paid $300 for their courier service from Fort Phil Kearny to Horseshoe Station. But this does not prove they rode together. No account, contemporary or reminiscent, mentions anyone with Phillips when he left Fort Phil Kearny, when he reached and left Fort Reno, when he left Horseshoe Station, or when he arrived at Fort Laramie. On this evidence, Portugee Phillips should be given credit for making most, at least, of this Herculean ride alone.

[9] It has been claimed that Red Cloud was present at this council, but he was not. On June 12 Comm. John B. Sanborn wrote to General Sherman, "Red Cloud is not here, nor is he the main man of influence among them." This letter is corroborated by a report from George P. Beauvais to the Secretary of the Interior on December 14, 1867. Both letters are in the National Archives.

[10] Such light casualties at the Rosebud are astounding when it is understood that the two forces—roughly equal in strength—fought each other on an open hillside for six hours. They charged and countercharged, taking only partial cover behind whatever rocks were handy. The soldiers were estimated to have fired somewhere between 10,000 and 25,000 rounds of ammunition. The Indians are said to have shot even more, probably because of their repeating rifles, although fewer of their empty shells have been found on the battlefield. Why were casualties so light?

It has been said that Crook's casualties were higher than reported, and the number was put at 28 killed and 56 wounded in a later biography of one of his scouts. But to credit this account (which is erroneous in many other particulars) one would have to dismiss not only the official reports of Crook and his officers but also other first-hand contemporary accounts.

The light casualties may be explained, first, by the battle being largely a cavalry fight, in which losses were normally much fewer than in infantry battles. The mobility of both sides minimized hand-to-hand encounters; in fact, there was none in the entire Battle of the Rosebud. Most of the Indians fought on horseback, rather than dismounting to improve aim. Hitting a moving target from the back of a running horse is almost impossible.

As for the soldiers, part of the reason for their inflicting comparatively few losses is that many were raw recruits, without sufficient target practice. Another factor was, of course, the difficulty of hitting Indians riding at breakneck speed on sloping and deceptive ground.

[11] After hostilities ended on the Western plains, the Government's treatment of the Sioux was as short-sighted in peace as it had been in war. Washington officials, supported by well-meaning champions of the Indian, assumed the solution was to make the Sioux become farmers, like white men. In 1887 the Dawes Act enabled individual Indians to receive up to 160 acres of "allotted" land, as distinct from tribal land. After a certain period, unallotted land would be open for sale by the government to anyone. To prevent land sharks from inducing the Indians to sell their allotments, these would each be held in trust for a period of years by the Indian Bureau. This precaution was subverted in 1891 when Indians were allowed to lease their allotted lands.

At first the Sioux were slow in taking allotments; most of the reservation land was, in fact, ill suited for farming. But under coercion the allotments were accelerated early in the 20th Century, peaking around 1917.

In 1906 the Indians were allowed to apply for full ownership of allotments. This led to rapid sales of the allotted lands by Indians to white settlers and land companies.

Between the opening of unallotted lands, the leasing of allotments, and finally the sale of such lands, many of the reservations were shredded. The relentless process, pushed alike by land-hungry interests and by reformers who believed farming was the Indians' salvation, was disastrous. Shorn of his traditional hunting livelihood, the plains Indian had been pacified with land; but as a result of U.S. policy he was now being shorn of that as well.

Genuine reform was in the air by the 1920s. In 1934 the Indian Reorganization Act halted the allotment of Indian land, provided for buying back reservation land, established loans for Indian farmers, authorized funds for Indian education, mandated preference to Indians for Indian Bureau jobs, and in general replaced the arbitrary, unilateral approach to Indian affairs with a bilateral approach that respected Indian rights and aspirations.

In the 1950s this enlightened policy was supplanted by one aimed at "termination" of government responsibility. For those tribes that were "terminated", the result was deplorable. Those remaining under government supervision suffered a return to the old paternalism.

Spurred by renewed cries for reform, Congress passed the Indian Self-Determination and Educational Assistance Act of 1974. Under this law, tribes can contract to manage the government programs themselves. Since 1991 the Tribal Self-Governance Program has offered still freer rein. By now the Indian Bureau itself, with 85 percent Indian employees, is largely under their control. The future of the Sioux will be decided, not by white soldiers or white officials, but by the Indians themselves. A Sioux elder declared in 1977: "We Indians will be Indians all our lives, we will never be white men."

BIBLIOGRAPHY

I. First-Hand Sources

Manuscripts

Anderson. William Marshall. *Journal.* This is the first of three separate accounts of Sublette's 1834 expedition written by Anderson all in the Henry E. Huntington Library, San Marino, California. The Journal is the day-to-day diary written on the trail. From this a Narrative was written, with changes and additions, after Anderson returned to St. Louis. Thirty-seven years later a third version, with still further changes, was printed in the Circleville, Ohio, *Democrat and Watchman,* September 29 and October 13, 1871. Part of the latter account was reprinted in *Frontier and Midland,* Autumn, 1938.

Bettelyoun, Susan. Manuscript. Rich reminiscences by the daughter of James Bordeau. Nebraska State Historical Society, Lincoln. Microfilm now in Western History Research Center, University of Wyoming Library, Laramie.

Bordeau, James, and Samuel Smith, Antoine Reynaud, Leo H. Pallardy, John S. Smith. Statement to J. W. Whitfield, Indian agent, at Fort Laramie, August 31, 1854 on Grattan massacre. Social and Economic Branch, Office of Civil Archives, National Archives, Washington, D.C.

Bureau of Indian Affairs. Letters Received from the Upper Platte Indian Agency, 1863–1867. Record Group 75, Microfilm reels, 891, 892. Office of Civil Archives, National Archives. Microfilm copies now at Western History Research Center, Laramie. *Note:* Some of the 1864 testimony on John Loree is in the 1866 file.

Capron, Cynthia, and Thaddeus H. Letters and papers. Western History Research Center, Laramie.

Carrington, Col. Henry B. Telegram to Maj. Gen. Philip St. George Cooke, Fort Laramie to Omaha, December 26, 1866. Telegrams Received, Department of the Platte, Army and Air Corps Branch, National Archives.

Chamberlain, William E. Diary, 1849. California State Library, Sacramento.

Claudey, Edward, John Savard, I. B. Didier, and Joseph Turgeon. Signed statement to J. W. Whitfield, Indian Agent, Sept. 1, 1854, on Grattan massacre. Social and Economic Branch, Office of Civil Archives, National Archives.

Fleming, Bvt. Lt. Hugh B. "Reporting difficulty with Indians, in carrying out orders respecting them," June 16, 1853. To 1st Lt. R. B. Garnett, Commanding, Fort Laramie. Army and Air Corps Branch, National Archives.

311

Fort Laramie. Wyoming Territory, Letters sent, 1848–1850, 1855–1858, 1866–1878, 1882–1887. Four microfilm reels from Fort Laramie Historic Site, National Park Service. Originals in Army and Air Corps Branch, National Archives (Record Group 98). Microfilm also at Western History Research Center, Laramie.

———. Post Records. Selected letters, received and sent, 1849–1857; selected telegrams received and sent, 1866–1867, 1875–1877; selected orders, Department of the Platte, Vol. 23½, pp. 164–168, 182–184 (1876–1877). Microfilm from Army and Air Corps Branch, National Archives. Now at Western History Research Center, Laramie.

———. Letters sent, 1888–1890. Typescript provided by Fort Laramie Historic Site, National Park Service.

Foster, Rev. Isaac, of Plainsfield, Ill. Journal, 1849. California State Library.

Garnett, 1st Lt. R. B. Report "Relating to Indian Affairs, respecting an engagement between the troops of Fort Laramie & 'Minny-Konjoe' Indians," June 30, 1853. To Maj. F. M. Page, Asst. Adjt. Gen., Jefferson Barracks, Missouri. Army and Air Corps Branch, National Archives.

Hall, O. J. Overland Diary, 1948. California State Library, Sacramento.

Harney, Bvt. Brig. Gen. William S. Reports, August 3, September 26, 1855, "Head Quarters Sioux Expedition," to Lt. Col. L. Thomas, Asst. Adjt. Gen., Headquarters of the Army, New York. Army and Air Corps Branch, National Archives.

———. "A Special Report to the Secretary of War, concerning the present position of the Sioux Indians, and submitting certain propositions, etc." November 10, 1855, Head Quarters Sioux Expedition, Fort Pierre. Army and Air Corps Branch, National Archives.

Hoffman, Maj. and Bvt. Lt. Col. W. Report "In Relation to Indian Affairs, etc.," February 9, 1855, and "Reporting Indian Depredations, etc.," February 14, 1855, to Major O. F. Winship, Asst. Adjt. Gen., Head Quarters, Department of the West, St. Louis, Missouri. Army and Air Corps Branch, National Archives.

Hunton, John. Letter to Clarence Rickmeyer, March 23, 1927, Torrington, Wyoming. Western History Research Center, Laramie.

Jacob, Norton. The Record of Norton Jacob, 1845–1851. Huntington Library.

Kirkpatrick, Charles A. A Journal of a Trip to California, 1849. Bancroft Library, University of California, Berkeley.

Lester, Pvt. Charles. Letters to his sister, Mrs. Lucy O. Stanley, from various western posts, 1867–1869. Fort Laramie Historic Site, National Park Service.

Lyman, Eliza Marie (Partridge) Smith. Life and Journal, 1846–1885. Huntington Library.

Man-Afraid-of-His-Horses. "Narrative of Particulars of Affair of 19th August last by the 'Man who is Afraid of his Horses.'" Noted by U.S. Army Department of the West, February 13, 1855. Photostatic copy provided by the Army and Air Corps Branch, National Archives. This is the only eyewitness Indian account of the Grattan Massacre. Now in Western History Research Center, Laramie.

Miller, Reuben G. Journal, 1849. Huntington Library.

Monerami, J. B., and Jean Savas, I. B. Didier, Joseph Turgeon, Leston Pratte, and Auguste Robuin. Letter to Col. Whitfield, Agent Sioux Nation,

Fort John [Laramie], September 1, 1854, on Grattan Massacre. Social and Economic Branch, Office of Civil Archives, National Archives.

Palmer, Bvt. Brig. Gen. I. N. Telegram to Maj. Gen. Philip St. George Cooke, Fort Laramie to Omaha, December 26, 1866. Telegrams Received, Department of the Platte, Army and Air Corps Branch, National Archives.

Ricker, Judge E. S. Tablets. Extensive interviews with Indians and ex-traders, 1906–1907. Valuable for reminiscent details, but uneven in accuracy; many recollections should be checked against contemporary records. Nebraska State Historical Society, Lincoln.

Russell, Majors, and Waddell Papers. Huntington Library.

Sanborn, John B. "Papers Relating to the Sanborn Commission Investigation of the Fetterman Massacre," found in the records of the Bureau of Indian Affairs, Office of Civil Archives, National Archives. More than 800 pages of minutes of commission meetings, speeches by commissioners and Indians, and testimony by Col. Henry B. Carrington, Capt. Tenodor Ten Eyck, Maj. Gen. Philip St. George Cooke et al. (Carrington's testimony was printed only in U.S. Senate Documents, 50th Congress, 1st Session, Executive Doc. 33, Vol. Serial No. 2504). Microfilm of pages (excluding Carrington's testimony) now at Western History Research Center, Laramie.

Schuyler, Lt. Walter Scribner. Letters, 1876. Huntington Library.

Vogdes, Ada Adelaide Adams. "Three years on the Plains, the personal diary of the wife of an Army Officer. Fort Laramie and Fort Fetterman, 1868–1871." A very illuminating journal by an alert and perceptive woman. Huntington Library.

Walker, George M. Statement to William E. Connelley, May 24, 1910, on Platte Bridge battle. Western History Research Center, Laramie.

Wessells, Bvt. Brig. Gen. H. W. "Report upon the massacre of Bvt. Lt. Col. Fetterman 18th U.S. Inf. and others." January 21, 1867. Fort Philip Kearny, D.T. Army and Air Corps Branch, National Archives.

Newspapers

Alta California, San Francisco. May 26, 1862. Microfilm. Huntington Library.

Deseret News, Salt Lake City, September 28, 1854. Microfilm. Huntington Library.

Emporia Gazette, Emporia, Kansas. August 9, 1934. Clipping. Indian Depredations Scrapbook, Vol. 3, "Emporian's Father Took Part in an Eventful Day of Kansas History." Kansas Historical Society, Topeka.

Guide-Review, Lingle, Wyoming. November 14, 1957–October 22, 1959. Excerpts from John Hunton's Diary, January 1, 1884–August 4, 1888, ed. L. G. Flannery. Western History Research Center, Laramie.

Kanesville Frontier Guardian, Council Bluffs, Iowa. February–June 1849. Microfilm. Huntington Library.

Kansas City Enterprise, Kansas City, Missouri. October 28, 1854. Huntington Library.

Leavenworth Daily Times, Leavenworth, Kansas. August 19, 1865. Article on Platte Bridge Battle: "The Indians the Strongest," by Jean Wilson. Typescript from publisher.

Liberty Weekly Tribune, Liberty, Missouri. September 15, 29, October 6, 1854, March 16, November 2, 1855. Microfilm. State Historical Society of Missouri, Columbia, Missouri.

Missouri Intelligencer and Boon's Lick Advertiser, Columbia, Missouri. April 12, 1834, July 25, 1835. State Historical Society of Missouri, Columbia, Missouri.

Missouri Republican, St. Louis. Extracts. Nebraska State Historical Society Publications, Vol. 20.

————. Correspondence, B. Gratz Brown, October 6, 17, 22, 23, 24, 26, November 2, 9, 30, 1851, issues. Typescript copy provided by Western History Research Center, Laramie.

National Tribune. Clipping. Kansas Scrap Book, Biography E., Vol. 2, "At Platte Bridge," by Ferdinand Ehrhardt (date ?). Kansas Historical Society, Topeka.

New York Times, December 7, 1854, September 25, November 1, December 19, 1855. Microfilm. U.C.L.A. Library, Los Angeles.

Niles' National Register, June 14, October 25, 1845, August 14, 1847. Huntington Library.

Omaha Arrow, Omaha City, Nebraska Territory. August 4, September 22, 1854. Microfilm. Omaha Public Library.

Riley County Democrat, Riley County, Kansas. August 26, 1909. Article: "The Platte Bridge Battle," by Charles Waring, Manhattan, Kansas. Kansas Historical Society, Topeka.

Western Bugle, Council Bluffs, Iowa. September 7, 1853. Microfilm. Council Bluffs Free Library.

Periodicals

Beam, D. C., "Reminiscences of Early Days in Nebraska," *Transactions and Reports of the Nebraska State Historical Society.* Vol. III (1892).

Bent, George, "Forty Years with the Cheyennes," edited by George Hyde. Part Four: "A Raid on the Platte." *The Frontier* (Colorado), Vol. IV, No. 7 (January, 1906), p. 3.

Bullock, Col. William G., transcribed and edited by Agnes Wright Spring. Old Letter Book (Papers and letters of William G. Bullock, sutler's agent at Fort Laramie, 1858–1871, *Annals of Wyoming,* Vol. XIII, No. 4 (October, 1941).

Capron, Cynthia J., Diary, 1876 (papers contain excerpts from letters of Lt. Thaddeus H. Capron), *Illinois State Historical Society Quarterly* (October, 1920, January, 1921).

Case, William M., "Reminiscences," taken by H. S. Lyman, *Oregon Historical Society Quarterly,* Vol. I (1900).

Collins, Catherine Wever, Letters, 1863–1864, "An Army Wife Comes West," *The Colorado Magazine,* State Historical Society of Colorado, Vol. XXXI, No. 4 (October, 1954).

Collister, Oscar, Life of, as told to Mrs. Charles Ellis, *Annals of Wyoming,* Vol. VII, No. 1 (July, 1930); No. 2 (October, 1930).

Cosgrove, Hugh, "Reminiscences," taken by H. S. Lyman, *Oregon Historical Society Quarterly,* Vol. I (1900).

Craig, Gen. James, Letter of, from Fort Laramie, July 11, 1862, *Annals of Wyoming,* Vol. XV, No. 2 (April, 1943), p. 150.

Crawford, Medorem, "An Account of his trip across the Plains with the Oregon Pioneers of 1842," *Sources of the History of Oregon,* Vol. I, No. 1 (1897).

Diehl, Charles, "Crazy Horse's Story of Custer Battle," *South Dakota Historical Collections,* Vol. VI, p. 224.

Drips, Major Andrew, "Letters while serving as Indian agent for the Upper Missouri, 1842–1848," *South Dakota Historical Collections,* Vol. IX.

Drum, Gen. Richard C., "Reminiscences of the Indian Fight at Ash Hollow, 1855," *Collections of the Nebraska State Historical Society,* Vol. XVI (1911).

Evans, W. H., "Fort Laramie," *Annals of Wyoming,* Vol. IX, p. 752.

Fairfield, S. H., "The Eleventh Kansas Regiment at Platte Bridge," *Kansas Historical Collections,* Vol. VIII (1904).

Gordon, Brig. Gen. David S., "The Relief of Fort Phil Kearny," *Journal of the Military Service Institutions of the United States,* Vol. XLIX (1911), p. 281.

Guthrie, John, "The Fetterman Massacre," *Annals of Wyoming,* Vol. IX, No. 2 (October, 1932), p. 714.

Harney, Bvt. Brig. Gen. William S., et al, "Official Correspondence Relating to Fort Pierre," *South Dakota Historical Collections,* Vol. I, p. 381.

Henry, Bvt. Brig. Gen. Guy V., "Wounded in an Indian Fight." *Collections of the Wyoming Historical Society,* Vol. I (1897), p. 190.

Hull, Lewis Byram, "Soldiering on the High Plains. The Diary of Lewis Byram Hull, 1864–1866." *Kansas Historical Society Quarterly,* Vol. VII, No. 1 (February, 1938), p. 3.

Hunton, John, Letter to Grace Raymond Hebard, February 20, 1919, *The Frontier* (Montana), Vol. XI, No. 2 (January, 1931).

Lee, Jason. "Diary of Jason Lee," *Oregon Historical Society Quarterly,* Vol. XVII (March, December 1916).

Lovejoy, Asa L., "Lovejoy's Pioneer Narrative," *Oregon Historical Society Quarterly,* Vol. XXXI (1930).

Matthieu, F. X., "Reminiscences," taken by H. S. Lyman, *Oregon Historical Society Quarterly,* Vol. I (1900).

Meyers, Augustus, "Dakota in the Fifties," *South Dakota Historical Collections,* Vol. X, p. 130.

Miller, George L., "The Fort Pierre Expedition," and "The Military Camp on the Big Sioux River in 1855," *Transactions and Reports of the Nebraska State Historical Society,* Vol. III (1892), pp. 110, 119.

Minto, John, "Reminiscences of Experiences on the Oregon Trail in 1844," *Oregon Historical Society Quarterly,* Vol. II (1901).

Murphy, William, "The Forgotten Battalion," *Annals of Wyoming,* Vol. VII, No. 2 (October 1930), p. 383.

Palmer, H. E., "History of the Powder River Expedition of 1865." *Nebraska State Historical Society Transactions,* Vol. II (1887).

Pattison, John J., Diary: "With the U.S. Army Along the Oregon Trail, 1863–1866," *Nebraska History Magazine,* Vol. XV, No. 1 (January–March, 1934), p. 79.

Pennock, Isaac, "Diary," *Annals of Wyoming,* Vol. XXIII (July, 1951).

Penter, Samuel, "Recollections of 1843," *Oregon Historical Society Quarterly,* Vol. VII (1906).

Riggs, Thomas Lawrence, "Sunset to Sunset: A lifetime with my Brothers, the Sioux," *South Dakota Historical Collections,* Vol. XXIX (1958).

Ryan, Benjamin William, "The Bozeman Trail to Virginia City, Montana in 1864: A Diary," *Annals of Wyoming*, Vol. XIX (July, 1947).

Sublette, William, "Fragmentary Journal," *Mississippi Valley Historical Review*, VI, p. 110.

Todd, Capt. John B. S. *Journal:* "The Harney Expedition Against the Sioux," edited by Ray H. Mattison. *Nebraska History*, Vol. XLIII, No. 2 (July, 1962).

Twiss, Thomas, Letters, *Annals of Wyoming*, Vol. XVII (1945), p. 148.

Walker, George M., "Eleventh Kansas Cavalry, 1865, and the Battle of Platte Bridge." *Kansas Historical Collections*, Vol. XIV (1918).

Whitman, Narcissa, Letters of. *Transactions of the Oregon Pioneer Association* (1893).

Wyeth, Nathaniel J., "The Correspondence and Journals of Captain Nathaniel J. Wyeth, 1831–1836." *Sources of the History of Oregon*, Vol. I, Parts 3–6 (1899).

Young, Will H., "Journals of Travel of, 1865." *Annals of Wyoming*, Vol. VII, No. 2 (October, 1930), p. 378.

Government Publications

Benton, Thomas Hart. Speech before the House of Representatives, February 27, 1855. Appendix to the Congressional Globe, 33rd Congress, 2nd Session, New Series, XXXI, p. 334.

Bryan, Lt. F. T. "Report of, Concerning His Operations in Locating a Practical Road Between Fort Riley to Bridger's Pass, 1856." Senate Executive Documents, 35th Congress, 1st Session, Doc. 11, p. 455, Vol. Serial No. 920. Also in *Annals of Wyoming*, Vol. 17, No. 1 (January, 1925).

Carrington, Col. Henry B. Affidavit on John "Portugee" Phillips' ride, June 5, 1894, House of Representative Reports, 55th Congress, 3rd Session, Report No. 1900, p. 2.

———. "Papers relative to Indian operations on the Plains." U.S. Senate Documents, 50th Congress, 1st Session, 1888. Executive Doc. 33, Vol. Serial No. 2504.

Commissioner of Indian Affairs. Annual Reports, 1845–1878. *Note:* the Report for 1854 includes correspondence of J. W. Whitfield, James Bordeau, et al concerning the Grattan Massacre.

Cooke, Lt. Col. Philip St. George. Report on "Battle of Blue Water," (September 5, 1855), Senate Executive Documents, 34th Congress, 3rd Session (1856), Vol. 8, Doc. 58.

Cross, Major Osborne. "A report in the form of a journal to the Quartermaster General of the march of the regiment of mounted riflemen to Oregon, May 10–October 5, 1849," Senate Executive Documents, 31st Congress, 2nd Session, Doc. 1, Part 2.

Custer, Col. George Armstrong. "Report on the Expedition through the Black Hills." Senate Executive Documents, 43rd Congress, 2nd Session, Doc. 32. Also in South Dakota Department of History Collections, Vol. 7, p. 583.

Dodge, Col. Henry. "Journal of the March of a detachment of dragoons, under the command of Colonel Dodge, during the summer of 1835." House Documents, 24th Congress, 1st Session, Doc. 181.

Frémont, Bvt. Capt. John Charles. "Report of the Exploring Expedition to the Rocky Mountains in the Year 1842 and to Oregon and North California in the years 1843–'44." Washington, D.C., 1845.

Garfield, James, et al. Debate on the Indian Bureau, February 4, 1869. The Congressional Globe, House of Representatives, 40th Congress, 3rd Session, Vol. 2, p. 880.

Harney, Bvt. Brig. Gen. William S. "Council with the Sioux Indians at Fort Pierre." Proceedings and correspondence. House Executive Documents, 34th Congress, 1st Session (1855–56), Vol. 12, Doc. 130, Vol. Serial No. 859. Also, Senate Executive Documents, 34th Congress, 1st and 2nd Sessions, Vol. 14, Doc. 94.

————. "Report of General Harney, Commander of the Sioux Expedition," September 5, 1855. Senate Executive Documents, 34th Congress, 1st and 2nd Sessions (1855–56), Vol. 2, Doc. 1.

Henn, Bernhart. Speech before House of Representatives, May 20, 1854. Appendix to the Congressional Globe, 33rd Congress, 1st Session, new series, Vol. 29, p. 885.

Hoffman, Lt. Col. William, James Bordeau, Obridge Allen, et al. "Indian Hostilities." Official correspondence and statements concerning the Grattan massacre. House Executive Documents, 33rd Congress, 2nd Session (1854–55), Vol. 5, Doc. 36, Vol. Serial No. 783; Vol. 8, Report No. 63, "Engagements Between United States Troops and Sioux Indians," Vol. Serial No. 788; Senate Executive Documents, 34th Congress, 1st and 2nd Sessions (1855–56), Vol. 14, Doc. 91, Vol. Serial No. 823. In this extensive material, the statement of Obridge Allen, who accompanied Grattan from the fort as far as Bordeau's and then watched the engagement from a rooftop, is the most objective and useful. Bordeau's statements are also valuable.

House of Representatives. Report to the President by the Indian Peace Commission, January 7, 1868, 40th Congress, 2nd Session, House Executive Doc. 97, Vol. Serial No. 1337, p. 21; also in Annual Report, Commissioner of Indian Affairs (1868).

————. Reports of Committees, 44th Congress, 1st Session (1875–76). Report No. 799: "The Management of the War Department"; subreport "Testimony and Statements Relating to the Sale of Post Traderships," (August 5, 1876), Vol. 8, Vol. Serial No. 1715.

————. Testimony before the Committee on Indian Affairs. 44th Congress, 1st Session (1875–76), House Misc. Doc. 167. "The Management of the Indian Department," Vol. Serial No. 1702.

Jenney, Prof. Walter S. "Report on the Mineral Wealth, Climate, and Rainfall and Natural Resources of the Black Hills of Dakota," Senate Executive Documents, 44th Congress, 1st Session, Doc. 51.

Kearny, Col. Stephen W. "Report of a summer campaign to the Rocky Mountains, etc., in 1845." Executive Documents, 29th Congress, 1st Session, Vol. 1, Doc. 2, p. 210.

Mallery, Garrick. 4th Annual Report, Bureau of Ethnology (1882–83), "Petrographs of the North American Indians" (includes Sioux Winter Counts), Washington, D.C., 1886.

Raynolds, Bvt. Brig. Gen. William Franklin. Report on the Exploration of the Yellowstone River, Washington, D.C., 1868. Also in Senate Executive Documents, 40th Congress, 1st [2nd] Session, Doc. 77, Vol. Serial No. 1317.

Senate of the United States. 34th Congress, 1st Session, "Statistical Report of Sickness and Mortality in the Army (1839–1855)." Senate Executive Document 96.

——. 39th Congress, 2nd Session. Reports of the Committees of the Senate of the U.S. (1866–67). Report No. 156: "Condition of the Indian Tribes," Report of the Joint Special Committee appointed under joint resolution, March 3, 1865, with an appendix. Vol. Serial No. 1279.

——. 40th Congress, 1st Session, "Indian Hostilities," Senate Executive Document 13, Vol. Serial No. 1308.

——. 44th Congress, 2nd Session. Senate Executive Document 9, Vol. Serial No. 1918, "The Report and Journal of Proceedings of the Commission appointed to obtain certain concessions from the Sioux Indians, December 18, 1876."

——. 49th Congress, 2nd Session. "Report of Select Committee on Condition of the Sioux and Crow Indians." Report No. 283, March 7, 1884.

Turner, Lt., and Franklin, Lt. "Abstract of journals kept by Lt. Turner, adjutant 1st dragoons, and Lt. Franklin, Top. Eng., during an expedition performed in the summer of 1845, by five companies of the 1st dragoons under the command of Colonel S. W. Kearny." 29th Congress, 1st Session Vol. 1, Doc. 2.

United States War Department Records. *War of the Rebellion: A Compilation of the Official Records of the Union and Confederate Armies.* Includes orders, correspondence, and reports of commands engaged in Indian fighting from 1861–1865. Vol. 22, parts 1, 2; Vol. 34, parts 1, 2, 3, 4; Vol. 48, parts 1, 2. Washington, D.C., 1880–1901.

Warren, Lt. Gouverneur Kemble. "Explorations in the Dakota Country in the year 1855." Washington, D.C., 1856. Also in Senate Executive Documents, 34th Congress, 1st Session, Doc. 76.

——. Letter to the Hon. George W. Jones, relative to his explorations of Nebraska Territory. Washington, D.C., January 29, 1858.

——. "Preliminary Report," November 24, 1858. House Executive Documents, 35th Congress, 2nd Session (1858–59). Doc. 2, Vol. Serial No. 998, p. 625.

Whipple, Henry B., Bishop of Minnesota. Letter to the President of the United States, in relation to Indian Affairs in that state, dated March 6, 1862. Misc. Documents of the Senate of the United States, 37th Congress, 2nd Session (1861–62). Doc. 77, Vol. Serial No. 1124, p. 2.

Books

Adams, Charles W. *Civil War Reminiscences Interestingly Told.* Greenfield, Ohio, n.d.

Allen, A. J. *Ten Years in Oregon.* Ithaca, 1848. The narrative of Dr. Elijah White, as told to the author.

Ball, John. *Autobiography.* Glendale, California, 1925.

Bandell, Eugene. *Frontier Life in the Army.* Edited by Ralph P. Bieber. Glendale, California, 1932.

Beadle, Erastus F. *To Nebraska in '57.* New York, 1923.

Bidwell, John. *Echoes of the Past.* Chico, California, 190?.

——. *A Journey to California.* San Francisco, 1937.

Bisbee, William H. *Through Four American Wars.* As told to his grandson, William Haymond Bisbee. Boston, 1931.

Bourke, John G. *On the Border with Crook.* New York, 1891.

Bruff, J. Goldsborough. *Gold Rush: The Journals, Drawings, and other Papers of J. Goldsborough Bruff*. 2 Volumes. New York, 1944.

Bryant, Edwin. *What I Saw in California*. Philadelphia, 1848.

Burnett, Peter H. *Recollections and Opinions of an Old Pioneer*. New York, 1880.

Burton, Richard F. *The City of the Saints*. New York, 1963.

Carleton, Lt. J. Henry. *The Prairie Logbooks*. Edited by Louis Pelzer. Chicago, 1943. The best account of Kearny's 1845 expedition.

Carrington, Frances C. *My Army Life and the Fort Phil Kearny Massacre*. Philadelphia, 1911.

Carrington, Col. Henry B. *The Indian Question*. Boston, 1909.

Carrington, Margaret Irvin. *Absaraka, Home of the Crows*. Philadelphia, 1878.

Catlin, George. *Letters and Notes on the Manners, Customs and Condition of the North American Indians*, Vol. I. London, 1844.

Chandless, William. *A Visit to Salt Lake*. London. 1857.

Clayton, William. *Journal of*. Salt Lake City, 1921.

Collins, John S. *Across the Plains in '64*. Omaha, 1904.

Coke, Henry J. *A Ride over the Rocky Mountains to Oregon and California*. London, 1852.

Cooke, Col. Philip St. George. *Scenes and Adventures in the Army*. Philadelphia, 1859.

Crawford, Lewis F. *Rekindling Campfires*. Bismarck, North Dakota, 1926. This is an autobiography of the scout, Ben Arnold, as told to Mr. Crawford.

Crook, Gen. George. *His Autobiography*. Edited by Martin F. Schmitt. Norman, Okla., 1946.

Cummins, Sarah J. *Autobiography and Reminiscences*. La Grande, Oregon, 1914.

Dawson, Nicholas. *Narrative of Nicholas "Cheyenne" Dawson*. Introduction by Charles L. Camp. San Francisco, 1933.

Delano, Alonzo. *Life on the Plains and at the Diggings*. Auburn and Buffalo, 1854.

Dodge, Maj. Gen. Grenville M. *How We Built the Union Pacific Railway* and *Other Railway Papers and Addresses*. *Council Bluffs* (n. d.).

Dodge, Col. Richard I. *The Black Hills*. New York, 1876.

Drew, Lt. William Young. Account of Platte Bridge Battle, *History of Natrona County, Wyoming, 1888–1922*. Chicago, 1923.

Egan, Major Howard. *Pioneering the West, 1846–1878*. Richmond, Utah, 1917.

Farnham, Thomas J. *Travels in the Great Western Prairies, the Anahuac and Rocky Mountains, and the Oregon Territory*. New York and London, 1843.

Ferris, W. A. *Life in the Rocky Mountains*. Edited by Paul C. Phillips. Denver, 1940.

Field, Matthew C. *Prairie and Mountain Sketches*. Edited by Kate L. Gregg and John Francis McDermott. Norman, Oklahoma, 1957.

Finerty, John Frederick. *War Path and Bivouac, or Conquest of the Sioux*. New edition. Norman, Oklahoma, 1961.

Forsythe, Brig. Gen. George A. *The Story of a Soldier*. New York, 1908.

Greeley, Horace. *An Overland Journey from New York to San Francisco in the summer of 1859*. New York, 1860.

Hafen, LeRoy R. (editor). *The Colorado Gold Rush: Contemporary Letters and Reports.* Glendale, California, 1941.

———. *Relations with the Indians of the Plains, 1857–1861.* Glendale, California, 1959.

———. and Ann W. (editors). *Powder River Campaigns and Sawyer's Expedition.* Glendale, 1961.

Hakola, John, and Merriam, H. G. *Frontier Omnibus.* Missoula, Montana, 1962.

Hancock, Samuel. *The Narrative of Samuel Hancock, 1845–1860.* New York, 1927.

Hastings, Lansford W. *The Emigrants Guide to Oregon and California.* Cincinnati, 1845.

Hoffman, Charles F. *A Winter in the West.* Vol. II. New York, 1835.

Hunton, John. *Diaries of, 1868–1883.* 4 Volumes. Edited by L. G. Flannery. Lingle, Wyoming, 1956.

Johnson, Overton, and Winter, William H. *Route Across the Rocky Mountains with a Description of Oregon and California.* Lafayette, Indiana, 1846.

Keller, George A. *A Trip Across the Plains, and Life in California.* Oakland, 1955.

Kelly, William. *An Excursion to California.* 2 Volumes. London, 1851.

King, Capt. Charles. *Campaigning with Crook.* New edition, Norman, Oklahoma, 1964.

Larpenteur, Charles. *Forty Years a Fur Trader on the Upper Missouri.* New York, 1898.

Latrobe, Charles Joseph. *The Rambler in North America.* London, 1835.

Leonard, Zenas. *Adventures of Zenas Leonard, Fur Trader and Trapper.* Edited by W. F. Wagner. Cleveland, 1904.

Lienhard, Heinrich. *From St. Joseph to Sutter's Fort, 1846.* Translated and edited by Erwin and Elizabeth K. Gudde. Norman, Oklahoma, 1961.

Lockwood, James D. *Life and Adventures of a Drummer Boy.* Albany, 1893.

Lowe, Percival G. *Five Years a Dragoon.* Kansas City, 1906.

Majors, Alexander. *Seventy Years on the Frontier.* Columbus, Ohio, 1950. Republished from 1893 edition.

Manly, William Lewis. *Death Valley in '49.* San Jose, 1894.

Marsh, James B. *Four Years in the Rockies; or, the Adventures of Isaac P. Rose.* Newcastle, Pennsylvania, 1884. Reprinted, Columbus, Ohio. These are Mr. Rose's reminiscences told to Mr. Marsh.

Maximilian, Prince of Wied. *Travels in the Interior of North America.* London, 1843.

Mills, Brig. Gen. Anson. *My Story.* Washington, D.C., 1918.

Morehead, Charles R. "Personal Recollections." Appendix C of *Doniphan's Expedition,* by William Elsey Connelley. Topeka, 1907.

Murray, Charles Augustus. *Travels in North America During the Years 1834, 1835, & 1836,* Vol. 1. London, 1839.

Ostrander, A. B. *After Sixty Years.* Seattle, 1925.

Palmer, Joel. *Journal of Travels over the Rocky Mountains, 1845–1846.* (Vol. XXX of *Early Western Travels, 1748–1846.*) Edited by Reuben Gold Thwaites. Cleveland, 1906.

Parker, Rev. Samuel. *Journal of an Exploring Tour Beyond the Rocky Mountains.* Ithaca, New York, 1838.

Parkman, Francis, Jr. *The California and Oregon Trail.* New York, 1857. Excellent material on Fort Laramie and environs in 1846.

Poole, De Witt Clinton. *Among the Sioux of Dakota.* New York, 1881.

Porter, Henry M. *Pencillings of an early Western Pioneer.* Denver, 1929.

Preuss, Charles. *Exploring with Frémont.* Translated and edited Erwin G. and Elizabeth K. Gudde. Norman, Oklahoma, 1958.

Pritchard, James A. *Overland Diary, from Kentucky to California in 1849.* Edited by Dale L. Morgan. Denver, 1959.

Richardson, Albert D. *Beyond the Mississippi, 1857–1867.* Hartford, 1867.

Root, Riley. *Journal of Travels from St. Josephs to Oregon.* Oakland, 1855.

Royce, Sarah. *A Frontier Lady.* New Haven and London, 1933.

Russell, Osborne. *Journal of a Trapper.* Boise, Idaho, 1921.

Sage, Rufus B. *Rocky Mountain Life.* Boston, 1859. A wealth of first-hand information on life around the Laramie forts in 1841.

Sage, Rufus B. *His Letters and Papers,* 2 Volumes, Glendale, California, 1956.

Smet, Pierre-Jean de. *Western Missions and Missionaries.* New York, 1863.

———. *Life, Letters and Travels.* Edited by Hiram Martin Chittenden, Albert Talbot Richardson. 4 Volumes, New York, 1905.

Stanley, Henry M. *My Early Travels and Adventures in America and Asia.* 2 Volumes, 1895.

Stansbury, Capt. Howard. *Exploration and Survey of the Valley of the Great Salt Lake of Utah.* Philadelphia, 1852–1853.

Talbot, Theodore. *The Journals of Theodore Talbot, 1843 and 1849–1852.* Edited by Charles H. Carey. Portland, Oregon, 1931.

Thornton, J. Quinn. *Oregon and California in 1848,* 2 Volumes, New York, 1849.

Tixier, Victor. *Travels on the Osage Prairies.* Edited by John F. McDermott. Norman, Oklahoma, 1940.

Townsend, John K. *Narrative of a Journey Across the Rocky Mountains to the Columbia River.* Philadelphia, 1839. A very descriptive account of Wyeth's 1834 expedition by a perceptive young scientist.

Vestal, Stanley. *New Sources of Indian History, 1850–1891.* Norman, Oklahoma, 1934.

Villard, Henry. *Memoirs,* Vol. I. Westminster, England, 1904.

———. *The Past and Present of the Pike's Peak Gold Regions.* Princeton, 1932.

Ware, Capt. Eugene F. *The Indian War of 1864.* New edition. New York, 1960.

Warren, Lt. G. K. *Explorations in the Dakota Country in the year 1855.* Washington, D.C., 1856. Also in Senate Executive Documents, 34th Congress, 1st Session, Doc. No. 76.

Webster, Kimball. *The Gold Seekers of '49.* Manchester, New Hampshire, 1917.

Whipple, Henry Benjamin. *Lights and Shadows of a Long Episcopate.* New York, 1912.

Whitman, Dr. Marcus. "Diary and Letters Relating to the Whitmans' Missionary Labors, 1835–1839," in *Marcus Whitman, Crusader,* Part 1, 1802 to 1839. Edited by Archer Butler Hulbert and Dorothy Printup Hulbert, Denver, 1936.

Williams, Joseph. *Narrative of a Tour from the State of Indiana to the Oregon Territory in the years 1841–2.* New York, 1921.

Wislizenus, F. A. *A Journey to the Rocky Mountains in the Year 1839.* St. Louis, 1912. An excellent account by an observant German doctor.

Wistar, Isaac Jones. *Autobiography, 1827–1905.* New York, 1937.

II. SECONDARY SOURCES

Anderson, Harry. "The Controversial Sioux Amendment to the Fort Laramie Treaty of 1851." *Nebraska History,* published by the Nebraska State
Historical Society. Vol. 37, No. 3, September 1956.

Annals of Wyoming. Various articles on Fort Laramie and related subjects,
particularly in Vol. VI–VII, p. 396, Vol. XIII, p. 331; Vol. XVIII, p. 93;
Vol. XXI, p. 176; and Vol. XXVII, p. 3.

Armstrong, Moses K. *The Early Empire Builders of the Great West.* St.
Paul, 1901. Part of this history is drawn from Armstrong's own experiences
in early Dakota Territory.

Athearn, Robert. *William Tecumseh Sherman and the Settlement of the
West.* Norman, Oklahoma, 1956.

Berthrong, Donald J. *The Southern Cheyennes.* Norman, Oklahoma, 1963.

Branch, E. D. *Hunting of the Buffalo.* New York and London, 1929.

Brininstool, E. A., and Grace Raymond Hebard, *The Bozeman Trail,* Vol. II.
Cleveland, 1922.

Brown, Dee. *Fort Phil Kearny.* New York, 1962.

———. *The Galvanized Yankees.* Urbana, Illinois, 1963.

Chittenden, Hiram Martin. *The American Fur Trade of the Far West.* New
York, 1935. 3 Vols. Though first published at the turn of the century,
this classic remains a source of much unique material.

———. *History of Early Steamboat Navigation on the Missouri River.* New
York. 1903.

Clarke, Dwight L. *Stephen Watts Kearny.* Norman, Oklahoma, 1961.

Coutant, Charles G. *History of Wyoming.* Laramie, 1899. While Mr. Coutant provides much unique material on Wyoming and Fort Laramie
history drawn from interviews with pioneers, some of his information is
inconsistent with primary sources.

Coy, Owen C. *The Great Trek.* Los Angeles and San Francisco, 1931.

David, Robert Beebe. *Finn Burnett, Frontiersman.* Glendale, California,
1937.

Deatherage, Charles P. *Early History of Greater Kansas City.* Vol. I, Chap.
19. Kansas City, Missouri, 1927.

De Barthe, Joe. *Life and Adventures of Frank Gruard.* Norman, Oklahoma,
1958.

DeLand, Charles E. "The Sioux Wars," South Dakota Historical Collections,
Vol. XV, 1930, Vol. XVII, 1934.

Dick, Everett N. *Vanguards of the Frontier.* New York, 1941.

———. *The Sod-House Frontier, 1854–1890.* Lincoln, 1954.

Dodge, Col. Richard I. *Our Wild Indians.* Hartford, 1882.

Fritz, Henry E. *Indian Assimilation Movement, 1860–90.* University of
Pennsylvania, 1964.

Gard, Wayne. *The Great Buffalo Hunt.* New York, 1959.

Gray, W. H. *A History of Oregon, 1792–1849.* Portland, Oregon, San Francisco and New York, 1870. Mr. Gray was a member of the Whitman party
of 1836; his book gives a first-hand account of that expedition.

Grinnell, George B. *The Fighting Cheyennes.* New York, 1915.

Griswold, Wesley S. *A Work of Giants: Building the First Transcontinental
Railroad.* New York, 1962.

Hafen, LeRoy R. *The Overland Mail, 1849–1869.* Cleveland, 1926.
———— and W. J. Ghent. *Broken Hand: The Story of Thomas Fitzpatrick.* Denver, 1931.
———— and Francis M. Young. *Fort Laramie and the Pageant of the West, 1834–1890.* Glendale, California, 1938.
Harvey, Robert. "The Battle Ground of Ash Hollow." *Collection of the Nebraska State Historical Society,* Vol. XVI, 1911, p. 152.
Hassrick, Royal B. *The Sioux: Life and Customs of a Warrior Society.* Norman, Oklahoma, 1964.
Hieb, David L. *Fort Laramie National Monument, Wyoming.* National Park Service Historical Handbook Series No. 20, Washington, D.C., 1954.
Hoig, Stan. *The Sand Creek Massacre.* Norman, Oklahoma, 1961.
Hoopes, Alban W. "Thomas Twiss, Indian Agent on the Upper Platte," *Missouri Valley Historical Review.* Vol. XX, p. 355.
————. *Indian Affairs and Their Administration, 1849–1860.* Philadelphia, 1962.
Hyde, George. *Red Cloud's Folk: A History of the Oglala Sioux Indians.* Norman, Oklahoma, 1937.
————. *Spotted Tail's Folk: A History of the Brulé Sioux.* Norman, Oklahoma, 1961.
Irving, Washington. *The Adventures of Captain Bonneville, U.S.A., in the Rocky Mountains and the Far West.* New York, 1856. This classic of the early West is based on Bonneville's own account given to Irving.
Jackson, W. Turrentine. *Wagon Roads West.* Berkeley and Los Angeles, 1952.
————. "The Army Engineers as Road Surveyors and Builders in Kansas and Nebraska, 1854–1858." *Kansas Historical Society Quarterly,* Vol. XVII, 1949, p. 37.
Lombard, Jess H. "Old Bedlam," *Annals of Wyoming,* Vol. XIII, No. 2, April 1941, p. 87.
Mattes, Merrill J. *Fort Laramie and the Forty-Niners.* Estes Park, Colorado, 1949.
————. "Fort Laramie, Guardian of the Oregon Trail," *Annals of Wyoming,* Vol. XVII, No. 1, January 1945, p. 3.
McCague, James. *Moguls and Iron Men: The Story of the First Transcontinental Railroad.* New York, 1964.
McCann, Lloyd E. "The Grattan Massacre," *Nebraska History,* Vol. 37, No. 1, March, 1956.
McDermott, John Dishon. "Fort Laramie's Iron Bridge," *Annals of Wyoming,* October, 1962.
————. "The Search for Jacques Laramee: A Study in Frustration," *Annals of Wyoming,* October 1964, Vol. XXXVI, No. 2, p. 169.
McGlashan, C. F. *History of the Donner Party.* Stanford, 1940. Republished from 1880 edition.
Miller, David Humphreys. *Ghost Dance.* New York, 1959.
Mokler, Alfred James. *Fort Caspar.* Casper, Wyoming, 1939.
Morton, J. Sterling, Albert Watkins, and Dr. George L. Miller. *Illustrated History of Nebraska,* Vol. I. Lincoln, 1905.
National Park Service. *Fort Laramie National Historic Site.* Government Printing Office Publication No. 836–645. Washington, D.C., 1962.
————. *Soldier and Brave.* Introduction by Ray Allen Billington. New York, 1963.

Olson, James C. *Red Cloud and the Sioux Problem.* Lincoln, 1965. A conscientious, thoroughly documented study.
————. "The Lasting Peace of Fort Laramie," *The American West,* March 1965, p. 46.
Powell, Maj. W. H. "Fort Laramie's Early History," *Collections of the Wyoming Historical Society,* Vol. I, 1897, p. 176.
Priest, Loring Benson. *Uncle Sam's Stepchildren.* New Brunswick, 1942.
Reavis, Logan U. *Life and Military Services of Gen. W. S. Harney.* St. Louis, 1878.
Rickey, Don. *Forty Miles a Day on Beans and Hay.* Norman, Oklahoma, 1963. An authoritative description of soldier life in the West.
Robinson, Doane. "A History of the Sioux Indians," *South Dakota Historical Collections,* Vol. II, 1904.
Sandoz, Mari. *Crazy Horse.* New York, 1942.
Scharf, J. Thomas. *History of Saint Louis City and County,* Vol. I. Philadelphia, 1883.
Schmeckebier, Laurence F. *The Office of Indian Affairs.* Baltimore, 1927.
Settle, Raymond W. and Mary Lund. *Empire on Wheels.* Stanford, 1949.
Spring, Agnes Wright. *Caspar Collins.* New York, 1927. Includes letters of Col. William O. and Lt. Caspar Collins.
————. *Cheyenne and Black Hills Stage and Express Routes.* Glendale, California, 1949.
Sunder, John E. *Bill Sublette, Mountain Man.* Norman, Oklahoma, 1959.
Taylor, Emerson G. *Gouverneur Kemble Warren: The Life and Letters of an American Soldier.* Boston and New York, 1932. Includes excerpts from Warren's diary.
Taylor, Joseph Henry. "Lonesome Charlie," *North Dakota Hist. Quarterly,* Vol. IV, No. 4, July 1930.
Trenholm, Virginia Cole. "The Bordeaux Story," *Annals of Wyoming,* Vol. XXVI, No. 2, July 1954, p. 119.
Utley, Robert M. *The Last Days of the Sioux Nation,* New Haven and London, 1963.
Vaughn, Jesse Wendell. *The Battle of Platte Bridge.* Norman, Oklahoma, 1963. Like Mr. Vaughn's other works, this definitive book represents a happy combination of modern scholarship and field exploration.
————. *The Reynolds Campaign on Powder River.* Norman, Oklahoma, 1961.
————. *With Crook at the Rosebud.* Harrisburg, 1956. Includes all reports of Crook and his officers on the Rosebud battle.
————. Indian Rights: New Facts on Seven Encounters. Norman, Oklahoma, 1966.
Vestal, Stanley. *Sitting Bull: Champion of the Sioux.* Norman, Oklahoma, 1932.
————. *Warpath and Council Fire.* New York, 1948.
Victor, Frances Fuller. *The River of the West.* Hartford and Toledo, 1870. Much of this is based on the recollections of the mountain man, Joe Meek.
Wennett, W. M. "Custer's Expedition to the Black Hills in 1874," *North Dakota Historical Quarterly,* Vol. VI, No. 4, p. 299.
Wilson, Maj. Frederick T. "Old Fort Pierre and its Neighbors," with editorial notes by Charles E. DeLand. *South Dakota Historical Collections,* Vol. I, 1902, page 259.
Young, Otis E. *The West of Philip St. George Cooke, 1809–1895.* Glendale, California, 1955.

Index

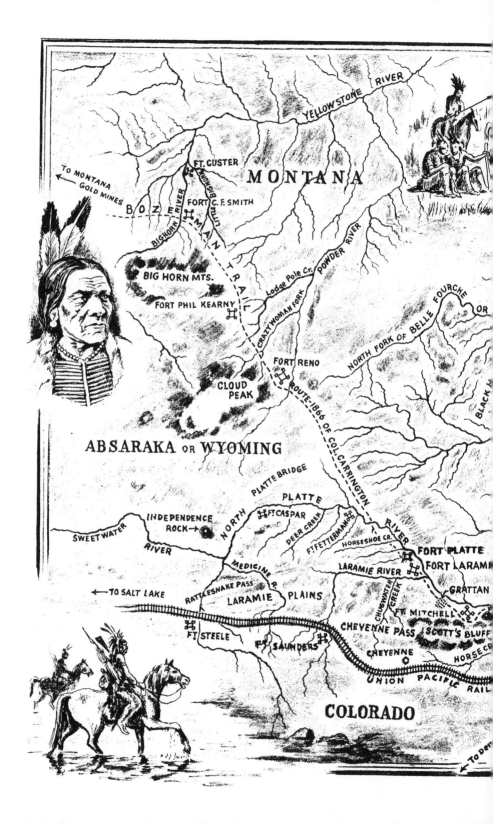

YELLOWSTONE RIVER

FT. CUSTER

MONTANA

FORT C. F. SMITH

TO MONTANA GOLD MINES

BOZEMAN TRAIL

BIGHORN RIVER

LITTLE BIGHORN

POWDER RIVER

BIG HORN MTS.

Lodge Pole Cr.

Crazy Woman Fork

NORTH FORK OF BELLE FOURCHE

OR

FORT PHIL KEARNY

FORT RENO

CLOUD PEAK

ROUTE 1866 OF COL. CARRINGTON

BLACK H

ABSARAKA OR WYOMING

PLATTE BRIDGE

PLATTE

FT. CASPAR

INDEPENDENCE ROCK →

NORTH

DEER CREEK

RIVER

SWEETWATER

RIVER

FT. FETTERMAN

HORSESHOE CR.

FORT PLATTE

FORT LARAM

LARAMIE RIVER

MEDICINE B

← TO SALT LAKE

RATTLESNAKE PASS

LARAMIE PLAINS

CHUGWATER CREEK

GRATTAN

FT. MITCHELL

FT. STEELE

FT. SAUNDERS

CHEYENNE PASS

SCOTT'S BLUFF

CHEYENNE

HORSE CR

UNION PACIFIC RAIL

COLORADO

TO Den

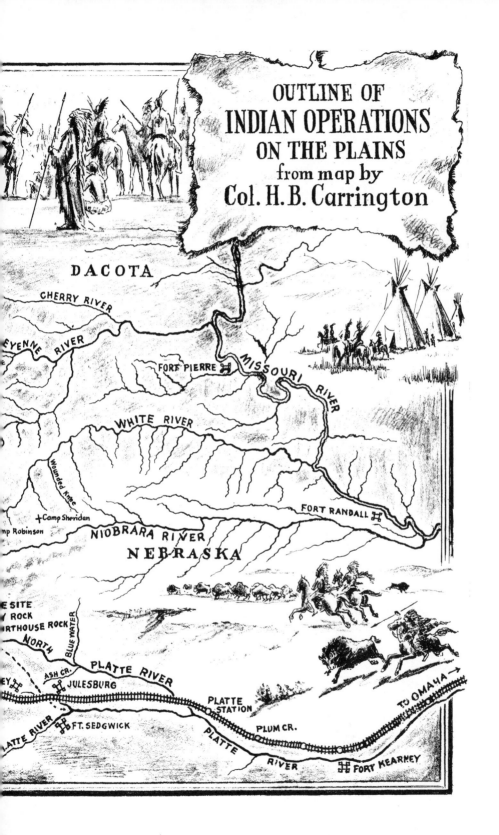

OUTLINE OF
INDIAN OPERATIONS
ON THE PLAINS
from map by
Col. H. B. Carrington

DACOTA

CHERRY RIVER

EYENNE RIVER

FORT PIERRE

MISSOURI RIVER

WHITE RIVER

Wounded Knee

Camp Sheridan

np Robinson

NIOBRARA RIVER

NEBRASKA

FORT RANDALL

SITE
ROCK
RTHOUSE ROCK

NORTH

BLUE WATER

PLATTE RIVER

ASH CR.

JULESBURG

EY

FT. SEDGWICK

LATTE RIVER

PLATTE
STATION

PLUM CR.

PLATTE
RIVER

TO OMAHA

FORT KEARNEY